The Louisiana Purchase

Landmark Events in U.S. History Series

The Declaration of Independence: Origins and Impact

Scott Douglas Gerber, Editor

The Louisiana Purchase: Emergence of an American Nation

Peter J. Kastor, Editor

Marbury versus Madison: Documents and Commentary

Mark A. Graber and Michael Perhac, Editors

The Louisiana Purchase
Emergence of an American Nation

Peter J. Kastor, Editor

CQ PRESS

A Division of Congressional Quarterly Inc.
Washington, D.C.

CQ Press
1255 22nd Street, N.W., Suite 400
Washington, D.C. 20037

202-729-1900; toll-free: 1-866-4CQ-PRESS (1-866-427-7737)

www.cqpress.com

Printed and bound in the United States of America

06 05 04 03 02   5 4 3 2 1

☺ The paper used in this publication meets the minimum requirements of the American National Standard for Information Sciences—Permanence of Paper for Printed Library Materials, ANSI Z39.48-1992.

Cover design: Debra Naylor

The quotation that appears on the front cover ("Let the land rejoice, for you have bought Louisiana for a song") is from a July 18, 1803, letter from General Horatio Gates to President Thomas Jefferson congratulating Jefferson on the Louisiana Purchase.

Library of Congress Cataloging-in-Publication Data

The Louisiana Purchase : emergence of an American nation /
    Peter J. Kastor, editor.
        p. cm. — (Landmark events in U.S. history series)
    Includes bibliographical references and index.
    ISBN 1-56802-706-0 (cloth : alk. paper)
    1. Louisiana Purchase.   2. Louisiana Purchase—Sources.
I. Kastor, Peter J.   II. Series.
E333 .L93 2002
973.4'6—dc21

2002010595

Contents

List of Documents

Preface

The Louisiana Purchase is a landmark historical event that Americans have some awareness of yet often do not fully understand. The basic details are straightforward: In 1803 the United States bought a vast area of land from France that doubled the size of the young republic. What became known as the Louisiana Purchase was the greatest diplomatic success of Thomas Jefferson's presidency. The purchase of this large territory was only the first in a series of steps taken by the United States on its road to continental dominance. Although these statements are true, each is somewhat misleading. Far from a cut-and-dried decision, the treaty that put the purchase into effect caused years of dispute and debate. The purchase may have been the great achievement of Jefferson's presidency, but it had little to do with Jefferson himself. And although it may have been a defining moment of U.S. expansion westward, it hardly reflected an unquestioning spirit of American expansionism.

The chapters and the documents in this collection help make sense of why the Louisiana Purchase happened and examine the tremendous changes that came in its wake. The introduction explains the details of the purchase. The chapters that follow are organized in three major groups. Chapters 1 through 3 investigate the political cultures on both sides of the Mississippi River in the years immediately preceding the Louisiana Purchase. These chapters are in part background, but they also help explain why the United States pursued the purchase and why the residents of Louisiana responded as they did. Chapters 4 through 7 examine the events immediately related to the Louisiana Purchase through the experiences of four men who felt those changes most acutely: Thomas Jefferson; Aaron Burr, Jefferson's controversial vice president; Dehahuit, the Caddo Indian chief; and Edward Livingston, a politician and legal theorist. The authors of these chapters take different approaches to their subjects. Mark Fernandez presents a biographical study of Livingston, while James Lewis's study of Burr focuses on what became known as the Burr conspiracy and the way Americans situated it within a broader consideration of the federal union. Finally, chapters 8 through 10 discuss the Louisiana Purchase's connections to American politics and constitutionalism. The authors use the Louisiana Purchase to look back to constitutional debates that started with American independence and forward to disputes that ended with the Civil War.

One of the goals of this reference anthology is to show that the same issues appear in a different light depending on one's perspective. For example, Sanford Levinson's discussion of constitutionalism in Chapter 8 and Robert Bonner's analysis of sectionalism in Chapter 10 show the complexity of political debates in the nineteenth century, where discussions about the structure of government coincided with, but never entirely overlapped, arguments about slavery. Likewise Andrew Trees in Chapter 1 and Peter Onuf in Chapter 9 describe a Thomas Jefferson who is not altogether the same as the one presented by James Sofka in Chapter 4. Each of these three chapters emphasizes Jefferson's search for appropriate political and diplomatic strategies. But whereas the Jefferson in Chapters 1 and 9 remains focused on defending a republican polity at home, the Jefferson who emerges in Chapter 4 is a pragmatist looking abroad.

These chapters assume no special knowledge of the Louisiana Purchase. The authors have approached their chapters as opportunities to introduce readers to the purchase and to situate it in a broader context. The primary documents that follow the chapters provide additional insight. Many of the documents are discussed in the chapters. Many date from the years after the Louisiana Purchase and shed light not only on the way the purchase transformed the United States but also on the way Americans came to remember it in the years that followed.

The range of chapters and documents should indicate the complexity surrounding the Louisiana Purchase. The treaty transformed not only the United States but also the whole of North America. The Louisiana Purchase generated no end of controversy, and many Americans believed it created as many problems as it had solved. In large part they were right because the Louisiana Purchase created ripples that continued long after 1803.

A Note on Terminology

"Louisiana Purchase" actually has two different usages in this anthology. First, the term applies to the agreement by which France sold its possessions on the North American mainland to the United States. Second, the Louisiana Purchase has acquired a more colloquial meaning that refers to the land itself. Although the boundaries of the Louisiana Purchase remained the subject of dispute, the purchase eventually came to encompass a rough triangle, with the Mississippi River, the Rocky Mountains, and the U.S.-Canadian border forming its outlines.

This anthology includes discussions of five major groups of people: white Americans (citizens of the United States whose nationality stemmed either from birth or from naturalization outside the Louisiana Purchase), white Louisianians (people of European ancestry who found their nationality transformed by the Louisiana Purchase), Indians, slaves, and free people of color. These terms are, of course, generalizations. As Jay Gitlin shows in Chapter 2, white Louisianians included French- and Spanish-speaking Creoles born in Louisiana as well as a large number of migrants from France, the French Caribbean, and other parts of the Atlantic world. Indians differed tremendously as well, depending on the villages from which they came, the languages they spoke, or the cultural networks to which they belonged. Some people who were slaves in 1803 eventually freed themselves, joining a population of free people of color whose attitudes toward slaves and free whites varied.

Acknowledgments

Anthologies can be a delight or a nightmare to bring to fruition. Many of my colleagues have told me stories of delinquent contributors or difficult editors. I wouldn't know about that because the collaborators on this project proved to be a delightful group, and I want to give them the thanks they deserve.

The first of those collaborators was Christopher Anzalone at CQ Press. Ever since he first contacted me about creating an anthology on the Louisiana Purchase, Chris has been a marvelous colleague. Once he got the project moving, Ann Davies at CQ Press and Steph Selice, an independent editor, kept things on course. Gwenda Larsen at CQ Press came on board in the final stages of editing and made certain that we resolved the numerous questions that emerge when pulling together so many essays and documents.

Working with the scholars who wrote the chapters for this anthology was equally rewarding. These people spend most of their time writing for an audience of fellow scholars, and they were extremely accommodating as we tackled the difficult task of converting the work of specialists into accessible essays that would not require extensive background in the particulars of the Louisiana Purchase, the history of the early American republic, or the nuances of American constitutionalism. Prompt in delivering their essays and making revisions, the authors were also willing to make adjustments on faith alone when I told them that a

particular change or addition would make their essays dovetail with the work of other contributors.

While the editors at CQ Press and the contributors to this anthology were doing their work, I was able to do mine through the support I received from the American Culture Studies Program in Arts and Sciences at Washington University in St. Louis. Wayne Fields, Carolyn Gerber, and more recently Deborah Jaegers all gave me the time and resources I needed to get this project finished. And when I had questions about how to assemble an anthology, David Konig in Washington University's History Department was as consistently helpful and supportive as he has been from the moment I arrived in St. Louis. Several undergraduates helped in many ways. My research assistant, Allison Oxley, helped collect the documents. Adam Eckstein, Joanna Franks, Megan Lindsay, Diana Raesner, and Jeff Waller all volunteered to read individual essays. Two recent Washington University graduates, Chris Kurpiewski and Diana Raesner, provided essential assistance in the final stages of preparing the manuscript.

I would also like to express special gratitude to the editors of the Papers of James Madison. Located in Alderman Library at the University of Virginia, this editorial project employed me as a graduate student and later helped me understand the immense documentation surrounding the Louisiana Purchase. Most relevant to this anthology, however, is what I learned about the editorial process. Committed to the best principles of presenting the past, the editors of the Papers of James Madison have created a terrific model for explaining documents while letting those documents speak for themselves. I hope I do justice to the standard they have set.

On a final note, I want to thank my wife, Jami Ake, and our son, Sam Kastor. Sam was born in April 2001, just as the process of creating this anthology got under way. From the moment he was born, Sam has made everything more fun. Of course, Sam needed atten-tion, and despite her own demands at work, Jami helped me carve out the time to complete this project. For that assistance—as well as countless other reasons—this book is dedicated to her.

Peter J. Kastor
August 2002

Contributors

About the Editor

Peter J. Kastor is assistant professor of history and American culture studies at Washington University in St. Louis. He is the author of *"An Acquisition of So Great an Extent": An Introduction to the Louisiana Purchase,* a general discussion of the purchase to be published by the Lewis and Clark Interpretive Association as part of the bicentennial commemoration of the Corps of Discovery. His current book project, *"An Apprenticeship to Liberty": The Incorporation of Louisiana and the Struggle for Nationhood in the Early American Republic, 1803–1820,* considers the way the Louisiana Purchase shaped people's conception of what it would mean to be American and a nation.

About the Contributors

Robert E. Bonner is assistant professor of history at Michigan State University. He is the author of *Colors and Blood: Flag Passions of the Confederate South* (Princeton University Press, 2002) and of articles in *Civil War History* and the *Journal of Southern History*. He is currently writing a study of slaveholders and American nationhood from the period of the Revolution through the defeat of the Confederacy.

Mark Fernandez is associate professor of history at Loyola University of New Orleans, where he teaches early American and southern history. A native New Orleanian, he received a Ph.D. in history from the College of William and Mary in 1991. He is the coeditor, with Warren M. Billings, of *A Law Unto Itself? Essays in the New Louisiana Legal History* (Louisiana State University Press, 2001). His book *From Chaos to Continuity: Evolution of Louisiana's Judicial System, 1712–1862* (Louisiana State University Press, 2001) received the Louisiana Literary Award.

Jay Gitlin is a lecturer in history and associate coordinator of the Howard R. Lamar Center for the Study of Frontiers and Borders at Yale University. He coedited *Under an Open Sky: Rethinking America's Western Past* (W.W. Norton, 1992) and contributed a chapter ("Empires of Trade, Hinterlands of Settlement") to *The Oxford History of the American West* (1994). His book, *Negotiating the Course of Empire: The French Bourgeois Frontier and the Emergence of Mid-America, 1763–1863* will be published in 2002.

Sanford Levinson is professor of government and holds the W. St. John Garwood and W. St. John Garwood Jr. Regents Chair in Law at the University of Texas Law School. He is the coeditor of a casebook in constitutional law, *Processes of Constitutional Decisionmaking* (Aspen Publishers, 4th ed., 2000) which is distinguished from most other casebooks by its emphasis on constitutional history. The holder of a J. D. from the Stanford Law School, Levinson received a Ph.D. in political science from Harvard, where he worked with Robert McCloskey. Levinson has updated McCloskey's classic 1960 volume, *The American Supreme Court,* for subsequent editions.

James E. Lewis Jr. is the author of *The American Union and the Problem of Neighborhood: The United States and the Collapse of the Spanish Empire, 1783–1829* (University of North Carolina Press, 1998) and *John Quincy Adams: Policymaker for the Union* (Scholarly Resources, 2001). He has taught at Hollins College, Louisiana State University, Widener University, and the University of Pennsylvania. His essay in this collection is drawn from his current research on the Burr conspiracy.

Peter S. Onuf is Thomas Jefferson Foundation Professor in the Corcoran Department of History at the University of Virginia. He is the author of numerous books on the history of the early American republic. His recent work on Thomas Jefferson's political thought, culminating in *Jefferson's Empire: The Language of American Nationhood* (University Press of Virginia, 2000), grows out of his earlier studies on the history of American federalism, foreign policy, and political economy. Onuf is also coauthor of *All Over the Map: Rethinking Re-*

gion and Nation in the United States (Johns Hopkins University Press, 1996), the editor of *Jeffersonian Legacies* (1993), and the coeditor of *Sally Hemings and Thomas Jefferson: History, Memory, and Civic Culture* (1999) and *The Revolution of 1800: Democracy, Race, and the New Republic* (2002), all published by University Press of Virginia.

James R. Sofka is assistant dean and assistant professor in the college of arts and sciences at the University of Virginia. He is director of the Echols Scholars Program, the honors program for undergraduates in the college. He teaches international law and specializes in eighteenth-century international relations. He is the author of *Metternich, Jefferson, and the Enlightenment: Statecraft and Political Theory in Early Nineteenth Century Europe and America* (forthcoming, Stanford University Press).

Andrew Trees recently completed a Ph.D. at the University of Virginia and has published numerous articles on the political culture of Revolutionary America. A former research fellow at the International Center for Jefferson Studies, his current book project, *The Politics of Character,* examines the founders' attempts to fashion personal and national character in the wake of the upheaval of the Revolution.

Betty Houchin Winfield, professor of journalism at the University of Missouri–Columbia, specializes in the mass media and politics. She is the author of three books, including *FDR and the News Media* (1990, 1994), eight book chapters, and more than sixty other scholarly writings consisting of journal articles, monographs, encyclopedia articles, and national/international papers.

The Louisiana Purchase

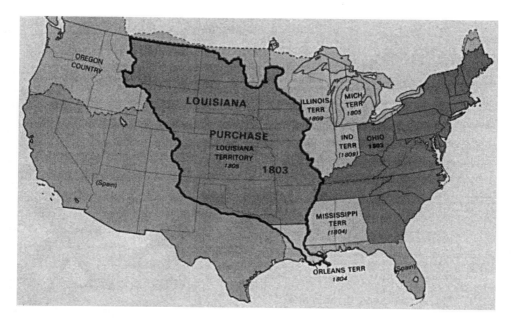

The April 1803 treaty between the United States and France, known as the Louisiana Purchase, added more than 800,000 square miles to the United States and nearly doubled the size of the young nation. Although the $15 million purchase would eventually involve all or portions of thirteen future states, the final boundaries were not settled by the treaty and would take years to resolve.

Source: Perry-Castañeda Library Map Collection, University of Texas Online (http://www.lib.utexas.edu/maps/united_states/us_terr_1810.jpg). Map compiled by H. George Stoll, Hammond Incorporated, 1967; revised by U.S. Geological Survey, 1970.

Introduction:
Framing an Endless Purchase

What was the Louisiana Purchase? This is not only a question that people might ask today but one that people asked in 1803, when American and French negotiators signed a treaty ceding French lands to the United States. Currently, many Americans understandably are unaware of the details of the treaty. But two centuries ago people on both sides of the Atlantic disagreed about the very definition of the land encompassed by the Louisiana Purchase. Its boundaries were difficult to discern, and settling the problems that came with the purchase seemed like an almost endless process for American policymakers, who devoted the better part of a generation to crafting an acceptable definition of what the Louisiana Purchase encompassed and to building a government within that space.

If the treaty was so ambiguous, why did the United States purchase Louisiana? Rather than actively pursue the provisions of the 1803 treaty with France, American negotiators agreed hesitantly to a treaty that was entirely at odds with both the instructions of their superiors and their own vision of American priorities. Once the treaty arrived in the United States, it generated no end of controversy, in large part because many Americans believed it

had created as many problems as it solved. Far from seeing the Louisiana Purchase as a breathtaking success, people throughout the United States in 1803 were more relieved than ecstatic about the transaction and more anxious than overjoyed. This proved to be the case in large part because the Louisiana Purchase created ripples that continued long after 1803. And for this reason the majority of the chapters and documents in this book actually cover later events. One reason for this approach is obvious: to explain the significance of the Louisiana Purchase. But another reason is more subtle, although no less important. It is impossible to understand how the Louisiana Purchase happened without explaining what came in its wake. The priorities and the concerns that led the U.S. government to pursue the Louisiana Purchase in the first place become all the more clear when considered in the context of events that followed.

Louisiana and the Contest of Empires

The best way to understand how the Louisiana Purchase came about is to begin by looking back to 1763, when France lost its North American possessions, and to consider what was happening then on both sides of the Atlantic. During a bloody conflict eventually known as the Seven Years' War in Europe (or the French and Indian War, as it became known in the United States), Great Britain seized the settlements that controlled French Canada. A second colony to the south, Louisiana, had always served primarily as a means to defend Canada and to guarantee passage down the Mississippi River for Canadian goods and settlers. Without Canada, Louisiana seemed to serve little purpose, especially since it had always been a money loser for the French treasury. Meanwhile, the Spanish government was eager to acquire its own buffer that would defend its North and Central American holdings from the British. So, in 1763, France acknowledged British possession of Canada and ceded Louisiana to Spain.

If the Spanish were worried about the British, the British were responding in kind. The Spanish colony of Louisiana was a matter of no small concern to settlers in British North America or their colonial rulers. When American settlers declared their independence in 1776, and secured British acknowledgment of that independence seven years later, the new government of the United States remained deeply concerned about Louisiana. The focus of their concern was not the land west of the Mississippi River but the river itself. Among the first diplomatic goals that officials of the new government set for themselves was to secure a guarantee from Spain that Americans could travel down the length of the Mississippi and bring their goods for transshipment from New Orleans, the largest port in the American West.

Americans came to care so much about New Orleans and the Mississippi because there

was more at stake than mere trading privileges. As Chapter 1, on the foundations of the American government shows, America's Mississippi River policy was deeply rooted in the most essential principles of the new republic. That policy responded to the changes in political culture and constitutional order, but it also propelled those developments. Americans concluded that the survival of the republican experiment itself depended in no small part on a successful arrangement on the Mississippi. New Orleans was the last stop for western settlers, most of whom raised crops that they planned to sell through a transportation system linking the rivers of the western United States to the Mississippi. American officials quickly came to believe that if they could not guarantee a prosperous trade, western settlers might well seek their fortunes elsewhere—either by forming a separate republic of their own or, worse still, by inviting trade with European empires that would have the power to offer what the settlers wanted. As Chapters 5 and 9 of this book make clear, these concerns about union remained at the center of American political debate in the half-century following independence.

In the 1780s advocates of the federal Constitution had argued that a more powerful central government would enable the United States to overcome both foreign and domestic dangers in the West. During the 1790s the Constitution seemed to deliver on its promise. In 1795 the United States and Spain ratified the Treaty of San Lorenzo, which guaranteed the American right to deposit goods free of charge in New Orleans. The treaty also included most of the land that now constitutes Alabama and Mississippi (with the notable exception of the

Gulf Coast and the Florida peninsula, a region more generally known as the Floridas). And while the Constitution provided new diplomatic muscle, the administration and Congress seemed to be governing the West more effectively than the states had in the 1780s. Whether by creating territorial governments in places like Ohio, Illinois, and Mississippi; by creating a uniform system for admitting new states like Tennessee; or by building a federal army that scored a number of victories against organized Indian resistance to white settlement, the federal government appeared to have the means of realizing a successful Mississippi policy.

Americans concluded that all those aspirations were in jeopardy in 1801, when news reached the United States that Spain had secretly returned Louisiana to France the year before in an act that soon became known as the retrocession. Not only did the retrocession threaten to invalidate the Treaty of San Lorenzo, but it also led many Americans to conclude that France had grand ambitions to create an empire on the American mainland. After all, anxious Americans observed, Napoleon Bonaparte had displayed similarly grand ambitions in Europe. As a general, he had led campaigns of occupation throughout the continent. In 1799 the thirty-year-old Bonaparte had helped form a new government, and less than a year later he had established himself as its supreme leader. Although many Americans had shown initial support for the French Revolution, they had soured at the excesses of the revolutionary regime. They had also concluded that Bonaparte had territorial ambitions in North America that might yet include the United States.

The news of the retrocession came just as Thomas Jefferson assumed the presidency in 1801. Given his decades-long concern about development in the West, Jefferson is a pivotal figure to many of the authors in this anthology. Much of the study of the Louisiana Purchase focuses on Jefferson, but James Madison was no less important to the eventual shape of the nation's Louisiana policy. Madison was Jefferson's secretary of state, closest political confidante, and successor during the years in which the Louisiana Purchase continued to pose challenges to the federal leadership. Jefferson and Madison both concluded that the retrocession constituted a dire threat to the United States. They were also in a quandary about how to proceed. The Treaty of San Ildefonso (the instrument of the retrocession) maintained an odd arrangement in which France legally owned Louisiana but Spain continued to govern the province. The Spanish accepted this arrangement because it allowed them to guarantee protection of other colonies in North America and the Caribbean. But how to achieve American goals with the Spanish monarchy and the French revolutionary government seemed a daunting challenge to the new administration in the United States. Madison immediately set to work, hoping to build a diplomatic strategy that would preserve American goals.

The situation went from bad to worse in 1802, when the Spanish intendant in New Orleans abruptly announced new restrictions on American merchants. In the process, he also implicitly announced that the Treaty of San Lorenzo was, as the Americans feared, null and void. As American policymakers had long predicted, threats from overseas created dangers at home. Western settlers once again were grumbling about the federal government's inability to act on their concerns. And once again, federal leaders feared internal dissent or foreign intervention.

The retrocession, together with the Spanish policy in New Orleans, persuaded many American policymakers to act more aggressively. Some Americans demanded that the United States declare war on France, Spain, or both, and take New Orleans by force. The documents in this anthology include Alexander Hamilton's bellicose editorials demanding a military resolution to what many Americans called the Mississippi crisis. The administration was more cautious. In 1802 the United States was in its second year of an unsuccessful naval blockade of Tripoli. If the nation's military could not defeat a small power that many Americans considered culturally deficient, how could it hope to defeat France or Spain in a campaign on a distant frontier? As the discussion in Chapter 4 shows, Jefferson was hardly averse to using force, but he considered it more efficient and effective to exploit disputes within the European community. So the Jefferson administration hoped to achieve a diplomatic settlement with France, Spain, or ideally with both. By 1803, however, these negotiations focused on France, and the goals began to solidify. As the architect of American foreign policy, Secretary of State Madison instructed his diplomats to seek the sale of New Orleans and the Floridas to the United States. Together, these possessions would consolidate American sovereignty east of the Mississippi and eliminate foreign control of the river once and for all. No document better details the administration's goals—or its means to those goals—

more thoroughly than the March 2, 1803, instructions that Madison composed for the American diplomats in France.

But the Americans had nothing to offer and no influence to wield. As a result, neither the French nor the Spanish showed any real interest in American goals. When the change came, it had less to do with American diplomacy than with French troubles. In 1791 free people of color in the French colony of Saint Domingue asserted that they, too, were citizens of the French Republic and should be treated accordingly. Meanwhile, slaves made their own demands that the republic deliver on its promise to eliminate human bondage. Slaves and free people of color had no tradition of alliance; many free people of color owned slaves themselves. As a result, the mobilization of these groups coincided but was not initially allied. Only when France showed no signs of changing its colonial policy did these groups combine forces and seek to impose change by force. When Napoleon dispatched a massive army to quell the revolt in 1802, he soon received staggering news that the army had fallen apart from disease and rebel attacks.

By March 1803 Napoleon had concluded he could no longer preserve control over Saint Domingue, and Saint Domingue had been among his primary reasons for acquiring Louisiana in the first place. Contrary to what the Americans believed, Napoleon was not intent on building a permanent American empire. Instead, he saw Louisiana as so many others had seen it: a strategic backwater that supported more important locales. In 1800 that meant defending and supplying Saint Domingue. When Napoleon heard that American diplomats were eager to acquire French possessions in North

America, he moved fast. In April 1803 he began making plans to sell Louisiana to the United States. The timing was remarkable, for on April 12 James Monroe arrived in Paris, there to act as minister plenipotentiary (or special envoy) in support of the American minister, Robert R. Livingston. Monroe brought with him the highly detailed March 2, 1803, instructions from Madison, which told Monroe and Livingston to acquire New Orleans and the Floridas. Instead, Napoleon's delegate, François Barbé-Marbois, minister of the treasury, informed the Americans that France would sell its holdings in North America. Barbé-Marbois was a logical choice. Before moving to the French ministry of the treasury, he had gained extensive experience as diplomat, including service in the United States.

Monroe and Livingston were shocked by the offer, but they responded with an immediate "yes," and within three weeks they had crafted a treaty with the French that became known as the Louisiana Purchase. In this agreement, the United States agreed to pay $11.5 million and forgive $3.5 million in debt that France owed to the United States for attacks on American shipping during the Quasi-War, a military confrontation between the two republics that lasted from 1798 to 1801.

Reactions

When news of the treaty reached the United States, Americans reacted in various ways. Although most were relieved by the resolution of the Mississippi crisis, others wondered about the constitutionality of the agreement and worried about the challenge of governing so much land and so many people. The purchase dominated political debate and the emerging print media of the young republic. Meanwhile, selections from the congressional debate show how difficult Americans knew it would be to incorporate Louisiana into the United States.

In late 1803 and 1804 Americans were asking a number of questions about the Louisiana Purchase. The most immediate constitutional issue concerned the executive branch's ability to negotiate treaties that expanded national boundaries. The question of presidential power did not last long. On October 20, 1803, the Senate ratified the Louisiana Purchase (the Constitution reserved to the Senate the power to approve treaties), and eleven days later, both houses of Congress passed a resolution permitting Jefferson to take possession of Louisiana. But other constitutional matters had a longer lifespan. American politicians had only begun to debate how—or even if—the constitutional structure could accommodate the long-term governance of Louisiana and the naturalization of its residents.

The Louisiana Purchase had come as a surprise, and it had come quickly. For all the relief brought by the peaceful end to the Mississippi crisis, the purchase was an imperfect treaty, and revising the treaty in a way that fit American goals took the better part of a generation. When that process was over, the ability of the United States to have an agreeable version of the purchase testified to the rising power of the American empire and the collapsing North American fortunes of the European empires that had once ruled the Western Hemisphere.

The most immediate problem of the purchase was that it did not say what "Louisiana" actually was. Instead of defining fixed geographic points, the treaty only stated that the

United States acquired what France had acquired through the retrocession. The boundaries of that land were anybody's guess. The only borders to which everybody agreed were the Mississippi River to the east and Canada to the north. France and Spain had never established a clear western boundary before 1763, and Spain saw no reason to do so afterward. But the greatest source of concern in the United States was the lack of any indication that Louisiana included the Floridas. Jefferson and Madison tried to convince themselves that it did. But the fact that Spain governed the Floridas in the years that followed reflected another fact: the United States acquired Louisiana only through the good graces of France, and there was no equivalent acquisition coming from Spain. So in the years after 1803 American diplomats tried without success to establish an American claim to the Gulf Coast.

There was little Jefferson or Madison could do. Besides, they were so far from European capitals that any change would have to be the work of their diplomats. Of more immediate concern was the daunting task of extending the U.S. government west of the Mississippi. Territorial administration fell to the secretary of state, and the incoming correspondence from the territories usually exceeded the amount from American overseas missions. Before 1803 U.S. secretaries of state governed an area larger than that controlled by any state governor. After 1803 Madison governed more land than all the state governors combined.

The task bedeviled Madison and Congress throughout Jefferson's presidency and continued long after Madison succeeded his friend as president in 1809. The first attempts to build a government met with mixed results. In 1804 Congress partitioned the Louisiana Purchase into the Territory of Orleans (which included most of the present state of Louisiana) and the District of Louisiana (which included everything else). The instrument of this change, the Governance Act of 1804, exemplified the federal government's effort to extend its reach. Neither the Territory of Orleans nor the District of Louisiana had any elected offices, and the District of Louisiana came under the jurisdiction of the Indiana Territory. White residents at both ends of the Mississippi Valley made angry protests, arguing that the Louisiana Purchase guaranteed them full citizenship and, therefore, statehood or at least treatment equal to that of other territories. Locally, residents of the Territory of Orleans opposed efforts to replace legal customs that had developed under colonial rule with the Anglo-American common law. Their concerns appear in this book in "Remonstrance of the People of Louisiana against the Political System Adopted by Congress for Them."

Congress responded by creating an elected House of Representatives in the Territory of Orleans and a Territory of Louisiana separate from Indiana. But these changes did not satisfy all Louisianians, many of whom continued to complain about what they saw as Anglo-American chauvinism against the new francophone citizens of the United States. As Chapter 7 explains, territorial officials also accepted a legal system that combined numerous influences, with local legal traditions governing civil procedure and American principles governing criminal law.

Resistance and Change

When the threat of disunion came, it was not actually from Louisianians but from Americans. In 1806 rumors floated throughout the United States that former vice president Aaron Burr had formed a conspiracy to separate a portion of the lower Mississippi Valley and, combining it with a portion of Texas, create an independent republic. The administration feared that Burr would find ready allies among local residents, but most of his collaborators seemed to be Americans of otherwise high standing. Only when the army found Burr and returned him to Washington on charges of treason did the administration relax. Although a court in Virginia acquitted Burr, the administration had made clear that it would brook no resistance among white residents. Still, Chapter 5 details the ongoing anxiety that surrounded the Burr conspiracy both before and after the trial.

At least the white residents of Louisiana protested in a civil manner. Other, more dangerous forms of resistance soon made white Louisianians seem calm by comparison. Although Indians in the far West proved welcoming to small teams of American explorers, like the Lewis and Clark expedition, Indians of the lower and mid–Mississippi Valley recognized the weakness of the American regime. They pressed their own terms on federal policy in ways that shocked, frightened, and even offended American officials committed to racial supremacy.

But the greatest danger to most federal officials, whether in Washington or in Louisiana, was a revolt by the black majority in the Territory of Orleans. Anglo-Americans were convinced that French and Spanish legal codes had withered the proper controls on slaves and free people of color. Drawing on their own experiences in Virginia—the home for the Jefferson-

ian leadership and for most of their delegates in Louisiana—the governments of the Orleans and Louisiana Territories soon established regulations that imposed new restrictions on slaves and limited their ability to establish their freedom.

Slaves had lost the most from the Louisiana Purchase, and they responded accordingly. In January 1811 hundreds of slaves joined a revolt on the outskirts of New Orleans. Although the exact number of participants is impossible to determine, it was probably the largest revolt in U.S. history. Armed mostly with field tools and led by makeshift banners, the slaves marched on the territorial capital. Even when federal troops and territorial militias dispersed the slaves following a brief battle, territorial officials continued to worry about renewed slave conspiracies.

These domestic problems were all the more disturbing because international affairs had become more precarious. In 1808 Napoleon broke with his old ally, Spain, and launched an invasion of the Iberian Peninsula, which made a shambles of American relations with both Spain and France. Tensions between the United States and Great Britain—an unending problem since independence itself—were rising as well. In 1812 Madison sought the nation's first declaration of war to pursue a military campaign against Great Britain designed to coerce a change in British policy toward the United States. So, in 1812, U.S.-Spanish relations were frozen, while Madison's war soon devolved into a chaotic series of failed efforts to launch an American assault on Canada.

This state of affairs clashed with every American effort to pursue diplomatic priorities through reasoned negotiations. Yet these changes were not always for the worst. As Spanish authority disintegrated throughout the Americas, Anglo-American residents in the area around Baton Rouge declared their independence and pronounced themselves the leaders of the Republic of West Florida. Madison responded by ordering the annexation of West Florida. His proclamation combined old claims that West Florida had always been part of the Louisiana Purchase with new assertions that Spain had abandoned whatever sovereignty to that land it had once claimed. The War of 1812 created similar opportunities for the United States to crush Indian power on the Gulf Coast and, eventually, to seize more territory. Even the last battle of the war would serve the interests of Louisiana's residents. When the British attempted to invade New Orleans in the winter of 1814–1815, numerous slaves exploited the situation by running away. And when local residents contributed to the overwhelming American victory over the British, white Louisianians claimed that they had proven their loyalty to the United States.

As their behavior during the Battle of New Orleans showed, white Louisianians had learned how to participate in American politics. They had also learned the rules of American constitutionalism. By calling conspicuous attention to their loyalty and their knowledge of federal principles, residents of the Territory of Orleans persuaded Congress to create the state of Louisiana in 1812. Their neighbors to the north were hard at work as well. By 1819 Congress was prepared to create the state of Missouri. Local residents crafted a constitution and submitted it to Congress, confident that it would be an easy process. They were not alone in failing to predict the firestorm that followed

as members of Congress argued over the expansion of slavery. Congress resolved the problem only through a compromise that permitted Missouri to enter the Union along with Maine, a free state, and by agreeing to restrict the future expansion of slavery to states located below latitude 36°30′. As Chapters 8 and 10 make clear, the ongoing effort to build new governments in the land acquired through the Louisiana Purchase defined the sectional debate during the decades that followed.

In the process, the Missouri crisis transformed the way Americans thought about the Louisiana Purchase in particular and westward expansion in general. For a half-century many Americans believed that the greatest sources of tension in the country were between East and West. They also believed the greatest challenge facing the federal government was to overcome the distances separating East from West. After 1820 Americans focused almost exclusively on the tension they saw between free and slave states, a relationship the Missouri crisis had forever defined as one between North and South.

Of course, federal leaders would continue to worry about the West, and western settlers would continue to complain that they felt isolated; threatened by the Indians, who they considered unfair impediments to western settlement; and ignored by those who commanded the centers of power. Nonetheless, western settlers had been so successful in voicing those concerns that they continued to draw federal resources at a level disproportionate to their population, fostering a relationship with the federal government that remains to this day. Western settlers had also so effectively proven their commitment to the United States that they only seemed likely to cause violence or chaos when they argued about the expansion of slavery. Western states would find their own political voice during these years. Andrew Jackson was the first in a series of western presidents, and the rough-and-tumble democratic politics that formed the backbone of his electoral majority was itself a by-product of frontier life.

Coincidentally and almost conveniently, the diplomatic controversies that came with the Louisiana Purchase came to a close at the same time that the Missouri crisis signaled a new era in domestic politics. In 1819, the same year that members of Congress were coming to blows, Spanish and American negotiators were finally coming to terms. In the Transcontinental Treaty, they attempted to create what French and American negotiators could not: a treaty that defined Louisiana with boundaries acceptable to both parties and that did not create any alarming rules for how the United States would govern the people who lived within its boundaries. The chief American negotiator, Secretary of State John Quincy Adams, was able to press his terms on the Spanish because the United States was now dealing from a position of strength. The Spanish were eager for a settlement because they believed an alliance with the United States would clear the way for Spain to reestablish authority over Mexico. Spain had also abandoned its last claims to the Florida peninsula. Besides, the vulnerability of Florida had been clear to the Spanish since 1817, when Andrew Jackson turned a war against the Seminole Indians into an invasion of the Florida peninsula, ignoring the Spanish altogether. Jackson had done much the same during the War of 1812, when he seized Pensacola to punish Spanish officials who had offered a safe haven to Creek Indians.

The Spanish could have saved themselves the trouble of negotiating with the United States. In 1821, when the Senate finally approved the Transcontinental Treaty, Spain was forced to acknowledge the independence of Mexico. The only remaining European power on the North American mainland was Great Britain, but as American relations improved, the U.S.-Canadian border became a locus of trade rather than a site of conflict.

During the 1820s the United States consolidated its power as the emerging empire of the Americas. Whether that meant asserting the Monroe Doctrine with a gumption that bore little relationship to actual power, or claiming that the Compromise of 1820 provided the means to create an almost unlimited number of states, Americans became increasingly comfortable with their redefined republic. Within a generation, evils had become virtues. During the 1830s and 1840s the architects of manifest destiny would claim that expansion was essential to the republic rather than a threat. Even as expansion heightened sectional disputes, the United States created new territories and, in 1848, acquired a vast new western preserve following a war of aggression against Mexico. The United States was governed by a Constitution that was almost unchanged from the document in place at the time of the Louisiana Purchase. (The only change had been the Twelfth Amendment, which provided for the separate designation of presidential and vice presidential candidates and which was also the subject of congressional debate at the time of the Louisiana Purchase and the Governance Act of 1804.) But the constitutional order had nonetheless been transformed in ways no less profound than domestic politics or international affairs.

Expansion had become so attractive in no small part because the Louisiana Purchase seemed like such a success. The fact that the United States had remained united despite the addition of unfamiliar white citizens, the resistance of slaves and Indians, and a series of wars—whether declared or not—indicated that expansion was not so dangerous as the founding generation had believed. In time, it was the vision of the 1830s and 1840s that became the conventional wisdom in the American imagination. At the very end of the nineteenth century, the United States acquired yet more land at the expense of Spain. But there the similarities ended. The Spanish-American War reflected a boisterous optimism among its advocates. Even the opponents had less to say about expansion per se than about the moral qualms of invading foreign lands.

In the twentieth century the Louisiana Purchase entered American textbooks in a form that remained almost unchanged. Those histories described the purchase as a product of Jeffersonian planning, a reflection of American expansionism, a harbinger of things to come. This was the case whether commentators intended to celebrate or condemn the purchase. Most commentators described it as a moment of progress for the United States in particular and for North America in general. Others pointed to the fact that acquisition of new territory by the United States was a critical step in the near-eradication of Indians and the expansion of slavery on a continental scale. Regardless of perspective, however, the purchase always seemed *planned*. What was lost in the process was the fact that the purchase the United States got was not the purchase Americans had sought. What was equally forgotten was the ambivalence and the fear that led so many people to believe that the Louisiana Purchase might be the nation's undoing or the almost surprised nature of the celebration when news of the purchase reached the United States.

Surprise often disappears with hindsight. That the Louisiana Purchase would happen and that it would seem beneficial for the United States appears obvious, so much so that it is hard to recapture the ambivalent mix of uncertainty and of opportunity that so many Americans experienced in 1803. It is also easy to forget just how new the American experiment actually was. The political, administrative, and judicial structures that would become hallmarks of the federal structure were still in their infancy. Those structures would face unprecedented challenges after 1803, as the Louisiana Purchase forced people to consider how the United States could become an American empire.

1

Building a New Nation: American Politics in a Revolutionary Age

ANDREW TREES

In the summer of 1776 the delegates to the Second Continental Congress offered a bold affirmation of a new national beginning: "THE UNANIMOUS DECLARATION OF THE THIRTEEN UNITED STATES OF AMERICA," justifying the rebellion against England based on "self-evident" truths that proved not only the nation's right but its "duty . . . to throw off such government." The Declaration of Independence seemed to foretell the unfolding of a plan for national success that was beyond doubt.

Beneath its confident words, though, lurked an anxiety about the nation. The emphasis on unanimity disguised the deep fissures within the country and within each state, where about one-third of the populace remained loyal to Great Britain and another third were tepid patriots at best. The remaining third seemed oblivious or uncommitted to the struggle for independence, but their allegiances potentially could go anywhere. In addition, the new truths expressed in the Declaration and in the debates about the form the government was to take were far from self-evident and revealed tremendous uncertainty about the nation's future.[1] Having rejected the political models of Great Britain and the nations of Europe, political leaders faced a stark challenge: How could the American people build a resilient political system while rejecting so many of the institutions essential to European politics?

The United States of America may have secured its independence on the battlefield by 1783, but its leaders still faced an ongoing struggle to define, establish, and secure the nation's revolutionary heritage. American leaders recognized that winning the war was only the first step in the long process of building a nation. In an open letter of farewell upon his retirement as commander of America's army, George Washington made clear that although the war was over, the crucial work of building a nation remained undone: "This is the time of [our] political probation, this is the moment when the eyes of the whole World are turned upon them, this is the moment to establish or ruin [our] national Character forever."[2] Washington believed that the very meaning of the Revolution was still an open question that would be decided in the crucial years to come. "It is yet to be decided," he wrote, "whether the Revolution must ultimately be considered as a blessing or a curse: a blessing or a curse, not to the present age alone, for with our fate will the destiny of unborn Millions be involved."[3]

In the decades that followed, Americans continued to think of themselves in such grand terms. That attitude proved as important as anything else in determining the political, diplomatic, and constitutional conditions that put the United States in a position to acquire the Louisiana Purchase and that shaped American attitudes toward incorporating it. This chapter addresses the political dynamics within the United States at that time—dynamics that, in the 1780s and 1790s, established a set of priorities and behaviors that shaped the new nation's constitutional and policymaking structure (which is the concern of the other authors in this anthology). In the wake of the Revolution, American leaders wrestled with how to sustain its principles. This essay offers a brief introduction to the major issues that dominated the American political landscape during those years, for the efforts to secure the promise of the Revolution would set the stage for the Louisiana Purchase.

Inventing American Politics

Americans faced many challenges as they began the work of building a new nation. Above all, they had to construct a new government. From the early days of the Revolution, John Adams, who played a leading role during the Revolution as both a member of the Continental Congress and as a diplomat for the fledgling nation, argued that creating a proper government was the "great and indispensable Work" of the Revolution, which he considered "the most difficult and dangerous Part of the Business Americans have to do in this mighty Contest."[4] But what sort of government could they create after a revolution rejecting the only model for government most of them had known? Although the Continental Congress created a committee to draft a constitution for the national government in July 1776, the demands of fighting the most powerful nation in the world left the founders with little time to worry about designing a new government. Even when the Continental Congress finally approved the Articles of Confederation in November 1777, it took four more years for the states to ratify the document, and the government that it created had sharply limited powers.

Unsurprisingly, with their deep distrust of centralized power because of their recent experiences as British colonials, the members of Congress designed a weak national government. The Articles of Confederation largely continued the government that had emerged from the Second Continental Congress, giving the legislative body the power to declare war and make peace, conduct diplomacy, regulate Indian affairs, appoint military and naval officers, require the states to provide soldiers or dictate orders to those soldiers, coin money, and issue paper currency. But Congress could not levy taxes or regulate trade. States not only held the purse strings, but they also had the ultimate authority to make and execute their own laws. Congress also had no executive branch to enforce its laws or carry out its policies. The Articles of Confederation can almost be thought of as a treaty uniting thirteen separate nations, rather than as a constitution creating one.

Although the United States eventually altered this constitutional order, the Articles of Confederation introduced principles that proved critical to the kind of domestic order and international system that Americans would attempt to create through the Louisiana Purchase. The Articles reflected the American obsession with securing a balance between local and national forms of power. The authors of the Articles were also deeply concerned with preserving an effective union of states, a union within which individual white citizens or families could pursue their own opportunities.

As Chapters 9 and 10 of this book show, these constitutional concerns came to dominate much of the political debate during the first century after independence. But along with the task of creating a government, Americans wrestled with the more nebulous one of creating a national political culture, a set of informal rules to guide political conduct. Although worries about political culture may seem far removed from the central duties of government, political leaders viewed political culture as integral to the success or failure of the government as a whole. The two were intertwined, each shaping the other. In this task, leaders also found themselves facing a daunting challenge. The thirteen states had developed largely independently of one another, and residents of many states were often more familiar with British standards than with the practices of other states. Suddenly, the practical necessity of a more effective constitutional order demanded that these different peoples begin to think of themselves as one nation. This created difficulties, as politicians unfamiliar with one another were forced to work together for the first time during the Revolution. Highlighting the complexity of the new national political arena, Adams wrote,

In a Provincial Assembly, where we know a Man's Pedigree and Biography, his Education, Profession and Connections, as well as his Fortune, it is easy to see what it is that governs a Man and determines him to this Party in Preference to that, to this System of Politicks rather than another, etc. . . . But here it is quite otherwise. We frequently see Phenomena which puzzles us. It requires Time to enquire and learn the Characters and Connections, the Interests and Views of a Multitude of Strangers.[5]

Sometimes Adams despaired of understanding this new arena, given its complexity: "A Mind as vast as the Ocean or Atmosphere is necessary to penetrate and comprehend all the intricate and complicated Interests which compose the Machine of the Confederate Colonies."[6]

National Shortcomings

With the end of the war, the shortcomings of the Articles of Confederation quickly became clear. After printing money indiscriminately to finance the war against Britain, the United States found itself in a precarious financial situation, which its limited financial powers left it unable to resolve. Many feared that state governments were only worsening the situation. After chafing under English rule, most states had created governments that gave nearly all power to popularly elected legislatures, a decision that contributed to the young nation's instability. No one spent more time analyzing these problems and thinking of possible solutions than James Madison, a young Virginian who had had firsthand experience with the shortcomings of America's early political institutions as a state representative to the Continental Congress under the Articles of Confederation.

After months of study, Madison drew up a document entitled "Vices of the Political System of the United States," which outlined what he saw as the major problems facing the new nation. Although he noted a number of serious flaws with the national government, he dwelled at even greater length on the shortcomings of the state governments in the wake of the Revolution. He pointed to the "multiplicity of laws in the several states" and complained of the "luxuriancy of legislation." Madison also pointed out the "mutability of the laws of the states." Such instability could never be the foundation for proper government because laws were "repealed or superseded, before any trial can have been made of their merits, and even before a knowledge of them can have reached the remoter districts within which they were to operate." Worst of all, Madison noted, was the "injustice of the laws of the states," which called "into question the fundamental principle of republican Government, that the majority who rule in such government are the safest Guardians both of public Good and private rights."[7] Although patriots had fought the Revolution, at least in part, to give voice to the will of the people, many leaders were beginning to recognize that building a lasting nation would require more stability than simple majority rule could provide. One of the most important debates in the early years of the government was over the role of the people in government.

The Revolution had created not just a new nation but new attitudes among the people about their own role in that nation—and Americans began to challenge traditional sources of political authority as never before. Many of the elite men who had created a rhetoric that celebrated challenges to British power in the 1770s began to fear similar challenges to

their own in the 1780s. Men from nonaristocratic backgrounds such as Daniel Shays, emboldened by revolutionary rhetoric, no longer deferred to elite rule—they questioned it. Americans had revolted to throw off the tyranny of the British Crown, but many now feared that they had merely exchanged that tyranny for that of the mob.

Foreign powers also exploited the weakness of the Articles of Confederation. British ministers secretly instructed Canadians to maintain their forts and trading posts inside U.S. territory, because they correctly assumed that, with the Continental Army disbanded, the Americans would be unable to force their withdrawal. The British also attempted to persuade Vermonters, who had been denied statehood, to join Canada as a province, a tactic that eventually pushed Congress to make Vermont a state. Spanish officials also tested the new nation by making treaties with various Indian tribes. And in 1784, the Spanish closed the Mississippi to American navigation. Western farmers were completely dependent on the Mississippi to get their products to market, and Spain's action aroused serious talk among westerners about detaching themselves from the United States and joining the Spanish.

Toward a New Constitution

In the summer of 1787 both the structural problems of the Articles and the social unrest in many parts of the country motivated leading politicians throughout the United States to craft a new constitutional system. The men chosen to revise the Articles could draw on a great deal of practical experience, because nearly all of the states had written constitutions after 1776. The most radical constitutional experiment was in Pennsylvania, where delegates in the early days of the Revolution had created a government that gave nearly unchecked power to the people by creating a powerful, directly elected unicameral legislature. The most influential state constitution was created by Massachusetts delegates (John Adams wrote the actual document). Ratified in 1780, the Massachusetts state government included a house and a senate, a popularly elected governor with the power to veto legislation, and property qualifications for officeholders and voters. The example of the Massachusetts constitution would strongly influence the work of the federal convention (with the preamble of the national constitution even echoing that of Massachusetts, which read, "We . . . the people of Massachusetts . . . agree upon, ordain, and establish . . . ").

Still far from having any uniform feeling about what sort of national government should be created, the delegates nonetheless managed to agree on a number of crucial compromises that allowed them to create a framework for a new government. One of the most significant compromises was between large and small states. The House of Representatives, apportioned according to population, favored the large states, while the Senate, which gave each state equal representation, favored the small ones. The founders compromised on a number of other crucial issues as well, many of which are largely forgotten today. For example, the role of the people in the new government was a contentious issue throughout the convention. The founders struggled with how to contain the sort of popular movements that seemed to threaten national stability

without eliminating the representative aspect that Americans considered essential to any political system.

The Constitution also created the framework that would one day shape the efforts to incorporate the Louisiana Purchase into the United States. Although they did not establish specific provisions, the authors of the Constitution gave Congress the right to create new states. Perhaps more importantly, the Constitution implied that new states would enter the union on the same footing as the existing ones. The framers were continuing the principles introduced earlier that summer by the Northwest Ordinance. The ordinance established the principles of the territorial system, by which the federal government took direct charge of new polities on the frontiers of the union, with the promise that those polities could enter the union equal to older states. By introducing this notion of jurisdictional equality, both documents made a profound break from European empires, in which new settlements never shared political equality with older centers of power. This decision was rooted as much in pragmatism as in idealism. Equality in all its forms was, of course, a key revolutionary principle. But equality also seemed the only means to secure support for the Constitution and to preserve the union. After all, many Americans concluded, it was inequality within the British Empire that had fueled the American Revolution in the first place.

The Fragile Republic

After a bruising state-by-state fight over ratification, Americans began life under a new constitution. The document was a model of brevity, and American leaders recognized that the early days of government would play a central role in shaping the Constitution's final meaning. The early years of Congress served almost as a second constitutional convention, because questions of policy quickly became entangled in larger questions about the type of government members were attempting to create. American leaders were engaged in nothing less than a wide-reaching debate about what sort of nation the United States was to be.

The Constitution established the United States as a republic, a form of government not seen since the ancient examples of Rome and Greece. Of republicanism, Adams once wrote, "I confess I never understood it, and I believe no other man ever did or ever will."[8] Based on historical precedent, many thought that republican government was inherently fragile and unstable and believed that the United States of America would only survive for a short time. Even Washington thought that the government would not last more than twenty years. During the 1790s, political leaders continued to struggle with their attempt to turn thirteen independent states into one nation. Given the beliefs about the fragility of republican governments, the decade became a period of violent and extremist rhetoric, as every decision seemed to forebode potential disaster.

These beliefs about republicanism made most of the founders deeply distrustful of politics. All the leading men disdained the figure of the politician. Alexander Hamilton wrote sneeringly in the *Federalist Papers* of "the little arts of little politicians," confident that such a feeling would find widespread support.[9] According to Samuel Johnson's *Dictionary,* the very word meant something unsavory. Johnson defined the politician as a "man of artifice, of deep contrivance." If politicians were dangerous individually, party or faction represented the institutionalization of these figures in a combined form that could ruin a republican government ostensibly based on the search for a common good. As one American political commentator wrote in 1775, "For every division in any degree, is in a Political, what we call a disease in a Natural Body, which as it weakens its strength, so it tends to its destruction."[10] Republican government, theorists agreed, was particularly susceptible to the dangers of faction. And when parties began to emerge, many were sure that it was a harbinger of the end. The hostility to politicians and parties in the early republic helped create a highly personalized manner of conducting politics. Each player's attempts to fashion a role for himself politically would have to be constructed on grounds that, at least ostensibly, eschewed politics, heightening the importance of political manners and political culture in the new government.

Regional differences also continued to complicate the project of building a nation. Each state and region had developed its own particular political etiquette to guide the behavior of its leadership, and these differences were frequently the source of misunderstanding and division among the nation's political leaders. For example, Pennsylvania senator William Maclay kept a detailed diary of his two years in the Senate that reveals the problems created by trying to meld thirteen political cultures into one. After only a short time in the Senate, he wrote "I have been a bird alone. I have had to bear the Chilling cold of the North, and the intemperate Warmth of the South. Neither of which are favourable to the Middle State from which I come. Lee & Izard hot as the burning Sands of Carolina hate US. Adams with all his frigid Friends cool and wary, bear Us no good Will."[11]

Each region exhibited certain faults, according to Maclay. Of New England, Maclay wrote, "[N]o People in the Union dwell more on trivial distinctions, and Matters of Mere form" (p. 9). He complained that New Englanders were "an unmixed people . . . used only to see Neighbours like themselves" (p. 9). Because of this provinciality, Maclay did not think much of New Englanders when they left their region: "[F]or should they ever go abroad, being early used to a ceremonious and reserved behavior, and believing that good Manners consist intirely in punctilios. They only add a few more stiffened Airs to their deportment, excluding Good humor affability of conversation, and accomodation of temper and sentiment, as qualities too vulgar, for a Gentleman" (p. 9).

But the South was little better. Maclay noted, "I have observed ever since we began to do Business that a Jehu like Spirit has prevailed with a number of Gentlemen, and with none more than with the Member from the Antient dominion" (p. 10). Maclay complained that this Virginian, Richard Henry Lee, wanted "a most expensive and enormous Machine of a Federal Judiciary, pompous Titles, strong efforts after religious distinctions coercive laws for taking the Oaths & ca. & ca." (p. 10). After dining with another Virginian, Maclay mocked the boastful gallantry of the southerner: "But the Frothy Manners of Virginia were ever uppermost. Canvasbacks ham & Chickens Old Madeira, the Glories of the Antient Dominion, all amazing fine, were his constant Themes. Boasted of personal Prowess, more manual Exercise than any Man in New England. Fast but fine living in his Country, Wine or Cherry bounce from 12 O'Clock to night, every day. He seemed to practice these principles too, as often as the bottle passed him" (p. 365).

Not surprisingly, Maclay thought that Pennsylvania was the best state, blending the ideal qualities in its middling position. "We have really more republican plainess, and sincere openess of behaviour in Pennsylvania, than in any other place I have ever been," he wrote (pp. 8–9). Maclay's regional prejudices were common among national leaders of the day—one more obstacle in the struggle to create an effective national government.

Maclay's diary also reveals the central importance of political culture in these early years. Although legislative debates occupy a large portion of his diary, Maclay devoted considerable attention to political manners. Anxious to detect if the republican government was being turned in a monarchical direction, Maclay carefully examined the behavior of those around him. When some members of Congress proposed giving titles to members of government as a way to increase respect for them, Maclay saw it as an example of creeping monarchism that would eventually muffle the voice of the people. When Washington instituted a weekly levee for people to visit him and thus free himself from the endless rounds of calling upon people to which he would otherwise be socially obliged, Maclay again saw signs of creeping royalism. "Indeed from these small beginnings I fear we shall follow on," he wrote, "nor cease till we have reached the summit of Court

Etiquette, and all the frivolities fopperies and Expence practised in european Governments" (p. 70).

Despite his criticisms, Maclay was no less confused than many others in his attempt to find a proper style for himself and for the government. Even as he fretted about these practices, he repeatedly worried that American political manners fell short of European standards. Maclay's ambivalence revealed the difficulties in developing an appropriate style for the new republic. Americans self-consciously rejected European court politics and manners, but they also remained anxious to show the world that they were as refined as their Old World counterparts. They were left with the ticklish task of living up to the ideals of gentility while at the same time creating a government by and for the people, a kind of paradoxical republican gentility that demanded both simplicity and refinement.

Domestic Debates

The profound disagreements of the 1790s soon led to the formation of two parties, the Federalists and the Republicans. These parties emerged from heartfelt disagreements over specific policy choices, but they also reflected and shaped the emerging codes of behavior of the national government. Of course, republican ideals dictated that neither of these two groups would call itself a party, and neither was willing to recognize the other as a legitimate opposition for that same reason. Both sides believed that they were in a struggle to the death over the fate of the new nation.

Numerous issues gave birth to the party divisions. The most important early battles were fought over the nation's finances, a debate that revealed vastly different ideas about the power and importance of the national government. Under the Articles of Confederation, the Continental Congress had been unable to levy taxes without the unanimous consent of the states. Throughout the war, Congress relied on foreign loans and requisitions from the state, and the national government desperately needed to put its financial house in order. The infant nation owed approximately $10 million to foreign nations and $42 million to its own citizens. In addition, many of the states were burdened with substantial debts.

Alexander Hamilton, the first secretary of the Treasury, proposed a bold solution intended not only to secure the nation's finances but also to help shape the powerful national government that he envisioned. Unlike many of his peers, Hamilton's loyalty was entirely commanded by the nation, not by any state. Born in the West Indies into relative poverty, Hamilton's formative experiences as a youth had come while serving in the Continental Army. Like many of his fellow officers, this experience made him into a supporter of a strong national government. At times humiliated by the Continental Congress's inability to prosecute the war more vigorously, Hamilton was determined to create a national government that could command respect and honor from other nations.

At the request of Congress in 1789, Hamilton issued a report on the public credit and proposed a bold plan to salvage the nation's finances. He recommended that the federal government fund the national debt—that is, sell new securities that would pay interest to cover the amount owed. He also proposed that the national government pay off the state debts. Hamilton hoped not only to secure the nation's debt but also to entice citizens of the upper classes to purchase the new securities and thus tie their fortunes to the success of the new nation.

Hamilton's plan created a storm of controversy. Many of the states in the South had paid most of their debts and saw Hamilton's plan as unfair. In addition, some argued that the least deserving would reap the largest benefits. Many patriots who had bought government securities to support the government during the war had been forced to sell them at a fraction of their value out of dire financial need. Under Hamilton's plan, speculators, rather than true patriots, would gain the most. Hamilton did not simply wish to enrich speculators, arguing instead that it was essential for the United States to get its financial house in order. In the end, Hamilton managed to secure enough support only by promising to move the capital south, from Philadelphia to the banks of the Potomac. In the process, he mollified southerners in particular, but particularly the influential Virginians.

Hamilton soon followed his early success with an even more controversial proposal in December 1790, his report on a national bank. The secretary of the Treasury proposed that Congress create a national bank that, while costing taxpayers nothing, would provide a place to deposit tax revenues as well as provide short-term loans to the government. In addition, the bank could help regulate state banks and offer much-needed credit to expand the economy. Hamilton also proposed raising capital for the bank through a $10 million public stock offering. Shares could be partially paid for with government bonds, a device that would further tie the interests of the propertied class to the new government.

This proposal generated even greater controversy, as some suggested that the bank was not only unconstitutional but would be a source of corruption. Unsure of whether or not to sign the bill, Washington asked Thomas Jefferson, the secretary of state, and Hamilton to advise him. Jefferson, fearing that the bank represented a dangerous step toward an excessive concentration of economic and political power in the national government, argued that the bank was fundamentally unconstitutional, because chartering a bank was not among the enumerated powers of Congress. He wrote, "To take a single step beyond the boundaries thus specifically drawn from the powers of Congress is to take possession of a boundless field of power no longer susceptible of any definition."[12]

Despite his strongly worded declaration, Jefferson would later prove willing to bend his political principles to achieve pragmatic political goals. Nothing exemplified this pragmatism better than the Louisiana Purchase. Jefferson believed the Constitution provided an important bulwark against policies that could thwart the principles of the Revolution. In the case of the national bank, Jefferson concluded that such a step threatened to return the nation to the kind of governmental tyranny that it had fought against only a few short years before. Hamilton took a much broader view of the Constitution. Citing Article I, Section 8, Hamilton argued that Congress could enact all measures "necessary and proper" and that only measures expressly forbidden in the Constitution were unconstitutional. Hamilton's argument carried the day, and Washington signed the bill, which chartered the Bank of the United States for twenty years—a harbinger, many feared, of a powerful national government. But Hamilton's early victories had helped create a growing coalition of congressmen who dreaded the direction that the national government seemed to be taking. The rest of the 1790s would be a period of profound political conflict, as Federalists and Republicans fought for the soul of the nation.

Foreign Policy

Nothing played a more important role in debates between the two emerging parties than foreign policy. In fact, foreign policy loomed far larger on the American agenda than at almost any other time in its history, for the simple reason that America was a small and inconsequential nation subject to the whims of others more powerful. Most important, America found itself caught in the ongoing struggle between France and Great Britain. Like the other conflicts of the 1790s, Americans attached enormous symbolic weight to the direction of foreign policy, seeing it as a crucial influence on the character of the nation. For Republicans, the government in revolutionary France represented the triumphal spread of republicanism and freedom abroad and made France a natural ally, a tie only strengthened by French assistance during the American Revolution. Federalists focused on different aspects of the new regime—namely its terror and violence—and saw the French example as a dangerous warning of the tendency of republican governments to descend to mob rule. Meanwhile, many Federalists looked to Great Britain as an example of a balanced government that protected the rights of its citizens. Republicans took a far darker view of this and saw attempts to link the country's fortunes to England as nothing less than a way to "worm out the elective principle."[13]

For both sides, a politician's sympathies for Britain or France became an indication of his partisan affiliation. Jeffersonian Republicans were by and large more sympathetic to the French Revolution than their Federalist opponents, but they were hardly zealous Francophiles. Instead, they were more fiercely anti-British than the Federalists. The foreign power toward which most American policymakers were uniformly hostile was Spain, primarily because they were so bitterly irritated by Spanish restrictions on American trade down the Mississippi. When Americans lost the right of deposit on the heels of the Treaty of San Ildefonso (the secret agreement by which Spain returned Louisiana to French hands), American policymakers of all stripes concluded that Spain was an inherently corrupt power that operated outside the acceptable rules of diplomacy. But shared diplomatic concerns did not lead to consensus on proper diplomatic measures. Not only did each party accuse the other of proposing foolish plans to resolve problems with Spain, but by 1800 the divisions within the American political elite were simply too deep to be overcome by the unifying anger at Spain.

Foreign policy continually pushed to the forefront of national debates throughout the 1790s. In the mid-1790s, as British ships began seizing American vessels trading with France and their crews boarded American vessels in search of deserters from the Royal Navy, the nation seemed poised for war with Britain.

Tensions were exacerbated by border disputes between America and Canada. In 1795, Congress narrowly approved a treaty negotiated by John Jay, chief justice of the United States. Although it proved unpopular because it restricted trade with the French and allowed Britain to violate American neutrality, the treaty eased tensions between the two countries. In response, America found itself increasingly drawn into conflict with France, which began to seize American ships carrying goods to British ports.

After failed diplomacy convinced them that war was imminent, the Federalist-dominated Congress passed extreme measures in preparing for the coming conflict. Along with a substantial tax hike and the creation of a large army, Congress passed four measures in 1798 that came to be known as the Alien and Sedition Acts. The Sedition Act was so broad that it made it virtually impossible to distinguish between sedition and legitimate political dissent—in one notorious example, a Republican congressman was jailed for comments made in a private letter. The principal target of the acts proved to be Republican newspapers. In response, Jefferson and Madison both anonymously wrote manifestos (later endorsed by the Kentucky and Virginia legislatures, respectively) that questioned the constitutionality of the acts and that asserted the rights of states to judge the constitutionality of federal actions. The careful construction of a new constitution and a new nation seemed to be on the verge of unraveling only a decade after it had begun.

Against the wishes of his cabinet, President John Adams sent one final diplomatic mission to France, which proved successful. Suddenly faced with peace, the Federalists had over-reached and found their popular support eroded by high taxes and distaste for the Alien and Sedition Acts. In a closely fought presidential battle, Jefferson defeated Adams, and the country braced for the first real transition in power under the Constitution. Despite the violent disagreements between Federalists and Republicans, the transfer was peaceful, a recognition that legitimacy could only be conferred through constitutionally mandated channels. Such success boded well for the young nation.

In his inaugural address, Jefferson viewed his victory as no less significant than the revolutionary triumph a quarter-century earlier. He claimed that his election was a return to "the essential principles of our Government . . . [which] form the bright constellation which has gone before us and guided our steps through an age of revolution and reformation." Addressing the divisions that had wreaked havoc on the new nation, he proffered a healing hand. "We are all republicans: we are all federalists," he said, inviting Federalists to join with the Republicans in a union based on "harmony and affection."[14] Of course, much as in the Declaration, Jefferson's words belied the deep divisions that continued to separate the nation. His election did reveal at least one major triumph, though: the triumph of a national political culture that, even if it could not guarantee unanimity, provided stability.

But Jefferson also had reason to worry. The experiences of the previous quarter-century of independence convinced him that the United States faced diverse threats, all of which threatened to render the states anything but united. Jefferson's challenge (and the nation's) would be to preserve unity. Foreign events would once again intrude to make that task more difficult.

The French Revolution triggered a generation of warfare, which repeatedly threatened to engulf the nation. And every major European power retaining a foothold in North America was a potential foe.

Not all of these dangers were external. The fears of popular unrest in the 1780s that proved so important in creating the federal Constitution still led some Americans to dread internal disputes that could rip the nation apart. And while the Constitution contained the tensions between large and small states, between East and West, or between North and South, national leaders recognized that those tensions would never be fully resolved. Members of the Jefferson administration worried that some crisis might yet fuel those tensions in ways that the constitutional order could not contain.

As Jefferson and his administration faced the challenges of governing, they struggled to chart their own path, one that avoided both the ineffectiveness of the 1780s and the consolidation and centralization of Hamilton and the Federalists in the 1790s. No sooner were they in office than they would face the new challenge of incorporating a new territory that doubled the size of the country—the Louisiana Purchase.

Notes

1. See Scott Douglas Gerber, ed., *The Declaration of Independence* (Washington, D.C.: CQ Press, 2002).

2. George Washington, 8 June 1783, "Circular Letter of Farewell to the Army," in *The Writings of George Washington,* ed. John C. Fitzpatrick (Washington: U.S. Government Printing Office, 1931–1944), XXVII: 8.

3. Washington Circular Letter to the States, 8 June 1783, *Writings of Washington,* XXVI: 485.

4. John Adams to Mercy Warren, 16 April 1776, Charles F. Adams, ed., *Correspondence Between John Adams and Mercy Warren* (New York: Arno Press, 1972), LXXII: 222. Hereafter cited as *Warren-Adams Letters.*

5. *Diary and Autobiography of John Adams,* ed. L. H. Butterfield et al. (Cambridge: Harvard University Press, 1961), I: 161.

6. Adams to James Warren, 24 October 1775, *Warren-Adams Letters,* I: 161.

7. James Madison, "Vices of the Political System," April 1787, *PJM,* IX: 348–357.

8. Adams to Warren, 20 July 1807, *Warren-Adams Letters,* LXXIII: 353.

9. Alexander Hamilton, "*Federalist* No. 11," Harold C. Syrett and Jacob E. Cooke, eds., *The Papers of Alexander Hamilton* (New York: Columbia University Press, 1961–1987), iv.

10. "Essay upon Government," 38, as cited in Gordon S. Wood, *The Creation of the American Republic 1776–1787* (New York: Norton, 1969), 59.

11. William Maclay, *The Diary of William Maclay and Other Notes on Senate Debates,* 25. All future references will appear in the text.

12. Thomas Jefferson, "Opinion on the Constitutionality of the National Bank," 15 February 1791, Merrill D. Peterson, ed., *Jefferson Writings* (New York: Library of America, 1984), 416.

13. Jefferson to Elbridge Gerry, 26 January 1799, *Jefferson Writings,* 1056.

14. Jefferson, First Inaugural Address, 4 March 1801, *Jefferson Writings,* 492–496.

2

Children of Empire or Concitoyens?
Louisiana's French Inhabitants

JAY GITLIN

With the purchase of Louisiana, the United States expelled its imperial rivals from a vast area and secured the main trade route of the North American interior for its western citizens. The port of New Orleans—long coveted by European policymakers—was now in the hands of the young republic. The upriver town of St. Louis now provided a gateway to the West and the promise of a limitless trade in furs. The vision of a republican empire was beginning to take shape. The glorious dreams of commerce and territory were tempered, however, by one potential nightmare. There was a human reality on this vast and fertile ground. Anglo-Americans were not the first people of European descent to stake their claim to Louisiana. Far from it; France may have sold Louisiana to the United States, but there were substantial French-speaking (francophone) communities in this territory. Shrewd and observant French businessmen called this land home, and they were following events closely.

Four decades earlier, the French empire in North America had fallen, and for roughly half a century, from 1763 to 1815, the boundaries of this western frontier were up for grabs. Two great empires attempted to establish their sovereignty over areas that had previously been part of that French empire. The Spanish had jurisdiction over Louisiana. But even defining what Louisiana was proved complicated. That colony consisted of three subregions: Lower Louisiana, including the great port of New Orleans; the Arkansas country; and Upper Louisiana—also known as Spanish Illinois—which contained the towns of Ste. Genevieve and St. Louis and a number of smaller settlements. The British gained jurisdiction over Canada, which, of course, contained the cities of Quebec and Montreal. They also controlled the former *pays d'en haut,* the Great Lakes region anchored by the settlements and forts at Detroit and Michilimackinac. Finally, the British had jurisdiction over the French villages in the present-day states of Illinois and Indiana. The villages in this last region—including Vincennes, Peoria, Kaskaskia, and Cahokia—were the weakest links in the imperial chain. They were removed from the centers of power, yet connected by ties of trade and family to both Spanish Illinois and New Orleans to the west and south and the Great Lakes and Montreal to the north and east.

The great show of imperial (and later, republican) plans and agents notwithstanding, the reality was this: The region was dominated by

Indian people who controlled the land, raised crops, and gathered fish and furs. The tribal majority cast a long shadow over the claims of non-Indian politicians. In between Indian communities were French villages and incipient cities such as Detroit, St. Louis, Natchez, and New Orleans, inhabited by fur traders and merchants who managed the commerce between Indian America and Europe. A plantation economy—mostly sugar, tobacco, and cotton—had emerged in Lower Louisiana, and the French in Illinois with the help of African slave labor raised a significant amount of wheat and maize. But this vast area was best described as a trading-post regime—a region of colonial towns within Indian country. French was literally the lingua franca that tied together this complex polyglot, multicultural mid-America.

This chapter explores the culture that emerged in the center of North America in the second half of the eighteenth century. At a time when every European power was trying to stake its claim to the place that became the Louisiana Purchase, the local residents were also hard at work protecting their own interests. The discussion in Chapter 1 showed how policymakers in the United States were struggling to craft a republic. During the same years, Europeans and colonial residents were struggling to craft empires that would serve their needs. Although focusing primarily on the eighteenth century, this chapter extends into the nineteenth to show the ways that residents in Louisiana responded to the purchase as well as to show the considerable continuities that transcended the purchase. Beyond those particulars, however, this chapter proposes another argument: that Louisiana had a history before the Louisiana Purchase. It was this history that shaped the way people in Louisiana responded to news of the purchase itself.

A Land of Empires: France, Spain, and Britain in North America

All the subregions within the former boundaries of French North America had much in common, and the leading merchants in towns from New Orleans to St. Louis to Vincennes to Montreal often corresponded—primarily about business matters, but also about the political events that affected trade. Children might be sent to Montreal, New Orleans, or to France to be educated. In the end, neither the Spanish nor the British were successful in controlling their new acquisitions. The Spanish retreated to Texas, the British to Canada. In the middle of this period, of course, a new player emerged— the republic of the United States. The French, in the meantime, went about their business. On the eve of the Louisiana Purchase, few Anglo-Americans in the East had even an imperfect understanding of how events had unfolded in the territories the nation had acquired. A quick review, then, is in order.

Spain accepted the port of New Orleans and the Trans-Mississippi portion of Louisiana through the Treaty of Fontainebleau in November 1762. Louis XIV ceded this territory to Charles III as compensation for the loss of Florida to Great Britain. France thus avoided British domination of the entire mid-continent of North America and left open the possibility of a French colonial comeback at a later date. Spain, after years of procrastination, finally sent Antonio de Ulloa to Louisiana in 1766 to serve as the colony's governor. After further delays in the formal transfer of sovereignty, Ulloa was essentially booted out by the French inhabitants, who feared Spanish trading restrictions and were battling a currency crisis. This Louisiana Revolt of 1768 anticipated the American Revolution by seven years. Several leaders of the revolt even suggested setting up a republic and hoped France would back them. (French ministers briefly considered this course, thinking that a Louisiana republic would encourage English colonists to follow suit.) Instead, the next year Spain sent an Irish officer in the Spanish service, Alejandro O'Reilly, to put down the revolt and establish Spanish rule once and for all. Five of the French rebels were executed.

Although Spain eventually played a constructive role in the growth of Louisiana, the Spanish always considered the province a defensive buffer zone between the British colonies and New Spain. Only that rationale allowed Spanish officials to justify the annual subsidy of 400,000 pesos the Crown spent to administer Louisiana. Even this amount of Spanish largesse proved insufficient. Officials in Louisiana were constantly facing budget deficits. Spanish Louisiana was neither a profitable nor an essential part of the empire. Few Spaniards ever visited the colony; even fewer settled there.

The British accepted Canada and the Trans-Allegheny portion of French Louisiana in 1763 with less reluctance. Indeed, they entered the West with confidence. The departing French governor of Louisiana, Jean-Jacques Blaise D'Abbadie, described the British as "men drunk with success, and who regard themselves as masters of the world."[1] The outbreak of Pontiac's War in the summer of 1763 destroyed those illusions. An Ottawa warrior named Pontiac coordinated the pan-tribal at-

tack on the British garrison at Detroit. His success inspired other tribal warriors in the West, who successfully attacked a number of British outposts, including the important fort of Michilimackinac. The British eventually abandoned smaller posts such as Green Bay, which they never reoccupied.

The British quickly realized that defeating the French empire did not mean that they had won the West. The British did not occupy the Illinois country until 1765—two years after the Treaty of Paris. By 1768 the British had admitted their weaknesses and were ready to dismantle many western posts in the backcountry. By the winter of 1771–1772 the British had abandoned Fort Pitt and Fort de Chartres in Illinois. Convinced that French traders in the West were partly responsible for their problems, Gov. James Murray of Quebec recommended that the British remove French inhabitants from the interior. The British eventually attempted to expel the French (which they had previously implemented in Acadia in 1755) in Vincennes, in present-day Indiana. A proclamation ordering the inhabitants on the Wabash to "quit those countries instantly and without delay" was issued on April 8, 1772. The French inhabitants protested that they were settlers with legitimate land titles, not "vagabonds," as they had been described, and they declared their fidelity to the British king, George III. Meanwhile, the French at Kaskaskia (in present-day Illinois), frustrated with the arbitrary and oppressive acts of their successive British commandants, Reed and Wilkins, sent a memorandum to British general Thomas Gage in 1772 that outlined a plan for a republican form of government modeled after the colony of Connecticut.[2]

Gage returned to England, and his reports and advice contributed to yet another change in British policy. The Quebec Act of 1774 restored civil law in Quebec and guaranteed tolerance of Catholicism. Indeed, this act (which infuriated Protestant Anglo-Americans) even granted key legal and political privileges to French Catholics in North America that were not extended to Irish Catholics back in Great Britain—a fact that did not go unnoticed. The Quebec Act also extended Quebec's boundaries to include Indian country between the Ohio and Mississippi rivers. In short, it restored much of the form and substance of the pre-1763 era.

Although the British seemed intent on putting their imperial house in order, the fact remained that both Britain and Spain had had great trouble fitting their costly new territories into their imperial systems. Spain and Great Britain also faced each other, with intermittent hostility, across uncertain and awkward boundaries. The Mississippi River had once been the central, unifying artery of Louisiana; it functioned considerably less well as a border. Spanish and British officials complained constantly that trade was being siphoned off to the opposite bank of the river. Contraband was a fact of life. It could hardly have been otherwise. The road that connected the two main settlements of Spanish Illinois—St. Louis and Ste. Genevieve—ran along the coast of British Illinois.

It was in the midst of this confusion that British settlers in the colonies south of Canada declared their independence. The American Revolution, and especially the war that came in its wake, had profound ramifications for the borderlands of the North American interior. In 1779 Spain joined with France and the American rebels and declared war on Great Britain. The Revolution crippled any Spanish attempts to benefit from the fur trade of Upper Louisiana. To make matters worse, a partial British blockade of the gulf disrupted the flow of goods in and out of New Orleans, and gangs of mostly Anglo pirates plundered boats traveling along the lower Mississippi. Until the 1790s Spanish officials in Upper Louisiana were forced to look the other way while French merchants under their jurisdiction traded illegally with British companies. Despite their economic advantage, British officials knew that British Illinois could never be secure while New Orleans was in Spanish hands. They considered war with Spain in 1779 a golden opportunity to seize control of the lower Mississippi Valley.

As the Revolution progressed, neither the British nor the Spanish felt secure. Could either power rely on the allegiance of the Indian and French inhabitants of this vast area? At this point in the region's history a new group took the stage: George Rogers Clark and his motley band of frontiersmen.

In the manner of a comic opera, George Rogers Clark and his small force of Virginians and Pennsylvanians conquered the French Illinois villages of Kaskaskia, Cahokia, and Vincennes in 1778 in the name of the Virginia government. Later that year, Lt. Gov. Henry Hamilton of Detroit and his British army retook Vincennes. Then, in February 1779, Clark and the Americans—after a march of some 180 miles in the dead of winter—recaptured Vincennes and took Hamilton prisoner, sending him in irons to a jail in Williamsburg, Virginia. It is a heroic episode that has been told and retold by historians and writers of historical fiction. In reality, half of Clark's troops were local French villagers and the majority of those commanded by Hamilton were also local Frenchmen. It seems that the French settlers of Vincennes had become old hands at taking oaths of allegiance during the course of this campaign.

Clark's so-called conquest—comic though it must have seemed to the French inhabitants—had important consequences. It established an American (or, at least, a Virginian) claim to the region that was pursued by the new republic at the peace table. Virginia governor Patrick Henry established the Illinois country as a part of Virginia in 1778, but following the precedent of the British empire, allowed civil government there to lapse in 1781. Virginia ceded the entire area to the United States in 1784. Together with smaller cessions from other states, this land would become the Northwest Territory of the United States. In the wake of its withdrawal from Illinois, Virginia left a legacy of political anarchy and unpaid debts. A number of substantial Illinois merchants who had supplied goods to the Virginians suffered financially for their support of the American cause. The United States, in turn, neglected the area and failed to send a civil representative to Illinois until 1790.

Francophone North America and the United States

Two new areas that were formerly part of the French empire became part of the United States in the 1790s—the Detroit region in 1796 and the Mississippi Territory in 1798. The French in Spanish Louisiana looked on with growing interest. Both in the Illinois country and in the De-

troit region during its first decade of American rule from 1796 to 1805, the United States did little to reassure the French inhabitants that the new regime would be either responsive or responsible. In both Vincennes and Detroit, only one American officer—John Francis Hamtramck, a native of Quebec and a Roman Catholic—managed to command respect and create a bond between the francophone citizens and their new government. If one had surveyed French opinion about Americans in the decade before the Louisiana Purchase, the results would not, in general, seem positive. Zenon Trudeau, the French lieutenant governor of Upper Louisiana under the Spanish regime, wrote to François Vallé at Ste. Geneviève in 1792 that the Americans were "un peuple sans loix ni discipline [a people without law or discipline]."[3]

If the French had already begun to forge their stereotypes of the Americans, the reverse was even more striking—and the prejudices of Americans writing from the centers of power on the Atlantic Coast were rarely informed by personal encounters. Although the incorporation of Louisiana into the republic was not the first instance of French inhabitants in the West becoming American citizens, the magnitude of this addition forced a systematic discussion of the issue for the first time. And Jeffersonians and Federalists alike publicly speculated about how to make good Americans out of the French inhabitants of the Mississippi Valley.

Ethnic and cultural biases aside, most American concerns were political. This continued through the 1790s and was still the case at the time of the Louisiana Purchase. Jefferson himself, writing to John Breckinridge in 1803, worried that "the Constitution had made no provision for our holding foreign territory, still less for incorporating foreign nations into our union."[4] The Constitution had clearly authorized the admission of new states into the Union and also implied that America might expand territorially, but the status of the inhabitants acquired by such expansion was open to judicial interpretation. Behind such constitutional concerns lay the assumption that American citizenship, like divine grace, was properly bestowed on those individuals who had made a conscious decision to deserve it. The common stereotype held by many American political leaders was that the French of the Mississippi Valley were, at best, indifferent to the rights and responsibilities of a free people. Simply put, they were French (strike one); they were ignorant of the principles of self-governance, being the "children" of empire (strike two); and they were Roman Catholic and therefore spiritual servants of the Pope (strike three). This last bias against Catholicism was rarely expressed in public, but it certainly festered in the minds of many. For example, Frederick Bates, a young Virginian and Jeffersonian bureaucrat who held appointive offices in Detroit and St. Louis, described the French in Missouri in a letter to his brother:

The very name of *liberty* deranges their intellects. . . .
If their Commandant spurned them from
his presence: deprived them of half their
Estate or ordered them to the black Hole, they
received the doom as the dispensation of
Heaven, and met their fate with all that
resignation with which they are accustomed to
submit indifferently. . . . Surrounded with
wretchedness they dance and sing; and if they have
their relations and friends within the sound of
their violin, they have nothing more to ask of the
Virgin; Provided her viceregent the Priest, will
deign to forgive those sins which perhaps they
never committed.[5]

Though Bates clearly had a low opinion of Catholicism, the point is that his religious bias informed his assessment of whether or not French Catholics were suitable as potential citizens of the republic. Bates assumed that they were in the habit of being submissive, spiritually and politically. Albert Gallatin, Jefferson's secretary of the Treasury, was a native French speaker, but he was from Geneva, the Calvinist heart of Europe. His opinion of the French in the Mississippi Valley, expressed in a letter to Thomas Jefferson, was that they were "but one degree above the French West Indians, than whom a more ignorant and depraved race of civilized men did not exist."[6] And so it went. Many American politicians would have agreed with Josiah Quincy, the Massachusetts Federalist, when he proclaimed that the people of Louisiana "may be girt upon us for a moment, but no real cement can grow from such an association."[7] Indeed, it is not too much of a stretch to assume that many Anglo-Americans, like the British before them, secretly hoped that the French would either disappear or, at the very least, be outnumbered as soon as possible so that the republic might progress unimpeded. One Anglo-American newcomer suggested at a cocktail party that it would take many French funerals to improve St. Louis.[8] It is worth noting here that some Jeffersonian territorial appointees were not above discrediting those French merchants who had trade priority and status in the western territories as a way of advancing their own interests in the race for political office and land.

"The Character of the Inhabitants"

But just how well did the Americans understand the inhabitants of Louisiana? How valid were these preconceptions? And how well are those francophone inhabitants understood two centuries later, given the relative absence of historical scholarship directed at this Creole society?

The first misconception was geographical. It is worth reiterating that this region, as a social and cultural entity, stretched beyond the boundaries of the Louisiana Purchase to include places such as Vincennes and Detroit. French customs and language predominated. English did not eclipse French as a common language in St. Louis and Detroit by the 1830s. It would take the Civil War to finally determine that struggle for language supremacy in New Orleans. The linguistic battle was complicated by racial boundaries, as people of African descent (both free and slave) might belong to either linguistic group. Add to this mix an incredible array of immigrants and Indian groups, and one can appreciate the reaction of William Keating, who made the following observations after traveling from Pennsylvania to Fort Wayne, Indiana, in 1823:

Not being previously aware of the diversity in the character of the inhabitants, the sudden change from an American to a French population, has a surprising, and to say the least, an unpleasant effect; for the first twenty-four hours, the traveller fancies himself in a real Babel. . . . The business of a town of this kind differs so materially from that carried on in our cities, that it is almost impossible to fancy ourselves still within the same territorial limits.[9]

Similar reactions could be heard throughout the region, where the sense of flow, literally, went from north to south, not east to west. And it was a region dominated by towns. Detroit and St. Louis were still small in 1803, neither place with much more than a thousand inhabitants. But both functioned as urban centers,

connecting the paths of goods and people. Merchants' wives in St. Louis looked to New Orleans and to Paris for the latest fashions, and Captain Amos Stoddard, the American officer in command at the transfer of sovereignty in 1804 described the people as "rich and hospitable. They live in a style equal to those in the large sea-port towns, and I find no want of education among them."[10] Further down the Mississippi travelers encountered another urban center, Natchez. Similar in size and culture to the other Creole towns, Natchez boasted a diverse citizenry. Underneath a patina of French customs, visitors discovered merchants who hailed from as far as Majorca and Genoa.

And then there was *la ville*, New Orleans. At the time of the transfer, it was already one of the largest urban centers in the young nation. By 1820 it was the largest city south of Baltimore and the fifth largest in the United States. By 1850 New Orleans had a population of more than 100,000. In 1835 the city's exports exceeded those of New York—though the latter would take back the lead by 1850. New Orleans had also eclipsed Montreal in population by 1820. But Montreal had a British majority from 1830 to 1860. It could therefore be argued that New Orleans, with its flourishing French-language schools, newspapers, and opera companies, was the preeminent French city in North America before the Civil War.

Who were these thousands of French residents? Were they, in fact, the descendants of ancient inhabitants of the region? Were they simple peasants? Conservative fur traders, or degenerate Creoles content to make a few dollars while more ambitious Anglo-Americans built a republican empire? Although the French had indeed inhabited parts of this vast region since the late seventeenth century, a surprising number of prominent merchants were recent arrivals from Canada, France, and Saint Domingue.

Consider the case of Gabriel Cerré, born in Côte-Saint-Paul near Montreal in 1734, who had volunteered to fight in the Seven Years' War. Having seen the Ohio country, he decided not to return to Canada and a life as a farmer, opting instead to test his abilities as a trader. He married into an old French Illinois family in 1764. Cerré himself became one of the most prosperous merchants in the region, ultimately settling in St. Louis. His daughter, Marie-Anne, attended a convent school back in Montreal and eventually married one of the most prominent French Canadians of the period, Pierre-Louis Panet, a supporter of the British regime and a member of the Governor's Executive Council. Panet kept the powerful Chouteau family business of St. Louis well apprised of events in Canada.

Other Canadians arrived much later. Pierre Menard, born in Montreal in 1766, found his way to Vincennes in 1786, serving as a clerk for Francesco Vigo. He ultimately settled in Kaskaskia and became the most important citizen and merchant in that community. Menard was perhaps the only Frenchman in the area with a true love of the young American republic. His father had raised a company of volunteers in Canada to support the revolutionary cause. Menard himself served as the first lieutenant governor of the new state of Illinois.

Neither of these French Canadians, Panet or Menard, were themselves natives of the western country, though they married into families with deeper roots. Both were clearly ambitious self-made men.

Immigrants from France continued to arrive in the region both before and after the Louisiana Purchase. Frenchman Nicolas Jarrot arrived in the Illinois country in the 1790s. A tireless land speculator, he died a wealthy man, and his wife, Julie Beauvais Jarrot, pursued the family business interests with great success after his death. Joseph Sire, born in 1799 in La Rochelle, arrived in St. Louis in 1821, served as a master aboard various American Fur Company steamboats and became an important partner in Pierre Chouteau, Jr. and Company in 1838.

Exiles from successive regimes in France sought asylum and opportunity in French America. Royalist Louis Philippe Joseph de Roffignac arrived in New Orleans in 1800 and served several terms as mayor in the 1820s. Exiles from the Bonapartist regime included the famous New Orleans lawyer Etienne Mazureau. After Waterloo, the architect Benjamin Buisson arrived in New Orleans. Ange Palms, a former officer under Napoleon, settled in Detroit, where his daughter Marie-Françoise married the son of Joseph Campau, the richest man in the territory. Statesman-politician Pierre Soulé, destined to achieve national prominence in the Democratic Party, fled Restoration France in 1825. The stream of immigrants from France to Louisiana actually increased from the 1830s to the Civil War. The census of 1860 listed more than 10,000 natives of France in New Orleans, making them the third-largest immigrant group in the city after the Irish and the Germans.[11]

Frenchmen from Saint Domingue arrived in both St. Louis and New Orleans in significant numbers from 1793 to 1804. Then, in 1809 and 1810, the largest wave of francophone refugees from Saint Domingue arrived in Louisiana, deported by officials in Cuba in response to the Bonapartist invasion of Spain. More than 10,000 emigrated in less than a year. Many of these newcomers stayed in New Orleans, but others found homes in French towns upriver. René Paul from Cap François married a daughter of Auguste Chouteau. Educated at the École Polytechnique in Paris, he served as the official surveyor of St. Louis from 1823 to 1838, a critical period of expansion that proved to be of great value to his new family.

Then there were those who defied categorization. Pierre Derbigny, born into the nobility in Laon, fled the French Revolution for Saint Domingue in 1793. He married the daughter of a prominent French Illinois family and settled in Louisiana in 1797, ultimately becoming governor of the state. The powerful "father" of Bayou Lafourche, Henry Schuyler Thibodaux, was born in Albany in 1769 of French Canadian and Dutch New Yorker stock. He landed in Louisiana in 1794 after "a youth spent in Scotland."[12]

Francophone Society in the New Republic

In every town and city in the region, these newcomers reinforced the linguistic, cultural, economic, and political staying power of the French community. Indeed, in New Orleans, the so-called Foreign French were sufficiently numerous as to constitute a distinct group within the city's ethnic and cultural politics. In other places, they simply blended into francophone society. The main point, however, is that these French towns and cities were works in progress both before and after the Louisiana Purchase. Despite the claims of various American observers and French Creoles, especially in New Orleans, there was little that was "ancient" about the francophone world of the Mississippi Valley. These were urban places subject to all the rampant changes and adjustments to be expected in such settings.

If these French towns were in fact experiencing social and demographic changes, were the values of the inhabitants nevertheless rather traditional? Were they prepared for the influx of enterprising and progressive Anglo-Americans? One historian has described Joseph Campau, who hailed from one of the oldest families in Detroit, as conservative and feudal—unable to adjust to the more modern values of incoming Yankees. (This despite the fact that Campau's estate was valued at $3 million at the time of his death in 1863.) Yet Campau—who never learned to speak English—founded the *Detroit Free Press,* and his nephew became the first mayor of the city in 1824 and a leader of Michigan's Democratic Party.

In 1800 Campau became the first Frenchman in Detroit to join the Zion Lodge, Number 10, of the Ancient Free and Accepted Masons. Following his lead, Gabriel Godfroy and six other Frenchmen had joined the lodge by 1805. Freemasonry, of course, was frowned upon by the church as being both anti-Catholic and dangerously liberal. Indeed, when Campau, in ill health by 1802, asked Detroit's Father Richard for spiritual aid, the priest made him promise, among other things, to withdraw from the lodge. That year Campau went to confession and took more active part in church affairs, even being chosen a *marguillier,* or churchwarden. Campau, apparently feeling much better—he died at the age of ninety-five—did not withdraw from the lodge and was reelected treasurer by his freemason brethren before the year was over. He would later lead the struggle spearheaded by the most prosperous portion of the parish over control of church property.

The Catholicism of the French is often taken as one measure of their traditional character. Putting aside the fairness of such an unwarranted interpretation, what are some interesting complications this assumption may in fact imply? Campau was not the only French Catholic in this region to become a freemason. Pierre Chouteau Jr., the head of the Creole family dynasty in St. Louis, was also a mason. French Catholic freemasons dominated the board of church trustees or *fabrique* controlling St. Louis Cathedral in New Orleans, resulting in a serious church schism in 1805. Such progressive or liberal tendencies may be attributable to Americanization—but the freemasons in New Orleans were resisting attempts by the church hierarchy to appoint priests sympathetic to the American cause and the needs of English-speaking Catholics. Disputes between middle-class francophones and church officials over liberal ideas and the control of church property were also becoming more common in Quebec at this time.

In short, there were many French inhabitants, especially among the commercial elite, who were enterprising parvenus and often complicated men and women. They were frequently well informed about events in the East, in Canada, and in Europe. They traveled and had correspondents in a variety of places. Their concerns were primarily economic, but they also followed the course of political events and ideas. The francophone inhabitants of

Louisiana had already had ample opportunity to analyze the acts of incorporation their neighbors and correspondents in Illinois, Michigan, and Mississippi had experienced before 1803. As already suggested, they were not much impressed by the swagger and lawlessness of their American neighbors.

Gauging the political sentiments of these French colonials is hard to do, given the relative scarcity of correspondence or published materials that address such concerns directly. The documents generated by the revolt of 1768 provide some intriguing early hints that the French were not necessarily inclined to be submissive or traditional. The memoir composed in his own defense by Pierre Carresse, a leader of the rebellion and a New Orleans merchant, is particularly noteworthy. Defending free trade, Carresse exclaimed:

One would have to be an unzealous citizen not to applaud these principles. M. Ulloa, however, never permitted us to put them to his review. We had to suppress even the cry of pain. The admission of our slavery was a potentially explosive challenge to authority. We were expected to shout "I am free," imitating the galley-slaves of Venice, whose chains bear the engraving "Liberty."[13]

Given such strong words, it should be no surprise that Alejandro O'Reilly had Carresse executed. Professing his devotion to the French king, Carresse referred consistently to himself and his fellow Creoles as "*citoyens* [citizens]," not "*sujets* [subjects]." The language of the Enlightenment had certainly penetrated this distant French colony.

Fighting for a Political Voice

British agents of empire, like their Spanish counterparts, were surprised by the French resistance they encountered in Canada. With American forces threatening Montreal and Quebec in 1775, Chief Justice William Hey wrote to Colonial Secretary Dartmouth:

Every day furnishes too many instances of it, and gives me an Idea of the real character of the Canadians very different from what I used to entertain . . . Your Lordship will remember how much has been said by us all of their Loyalty, obedience & Gratitude, of their habitual submission to Government . . . but time and accident have evinced that they were obedient only because they were afraid to be otherwise. . . .[14]

Governor Carleton noted that a bust of King George III in Montreal had been "smeared with soot and decorated with a collar of potatoes and a wooden cross with the inscription: 'Voilà le pape du Canada et le sot anglais' (Behold the Pope of Canada and the English fool)."

Often pictured as infantilized and backward peasants and fur traders, quite literally the children of empire, the French have appeared in many a historical novel as passive spectators to the noble exploits of Anglo-American liberators such as George Rogers Clark and Andrew Jackson. However, any perceived American attempt to deprive the French of their political voice or their property drew their immediate response. Consider the numerous petitions sent by the inhabitants of Indiana, Illinois, and Michigan in the 1780s and 1790s. The Governance Act of 1804 also prompted lengthy memorandums from the leading francophone citizens of Lower and Upper Louisiana and delegations to deliver the documents to Washington from both New Orleans and St. Louis. Loathing the prospect of a dictatorship of Jeffersonian bureaucrats and the imposition of anglophone institutions, the writers chided

Congress for not extending to them the essential privileges of a free people—including, of course, any form of representative government. Speaking a language eastern politicians could easily recognize, the French sounded much like other groups of disenfranchised westerners chafing at the territorial bit. They had, of course, special concerns, noted in the memorandum sent from St. Louis with a fair measure of sarcasm:

[T]he records of each county, and the proceedings of the courts of Justice in the District of Louisiana, should be kept and had in both the English and French languages as it is the case in a neighboring country under a monarchial Government and acquired by conquest.[15]

The French, were more than ready to play the game of republican politics, as their subsequent actions in Louisiana and elsewhere amply demonstrate. In Detroit the alienated French majority grew so exasperated with territorial governor William Hull that they sent a petition to President Madison requesting Hull's removal in 1809. In that city Joseph Campau's nephew wrote to François Navarre in 1819 about an upcoming election and observed with great passion that the "natives of the country" must guard against the "strangers" who would "insolently ravish our rights and our natural privileges."[16] Though presented to some degree as an ethnic struggle, the contest was framed as a political one, a struggle of *"concitoyens"* (fellow citizens) in defense of their status as free members of the republic. Bernard Marigny, perhaps the most ardent defender of the status of French Creoles in Lower Louisiana, understood quite clearly what the change from an imperial regime to a republican one implied. Chiding the former French aristocrat Mayor

Roffignac of New Orleans for his obsequious behavior during a formal visit of Andrew Jackson to the city, Marigny observed that "servile flattery" was unbecoming in a republican nation. In Marigny's words: "the compliments of our Mayor are of the kind, called, in good French *de l'eau bénite de cour* [holy water of the court]."[17] Times had changed, and the French in this region, especially those from the dominant commercial class, had heard the news.

The Resurgence of French Pragmatism

Given that the most important Frenchmen of means in the region were merchants, it should not be surprising that their political efforts were channeled first and foremost into practical concerns. Land claims topped the list. The French were bound and determined to profit by their priority and understood full well that the influx of Americans would increase the value of their holdings substantially. Indeed, the anticipation of American sovereignty provoked a flurry of private Indian purchases in Michigan from 1794 to 1796 and a rush for Spanish land grants in Upper and Lower Louisiana from 1795 to 1803. The Jefferson administration began dealing with private claims by setting up Boards of Land Commissioners in the Illinois, Orleans, Louisiana (Missouri), and Michigan territories from 1804 to 1806. Protests over the terms and procedures of confirmation forced it and subsequent administrations to continually revise and liberalize the process. In the end, powerful French citizens learned and even perfected the art of lobbying. In Missouri, they sponsored the rapid rise of Thomas Hart Benton to political

prominence. Elected as a Jeffersonian Republican to Missouri's first Senate delegation in 1821, he served five terms during which he joined the Jacksonian Democrats. Two years after leaving the Senate in 1851, he returned two years later for a single term as a member of the House of Representatives. Throughout his extended political career, Benton never failed his patrons on land issues or on fur trade and Indian treaty interests. Perhaps this could be seen as an influence of *ancien regime* politics on the republic.

A Question of Law

Other French concerns were addressed at the local level. The question of law, its substance and its procedures, was one of critical interest. As Chapter 7 shows, matters of law proved critical to the political landscape of Louisiana after the purchase. The French throughout the region were generally concerned that Anglo-American jurisprudence would bring with it prolonged trials by jury that would impede the smooth flow of commerce. As Louis Nicholas Fortin, a merchant near Baton Rouge, wrote to his brother-in-law Antoine Marechal of Vincennes:

[T]hey will bring with them, in a free and peaceful country, the discord and disunion of families through lawsuits and taxation. Lawyers, sheriffs, and constables will come crowding in here. . . . [T]hese idle worthless fellows, that carry a little green satchel filled with useless old papers, [will] come here and seek their fortune in their shabby motheaten black suits, and their Blackstone under their arms! They won't be the most welcome.[18]

In Louisiana, where sheer numbers and a professional class of francophone lawyers (mostly immigrants) supported the effort, the

French managed to hold on to their civilian legal tradition in the sphere of private substantive law. Criminal law and criminal procedure, on the other hand, followed common-law tradition. The Quebec Act of 1774 had enacted a similar compromise in Canada, much to the dismay of British merchants in Quebec. A contemporary Canadian political cartoon viewed the result of this unholy alliance of French and English legal traditions as producing an illegitimate child. In Louisiana, francophone planter Julien Poydras used the phrase "mongrel offspring of injustice and chicane." Nevertheless, the Louisiana French could look back with some satisfaction after civil codes were adopted in 1808 and 1825. Chapter 7 chronicles how Louisianians in the lower Mississippi Valley became powerful figures in determining regional legal practice. Codification of the civil law in Quebec did not occur until 1866, however, and the final product was less progressive than Louisiana's earlier efforts.[19]

Life a la Française

Attempts to preserve aspects of the civil law went down in flames in Missouri. However, the Creole members of the Board of Trustees of St. Louis did resist the attempts of American Protestants to abolish the "Creole Sabbath" in that town—that is, the inclination of the inhabitants to amuse themselves after church. Similar attempts to restrict what activities would be considered allowable on Sunday in New Orleans were defeated time and time again. By the 1830s, Anglo-Americans in that city had adapted, and doing things *a la française* had become fashionable. In Detroit, the first Board of Trustees with an Anglo majority in 1803 passed a Sabbatarian ordinance. French leaders in that city, however, became leaders within Michigan's Democratic Party. They supported the electoral rights of Catholic immigrants, resisted the attempts of Whig politicians and evangelicals to impose temperance laws, and forced a compromise on the reading of the Bible in public schools.

A Place at the Table

In the end, French citizens in the lands of the Louisiana Purchase and nearby regions that had previously been joined to the United States challenged the republic to address their specific needs and to live up to the promise of political empowerment. As westerners, they grew impatient with federal guardianship. As urban businessmen, they sought stability, resented interference, and demanded public improvements. Through all of this, their behavior was more predictable than exceptional. Yet they also expressed themselves culturally, socially, and legally as Frenchmen. This distinctiveness asserted itself in complex ways throughout the nineteenth century. In the 1890s, Louisiana's Afro-Creole leaders such as Aristide Mary, Rodolphe Desdunes, and young Homer Plessy—also the heirs of this distinctiveness—would challenge the constitutionality of the state's segregation law.

Pierre-Louis Panet of Montreal wrote a letter to his brother-in-law Auguste Chouteau of St. Louis on May 18, 1804. "Vous etes actuellement citoyens [des États Unis]. Je souhaite que vous vous trouviez bien de le changement inattendu." [You are now citizens of the United States. I hope that you like this unexpected change.][20] In this same letter, Panet reported that Chouteau's son, in school at Montreal, had learned to read and speak English fairly well. The change may have been unexpected, but the French were not unprepared for it.

Ready to speak English, the French were consistently frustrated by the refusal of Anglos to return the favor. Prepared to enjoy the blessings of freedom and exploit the opportunities in an expanding American empire, the French of the Mississippi Valley had more success in pursuing profit and expanding influence. To their credit, Jeffersonian officials exhibited some flexibility on a variety of related issues. They may have underestimated their new fellow citizens, but they were prepared to recognize the political and economic interests they all had in common.

Notes

1. Quoted in Robert R. Rea, *Major Robert Farmer of Mobile* (Tuscaloosa: University of Alabama Press, 1990), 37.

2. *Invitation Serieuse aux Habitants des Illinois par Un Habitant des Kaskaskias (1772),* ed. Clarence W. Alvord and Clarence Edward Carter (New York: Burt Franklin, 1968). For more on Vincennes, see Andrew R. L. Cayton, *Frontier Indiana* (Bloomington: Indiana University Press, 1996), chap. 3.

3. Zenon Trudeau to François Vallé, December 1792, *Vallé Papers* (St. Louis: St. Genevieve Archives, Missouri Historical Society). The French in Upper Louisiana had ample opportunity to observe Anglo-Americans. A generous Spanish land policy attracted immigrants from the United States. By 1804, three-fifths of the 10,000 inhabitants of Upper Louisiana were Americans. The French still occupied most leadership positions and dominated the fur trade and commerce of the region.

4. Quoted in George Dargo, *Jefferson's Louisiana: Politics and the Clash of Legal Traditions* (Cambridge: Harvard University Press, 1975), 82.

5. Frederick Bates to Richard Bates, 17 December 1807, in *The Life and Papers of Frederick Bates,* vol. 1, ed. Thomas M. Marshall (St. Louis: Missouri Historical Society, 1926), 237–247.

6. Albert Gallatin to Thomas Jefferson, 20 August 1804, in *Writings of Albert Gallatin,* vol. I, ed. Henry Adams (Philadelphia: Lippincott, 1879), 202.

7. Quoted in Dargo, *Jefferson's Louisiana,* 182.

8. Address by Eugenie Berthold, "Glimpses of Creole Life in Old St. Louis" (St. Louis: Missouri Historical Society, 1933).

9. William H. Keating, *Narrative of an Expedition to the Source of St. Peter's River* (Minneapolis: Ross and Haines, 1959), 75.

10. Quoted in William E. Foley, *The Genesis of Missouri: From Wilderness Outpost to Statehood* (Columbia: University of Missouri Press, 1989), 85.

11. Much of this information comes from Paul F. Lachance, "The Foreign French," in *Creole New Orleans: Race and Americanization,* ed. Arnold R. Hirsch and Joseph Logsdon (Baton Rouge: Louisiana State University Press, 1992).

12. Joseph G. Tregle, *Louisiana in the Age of Jackson: A Clash of Cultures and Personalities* (Baton Rouge: Louisiana State University Press, 1999), 100.

13. Memoir of Pierre Carresse, 1769, in Wilbur E. Meneray, ed., *The Rebellion of 1768: Documents from the Favrot Family Papers and the Rosamonde E. and Emile Kuntz Collection* (New Orleans: Howard-Tilton Memorial Library of Tulane University, 1995), 103.

14. This quote and the one that follows are taken from Jean-Paul de Lagrave, *Voltaire's Man in America* (Montreal: Robert Davies, 1997), 55–56.

15. Quoted in Louis Houck, *A History of Missouri* (Chicago: R. R. Donnelley, 1908), 391.

16. John R. Williams to François Navarre, 31 August 1819, Navarre Family Papers, Burton Historical Collection, Detroit Public Library, Detroit, Michigan.

17. Bernard Marigny, "Memoire of Bernard Marigny Resident of Louisiana addressed to His Fellow-Citizens" (New Orleans: Howard-Tilton Memorial Library, of Tulane University), 20–21.

18. Louis Nicholas Fortin to Antoine Marechal, 25 July 1803, *Lasselle Papers* (Indianapolis: Indiana State Library, Indiana Division).

19. For more on the legal history of Louisiana and Canada, see Dargo, *Jefferson's Louisiana;* F. Murray Greenwood, *Legacies of Fear: Law and Politics in Quebec in the Era of the French Revolution* (Toronto: University of Toronto Press, 1993); Edward F. Haas, Jr., ed., *Louisiana's Legal Heritage* (Pensacola: Perdido Bay Press, 1983); *A Law unto Itself? Essays in the New Louisiana Legal History,* ed. Warren M. Billings and Mark F. Fernandez (Baton Rouge: Louisiana State University Press, 2001); Brian Young, *The Politics of Codification: The Lower Canadian Civil Code of 1866* (Montreal: McGill-Queen's University Press, 1994).

20. P. L. Panet to Auguste Chouteau, 18 May 1804, *Chouteau Collections* (St. Louis: Missouri Historical Society).

3

Public Perception and Public Events: The Louisiana Purchase and the American Partisan Press

BETTY HOUCHIN WINFIELD

In 1803, without well-developed transportation systems, the telephone, the telegraph, the Associated Press, or the Internet, the American people depended on other forms of communication to learn of the Louisiana Purchase. The purchase came at a time when Americans were rapidly moving from a dependence on an oral communication tradition, as found in taverns, churches, and coffeehouses, to a more literate, written culture with its public notices, newspapers, and other periodicals. The newspapers, growing in numbers and circulation each year, signaled the initial news of the Louisiana Purchase in 1803, defined what it was, and (above all) explained what it meant. All this happened through a strongly partisan lens, with newspapers embracing the notion of bias so that they could advance specific political goals.

This chapter examines public perception of the Louisiana Purchase, as found in the era's press, primarily the partisan newspapers. While members of Congress and the administration were arguing about what policies to pursue, newspapers brought those policies to a broader public. Unlike other chapters of this book in which the actors in this drama are historical figures, the newspapers themselves play the actors' roles here. American newspapers created their own interpretation of the Louisiana Purchase, an interpretation that could take form within the particular genre of early print journalism. Newspaper articles from a time before public opinion polling offer bits of proof (albeit limited evidence) about contemporary public perception: in this case, knowledge of the Louisiana Purchase and a range of opinions about the acquisition. If public perception can also be public opinion, then the latter became crucial to the Jefferson administration's effort to build support for the Louisiana Purchase.

The Press, the People, and the Parties

The development of the American constitutional system that other chapters discuss was inseparable from the rise of American journalism. That the First Amendment to the Constitution established freedom of the press is only the most obvious example of this parallel de-

The author wishes to acknowledge Asia Zmuda's library assistance and microfilm reading and copying. Ms. Zmuda is a senior at the University of Missouri-Columbia.

velopment. Equally important was the fact that the role of print media proved crucial to the way Americans conceived of politics in the years before the purchase. As the discussion in Chapter 1 showed, American politicians believed they were creating a new system of politics. Those same founders believed that newspapers would be critical to the process.

Public awareness was so important in establishing a democratic nation that when the Constitution was being ratified almost fifteen years before the Louisiana Purchase, Alexander Hamilton referred to the preeminence of public opinion—what the people thought—in *The Federalist Papers*. In particular, in *Federalist* No. 84, Hamilton noted that a Bill of Rights and press freedom "must altogether depend on public opinion, and on the general spirit of the people and of the government." Jefferson too valued the public's voice: "The force of public opinion cannot be resisted, when permitted freely to be expressed."[1]

Jefferson, along with the country's earliest political leaders, depended on public support and relied on newspapers—not just as a reflector of public opinion, but also as a purveyor of political communication as well as an advocate of the Jeffersonian Republican Party. The newspapers, as a vital part of the nation's political life during this period, devoted a large amount of space to political discussions. As the two major parties crystallized during the 1790s, so too did press affiliations. By 1800 most newspapers openly supported either the Federalists or the Republicans. Such a relationship was not just ideological; these early newspapers needed their connection to printing contracts and legal notices to survive. Even though "Advertiser" might be part of a news-

paper's masthead name, such as the *National Intelligencer and Weekly Advertiser*, most newspapers had relatively little advertising and depended primarily on a party's financial backing for survival.

As a forum for information and opinions, most newspapers not only supported a party's ideals and policies, but also helped develop the arguments that party members used to defend their views. In addition, newspapers openly advocated party benefits in an attempt to win more political adherents. Often backed by major politicians of the day, the fledgling press attacked opponents as they preached the party line to the faithful and campaigned for more elected party adherents. With such an intense political partnership, newspapers often printed abusive political attacks as well as personal invective directed at politicians other than those the party line supported. The battle of printed words was so strong that many scholars now see the era as either a golden age of public knowledge and civic interest or as a dark era of American politics because of the vicious political attacks.[2]

Press Technology: Partisan Words into Type

The newspapers of the early nineteenth century looked very different from their modern counterparts. This was as much a product of the era's printing technology as of its contemporary journalistic ethics. Technically, there was no ability for a newspaper's typesetters to cross columns of type. Headlines, if any were set at all, were laid out within a narrow column and usually had somewhat larger type or a different typeface made up of capital letters. For example, on July 4, 1803, the *National Intelligencer* announced the Louisiana Purchase with this kind of (typical) headline:

Paris, 13th May

"LOUISIANA IS CEDED TO THE UNITED STATES ON THE MOST HONORABLE TERMS, & INDEMNIFICATION WILL BE MADE FOR FRENCH SPOLIATIONS.

As noted from the *Intelligencer* publication dates, a newspaper reported important events from Europe as well as other parts of the country weeks or even months after they occurred. For example, diplomatic nuances in the American negotiations with France in 1802–1803 would have taken place a month or six weeks before the president learned of these developments. Without a telegraph, editors depended on late ships and the slow-moving mails for information.

These early newspapers were printed before typesetters could include images and before photography existed. If any visual designs were used, they often were simple woodblock cuts for advertisements, such as ships for sailing announcements, or crude graphics for a paper's masthead.

Moreover, although commentators in other countries marveled at how many newspapers began operation in the years following the American Revolution, the total number was still relatively small by modern standards. In 1800 some 234 newspapers were published in the United States, most as weeklies (there were only 24 dailies). Today, these newspapers would seem either elitist or provincial in scope, since they emphasized political news for party members. These newspapers would also be considered elitist today because of their low circulation figures and limited access, as well as the prohibitive costs of subscribing to them. (In a period before cheap paper and mechanized printing, subscriptions ranged from $2 to $10 a year at a time when the average annual salary was less than $60.)[3] Although some estimates put the literacy rate among whites in the United States in 1800 at 70 percent, voters were limited to white adult property-owning males.[4] Mostly sent through the mail, early American newspapers had an estimated circulation of 145,000[5] among a population of 5.3 million, 40 percent of whom were white adult males.[6] Yet access to the press may have been somewhat larger than the circulation figures, because newspapers were often passed along to others and shared in coffeehouses and taverns.

Content Before Copyright, Correspondents, or Cooperation

As a vital part of the new nation's political communication system, newspaper columns helped set the agenda for political discussions. The content depended on official announcements, public and private letters, editorials, political official messages and proceedings, and the content and editorials of other newspapers. The press lacked specified correspondents or the cooperative newsgathering organizations that later came to define American journalism. In the absence of a distributed collection of professional journalists working for particular publications, newspapers shared stories and editorials. Often, like-minded newspapers just copied content, verbatim, from other newspapers without worry over copyright or even attribution. The connection between politicians and the newspapers that supported them was close during this period. Leading political figures often wrote editorials, employing pen names for anonymity. For example, many Federalist newspapers just lifted columns by "Pericles," Alexander Hamilton's pseudonym for the strong editorials he contributed to the *New York Evening Post*.[7] In fact, Hamilton financially supported the *New York Evening Post*, which became a major newspaper and in many ways a representative of the Federalist press.

The Press and the Politicians

Politicians paid close attention to the editorials and the political slant of newspaper columns. A major political figure would read more than one newspaper and would pay particular attention to the views of the opposition. For example, after Republican victories at the state and federal level in 1800, which eventually included Jefferson's victory in the presidential election, the newly elected president estimated that up to three-fifths of the nation's newspaper editors continued to support Federalist policies.[8] Jefferson carefully observed the news content of the time and even took an active, behind-the-scenes role to ensure positive press coverage of himself and his administration. In November 1803, for example, Jefferson wrote Meriwether Lewis about the success of congressional approval for the treaties and additional funds for the Louisiana Territory and apologized for his late correspondence: "the present has been long delayed by an expectation daily of getting the inclosed 'account of Louisiana' through the press."[9]

Moreover, when Jefferson became president, he so valued the newspaper's political role that he urged the founder of the *National Intelligencer* to move from Philadelphia to Washington, D.C., to ensure that the *National Intelligencer* would become the semiofficial organ of his administration. Much to Jefferson's chagrin, the *National Intelligencer* proved so objective in its reporting of the proceedings of Congress that it served the needs of newspapers representing various political factions outside Washington.[10] In fact, with the moderate and more neutral stand of the *National Intelligencer*, Jefferson had to rely on the more combative *Philadelphia Aurora* as a leading party newspaper.[11] Acknowledged in 1803 as "the most complete channel of Republican communication in the United States" by *Kline's Carlisle Weekly Gazette* on August 31 and December 14, the *Aurora* was among the most partisan of the Republican newspapers.

The Foreign Press and Fear of Foreign Intrigue

The party newspapers, also major public sources of international news, repeated the slowly transmitted dispatches from European newspapers covering political actions and military successes, especially those of Napoleon Bonaparte. They provided extensive coverage of the Mississippi crisis in 1802–1803, as well as rumors that Napoleon intended to evict the Spanish and dispatch French troops to Louisiana. On April 3, 1802, for example, the *Richmond Recorder* reported, "The French are now masters of the Western waters. Tennessee and Kentucky cannot send a single barrel of flour to the West Indies . . . Bounaparte sends two seventy-four gun ships to the mouth of the Mississipi, and there is *an end of your Western trade to the West Indies*."

Other newspapers expressed similar fears about foreign intrigues in Louisiana or the threat that came from the lack of accurate information on the West. For example, the *Aurora* pointed out the lack of knowledge on March 26: "Concerning Louisiana, about which so much has been said . . . no definite knowledge can be possessed in America at this time." The newspapers could not clarify or verify some of what they printed, and true to their partisan nature, they stepped up their attacks on one another. The *New York Evening Post* went after the *Aurora* in the fight over who ceded what to whom. Ever combative toward the Federalists, the *Aurora* focused on the original source of contention between the parties by pointing out the dangers of British forts along the northwestern border of the United States: "The tory prints, have talked much about *Louisiana* and the *Mississippi,* but they have taken no notice whatsoever of the stipulation in the *British treaty* concerning that river, which may one day prove one of the most serious and injurious parts of that most imbecile and *wicked* of all our diplomatic transactions."

By March 29, when the *Aurora* announced the Spanish transfer of Louisiana to the French with certainty, the Philadelphia newspaper was particularly strident toward the opposition press. "The treaty between Spain and France which we publish this day, will afford the anti-republican scribes a new theme for the display of *their talents*—the Boston Centinel and the Washington Federalist—and the anti-Democrat and the New-York Evening Post, will unsay all their former sayings, and say a great number of things which they will have to unsay again. . . . They will now say further, that all

the Aurora has published concerning *Louisiana,* is not true, because what is in this treaty corroborates it!"

Yet just as American newspapers feared and had even warned, the trade closure did happen. The *National Intelligencer* announced on November 26 that the port of New Orleans had been closed "against foreign vessels from the ocean, including American, and that the right of depositing American property there had been prohibited, without any other establishment being assigned in lieu of it. . . ." In his December 1802 message to Congress, Jefferson posed the possibility of the French occupation of Louisiana. Many of the articles discussing the Mississippi crisis appeared with the sort of classical pseudonyms that were so common in early American newspapers and pamphlets. For example, "Pericles" in the *New York Evening Post* pointed out that "Napoleon's control of Louisiana threatens the only dismemberment of a large portion of the country; more immediately, the safety of all Southern States; and remotely, the independence of the whole Union." The dangers were imminent. While the French troops were awaiting their transfer from the ports of Holland, the president and Congress continued to push for a U.S. military buildup along the eastern bank of the Mississippi. Such military actions pleased many Federalists, particularly Alexander Hamilton. The *New York Evening Post* justified a military solution on January 28, 1803: "*It* belongs of *right* to the United States to regulate the future destiny of *North America.* The country is *ours;* ours is the right to its rivers and all the sources of future opulence, power and happiness."

By April 7, 1803, the *Times* of London, which was widely reprinted in the United

States, pointed out: "The government and people seem to be aware that a decisive blow must be struck before the arrival of the expedition now awaiting in the ports of Holland." Many Federalist newspapers agreed with William Coleman, editor of the *New York Evening Post,* who wanted the country to go to war with France over the issue.

When the Federalists learned that Jefferson was also negotiating with the French for the possible purchase, a *Post* column signed by "Pericles" argued for a military solution: "This event threatens the early dismemberment of a large portion of our country; more immediately the safety of all the Southern States; and remotely the independence of the whole union." In that February 8 issue, "Pericles" rhetorically asked what should the United States be doing and then answered: "seizing New Orleans and the Floridas at once and negotiating later." "Pericles" added: "War is undoubtedly a calamity, but national degradation is a greater, and besides, is always inevitably followed by war itself."

The "Pericles" of this article, none other than Alexander Hamilton, used the *Evening Post* as a means to remain a voice in national politics after leaving the Washington administration's cabinet. In the same article, Hamilton criticized the president's appointment of James Monroe as a special envoy to work with the U.S. minister to France, Robert Livingston: "The appointment of an Envoy Extraordinary, at this time, and under present circumstances, is in every respect the weakest measure that ever disgraced the administration of any country."

More and more American newspapers began to provide details of the Jefferson ad-

ministration's plans. By early 1803 newspapers gave word that Jefferson was instructing James Monroe to purchase New Orleans and West Florida, rather than go to war. The newspapers wrote of rumors about the negotiations. The *Kentucky Palladium,* a Republican newspaper, reported that Bonaparte was considering the sale of Louisiana to the United States.[12] Diplomacy was an important news topic, with speculation as well as rapprochement of the British for permitting "that vast country to fall into the hands of France."

Newspapers also warned of geopolitical implications for the administration's efforts. They reprinted the *Times* coverage of Lord Hawkesbury's declaration in the British House of Commons "that it was sound policy to place the French in such a manner with respect to America as would keep the latter in a perpetual state of jealousy with response to the former, and of consequence unite them in close bonds of amity with Great Britain." Jefferson himself expressed the same thought in a private letter to Livingston.[13]

Front-Page News

The *Boston Independent* first broke the news of the purchase on June 30 under the headline "Louisiana Ceded to the United States!" The *Independent* expressed Republican joy: "Our former anticipation have not only been realized, but exceeded; and thus the wise, seasonable and politic negociation of the President, approved and confirmed by Congress, has gloriously terminated to the immortal honor of the friends of peace and good government, and to the utter disappointment of the factious and turbulent throughout the Union." Five days later the *National Intelligencer* printed an announcement on July 4:

WASHINGTON CITY
———0———
MONDAY, JULY 4
——— 0 ———
OFFICIAL.
— 0 —

The Executive have received official information that a Treaty was signed on the 30th of April, between the Ministers Plenipotentiary and Extraordinary of the United States and the Minister plenipotentiary of the French government, by which the United States have obtained the full right to and sovereignty over New Orleans, and the whole of Louisiana, as Spain possessed the same.
— 0 —

Other Republican newspapers followed the *Intelligencer's* announcement about the agreement. The *Boston Independent Chronicle,* along with the *Aurora* and the *National Intelligencer,* heralded the event for the rest of the nation. The *National Intelligencer* set an agenda for the Republican newspapers' announcement on July 4 and the interpretation of the acquisition: "We have secured our rights by pacific means. Truth and reason have been more powerful than the sword." Yet the (Frankfort) *Kentucky Gazette* later stated that "the differences of political opinion were forgotten."[14]

Federalists led by Hamilton had clamored for a war of conquest for Louisiana in 1803. This marked a decided shift from 1796, when the Federalists had been in power and when newspapers that supported them considered a negotiated settlement possible. One Federalist newspaper claimed that the United States could someday obtain the western province "by purchase or amicable means."[15] While the Federalists denounced the treaty, the *Boston Independent Chronicle* retorted on July 4, 1803: "How must the President smile at the absurd paragraphs in the tory papers on his conduct! They want war, he wishes peace; and it lies with the people to approve or disapprove his policy."

The *Chronicle* article came as part of a shift in the newspaper's emphasis. In the weeks preceding news of the purchase, the *New York Evening Post* had interrupted its serial reprinting of scandalous stories on Jefferson's private life to cover important international developments, including the cession of Louisiana to the United States. The *Post* strayed from its usual warmongering to remark on the momentous news, without pausing to add Hamilton's usual pseudonym: "At length the business of New-Orleans has terminated favourably to this country. Instead of being obliged to rely any longer on the force of treaties, for a place of deposition, the jurisdiction of the territory is now transferred in our hands and in the future the navigation of the Mississippi will be ours unmolested."[16]

After announcing the treaty, Federalist newspapers immediately questioned the secrecy surrounding the acquisition. The *Aurora* retorted that the treaty could not be published until the Senate so authorized or had acted upon it as it was not yet binding to the country. The Republican newspaper also said, "upon the whole the public are already informed to the full extent which is authorised by the constitution; that is, that the *negociation set on foot by our executive has been successful.*" Along with other newspapers, the *Aurora* rejoiced in its issue of July 9, 1803, "that the objects for which was so violently advocated have been obtained without bloodshed or the creation of an enemy."

Subsequent articles on July 21, while complimenting "an opening of a free and valuable market to our commercial states," also helped set a negative news agenda all summer for the Federalist responses. The greatest volume of criticism in newspapers and pamphlets came from Boston, Hartford, New York, and Philadelphia. In fact, slightly less than 25 percent of the publications commented on any advantages to be gained by an expansion of the population into the new territory. About 66 percent of the rural press had a favorable opinion of the acquisition of the new territory.[17]

The negative arguments were hardly surprising to the Jefferson administration. Federalist newspapers charged that the price of the purchase was too high; that Britain deserved the credit for forcing the hand of Napoleon, rather than Jefferson; and that the territory was of little value, except for possible future barter with Spain for both East and West Florida. Finally, as the *Post* pointed out on July 5 and July 21, 1803, the vast territory was actually now a threat to the United States, as it offered the possibility of too wide a dispersion of the population.[18] The Federalist *Boston Columbian Centinel* had in its columns on July 20, "It has not transpired at what price the United States has purchased *Louisiana*. It rises daily." The *Centinel* went on to criticize the settlement as unnecessary:

the payment of fifteen millions of Dollars to France for the restoration of our rights will not be thought wise by the American People, when they have time to consider it; —they will easily perceive that FRANCE COULD NOT KEEP NEW-ORLEANS and must have been glad to cede it to the U.S. that it might not fall into the hands of the English; —they will see that THE ADDITION OF LOUISIANA IS ONLY A PRETENCE FOR DRAWING AN IMMENSE SUM OF MONEY FROM US. . . .

For a Federalist criticism, the Republican press would have an answer. By July 21, the *Aurora* responded to the cost argument in the *Centinel,* "the *democratic* government has obtained a territory as large as France, for the amount of one year's public expenditure under the any thing of nothing administration." And, by August 17, the *Intelligencer* pointed out that the Federalist newspapers had once valued the Mississippi waterway so much that they had stated "that too great a price could not be given for New-Orleans."

Another major Federalist argument against the purchase was that the country did not need more land. As the *Boston Columbian Centinel* repeated in an editorial criticism on July 13, 1803: "We are to give money of which we have took little for land of which we already have too much." The newspaper called Louisiana "a great waste, a wilderness unpeopled with any beings except wolves and wandering Indians" that "may be cut up into States without numbers, but each with *two votes in the Senate.*" This latter argument pointed out another major fear—a loss of power to the West. Other newspapers acknowledged the potential political fight; the *Carolina Gazette* hoped on August 11 that the westerners would be of "one body" with easterners, "when necessary."

The *Philadelphia Aurora* carried a response on July 8: "The policy of our possession does not so much arise from a *want of land,*" read one article, "as from a prudential and early precaution to guard against dangerous or perfidious neighbours." On the same day, the *National Intelligencer* lauded the possibilities: "By the cession of Louisiana, we shall preserve peace, and acquire a territory of great extent, fertility, and local importance."

The August 1, 1803, issue of the *Intelligencer* celebrated "the acquisition of a vast territory without the effusion of a drop of blood;" the agreement had not incurred a large army and the related expense nor the waste of human life. Into 1804 the *Intelligencer* kept to the same message: "Never have mankind contemplated so vast and important an accession of empire by means so pacific and just, and never, perhaps, has there been a change of government so agreeable to the subjects of it."[19]

To Purchase or Not to Purchase: The Ongoing Debate

The criticism did not cease, no matter what Republican supporters wrote. On July 14, 1803, the *Boston Independent Chronicle* noted that "The cession of *Louisiana* . . . has not lessened the malignity of *opposition*, but on the contrary, federalism, if possible is this moment more rancorous than ever. The more perfectly successful, & the more eminently beneficial to the country, the measures of the present administration are hourly becoming, the more virulent becomes the abuse and outrage which is daily displayed in the federal papers." By August 8, the *Chronicle* was observing that "[a]nother opportunity recurs for the enemies of the administration to sheathe the sword. Will they embrace it." They did so even as the country appeared to approve the treaty.

The attacks became personal, and newspapers such as the *Boston Columbian Centinel*

went after the U.S. ministers. On August 10, 1803, the *Centinel* claimed: "Great pains have been taken to give a popular complexion to the purchase of Louisiana; and a contest is maintained by the respective friends of LIVINGSTON and MONROE for the exclusive honor of the transaction." The *Centinel* went on to indirectly accuse the men of treason by implying they were too close to French interests: "France has no reason to complain of either of them. Both have discovered a zeal to serve her in her conflict with England which could hardly be exceeded if we were a colony of France and those men our agents at the Directorial and Consular Court."

Rather than give Jefferson credit, those Federalists who approved of the purchase lauded the administration's ministers. In fact, the *Intelligencer* noted on July 11, 1803, "the pitiful attempts, made in some of the federal prints to derogate from the merit due to the President of the United States" for the acquisition. The *Intelligencer* pointed out that "Mr. Livingston's merit may have been great, but his merit consists, not in standing alone, but in carrying into effect the will of those he represented." These public recriminations were fueled in no small part by the private dispute between Monroe and Livingston over who should receive credit for the purchase. Indeed, both men found themselves arguing all the more when they learned what was being published in the newspapers.

The arguments continued in the fall of 1803 as Congress debated the purchase. While members of Congress considered the challenges of governing so much land and so many people, much of the discussion in American newspapers focused on whether the land was worthless or valuable, or as the *Intelligencer* touted on October 24, "a better soil to expose to its [the sun's] rays; or a soil capable of higher cultivation, or a richer or greater variety of produce." Newspapers advocating for the purchase claimed that it would deliver considerable benefits to the West.

The debate over the Louisiana Purchase was hardly limited to American newspapers, and some examples from Great Britain provide a revealing counterpoint. By October 3, 1803, the *London Times* expressed the fear that Britain would lose its favored trade status in New Orleans: "The cession of Louisiana to the United States continues to engross public attention in America. It is expected that it will occasion a great deal of discussion at the meeting of Congress. By one article, New Orleans is declared to be a free port for France and Spain, but no mention is made of Great Britain." The *Times* noted the acrimony among the American political parties as the election of a new president approached and "among the opponents of the President, some dissatisfaction prevails respecting the policy of obtaining the cession of Louisiana by purchase. They conceive that such a proceeding was inconsistent with the honour and dignity of the United States."

In its October 15 issue, the *Times* cautioned against using Anglo-American terms and principles and English language in the formerly French territory. For keeping French language and customs, the *Times* warned, "If the Americans encourage this foreign language, and let it become the vernacular dialect of Louisiana, French books, of course, will be read by the vulgar, and everything will, by degrees, be perfectly *Frenchified*: the name of the Province, and of its chief towns too, are French." The

Times further claimed that "America will find, in the consequences of her new fraternization, that she is only . . . to be made use of as an instrument in the hand of her most dangerous enemy, for intriguing and cabling in the Senate and Legislature."[20]

London's assessment raised potential concerns that Americans were also debating. Although white residents of Louisiana soon concluded that the Louisiana Purchase offered them considerable benefits, newspapers were not so sure. Republican newspapers were less pessimistic, however, searching for evidence of loyalty among the Louisianians. By Independence Day in 1804, for example, the *Mississippi Herald and Natchez City Gazette* reported from Natchitoches, a small town in what is now northwestern Louisiana, that "forty gentlemen heard the Declaration of Independence read in French as well as English." The Frenchmen present "reacted with pleasure and astonishment."[21]

What was missing from this coverage proves no less interesting. In the midst of this journalistic concern, articles discussing the constitutionality of the Louisiana Purchase were few and far between. One rare exception was the December 31, 1803, issue of the *New York Evening Post,* which reported on cabinet rumors during the fall congressional debates. The *Post* told of a letter writer hearing both the secretary of the Treasury, Albert Gallatin, and the attorney general, Levi Lincoln, say, "that without question the third article of the treaty incorporating Louisiana into the Union, was not warranted by the constitution; but they thought the constitution might be amended as to cure this objection."

From July through October 1803, rather than acknowledging a possible constitutional question, the Republican newspapers followed the general party news interpretation of this peaceful means of land acquisition and the benefits of the new territory. Those few Federalist papers that raised the constitutional issue took an inconsistent and strictly constructionist stand. By October, the Senate approved the treaty and Congress passed on the expenditures in time for the United States to take formal possession of Louisiana by December 20, 1803.

When the *National Intelligencer* broke the news of the completion of the transfer and the bonds of payment to the French in December 1803, it repeated the sentiments so often expressed by Republicans and Republican newspapers. "The acquisition is great and glorious in itself; but still greater and more glorious are the means by which it is obtained. . . . Never have mankind contemplated so vast and important an accession of empire by means so pacific and just."[22]

The acquisition did not seem as just to the Federalists and their political newspapers. Rather, they saw the political ramifications for themselves and their party. The Louisiana Purchase raised Jefferson's popularity to a high level. The Federalists had already suffered setbacks in the 1802 election cycle, and with the upcoming 1804 election in mind, the Federalists worried that the purchase would assure the president's reelection. They also feared the longer-term consequences of a territorial expansion of the United States in two ways: primarily, that the sectional balances built into the Constitution would change and would diminish the eastern control of power by increasing the power of the West. Each new added state would have two more senators, more than

likely Republicans. New England would be ruined, and eastern cities would be depopulated, their streets emptied, and their shops closed.[23] Moreover, the Federalists saw the possibility of more slave states, the dangers of the mixed races of Louisiana and the Floridas, as well as the potential for military clashes with England and Spain.

After the announcement of the treaties, two well-known Federalists supported the purchase: former president John Adams and, surprisingly enough, Federalist leader Alexander Hamilton. Hamilton's *New York Evening Post* may have been critical of each phase of the acquisition, yet the former secretary of the Treasury did write editorials copied by many other Federalist newspapers. He disagreed with *Post* editor William Coleman as to the overall national worth of the acquisition. Viewing the acquisition from a national perspective, Hamilton saw the commercial advantages and a financial potential for markets as well as a benefit for U.S. foreign relations. Coleman ridiculed the acquisition of Louisiana, especially the territory's potential merits, so touted by Jefferson.

Jefferson's Grand Achievement: The Press and the Road to Empire

In January 1804 Republican members of Congress planned a great dinner in Washington to honor the president and his cabinet and to celebrate this Jeffersonian achievement. The Republican news coverage, taken from the *Intelligencer,* said, "Louisiana Jubilee, as the Federalists called it, began with a dinner on January 27, 1804, where about a hundred guests cheered and drank numerous toasts while three cannons boomed." Four days later, the Republicans held a ball for 500 people in Georgetown. The February 2 *Intelligencer* emphasized the simplicity of the event: "But when humanity rejoices in the extension of the empire of freedom, and of peace, the superficial effects of the arts of the painter, and of the gilder, vanish before the splendor of the even, and put place and form out of consideration."

Republican newspapers called for a national festival and wanted the entire nation to celebrate the purchase. In many parts of the country, Republicans set aside Saturday, May 12, for a "National Jubilee." The festival did create an occasion for easterners and westerners to toast each other and gave the regional newspapers much material for readers to digest over the next few weeks. Even so, the Federalists denounced the celebration as a "paper affair manufactured by the printers and made to look national when it was really sectional and partisan." The enthusiasm for the acquisition of the Louisiana Territory carried over into the July 4 celebrations and the 1804 campaign, contributing to Jefferson's landslide victory.

At the July 4, 1804, celebrations, patriots gave orations filled with wild enthusiasm over the acquisition of Louisiana and full of anticipation of an empire stretching from sea to sea.[24] Close observers and readers of geographic explorations such as Jefferson knew of Robert Gray's discovery of the mouth of the Columbia River in 1792 and Captain George Vancouver's narrative of his voyage to the North Pacific.[25] Jefferson had long been curious about the West, and for twenty years he had been thinking about a transcontinental expedition. Yet little was known about the far reaches of the Northwest and the headwaters

of the Missouri River. During the fall of 1803 the *Intelligencer* had explained to its readers that the lower Missouri River was filled with dangers: "the Missouri is attended with difficulty and danger, danger from its numerous quicksands, and the difficulty from the obstinacy of the current" (October 21). Jefferson had feared a British foothold west of the Mississippi. Thus, the Louisiana Purchase would be strategically important.

Yet it was equally important to know what existed beyond the Mississippi River. Before the purchase, Congress had already appropriated funds for an exploration of the Missouri River region and beyond. The president had already chosen Meriwether Lewis to lead such an expedition, and Lewis was crossing the Appalachians when Jefferson sent him word of the U.S. diplomatic success in Paris.[26] By the time of those celebrations on July 4, 1804, Lewis (along with William Clark and thirty-one others) was already on the Missouri and exploring the Nebraska region as the expedition sought a possible transcontinental water route. By 1805 the newspapers would tell of their findings halfway through their journey, after they left Fort Mandan. During the fall of 1806 the newspapers would announce the expedition's return.

The Federalist-leaning press had been for the most part nonexpansionist (unless the method was to gain territory by waging war) and would ridicule the findings of the Lewis and Clark expedition. The Republican-leaning press had been expansionist in nature and would laud the Corps of Discovery efforts and reports. The partisan press would continue to alert the reading public, interpret events for them, and express opinions for them, just as newspapers had during the period of the Louisiana Purchase.

Notes

1. James Madison, Alexander Hamilton, and John Jay, *The Federalist Papers*, ed. Isaac Kramnick (New York: Penguin Books, 1987), 476–477

2. For the golden era, see William E. Ames, *A History of the* National Intelligencer (Chapel Hill: University of North Carolina Press, 1972). For the dark ages, see Frank Luther Mott, *American Journalism: A History, 1690–1960* (New York: Macmillan, 1962); and Frank Luther Mott, *Jefferson and the Press* (Baton Rouge: Louisiana State University Press, 1943). In his new book, historian Jeffrey Pasley places the editors in a much more independent power role than most mass media scholars do and leans more toward the "dark ages" viewpoint. See Jeffrey L. Pasley, *The Tyranny of Printers: Newspaper Politics in the Early American Republic* (Charlottesville: University Press of Virginia, 2001).

3. William David Sloan and James D. Startt, *The Media in America: A History*, 4th ed. (Northport, Ala.: Vision Press, 1999), 70.

4. Dora L. Costa and Richard H. Steckel, "Long-Term Trends in Health, Welfare, and Economic Growth in the United States," in *Health and Welfare during Industrialization*, ed. Richard H. Steckel and Roderick Floud (Chicago: University of Chicago Press, 1997), 47–89.

5. Sloan and Startt, *The Media in America*, 70.

6. *The Statistical History of the U.S., from Colonial Times to the Present* (New York: Basic Books, 1976), A57–A81.

7. Michael Emery and Edwin Emery, *The Press and America: An Interpretive History of the Mass Media* (Englewood Cliffs, N.J.: Prentice Hall, 1992), 74.

8. Ibid., 71.

9. Jefferson to Meriwether Lewis, 16 November 1803, in *Letters of the Lewis and Clark Expedition, with Related Documents 1783–1854*, vol. I, ed. Donald Jackson (Urbana: University of Illinois Press, 1978), 136.

10. Emery and Emery, *The Press and America*, 82.

11. Sloan and Startt, *The Media in America*, 285.

12. Alexander DeConde, *This Affair of Louisiana* (New York: Scribner's, 1976), 113.

13. Ibid.

14. *Kentucky Gazette*, 16 August 1803.

15. Ibid.

16. "Hamilton on the Louisiana Purchase: A Newly Identified Editorial from the *New York Evening Post*," *William and Mary Quarterly* 12 (1955), 273.

17. John L. Allen, "Geographical Knowledge and American Images of the Louisiana Territory," in *Voyages of Discovery, Essays on the Lewis and Clark Expedition*, ed. James P. Ronda (Helena: Montana Historical Society Press, 1998), n. 30, 57.

18. Ibid., 202.

19. *National Intelligencer*, 1 August 1803.

20. *Times*, 18 October 1804. The *Times* continued its negative response to the purchase and during the fall of 1804 pointed out, "while—they talk of the *equality* of the *rights of mankind*, they are absolutely striving to stipulate for liberty to continue the importation of *slaves*. . . . Such are the inconsistencies into which all the visionary theories of politics infallibly lead those who profess to frame Governments by their maxims."

21. *Mississippi Herald and Natchez City Gazette*, 24 August 1804.

22. *National Intelligencer*, 15 January 1804.

23. Frederick Merk, *Manifest Destiny and Mission in American History* (New York: Knopf, 1963), 11; Jerry W. Knudson, "Newspaper Reaction to the Louisiana Purchase, 'This New, Immense, Unbounded World,' " *Missouri Historical Review* LXIII (1969).

24. Merk, *Manifest Destiny and Mission in American History*, 13.

25. Donald T. Jackson, *Thomas Jefferson and the Stony Mountain: Exploring the West from Monticello* (Urbana: University of Illinois Press, 1981), 86–96.

26. Gary E. Mounton, ed., *The Journals of the Lewis and Clark Expedition*, vol. I (Lincoln: University of Nebraska Press, 1983–), 3.

4 Thomas Jefferson and the Problem of World Politics

JAMES R. SOFKA

In the nineteenth century few issues besides slavery dominated American politics more relentlessly than the debate over westward expansion. As early as the Seven Years' War, American colonists had fought France to open the Ohio frontier to settlement, and the drive across the mountains only intensified after the Revolution. The Louisiana Purchase, which doubled the size of the United States with a pen stroke, is traditionally understood in the context of the ideology of manifest destiny, a broad term that by the 1840s came to mean American control over much of North America. In reality, Thomas Jefferson viewed the western question through the intersecting lenses of commerce and national security. He intended to project American influence westward in order to prevent any foreign power from suffocating the nascent economy of the United States. From the 1780s through his retirement from public life, Jefferson relentlessly maintained that the United States could not mature and prosper while its trade was at the mercy of the European powers.

Unlike later proponents of manifest destiny, for whom expansionism became its own end, Jefferson's western objectives were tangible in nature and formed an indissoluble strategic trinity: American control over the mouth of the Mississippi at New Orleans, free navigation of the river itself, and mastery of the shipping lanes along the West Florida territory. If the United States failed to realize these three ambitions, he argued, the economy and national security of the United States was in jeopardy. In Jefferson's eyes, most of the vast acreage of Louisiana he acquired in 1803 was gratuitous, and he offhandedly noted that it would take a thousand years to populate. Indeed, the interests at stake in the region were so high that Jefferson prepared for a potential war with Napoleonic France in 1802–1803 to ensure that the economic aorta of the West would be safely under American control.

This chapter explains Jefferson's actions during the Mississippi crisis by setting them in a broader context of transatlantic statecraft. If the terms in this chapter seem familiar, that should be no surprise. Policymakers at the turn of the nineteenth century faced decisions quite similar to those challenging world leaders today: They sought the best means to promote their national interests and to protect their security. In the early years of the American Republic, that meant preserving a specific set of interests in a world of significant threats.

Genesis of Jefferson's Western Strategy, 1786–1801

In *The Spirit of the Laws* the French philosopher the Baron de Montesquieu observed that most states "have made commercial interests give way to political interests," while England alone "has always made its political interests give way to the interests of its commerce."[1] Montesquieu might have said the same about the foreign policy of the United States under Thomas Jefferson. Jefferson approached foreign policy questions as a disciple of eighteenth-century (and almost exclusively European) thinking about the nature and workings of the international system and based his administration's policies on this tradition. Like many of his contemporaries, Jefferson maintained that commerce was a decisive if not determining factor propelling America's gradual ascent to the status of a great world power. How best to develop the wealth of the United States was a political question that sparked vigorous debates in the new republic. The diplomatic task Jefferson faced, however, was to protect these resources and exploit their uses in negotiations with other powers.

This labor was compounded by the severity of international conflict during the years when Jefferson served as secretary of state (1790–1793) under George Washington and as the third U.S. president (1801–1809). The French Revolution, which remained a purely internal problem for two years following its outset in 1789, escalated to the international level in late 1791. War erupted between France, Austria, and Prussia in the spring of 1792. By 1793 Britain and Spain had joined the growing conflict, which would rage across Europe among

various alliances until Napoleon's defeat in 1815. Indeed, in this twenty-five-year period there were only two years of relative calm: the Peace of Amiens of late 1801 suspended hostilities but rapidly disintegrated in 1803. It was this two-year period, as this discussion will show, that marked the most intense phase of Jefferson's western diplomacy. American political leaders were compelled to manage their nation's affairs in an era of incessant war, a seemingly insurmountable task given the poor state of American finances and the conspicuous absence of a significant national army or navy.

Despite their many political differences, both Federalist and Republican leaders at the time agreed on several national security questions. First, the new nation was economically and militarily weak and therefore vulnerable in an international system dominated by the European powers. America also needed time to develop key sectors of its economy. Finally, they believed that neutrality best served American interests during a period of European war and internal political and economic disarray. Neutrality was the only realistic means of keeping the nation out of a potentially catastrophic conflict, gaining access to markets, and (most optimistically) possibly manipulating the European conflict to American advantage.

Where Alexander Hamilton and Jefferson—the chief spokesmen of the Federalists and the Republicans, respectively, in foreign policy debates—differed was in their emphasis on the immediate rather than future status of American power. Hamilton accepted American economic and military inferiority as an unfortunate but real dilemma that severely constrained the new nation's options. In his view, while America was weak it must compromise; and in a predatory international system, it must seek external guarantees of security. Hamilton's preferred model was an *entente* with Great Britain that would allow the United States the protection of the Royal Navy and access to English markets. The ties of culture, language, and creditors bound the American and British markets, Hamilton reasoned. He believed that the United States should therefore largely accept London's restrictions on American trade in exchange for a workable commercial treaty that could afford the Americans protection. Hamilton's logic became the conceptual basis for the Jay Treaty of 1794, the terms of which were directed by Hamilton himself, and in which the United States remained neutral but "tilted" in favor of British policy. The cost of the Jay Treaty to the United States was that Americans were compelled to concede key advantages in trade to the British. But in Hamilton's view, with the United States hobbled by exorbitant debt, limited military power, and partisan cleavages, compromise with Britain was essential to securing a stable financial system for the new nation.

The Jeffersonian vision of American national security, on the other hand, was based on equally rational calculations, but it arrived at a radically different strategic premise. In Jefferson's view, American neutrality itself could become a potential weapon to be used in negotiating with the Europeans over increased access to markets. Although Jefferson concurred with Hamilton's assessment of America's immediate weakness, he was optimistic about the nation's potential leverage in the international system. His criticism of Hamilton's strategy was that American acquiescence to British policy would forever relegate the United States to the status

of being a client of London—in his words, "a second Portugal."[2] Once the interests of the United States were subjugated to those of European trade policy, the nation would forever remain a pawn in continental power politics. The European war, which so worried Hamilton, was in Jefferson's eyes a source of American power: Distracted governments and already overburdened militaries starved for raw materials would be compelled to bargain with the United States.

Jefferson articulated the relationship of economic and national power in his "Report on Commerce," which he presented to Congress in December 1793. This document represents Jefferson's most systematic formulation of his national security policy, and it is all the more striking for doing so in a manner consistent with European practices of the eighteenth century.

As a branch of industry [commerce] is valuable, but as a resource of defense, essential. . . . Its value, as a branch of industry, is enhanced by the dependence of so many other branches on it. In times of general peace it multiplies competitors for employment in transportation . . . and in times of war . . . when those nations who may be our principal carriers, shall be at war with each other, if we have not within ourselves the means of transportation, our produce must be exported in belligerent vessels, at the increased expense of warfreight and insurance, and the articles which will not bear that, must perish on our hands . . . it is as a resource of defense that our navigation will admit neither negligence nor forbearance. The position and circumstances of the United States leave them nothing to fear on their land-board, and leave them nothing to desire beyond their present rights. But on their seaboard, they are open to injury, and they have there, too, a commerce *which must be protected*.[3]

In substance this argument could have been advanced by most French or British statesmen after 1650. Distilled to its fundamentals, Jefferson held that a small but increasingly prosperous state dependent on trade for a large share of its national revenue could not compete globally as long as its commerce was vulnerable to attack, seizure, or prohibitive duties. This was common wisdom among most diplomats and mercantile interests in the eighteenth century—indeed, so common as to be almost taken for granted.

Throughout a political career spanning half a century, Jefferson consistently argued that the paramount national interest of the United States was not a crusade for republican liberty or a struggle for political hegemony in the Western Hemisphere, but rather the attainment and preservation of a respectable share of the balance of trade and the protection of American commercial and maritime rights. Having grown to political maturity in an era of incessant European competition for American resources, it is not surprising that Jefferson regarded the developing American economy as a source of pride and, above all, national power. In his own lifetime, England and France had fought three wars for control of the North American continent. In Jefferson's view, this recent history was ample proof of America's strategic and commercial importance and led him to believe unfailingly that the United States would enjoy vast promise in the international system.

The extension of this reasoning was that the United States was an important (and indeed, in time of war, critical) component of what Jefferson perceived as an Atlantic balance of power that included the European trading powers of Spain, Britain, and France. The United States could manipulate the economic

and strategic networks that composed this balance to serve American ends during a European war. Jefferson never ceased to maintain that if America properly managed its independence, lucrative resources, and freedom from "entangling alliances" (an argument articulated by George Washington but one that Jefferson also employed), the United States could not only secure its borders but could also prosper in a polarized international system. Convinced that North America possessed assets too valuable for the European powers to lose, Jefferson held fast to a neutral policy that allowed the United States some latitude to bargain with belligerent states to gain concessions for itself.

Jefferson viewed this intricate transatlantic relationship as a "natural" component of the international system of the late eighteenth century—one that could not be disregarded by American politicians preoccupied with partisan and ideological cleavages. Although he sarcastically endorsed a "meridian of partition" between the continents and a "divorce" from Britain, Spain, and France, he was too well aware of the workings of the American economy to seriously consider fostering an isolationist policy. The political realities of the early 1790s mandated that he publicly distance himself from Alexander Hamilton's financial program, but Jefferson realized fully that the United States depended on customs duties for a large percentage of its national revenue and that the economy of the South was sustained by exporting cotton, tobacco, and produce to Europe and the Caribbean. In more thorough analyses Jefferson rejected an isolationist course as

theory only, and a theory which the servants of America are not at liberty to follow. Our people have a decided taste for navigation and commerce. They take this from their mother country: and their servants are in duty bound to calculate all their measures on this datum: we wish to do it by throwing open all the doors of commerce and knocking off its shackles.[4]

Jefferson's prototype of an "open door" policy required deft calculations, counter-restrictions, and occasional force to be effective. Although the Atlantic remained the primary source of his concern, American trade nevertheless faced significant obstacles closer to home. Before many American goods produced in the Ohio Valley could be shipped abroad from ports on the eastern seaboard, they first had to navigate a journey from the interior of the country down the Mississippi to New Orleans. As a result, Jefferson's mission to secure American trade—the source of the nation's power in international politics—began in the muddy flats of the Mississippi Delta. But Jefferson was hardly alone in underscoring the critical importance of the Mississippi to the national security of the United States. Even before the Treaty of Paris, in 1783, reaffirmed Spanish sovereignty in Louisiana, the American government sought to limit European control of North America's most vital commercial artery. As early as 1780 Benjamin Franklin observed: "The very proposition [of yielding to Spanish control of the Mississippi] can only give disgust at present. Poor as we are, yet, as I know we shall be rich, I would rather agree with them to buy at great price the whole of their right on the Mississippi than to sell a drop of its waters. A neighbor might as well ask me to sell my street door."[5]

Jefferson devoted considerable attention to the Mississippi question after his appointment as the nation's first secretary of state in 1790. He argued that Spain posed only a modest obstacle to the growing United States, and he was fond of repeating Montesquieu's assertion that Spain and Turkey were useful actors in world politics because they were capable of holding empires that were of "utter insignificance." While American military and economic power matured, the territories of the West "could not be in better hands." Jefferson reasoned that the advancing volume of settlers and trade would soon make American control of the region a fait accompli, and he agreed with James Madison's view that Spain "can no more finally stop the current of trade down the river than she can the river itself."[6]

Nevertheless, the vagaries of European politics, and the possibility that Britain or France might seize, purchase, or barter for Spain's North American territories, were a constant worry to Jefferson and other American leaders. In the Nootka Sound crisis of 1790, when Britain and Spain seemed on the brink of war over an obscure territory in the Pacific Northwest, Jefferson expressed alarm that in the event of hostilities Britain might occupy New Orleans. His apprehension was sufficient to turn him from his policy of neutrality in European quarrels. "I am so deeply impressed with the magnitude of the dangers which will attend our government if Louisiana and the Floridas be added to the British Empire," he argued to President George Washington, "that in my opinion we ought to make ourselves parties in the *general war* expected to take place, should this be the only means of preventing this calamity." Although this European crisis ended peacefully, it presaged future incidents and convinced Jefferson that the only way to guarantee the transit of the river was to ensure that New Orleans and West Florida were under American sovereignty. "The navigation of the Mississippi," he declared succinctly, "we must have."[7]

Serving in a Federalist administration reluctant to contest the Europeans or drain the U.S. Treasury to acquire remote Spanish territory, Jefferson was not in a position to carry out his more ambitious western policies. Nevertheless, as secretary of state he laid the conceptual foundation for the course he would follow as president ten years later. His draft of an "Outline of Policy on the Mississippi Question" in August 1790 proposed a "natural" American claim to the river, given the volume of American trade in the West. Although Jefferson realized that his case for legal title to the Mississippi was tenuous at best, framing the issue in juridical language was his way of clothing an essentially acquisitive policy. In his more ambitious 1792 "Report on Negotiations with Spain," he flatly stated that with respect to the navigation of the river, "it is a principle that the right to a thing gives a right to the means without which it could not be used. That is to say, that the means follow their end."[8]

In Jefferson's opinion, American national security suffered because European powers had the ability to choke the trade of western states and territories. "The use of the Mississippi [is] so indispensable, that we cannot hesitate one moment to hazard our existence for its maintenance," he argued. Economic and political calculations convinced Jefferson that it was imperative that the new republic secure its trade routes and place them beyond the reach of "accident." As he observed later, "The occlusion of the Mississippi is a state of things in which we cannot exist. . . . Whatever power, other than ourselves, holds the country east of the Mississippi becomes our natural enemy."[9] Through such lucid and concise geopolitical reasoning, Jefferson outlined the ends of his western policy.

In the 1790s, however, Jefferson saw no reason to embark on military preparations to seize western territory or even to float serious purchase offers to the European powers. With the advancing sclerosis of Spain's North American empire, Jefferson believed that time was on his side. The relatively static Spanish population would soon be overwhelmed by the steady incursion of American settlers. Demographics alone would likely compel Spain to negotiate the dispensation of New Orleans and the Mississippi. When he learned that Spain was inviting Americans to settle in the Floridas as a means of increasing the population of their territories, Jefferson was ecstatic. In Machiavellian fashion, he noted in a letter to Washington in 1791 that "I wish a hundred thousand of our inhabitants would accept the invitation. It will be a means of delivering to us peaceably, what might otherwise cost us a war. In the meantime we may complain of this seduction of our inhabitants just enough to make them believe we think it very wise policy for them, and confirm them in it. This is my idea of it."[10]

In Jefferson's view it was unpardonably inefficient to wage a costly war to achieve what would come to pass "naturally" through the inexorable growth of the American population. As he noted later, Spain's "feeble state would induce her to increase our facilities [in New Orleans], so that her possession of the place would hardly be felt by us, and it would not perhaps be long before some circumstance might arise which might make the cession of it to us the price of something of more worth to her." Indeed, by 1800 the United States had absorbed most of the commerce of the province of Louisiana. Jefferson began to view the exponential growth in American settlers of the territory as a sign that the province would soon fall into American hands.[11]

When Jefferson was inaugurated president in March 1801, his approach to the western question remained unchanged. But the dynamics of world politics had undergone a tectonic shift since his 1792 "Report on the Mississippi." Spain, drained by the war in Europe and eager for continental gain, was becoming increasingly aware that Louisiana was a "square peg in the round hole" of its European diplomacy.[12] Yet rather than offer the province to the United States, as Jefferson had expected, the circumstances of the Napoleonic Wars made it far more profitable for Madrid to make a deal with France. Through the Treaty of San Ildefonso, in October 1800, Spain traded the North American province to France in exchange for several Italian duchies. Jefferson's complacency toward the West was shattered when he found the Mississippi under the control of Napoleon, and he was forced to adopt a more activist—and militaristic—policy to secure his objectives.

Executing Jefferson's Western Strategy: The Louisiana Purchase, 1801–1803

Jefferson was terrified by the prospect of the critical port of New Orleans under the control of a French garrison. "It completely reverses all the political relations of the U.S. and will form a new epoch in our political course," he in-

formed Robert R. Livingston, the American minister to France, in 1802. Whereas France had once been the nation that "has offered us the fewest points on which we could have any conflict of right," its interposition on the aorta of American trade radically disturbed the balance of power in the West and led Jefferson to challenge America's oldest ally as fiercely as he had Spain. He laid out his strategic reasoning with brilliant clarity to Livingston:

There is on the globe a single spot, the possessor of which is our natural and habitual enemy. It is New Orleans, through which the produce of three-eighths of our territory must pass to market, and from its fertility it will [before] long yield more than half our whole produce and contain more than half our inhabitants.

Reflecting on the San Ildefonso cession, Jefferson further observed that

France placing herself in that door assumes to us the attitude of defiance. Spain might have retained it quietly for years. . . . Not so can it ever be in the hands of France. The impetuosity of her temper, the energy and restlessness of her character, placed in a point of eternal friction with us. . . . These circumstances render it impossible that France and the U.S. can continue long friends when they meet in so irritable a position.[13]

This appraisal serves as a cogent summary of Jefferson's sophisticated grasp of power politics: The United States would relentlessly advance its interests in the West and would oppose any European state that impeded them.

When he heard that Spain had ceded Louisiana to France Jefferson embarked on a two-tracked strategy aimed at defusing an economic and diplomatic crisis. First, he instructed his ministers in Europe to inquire about the details of the San Ildefonso agreement and to try to discern Napoleon's intentions. Specifically, Jefferson was interested in learning whether the emperor of the French might be willing to sell New Orleans and its environs to the United States. He then made military preparations in the event of a French landing and ordered a military reconnaissance of the region. These measures were designed to enhance American capabilities in the West and to impress upon the French how seriously Jefferson viewed the San Ildefonso agreement.[14]

In early 1802 it was clear that the French intended to occupy New Orleans. The cession coincided with the Amiens peace agreement that, by suspending hostilities, made it feasible for Napoleon to dispatch a 40,000-man army to North America. Jefferson was concerned that the French would suspend the American right to deposit goods at New Orleans, charge exorbitant duties on American products, or strangle American trade on the Mississippi altogether. Whether or not Jefferson considered the suspension of the right to deposit goods or the simple landing of French troops as a *casus belli* is a question that scholars continue to debate. The larger and more critical point is that by spring 1802 there was no doubt that Jefferson was willing to fight to assert American commercial rights on the Mississippi.[15]

Nevertheless, Jefferson was aware that until his preparations were completed, he could not compel France to terms unilaterally. It would be necessary to take advantage of the dynamics of the Atlantic balance of power and seek British assistance in accomplishing his objective. With the Royal Navy on America's side, it was unlikely that the French could reinforce or resupply the province. On April 25, 1802, Jefferson flatly warned Pierre Samuel Du Pont de Nemours, his unofficial emissary to the French

government, that French interference with American shipping "will cost France, & perhaps not very long hence, a war which will annihilate her on the ocean, and place that element under the despotism of two nations, which I am not reconciled to the more because my own would be one of them." Jefferson had been even more explicit in his letter to Livingston a week earlier:

the day that France takes possession of New Orleans fixes the sentence which is to restrain her forever in her low-water mark. [Further, the occupation] . . . seals the union of two nations who in conjunction can maintain exclusive possession of the ocean. From that moment we must marry ourselves to the British fleet and nation. We must turn all our attentions to a maritime force . . . and having formed and cemented a power which may render reinforcement of her settlements here impossible to France, make the first cannon which shall be fired in Europe the signal for tearing up any settlement she may have made, and for holding the two continents of America in sequestration for the common purpose of the united British and American nations.[16]

In the corpus of Jefferson's diplomatic writings, few more lucid illustrations of his mastery of balance of power politics exist. For this reason, the proposed English alliance of 1802 remains one of the most controversial aspects of Jefferson's diplomacy. Analyzing this controversy in the larger context of his approach to international relations leads to the logical conclusion that Jefferson's threat of an alliance with England (or at least his professed intent to seek one) was serious. He correctly reasoned that Britain had no interest in Louisiana except to "keep the French out." In the event of a European war, which Jefferson desired by the summer of 1802, the Royal Navy could intercept French shipping and reinforcements to North America as it had during the Seven Years' War. Although Jefferson acknowledged that a union with Britain "is not a state of things which we seek or desire, it is one which this measure, if adopted by France, forces on us, as necessarily as any other cause, by the laws of nature, brings on its necessary effect."[17] It is interesting that he alluded to the Atlantic balance of power in the Newtonian language of "natural" action and reaction. In political terms, the enemy of Jefferson's enemy became, albeit reluctantly, his friend.

This reasoning evoked traditional eighteenth-century Realpolitik and would have been thoroughly familiar to its practitioners. Jefferson was determined to maintain American independence in the international system, but if the only way to accomplish his goal was to make a pact with the "harlot England," then so be it. His eye was always on the broader strategic logic of the Louisiana issue: the protection of commerce. This end had been fixed in Jefferson's mind for twenty years, and it was inextricably linked to preserving the objectives of the Revolution, but his means adapted cleverly to diplomatic fortunes in Europe. Resumption of war would divert Napoleon's attentions from America and make an Anglo-American coalition against the French workable. Any doubts about his true intentions are quelled by a private letter Jefferson wrote on July 11, 1803, in which he stated that "we could not say when war would arise, yet we said with energy what would take place when it should arise."[18]

To Jefferson's good fortune, the English alliance proved unnecessary. The resumption of war in early 1803, coupled with the deaths of thousands of French troops on Saint Domingue, led Napoleon to decide his interests were better served by selling the province to the United States. The extent to which Jefferson's bellicosity influenced Napoleon's decision is debatable, but the fact remains that the emperor had no desire to relive Louis XV's misfortune of fighting a transoceanic war against a combined Anglo-American force and in the face of guerrilla-style attacks on his garrison forces. Du Pont de Nemours objected to Jefferson's militaristic tactics and warned the president that "To say 'Give us this country; if you do not we will take it' is not at all persuasive." But even he must have been influenced by the tone—if not the substance—of the Livingston letter, as he suggested a possible sale of New Orleans to the Americans if the price was right.[19]

Under the Louisiana Purchase, the United States acquired all of formerly Spanish Louisiana, including New Orleans. Jefferson had gained far more than he had expected, and his announcement of the purchase on Independence Day 1803 was, without question, his greatest diplomatic coup. He had successfully studied, manipulated, and exploited the Atlantic balance of power to his advantage. Even James Madison was surprised at how quickly Jefferson reversed decades of hostility to England so he could force Napoleon's hand. In Jefferson's view, the Louisiana issue was but one component of the larger European conflict, and he owed his success in large part to his ability to examine the broader strategic dimensions of world politics and foresee the consequences of a renewed Anglo-French war. As he observed in a postscript on the Louisiana Purchase, "We did not, by our intrigues, produce the war: but we availed ourselves of it when it happened."[20]

Jefferson's western diplomacy was not an unqualified success, however. The problem with the Louisiana Purchase was that Jefferson had bought the wrong real estate, and too much of it. His original goal was to acquire New Orleans and the narrow strip of land known as West Florida, which extended to the Perdido River. Through the deal with France he had gained the first objective but not the second. The West Florida territory controlled the sea approach to New Orleans and contained the strategic ports of Mobile Bay and Pensacola. When he began his quest to obtain Louisiana late in 1801, Jefferson believed that the province had been included in the San Ildefonso cession to France. However, Spain had administered this territory as a distinct entity, and it had been insulated from the 1800 treaty. The Spanish minister to the United States, Count Carlos Martinez de Yrujo, made this emphatically clear to Jefferson and Madison. By July 1803 both were aware that the Floridas were outside the legal boundaries of Louisiana.

Convinced that without French support Spain would quickly sell the province to the United States, Jefferson repeated his Louisiana policy of intimidation, coupled with offers to negotiate. But in the case of West Florida, where no threat of intervention by the great powers existed given the fortunes of the European war, Jefferson saw no reason to offer Madrid generous sums. Jefferson realized that the military balance in North America favored the United States. The military preparations he had begun against the French could also be used against the small Spanish garrison in West Florida. The United States with its superior military force, he reasoned, could seize the territory at will. Madison expressed this view with brutal candor to Charles Pinckney, American minister to Spain, in which he noted that Madrid

dreads, it is presumed, the growing power of this country, and the direction of it against her possessions within its reach. Can she annihilate this power?—No. Can she sensibly retard its growth?—No. Given this reality, does not common prudence then advise her, to conciliate with every proof of friendship and confidence the good will of a nation whose power is formidable to her; instead of yielding to the impulses of jealousy, and adopting obnoxious precautions, which can have no other effect than to bring on prematurely the whole weight of the Calamity which she fears? Reflections such as these may perhaps enter with some advantage into your communications with the Spanish Government, and as far as they may be invited by favorable occasions, you will make that use of them.[21]

Jefferson was so certain of American superiority that he believed that the actual exercise of force would be pointless. In his opinion, since Spanish authority was destined to collapse under the weight of advancing American settlement into the territory, it would be imprudent for America to risk the fortunes of a war, especially given the likelihood of Federalist opposition. Such a conflict "would be a mere destruction of human life," he wrote Gen. James Wilkinson, "without affecting in the smallest degree the settlement, or its conditions." To understand Jefferson's plan, it is essential to realize that he hoped settlement would serve diplomatic goals, rather than the other way around. Jefferson's policy was to make clear to Madrid (as James Monroe phrased it) that Spain should peaceably accede to Washington's demands as "her government must know that at no distant period we should acquire [West Florida], the United States being a rising and Spain a declining power."[22]

Having decided that war was unnecessary and politically inexpedient, Jefferson changed course. He asked Congress for an appropriation of two million dollars for "extraordinary expenses" in early 1806, money he intended to use as a bribe to persuade Napoleon to approach his Spanish ally about a possible sale of the province. This policy backfired. Napoleon considered the sum too small, the Spanish refused to negotiate, and both Federalists and Republicans attacked the president's policy of "sordid bribery." One prominent Republican captured the opposition viewpoint well: "I consider it a base prostration of the national character to excite one nation by money to bully another nation out of its property."[23]

When the "Two-Million Dollar Act" failed, Jefferson lost the opportunity to acquire the Floridas during his second term. He played for time, but the fortunes of the European war soon brought to simmer a dispute with England. The nations' disagreements over the impressment of American sailors and access to foreign markets brought these issues to the fore of American diplomacy and relegated the Floridas to a lower priority. Although American forces occupied West Florida in 1810–1813, the Spanish did not cede the peninsula to the United States until 1819.

Conclusion

The Florida episode may be most accurately interpreted as an extension of the Louisiana strategy of 1801–1803, which itself grew from the seeds of Jefferson's 1792 analysis of the western question. In all cases the president pursued the same basic objective: to protect vital commercial arteries along the Gulf of Mexico and the Mississippi. Even in his retirement, Jefferson was extending this logic to include the Gulf Coast of Texas. He advocated that President Monroe delay ratification of the Transcontinental Treaty of 1819 and attempt to persuade Spain to include Texas in the pact.[24] A few days earlier, Jefferson had written to Monroe to push for the annexation of Cuba for "strategic reasons"—chief among them the port of Havana, with its proximity to Florida and shipping lanes to the Caribbean.[25]

There were few limits to Jefferson's appetite for asserting American sovereignty in the West and the Gulf of Mexico. However, it is worth noting that he did not value such expansion for its own sake and was blithely unconcerned with the vast majority of the land he purchased from Napoleon in 1803. Jefferson's unwavering fixation with the Mississippi, New Orleans, and West Florida was based on cold-blooded Realpolitik, not hazy dreams of an American "empire of liberty." This does not mean that Jefferson had abandoned his commitment to equality and freedom in the United States, but rather that the end remained for him entirely pragmatic. Put another way, New Orleans was to Jefferson what Danzig had been to Frederick II in the 1780s or the Dardanelles would prove to be to nineteenth-century Russian tsars.

In sum, Jefferson conceived and executed his western policy in the style of traditional reason of state, a pattern inherited from the European *ancien regime*. He was ruthless, duplicitous, and predatory in his dealings over

Louisiana and the Floridas, and at no time was his statecraft informed by idealistic pretensions or moral imperatives. His ambition was to secure the commerce of the Mississippi for the United States, and he was willing to negotiate with whatever power—including the nascent nation's old antagonist Britain—could best help him achieve this objective. Tactically, Jefferson remained abreast of European developments and shrewdly kept all diplomatic options open. In the case of Louisiana, he was able to reinforce Napoleon's deepening conviction that selling the territory served French interests. Had this strategy failed and had the French managed to assert sovereignty over the Mississippi trade, Jefferson was prepared to use force against the French garrison in New Orleans. This would have required an alliance with Britain to choke French supply lines to North America. Jefferson's equanimity in discussing this prospect with Livingston indicates he would have pursued this course had it been the only remaining option.

As in other areas of policy, Jefferson's ends in the West remained governed by the map, but his means were contingent and flexible. Against a relatively impotent Spain, he refused to waste or even expend much effort in terms of military power or expensive purchase arrangements. Believing that the effect of a surging population on a declining empire would carry the day, Jefferson maintained a complacent optimism that was violently shattered by the San Ildefonso cession. Although Jefferson preferred to avoid direct confrontation with France or Britain, the stakes were high enough in the case of New Orleans to warrant a potential military response. His willingness to even conceive of such a measure illustrates how vital he considered the national interests that were at risk. Jefferson's policy toward western North America, with its emphasis on power projection and the security of commerce, established the foundation for American dominance of the central continent by the middle of the nineteenth century.

Notes

1. Anne Cohler et al., eds., *The Spirit of the Laws* (1748; reprint, Cambridge: Cambridge University Press, 1989), 343.
2. Thomas Jefferson to James Madison, 30 June 1793, in *The Works of Thomas Jefferson*, vol. 7, ed. Paul Leicester Ford (New York: G. P. Putnam's Sons, 1904–1905), 421.
3. "Report on the Privileges and Restrictions of the Commerce of the United States," 16 December 1793, Ford, vol. 8: 112–113 (emphasis added).
4. Thomas Jefferson to G. K. van Hogendorp, 13 October 1785, in *The Papers of Thomas Jefferson,* vol. 8, ed. Julian Boyd, et al. (Princeton: Princeton University Press, 1950–), 633.
5. Benjamin Franklin to John Jay, 2 October 1780, quoted in Carl Van Doren, *Benjamin Franklin* (New York: Viking, 1938), 621.
6. James Madison to Jefferson, 20 August 1784, Boyd, vol. 6: 403; Jefferson to Archibald Stuart, 25 January 1786, Boyd, vol. 9: 218.
7. Jefferson to George Washington, 27 August 1790, Boyd, vol. 17: 129 (emphasis in original); Jefferson to Stuart, 25 January 1786, Boyd, vol. 9: 218.
8. "Outline of Policy on the Mississippi Question," 2 August 1790, Boyd, vol. 17: 113; "Report on Negotiations with Spain," 18 March 1792, Boyd, vol. 23: 299, 303. Similar arguments were put forward routinely by European foreign ministries throughout the eighteenth century: Frederick II's claim to Silesia in 1740 and Catherine II's defense of her Crimean policy in 1775–1783 employed equally questionable interpretations of international law to ornament a policy of annexation.
9. Jefferson to Du Pont de Nemours, 1 February 1803, *Correspondence between Jefferson and Du Pont de Nemours 1798–1817,* ed. Dumas Malone (Boston: Houghton Mifflin, 1930),

74–76. See Alexander DeConde, *This Affair of Louisiana* (New York: Scribner's, 1976), ix–x, for the argument that Jefferson's western policy was "a kind of pious imperialism" and forerunner of "manifest destiny."

10. Jefferson to Washington, 2 April 1791, Boyd, vol. 20: 97.

11. Jefferson to Robert R. Livingston, 18 April 1802, Ford, vol. 9: 364–365.

12. Arthur Preston Whitaker, *The Mississippi Question, 1795–1803* (New York: Appleton-Century, 1934), 181.

13. Jefferson to Livingston, 18 April 1802, Ford, vol. 9: 364–365.

14. This reconnaissance was the genesis of what later became known as the Lewis and Clark Expedition, which was originally intended as a military venture and assumed its scientific mission as the "Corps of Discovery" only after the crisis with France ended with the Louisiana Purchase in 1803. See Mary P. Adams, "Jefferson's Reaction to the Treaty of San Ildefonso," *Journal of Southern History* 21 (1955): 173–188 for Jefferson's military preparations.

15. A careful reading of Madison's correspondence during this period supports this interpretation of the Jefferson administration's policy. He wrote to Livingston in May 1802 that "the worst events are to be apprehended" from the simple French "*possession* of the mouth of the Mississippi." He makes no mention of the right of deposit as a potential *casus belli*. Madison to Livingston, 1 May 1802, *PJM-SS*, vol. 3: 176.

16. Jefferson to Du Pont de Nemours, 25 April 1802, *Correspondence between Jefferson and Du Pont de Nemours 1798–1817*, 47; Jefferson to Livingston, 18 April 1802, Ford, vol. 9: 365–366.

17. DeConde, *This Affair of Louisiana*, 173; Jefferson to Livingston, 18 April 1802, Ford, vol. 9: 366.

18. Jefferson to Philip Mazzei, 24 April 1796, Ford, vol. 7: 76; Jefferson to Horatio Gates, 11 July 1803, Ford, vol. 10: 13.

19. In a related dimension of his Louisiana policy, Jefferson did his best to make life for the French on Saint Domingue miserable and to tie down their troops there as long as possible to delay their arrival at New Orleans. He secretly funneled American arms to the slaves and free people of color fighting the French, an ironic policy indeed for a southern slaveowner. But the real causes of the French setbacks on the island were malaria and yellow fever, which reduced the occupation army by more than 50 percent. See Carl Lokke, "Jefferson and the Leclerc Expedition," *American Historical Review* 33 (1928), 322–338, for an overview of Jefferson's covert operations against the French. See also Du Pont de Nemours to Jefferson, 30 April 1802, *Correspondence between Jefferson and Du Pont de Nemours 1798–1817*, 59.

20. Jefferson to Gates, 11 July 1803, Ford, vol. 10: 13.

21. Madison to Charles Pinckney, 12 October 1803, Hunt, vol. 7: 74.

22. Jefferson to John Breckinridge, 12 August 1803, Ford, vol. 10: 5; Jefferson to James Wilkinson, 8 November 1806, DeConde, *This Affair of Louisiana*, 215; *Jefferson Papers*, Reel 59.

23. DeConde, *This Affair of Louisiana*, 227.

24. Upon learning of this development from Monroe, John Quincy Adams—architect of the treaty—privately seethed that Jefferson was quibbling with his work to reduce its significance against that of the Louisiana Purchase. Jefferson behaved, in Adams' words, "like an old sea captain who never liked to see his mate make a better voyage than himself." See Harry Ammon, *James Monroe: The Search for National Identity* (Charlottesville: University Press of Virginia, 1990), 444.

25. On Cuba, see Jefferson to James Monroe, 14 May 1820, Dumas Malone, *Jefferson and His Time: The Sage of Monticello* (Boston: Little, Brown, 1981), 22; Ford, vol. 10: 158–159.

5

The Burr Conspiracy and the Problem of Western Loyalty

JAMES E. LEWIS JR.

Did the Burr conspiracy threaten the American union? This question preoccupied those who tried to understand former vice president Aaron Burr's movements in the West in 1806 and 1807. The same question has absorbed the biographers and historians who have attempted to explain Burr's actions in the nearly two centuries since. In attempting to answer it, the question of whether the Burr conspiracy threatened the American union was often rephrased into a somewhat different one: "Did Burr intend to dismember the union?" As they worked to discover Burr's plans, contemporaries—and, later, historians—hoped that each new letter, official message, or newspaper would finally provide unequivocal evidence of his intent. None ever did. After Burr's effort had collapsed, more than one observer "wish[ed] that it had not so far matured as to leave no doubt as to his real design."[1] Even with access to thousands of letters written by Burr himself, his supporters, and his contemporaries, Burr's intent remains unclear to this day. The existing evidence makes it almost impossible to know exactly what Aaron Burr intended to accomplish.

For contemporaries, however, the question of whether the Burr conspiracy threatened the American union was also very much a question about loyalty. Were westerners—whether in the trans-Appalachian region in general, or in the new trans-Mississippi Louisiana Purchase, in particular—loyal to the United States? What processes would be required to divide the union at the Appalachians or the Mississippi River? Contemporary correspondence may only leave uncertainty as to Burr's designs, but it provides valuable evidence of the kinds of threats that Americans believed still faced the union after almost two decades under the Constitution. Where Chapter 4 examined the geopolitical concerns that shaped the Jefferson administration's goals and strategies, this chapter focuses on a threat that was at once domestic and foreign.

Discussions of disunion in the context of the conspiracy pointed to two distinct concerns. The first emerged from the basic recognition that regional differences existed in a diverse and extensive union. This analysis was not peculiar to either the trans-Appalachian West or the early years of the new nation. The second, and more worrisome, concern applied only to the West and lasted only to the mid-1820s. Its origins could be traced to the alarm over western loyalties triggered by the first rumors of France's recovery of Louisiana in early 1801.

The response to the Burr conspiracy demonstrated that the Louisiana Purchase in 1803 had not put these fears entirely to rest. If we cannot clearly identify Burr's intentions, we can use the conspiracy to understand the anxieties many of his contemporaries felt about the loyalties of westerners and the sources of disunionism even after the purchase.

The West and the Potential for Separatism

Americans saw an inherent threat of division in a union that included not only diverse peoples, but also distinct sections or regions. The boundaries assigned to these regions changed over time, as did the salience of their differences. But as long as there were regional variations, the potential for a separatist movement with widespread popular support would persist. Amidst the swirl of rumors and doubts that surrounded Burr's actions, some commentators voiced concerns about the West's attachment to the union that reflected this separatist model. Usually, however, the danger of this form of separatism was viewed with skepticism. Looking back twenty-five years later, Henry Marie Brackenridge expressed a view that was common even at the peak of the crisis. "It is absurd to suppose that a separation of the Western States entered into [Burr's] plan," he asserted, "when the bare suggestion of it would have excited universal indignation" among westerners.[2]

This separatist model took various forms over time and for different regions. In its most basic form, the potential for disunion arose from what seemed to be unchanging conditions. The size of the union might encourage separatism—particularly when distance was compounded by physical barriers, as with the trans-Appalachian West. More alarming was a sectional segregation of the interests and attitudes that arose from what were often viewed as permanent differences of ethnicity, religion, social structure, economic activity, and political preference among Americans. How the actual impetus for disunion would emerge from these long-standing sectional differences was rarely explained, however. Traveling in the West in 1805, for example, Josiah Espy noted "that before many years the people of that [region] would separate themselves from the Atlantic states and establish an independent empire." But he could not speculate on how this would happen: "What will be the proximate cause producing this great effect is yet in the womb of time."[3]

More fully elaborated forms of the separatist model could more easily answer questions about how the process of disunion could come about. A more sophisticated version added a vertical axis to what can be imagined as a horizontal conflict between theoretically equal geographical sections of the nation. This view recognized that each section of the United States interacted not only with every other section, but also with the federal government. Differences between sections formed an essential foundation for disunion, but grievances against the federal government could hold the missing proximate cause. Whether the West in the 1790s or New England during the embargo and War of 1812 or the South in the 1850s, a geographical section of the nation that viewed the government as under the control of another section or sections and as neglecting or sacrificing its interests appeared ripe for disunion. When the Republicans under Jefferson's leadership imposed the embargo (1807–1809), prohibiting foreign trade in an effort to coerce a change in British policy, New Englanders were outraged by a policy that seemed likely to destroy the regional economy. At the height of the embargo, for example, John Quincy Adams worried about efforts in New England to foment disunion by "paint[ing that] part of the Union, as under oppression from the rest" through the workings of a federal government that seemed willing to sacrifice the foreign trade that formed the basis of the region's economy.[4] Adams suggested another aspect of the more developed separatist model when he warned that ambitious leaders would try to turn such grievances into acts against the union.

Most of these elements of the separatist model were in place when contemporaries began to assess the threat of Burr's designs. The West had long been seen as a region with a strong separatist potential, shaped largely by the physical barriers that prevented easy trade, travel, and communication with the East. During the 1780s and 1790s the Franklin movement (a separatist revolt in western North Carolina designed to create a new state in land that eventually became East Tennessee), the Spanish conspiracy (an effort by the Spanish colonial government in Louisiana to build influence in Kentucky), the Whiskey Rebellion (a brief but violent uprising of settlers in western Pennsylvania irate about increased taxation on alcohol), and the Blount conspiracy (an effort to organize an armed force that would eject the Spanish from Florida and Louisiana, replacing them with British rule) had highlighted this potential. There was widespread suspicion, more-over, that Burr was just the type of ambitious man who could turn a vague separatist potential within the nation into a true disunionist act. A reputation for ambition had long dogged Burr. As early as 1792 Alexander Hamilton had described him as "an embryo-Caesar."[5] For many, the election of 1800, when Burr had apparently schemed to steal the presidency from Thomas Jefferson when an electoral tie sent the decision to the House of Representatives, provided unequivocal proof. "Burr's unbounded ambition, courage, and perseverance," Manasseh Cutler remarked shortly after the election, might "prompt him to be a Bonaparte, a King, and an Emperor, or any thing else which might place him at the head of the nation."[6]

Even with Burr (that "Master piece of Intriague," as Philip Van Cortlandt described him) in the West, however, a key element of the separatist model in its more developed form seemed to be missing.[7] The conviction that there were distinct western interests remained, as did the problems of the West's distance from the East and of barriers to travel. But all of the grievances that westerners had articulated against the government in the 1780s and 1790s had been resolved by 1806. The absence of local governments, the threat from the Indians, the closure of the Mississippi, the high price of land, and the tax on distilled spirits—all had been addressed in the preceding fifteen years. Republican control over the federal government, most westerners believed, guaranteed a continued solicitude for their region's interests.

Still, at the peak of the Burr crisis, a few contemporary commentators expressed concerns for the union that suggested their awareness of the force of a separatist model that combined distinct sectional interests, broad popular support, and ambitious leaders. In late October 1806, as President Jefferson met with the cabinet and dispatched instructions, one Virginia Federalist opined: "if Two Million of People are determined not to be under the Government of the United States, I dont know what King Tom will do."[8] It was not only eastern Federalists who feared western separatism, however. A Kentucky Republican confessed to Secretary of State James Madison that he was surprised that "the Idea of a separation [met] the countenance it does" and suggested "that designing bad men [could] do a great deal of Mischief in this country."[9] Similar fears about popular separatism and ambitious leaders shaped New Yorker John Nicholson's warning about a "sentiment of disunion" that "pervade[d] many of our western Citizens" and was "probably encouraged by some who might thereby promote their own views." Nicholson's long-term solution is as revealing as his immediate concern. He urged Jefferson to counteract this "sentiment" by beginning "the Grand national undertaking of opening avenues for Commerce" by constructing canals linking the Hudson and Ohio rivers, using the Great Lakes. By facilitating travel and trade, these canals "would convince our western Citizens that their Interest would be to remain united with us."

Most people, however, viewed the prospect of western separatism with great skepticism. Even Nicholson couched his warning in tentative terms: "*Possibly an attempt* at a separation is an event still *somewhat* to be feared."[10] Other commentators from across the nation discounted any thought of western disloyalty.

John Adams decided that Burr "must be an idiot or a lunatic" if he "thought that the trans-Alleghenian people would revolt with him."[11] To westerners, Burr's apparent intention of breaking the union through broad popular support could only be described as "chimerical," "a *mad, extravagant project,*" a "wild[,] desperate plan."[12] Many commentators could simply find no grounds for complaint against the U.S. government that could justify even a fear of disunion. Westerners enjoyed the prosperity of "well stored Barns and Corncribs" and "the protection of life and liberty," according to one Ohioan.[13] Another dismissed any thought of western separatism by noting that "the people are happy and highly pleased in the present order of things."[14]

Even if it was usually met with skepticism, the idea that the Burr conspiracy might include the kind of threat to the union embodied in widespread disloyalty was certainly troubling to some at the time. Fervent denials, no less than tentative admissions, showed that some people saw a prospect of western separatism that needed to be evaluated, even if it were only to be rejected. Among even the most strident defenders of western loyalty, moreover, few disputed that geography and shared interests marked the West as a distinct region. Ultimately, however, almost everyone who voiced these fears had to admit that westerners were too satisfied with the union and with the federal government *at that time* to consider disunion. "And unless it becomes a popular measure," a Kentuckian observed, "who is to effect it?"[15] No matter what Burr's intentions, the rise of a popularly supported movement in the West against the union seemed almost unthinkable in 1806–1807.

The Mississippi Crisis, the Louisiana Purchase, and the New Fears of Western Separatism

If separatism had provided the only foundation for concerns about disunion, it seems unlikely that Burr would have triggered much anxiety. A disunionist movement that required the level of popular support suggested by separatism seemed improbable even under optimal conditions. But when it came to the West, many of Burr's contemporaries could imagine disunion in a different form—one that did not require widespread support and that therefore seemed less improbable. Five years before the Burr conspiracy, rumors that Louisiana would be returned to France had also provoked fears for the union of East and West. During this crisis, many Americans had recognized that, if a strong national power held the mouth of the Mississippi, it could control the trade of the entire West. Offers of special privileges or threats of closed trade could be used to entice or force the West from the union. An otherwise loyal populace might be pressured into separatism by playing on the people's economic interests. During the winter of 1806–1807 many observers, including key policymakers, expressed fears for the union that were rooted in the Mississippi crisis.

Policymakers had quickly seen the threat that French control of the mouth of the Mississippi posed to the union. As events played out between the spring of 1801 and the summer of 1803, the Jefferson administration grew increasingly worried that Napoleon might have reacquired Louisiana precisely to gain influence over the West. Madison stated this concern clearly. He worried that France calculated

"that by holding the key to the commerce of the Mississippi, she [could] command the interests and attachments of the Western portion of the United States." With this leverage, France would try to "controul the Atlantic portion also; or if that [could not] be done, to seduce the [West] into a separate Government, and a close alliance with herself."[16] Policymakers were not alone in viewing the danger in this manner. William T. Barry, a nineteen-year-old from around Lexington, Kentucky, understood the threat as clearly as Madison. "Having in their possession the sea ports on the Mississippi, which are the only marts for the commerce of these States," he explained, the French would "have hold of a lever with which they can wield and regulate our interests as they please." In time, they would "try to separate [the western states] from the Eastern."

Four years later, Barry expressed exactly the same concern in the face of the Burr conspiracy. "The first object" was New Orleans, Barry concluded; with that in his possession, Burr would attempt first "to revolutionize the Spanish provinces, and establish an independent Govt. distinct from the U.S. and ultimately to bring about a separation of the Union."[17] As had also been the case earlier, this analysis proved especially powerful among policymakers and government officials. Joseph Hamilton Daveiss, the federal district attorney in Kentucky, noted in one early warning about Burr: "No doubt all the western waters are calculated on, as falling in with the power possessing the mouths of those waters."[18] Congressman George W. Campbell offered a similar analysis. He believed Burr hoped to seize New Orleans, invade Mexico, "and if successful in this, shut up the mouth of the Mississippi . . .

and thereby compel [the West] to join his newly created empire."[19] Jefferson also revived the logic of the Mississippi crisis to comprehend Burr's plans. Burr's intention, as the president understood it at one point, was to "extend his empire to the Alleghany, [by] seizing on New Orleans as the instrument of compulsion for our western States."[20]

But was Burr any more likely to succeed in "seizing on New Orleans" than in securing the broad popular support separatism would demand? Many observers thought so. Their anxious comments suggested at least four ways Burr might have taken New Orleans: with a large force raised in the West, with the support of the U.S. Army, with the aid of a foreign power, and with the backing of a disloyal local populace. Each of these ideas received serious consideration in the letters of private citizens and public officials.

Burr's Men: Rumors Run Rampant

Estimates of how many recruits Burr had, for example, filled contemporary correspondence. Even a fairly small force might have defeated the tiny regular army in the Southwest; but few of the estimates people suggested were even remotely small. Most accounts gave figures at least three times the size of the regular forces: 3,000 men according to one; 2,500 to 3,000, with 1,500 more on the way, according to Ohio governor Edward Tiffin; 5,000 and "daily increasing," according to news that reached Benjamin Hawkins at the Creek agency in Georgia.[21] Other reports estimated even higher. In late December 1806 Thomas Freeman alerted the War Department to rumors in Natchez that Burr "with an armed

force of nearly 8000. armed men" would arrive within days; Freeman's slip of the pen about Burr's doubly "armed" force probably more clearly conveyed his state of mind than did his assertion that the few nearby troops were determined to "do their duty."[22]

It was commonly assumed, however, that Burr would not need to raise a large force, or possibly even fire a shot, if he intended to seize New Orleans because the army had been corrupted to his purposes. Most of these fears centered on Gen. James Wilkinson, whose loyalty to the union had long been doubted. Wilkinson had been a key figure in Kentucky's Spanish conspiracy in the late 1780s and was widely considered (correctly, it was later learned) to be in the pay of Spain. As the first rumors of the conspiracy spread, one Virginian flatly asserted that Burr had "Wilkinson at the head of the Army, in league with him."[23] Speculation in the West in mid-January 1807 added many more details. Burr's force would unite in New Orleans with "Wilkason, and the federal troops there, together, with a detachment from New-York, which [was] to act by water."[24] News that "Wilkinson's Army have gone with him at their head, to N. Orleans" should have been reassuring; instead, it proved alarming. "This movement is unaccountable, and it is supposed to be unauthorized by Govt," William T. Barry wrote; "if so, a blow is struck at N. Orleans e'er this."[25]

As many observers saw it, foreign armies or navies that would supplement or supplant a corrupted American army were the means that would allow Burr to seize New Orleans. Relations with both Spain and Great Britain were tense; either of these powers might hope to cripple their American rival by encouraging disunion. That Burr had arranged foreign assistance seemed certain to many observers; what remained unclear was from which power. While his brother John thought "that the British Government and B[urr were] co-operating," William T. Barry believed differently: "I would rather conjecture that it is the Spanish and French Govts."[26] Thomas Rodney warned that the conspirators "Expect[ed] a Brittish Fleet to aid them," but John Randolph insisted that "no man, in his senses, [could] doubt that the schemes of Burr [were] now carrying on in concert with the cabinet of Madrid & with Spanish money."[27] Others thought that, though they were at war with each other in Europe, both Great Britain and Spain were aiding Burr.

The People of New Orleans

New Orleans could fall to Burr without either a large force under Burr's command or a corrupted army under Wilkinson or a foreign navy, however. Even as most observers considered the West to be loyal as a whole, they viewed the people of New Orleans and its environs as, at best, loosely attached to a nation that had only recently acquired them through the Louisiana Purchase. In the three years since the transfer of Louisiana, Governor William C. C. Claiborne had had reason to worry about each element of the city's mixed population—Spanish, French, Americans who had lived in the province before the transfer, Americans who had arrived since, free people of color, and slaves. It seemed likely that Burr could win enough local support to take the city almost unopposed. Joseph Hamilton Daveiss warned Madison that "you will upon an emergency find the settlement at Orleans perfectly

rotten."[28] With the crisis upon him, Claiborne admitted his doubts about whether "a majority of the People . . . would rally to the call of Government." He would only "cherish a hope" that the local militia would defend the city against Burr.[29]

In a November 1806 letter, Andrew Jackson suggested how all of these potential sources of support for the seizure of New Orleans could work together to bring about disunion. Writing to Tennessee senator Daniel Smith, Jackson assembled known facts and reasonable suppositions into a coherent picture of Burr's design. If "a plan for separating the Union is actually on foot," Jackson began, "how is it to be efected?" Given "the attachment of [th]e western people collectively to the government," "a designing man" would try to take advantage of the tensions on the southwestern frontier by "form[ing] an intrigue" with the Spanish minister. "[T]he general of your army" would be drawn into this intrigue as well. Spanish and American troops, under the "pretext" of a war scare, would come together at a point "within two hundred miles of New-orleans." As "the two armies . . . forme[d] plans of cooperation," Burr's force would descend "from the ohio and uper Louisiana." With "two thirds of its inhabitants into the plan," New Orleans would be in "a defenceless situation." Facing the combined forces of Burr's men from upriver, the American and Spanish armies, and local support, the city would "fall an easy pray." The two armies as well as Spanish naval vessels would allow Burr to hold the city. He would, then, "Shut the Port against the exportation of the west, and hold out alurements to all the western world to Join [in order to] enjoy free trade and profitable commerce." Convinced that most westerners remained committed to the union, Jackson nonetheless feared that Burr could force a division at the Appalachians.

Many people would have questioned Jackson's assertion that "no other plan presents itself . . . that could furnish [hope] of success" given all the elements that had to come together in his elaborate scenario.[30] Some clearly believed that with even just one of these potential sources of support, Burr could seize New Orleans. Still, concerns about disunion that derived from the logic of the Mississippi crisis, like those that derived concerns over separatism, were often voiced with skepticism. In the same letter in which he used this reasoning to explain Burr's plans, for example, Jefferson described this "enterprise [as] the most extraordinary since the days of Don Quixote."[31] Such skepticism seems well founded. Even if Burr had managed to gain possession of New Orleans, he still would have had to hold it long enough to use his newly acquired control over western trade to put pressure on the union. In the end, none of the potential sources of support for the seizure of New Orleans materialized in 1806–1807. And without control over western commerce, according to the logic of the Mississippi crisis, there was no threat to the union.

Conclusion: The Union Preserved, the Union Endangered

Contemporary responses to the Burr conspiracy reveal ongoing anxieties about the durability of the union between East and West nearly two decades after the Constitution and more than three years after the Louisiana Purchase. Some observers identified the threat as one of western separatism, relying on a model of disunion that had already been applied to New England, the South, and the West. Although the prospect of losing the West through disunion was viewed with skepticism, neither the abrupt end of the Burr conspiracy nor the effusive displays of western loyalty that it generated brought an end to separatist fears about that region. When depression supplanted prosperity in the nation and new grievances arose over policies about federal banking, land issues, Indians, and foreign relations, such concerns over separatism and disunion returned. Writing during the crisis created by the Panic of 1819, the Missouri debates, and the Transcontinental Treaty, Henry Clay warned that there were "several powerful local causes operating in the West" that threatened a "disseverance" of the union.[32] It took the opening of the Erie Canal in 1825 and the shifting of political power to the West after Jackson's election in 1828 to finally excise this perceived danger.

Other observers traced the threat to circumstances that were unique to the West, reviving the logic of the Mississippi crisis. As with separatism, the failure of the Burr conspiracy did not result in the final rejection of this line of reasoning. Its central premise reappeared in Jefferson's thinking as late as December 1820, nearly two decades after the Louisiana Purchase should have obviated it. As the Missouri crisis threatened to cleave the union between free states and slave states, the former president suggested that the division might end instead at the Appalachians. Ohio, Indiana, and Illinois would remain with the South, he argued, since they could "scarcely separate from those who would hold the Mississippi from its mouth to its source."[33] Over time, moreover, this logic was applied to new areas that seemed to pose a similar threat to western commerce. With New Orleans safely in American hands, concern shifted to West Florida and Cuba. As Thomas Sidney Jesup explained in August 1816, Cuba "constitute[d] the Key to all Western America"; if Cuba were passed from Spain to a stronger power, the response of westerners would show "that men are oftener governed by their interests, than love of country."[34]

Throughout the crisis generated by the Burr conspiracy, as during the earlier crisis sparked by the return of Louisiana to France, concern about disunion highlighted a persistent anxiety among some Americans about the loyalty of westerners. Whatever form their concerns took, Americans showed clearly that they understood loyalty to be calculated rather than natural, and rooted in economic self-interest rather than in political principles. If neither form of disunion seemed especially likely in the context of the Burr conspiracy, uncertainties about the loyalties of other Americans (in this case, those in the West) were strong enough that neither separatism nor disunion appeared entirely preposterous.

Notes

1. Thomas Tudor Tucker to John Page, 5 March 1807, *Thomas Tudor Tucker Papers* (Washington, D.C.: Library of Congress). Hereafter cited as *DLC*.
2. H. M. Brackenridge, *Recollections of Persons and Places in the West* (Philadelphia: J. Kay, Jun., and Brother, 1834; 2d ed., Philadelphia: J. B. Lippincott, 1868), 104.
3. Josiah Espy, *Memorandums of a Tour Made by Josiah Espy in the States of Ohio and Kentucky and Indiana Territory in 1805* (Cincinnati, Ohio: Robert Clarke & Co., 1870), 25.
4. John Quincy Adams, *American Principles: A Review of Works of Fisher Ames, Compiled by a Number of His Friends* (Boston: Everett and Munroe, 1809), 38.
5. Alexander Hamilton to unknown correspondent, 26 September 1792, in *The Papers of Alexander Hamilton,* vol. 12 (New York: Columbia University Press, 1961–1987), 480.
6. Manasseh Cutler to Ephraim Cutler, 21 March 1801, in *Life, Journals and Correspondence of Rev. Manasseh Cutler, Ll.D.,* vol. 2, ed. William Parker Cutler and Julia Perkins Cutler (Cincinnati, Ohio: Robert Clarke & Co., 1888), 44.
7. Philip Van Cortlandt to Pierre Van Cortlandt Jr., 30 December 1804, in *Correspondence of the Van Cortlandt Family of Cortlandt Manor,* vol. 3, ed. Jacob Judd (Tarrytown, N.Y.: Sleepy Hollow Restorations, 1981), 183.
8. "Extract of a letter from Alexandria in Virginia," 29 October 1806, enclosed in Jonathan Hamilton to Duncan Cameron, 4 November 1806, *Cameron Family Papers* (Chapel Hill.: Southern Historical Collection, University of North Carolina). Hereafter *NcU*.
9. John Taylor to James Madison, 13 October 1806, in "The Letters of James Taylor to the Presidents of the United States," ed. James A. Padgett, *Register of the Kentucky State Historical Society* 34 (April 1936): 115.
10. John H. Nicholson to Thomas Jefferson, 14 October 1806, in *Thomas Jefferson Correspondence: Printed from the Originals in the Collections of William K. Bixby,* ed. Worthington Chauncey Ford (Boston: Plimpton Press, 1916), 136.
11. John Adams to Benjamin Rush, 2 February 1807, in *The Spur of Fame: Dialogues of John Adams and Richard Rush, 1805–1813,* ed. John A. Schutz and Douglass Adair (San Marino, Calif.: Huntington Library Press, 1923), 76.
12. John Bigger Jr. to James Findlay, 17 January 1807, in "Selections from the Torrence Papers," ed. Isaac Joslin Cox, *Quarterly Publications of the Historical and Philosophical Society of Ohio* 4 (July–September 1909): 120; George Washington Campbell to Andrew Jackson, 6 February 1807, in *The Papers of Andrew Jackson,* vol. 2, ed. Sam B. Smith et al. (Knoxville:

University of Tennessee Press, 1980), 151 (hereafter Jackson, *Papers*); Thomas Worthington to Nathaniel Massie, 29 January 1807, in *Nathaniel Massie, A Pioneer of Ohio: A Sketch of His Life and Selections from His Correspondence,* ed. David Meade Massie (Cincinnati, Ohio: Robert Clarke, 1896), 241.

13. John Bigger Jr. to James Findlay, 17 January 1807, in Cox, ed., "Torrence Papers," 120.

14. Thomas Worthington to Nathaniel Massie, 29 January 1807, in Massie, *Nathaniel Massie,* 241.

15. Nick Warfield Jr. to John Payne, 14 January 1807, *John Payne Papers, DLC.*

16. James Madison to Robert R. Livingston and James Monroe, 2 March 1803, in *The Papers of James Madison: Secretary of State Series,* vol. 4, ed. Robert J. Brugger et al. (Charlottesville: University Press of Virginia, 1986–), 366.

17. William T. Barry to John Barry, 9 May 1803, *William T. Barry Letters* (Charlottesville: Alderman Library, University of Virginia) [hereafter *ViU*]; William T. Barry to John Barry, 2 January 1807, *ViU.*

18. Joseph Hamilton Daveiss to James Madison, 14 August 1806, in "View of the President's Conduct Concerning the Conspiracy of 1806," ed. Isaac Joslin Cox and Helen A. Swineford *Quarterly Publication of the Historical and Philosophical Society of Ohio* 12 (April–June/July–September 1917), 93 [hereafter Daveiss, "View"].

19. George W. Campbell, 25 February 1807, "Circular Letter to Constituents," in *Circular Letters of Congressmen to Their Constituents, 1789–1829,* vol. 1, ed. Noble E. Cunningham Jr. (Chapel Hill: University of North Carolina Press, 1978), 495.

20. Thomas Jefferson to Charles Clay, 11 January 1807, in *The Writings of Thomas Jefferson,* Definitive Edition, vol. 11, ed. Andrew A. Lipscomb and Albert Ellery Bergh (Washington, D.C.: Thomas Jefferson Memorial Association, 1905), 133. Hereafter Jefferson, *Writings.*

21. Benjamin Hawkins to Henry Dearborn, 18 February 1807, in *Letters, Journals, and Writings of Benjamin Hawkins,* vol. 2, ed. C. L. Grant (Savannah, Ga.: Beehive Press, 1980), 512. For the other reports, see James Finley to Thomas Worthington, 31 January 1807, and Edward Tiffin to Thomas Worthington, 9 January 1807, *Thomas Worthington Papers* (Columbus: Microfilm Collection, Ohio Historical Society).

22. Thomas Freeman to Peter Hagner, 30 December 1806, *Peter Hagner Papers, NcU.*

23. "Extract of a Letter from Alexandria in Virginia," 29 October 1806, enclosed in Jonathan Hamilton to Duncan Cameron, 4 November 1806, *Cameron Family Papers, NcU.*

24. William Martin to Daniel Smith, 16 January 1807, in *Correspondence of Andrew Jackson,* vol. 1, ed. John Spencer Bassett (Washington, D.C.: Carnegie Institution of Washington, 1926–1935), 164 n.1.

25. William T. Barry to John Barry, 2 January 1807, *William T. Barry Letters, ViU.*

26. William T. Barry to John Barry, 2 January 1807, *William T. Barry Letters, ViU.*

27. Thomas Rodney to Caesar A. Rodney, 21 November 1806, in "Thomas Rodney," ed. Simon Gratz, *Pennsylvania Magazine of History and Biography* 44 (October 1920): 289–308; John Randolph to George Hay, 3 January 1806 [sic, 1807], *John Randolph of Roanoke Papers, DLC.*

28. Joseph Hamilton Daveiss to James Madison, 14 August 1806, in Daveiss, "View," 93.

29. William C. C. Claiborne to James Madison, 5 December 1806, in *Official Letter Books of William C. C. Claiborne, 1801–1816,* vol. 4, ed. Dunbar Rowland (Jackson, Miss.: State Department of Archives and History, 1917), 42.

30. Andrew Jackson to Daniel Smith, 12 November 1806, in Jackson, *Papers,* vol. 2: 118.

31. Thomas Jefferson to Charles Clay, 11 January 1807, in Jefferson, *Writings,* vol. 11: 133.

32. Henry Clay to Langdon Cheves, 5 March 1821, in *The Papers of Henry Clay,* vol. 3, ed. James F. Hopkins et al. (Lexington: University Press of Kentucky, 1959–1992), 58.

33. Thomas Jefferson to Albert Gallatin, 26 December 1820, in *The Works of Thomas Jefferson,* vol. 12, ed. Paul Leicester Ford (New York: G. P. Putnam's Sons, 1904–1905), 188.

34. Thomas Sidney Jesup to Andrew Jackson, 18 August 1816, and Thomas Sidney Jesup to James Monroe, 8 September 1816, *Thomas Sidney Jesup Papers, DLC.*

6

Dehahuit and the Question of Change in North America

PETER J. KASTOR

Dehahuit had seen empires come and go. His village near the banks of the Red River could not have seemed more distant from the cities where diplomats negotiated the Louisiana Purchase, yet Dehahuit was all too familiar with the way Europeans operated. Equally important, Dehahuit was quick to ask how those decisions would affect him, the village in which he lived, and the villages that surrounded him. As a chief—or *caddi*—of the Caddo Indians, Dehahuit correctly concluded that the domestic politics as well as the international relations of his own people were inextricably linked with those of the Europeans and, eventually, to the newfangled empire called the United States.

In the years following the Louisiana Purchase, Dehahuit emerged as one of the critical political and diplomatic leaders on the borderlands between the United States and Spanish North America, his policies shaping the way the United States responded to the Louisiana Purchase. Examining his life is also a way to understand what the Louisiana Purchase meant to other Indians, because Dehahuit's experience was not unique.[1] Throughout North America, Indians asked themselves the same question: What would the French decision to sell land to the United States mean for us?

Many concluded that the decision meant nothing, and rightly so, for throughout much of the North American interior, it was Indians—not the Americans, the Spanish, or the French—who exercised sovereignty. Other Indian leaders concluded that the Louisiana Purchase might create new opportunities to advance their domestic and foreign agendas. Still others were worried, for they believed the Louisiana Purchase created new threats.

In the end, those Indians who were most anxious proved to be the most accurate. Territorial expansion by the United States would lead to the near-eradication of the Indians living in the Southeast and in most of the North American West in ways so stark that the disadvantages of the Louisiana Purchase to Indians seemed no less obvious than the benefits to the United States. In 1803, however, nobody was so certain. Dehahuit provides a case study in the contingency that abounded in North America at the turn of the nineteenth century. He also shows just how relative "contingency" could be. The Louisiana Purchase offered considerable benefits to Dehahuit as well as to other Indians, but for reasons that were entirely in conflict with the objectives of federal policymakers in the United States. A half-century

later, long after American policymakers concluded that the foreign threats posed by
the Louisiana Purchase had come to an end,
the Caddo were suffering from the results of
the Louisiana Purchase.

No one was more familiar with the realities
of empire than the Indians of North America.
As Chapter 9 shows, after 1803 the Louisiana
Purchase enabled the United States to continue
its effort to rework the meaning of empire, removing the sort of inequality and eventual dis-
integration associated with European models
of empire. But as Chapter 10 suggests, the
American empire would also unleash new
forms of racial inequality. In the era that the
Louisiana Purchase expanded the reach of
slavery, so too would the American empire in
the West eventually cause the near-annihilation
of Indians.

This is an unfamiliar story to many Americans, even those who study Indian history.
Most Americans of nonnative ancestry learn
about Indians through a focus on their culture,
whether agricultural practices, spirituality, or
tribal identities. Many scholars have shown
that spirituality played a critical role in the call
for—or rejection of—alliances among villages
or with Europeans.[2] In keeping with the goals
of this book, however, this chapter examines
the political and diplomatic principles that Indians developed in response to the Louisiana
Purchase. The goal is to outline the contours of
alternative forms of federalism in North
America as Indians proposed ways that their
own sovereignty could coexist or overlap with
that of Europeans or the United States. I take
this approach with some trepidation. Scholars
argue whether to study Indians in this way is
to impose European perspectives onto them. In

many cases the conflict between Indians and
Europeans emerged from profoundly different
ways of interpreting the world. Yet, I argue
here that it is striking how similar Indians,
Europeans, and Americans could be when it
came to political and diplomatic initiatives.

Dehahuit occupies center stage in this account because his own story is so telling. But
his biography becomes all the more clear in
comparison with the lives of other Indian leaders, or for that matter, the leaders of the United
States. These men all revealed a similarly pragmatic approach to international affairs. All of
them pursued commercial and strategic
arrangements that would serve their people. To
this end, Indians as well as leaders of the
United States sought constitutional arrangements that delivered unprecedented consolida-
tions of power. For Indians, these arrangements did not take the form of written
constitutions. But Indians did concern themselves with representation, distribution of
power, or systems of authority that they hoped
to impose on the North American landscape.

That Indian and U.S. leaders would reach
the same conclusions only made sense. Both
were reacting to unprecedented changes on
both sides of the Atlantic; both were attempting to fill the vacuum of power that came with
the disappearance of European authority in
much of North America. But their policies were
still on a collision course. The United States intended to establish its sovereignty over land on
which Indians lived; Indians wanted nothing
more than to preserve their autonomy. White
settlers eventually attempted to establish more
localized sovereignty in the form of farms or
towns; meanwhile, Indians had become deeply
suspicious of those white settlers. In the years

after 1803 Indians would pursue diplomatic as well as political policies of aggressive engagement, militant resistance, and complete disregard when it came to dealing with the United States. All of those policies would emerge from the potential repercussions that Indians associated with the Louisiana Purchase.

Union and Independence

They were such simple words, union and independence—but they were loaded. They were the words that guided much of the political debate in the United States in the quarter-century after independence. In fact, the United States pursued its Mississippi policy—a policy that led to the Louisiana Purchase—to bolster the union and to preserve independence. But union and independence were equally important concepts to Indians, who had been arguing about how much unity and how much independence they should seek long before the British colonies declared their independence in 1776. In the West, particularly on the eastern and northern Plains, Indians had established complex relationships among themselves as they attempted to dominate the North American interior. These relationships often had little to do with Europeans or with the United States. Later, Indians in the East would engage in their own reconfiguration, but for them the Europeans would prove critical.

Like the Europeans who descended on the Americas, Indians identified themselves in local terms. Villages—whether individually or as part of local clusters—were the communities that mattered most to Indians, not the tribal labels that Indians and whites would later use.[3] In this they were quite similar to Europeans,

especially British settlers. In 1776, for example, few British settlers were prepared to call themselves "Americans." Instead, they started by calling themselves "Virginians" or "Pennsylvanians." Since the arrival of Europeans on the American mainland at the turn of the sixteenth century, Indians had debated how best to respond to the newcomers. Some Indians believed that they could benefit from alliances with Europeans that would bring assistance from European armies and trade networks. Other Indians claimed that close association with Europeans *was* the problem. They argued instead for building coalitions among Indians. Although these alliances proved short-lived throughout much of the sixteenth and seventeenth centuries, by the mid–eighteenth century the movement for Indian unification gained new strength. Some Indians began to argue that they could only achieve spiritual revitalization and long-term survival by separating themselves from the Europeans and through closer ties and unity among themselves. Although Europeans were the catalyst to this debate, it was an internal argument, especially among chiefs who disagreed over how militant their policies should be. While some Indians advocated violent reprisals against Europeans, others sought to maintain political and commercial ties.[4]

The United States came into being just as the militant movement began to build steam, and the United States only provided more fuel for it. As Anglo-American settlers began moving to the Ohio Country—the center of militant resistance to the federal government—they further reinforced the belief among Indians that people of European ancestry were untrustworthy characters intent on stealing Indian land. Indian resistance in turn shaped the new government of the United States. United Indians created larger military forces that they hoped could stem the influx of American settlers, either through intimidation or violence. The United States responded in turn by creating its own military structure—a standing army that, although also designed as a defense against Europeans, spent most of its time on the frontiers of North America attempting to frighten Indians or to subdue and conquer them.[5]

Other Indians to the west were also reconstituting themselves, and had begun to do so long before the United States came into being. Throughout the sixteenth and seventeenth centuries, Indians had moved west as disease, European settlers, and European armies made life in the East increasingly difficult. As Indians from the eastern seaboard and Appalachia traveled west, those Indians already living in the Ohio and Mississippi valleys found their own lands increasingly crowded by these newcomers. For some, the decision was to head even farther west, to the Plains and the Rockies. They were able to do so because the arrival of horses, most of them from Spanish colonies to the south, gave them the mobility necessary for life on the unforgiving landscape of the continental interior.[6]

As Indians moved about and created new communities, they forged alliances as well as antipathies. For example, Indians continued to argue over which policy to follow in the East. Likewise, the Mandan and Hidatsa Indians of the upper Missouri River grew increasingly resentful toward the Teton Sioux who controlled the lower Missouri and, in turn, access to trade farther east. Meanwhile, Indians built elabo-

rate diplomatic alliances with different European powers. Although white governments acknowledged the Spanish claim to Louisiana, few Indians of the continental interior had much reason to care about Spain. The absence of Spanish officials or Spanish settlers meant that Indians continued to concern themselves with the outsiders who had come through the region throughout the eighteenth century: French and British traders—some of them individual entrepreneurs, others official representatives of their governments.

It was in this context of dynamic activity among Indians that the United States acquired Louisiana from France and set out to convince all the residents of North America that Louisiana was federal property.

Neutral Ground?

Dehahuit was probably born around 1760 in a region now known as Texarkana, at the intersection of Texas, Arkansas, and Louisiana. The land was home to a series of Indian villages connected by elaborate trade networks, linguistic similarity, and historical affiliations. Anthropologists would eventually use the word "Caddo" to define these villages, but that single word should not be misinterpreted as evidence of a unified society. For these Indians the village remained the locus of daily life and political identity.[7]

By the mid–eighteenth century, the Caddo were organized in three major village confederacies, with the Kaddohadacho villages emerging as the most powerful, primarily because of the ambitions and leadership of a series of Kaddohadacho chiefs. The first of these was Tinhioüen. His successor, Bicheda, continued Tinhioüen's policy of village coordination. Like Tinhioüen, he increased his own power—and that of his village—accordingly. The Kaddohadacho chiefs argued for a united front in the second half of the eighteenth century largely because they faced greater external enemies. So long as France and Spain jockeyed for control of the North American West, boundary disputes over the Red River valley had prevented any one European power from exerting particular pressure on the Indians who lived there. With France's decision to cede Louisiana to Spain in 1763, however, Spanish claims enveloped the Indians' land. This sort of unification was not without benefits for the leading *caddi*. External pressures had created political leaders of unprecedented power. Leaders of this sort were common throughout North America, whether they were of native or European ancestry.[8]

When Bicheda died in 1800, his son, Dehahuit, became *caddi*. Surrounded by encroaching Spanish officials, Dehahuit continued his father's efforts to preserve Indian autonomy through political unification. For Dehahuit, news of the Louisiana Purchase came fast but not a moment too soon. The eviction of Spanish authority from the Mississippi Valley transformed the diplomatic landscape in ways that seemed immediately beneficial to the Caddo.

The absence of a clear western boundary of Louisiana created its own set of problems for Spain and the United States, but occupying this nexus of confrontation were none other than the Caddo Indians. Theirs was obviously a position of great risk. Should the United States and Spain come to blows, the Caddo villages could find themselves trapped between two warring armies. But it was also a moment of opportunity that Dehahuit was quick to grasp. He actively courted the United States, hoping to build alliances with the new power to the east. But he was equally comfortable reforming his relations with Spain. Dehahuit soon decided that his own domestic and foreign policies depended on effective manipulation of the Spanish-American conflict.

Dehahuit was fortunate to find a sympathetic conduit to the leaders of the United States. Dr. John Sibley was a physician and amateur anthropologist. He was also a federal Indian agent with a vaguely defined jurisdiction consisting mostly of the western fringes of the Territory of Orleans, the jurisdictional predecessor to the State of Louisiana. Sibley and Dehahuit soon cultivated a cordial relationship based on repeated visits. Sibley often blamed Indians for what he considered irrational acts of anger. Yet he was also willing to act as their defender, a position which eventually brought him the ire of federal officials and white settlers.[9]

By 1806 Dehahuit was ready to express his own vision of the Louisiana Purchase. Sibley arranged a meeting with William C. C. Claiborne, the governor of the Territory of Orleans and the leading American official in the region. In a speech to the American governor and, in turn, to the U.S. government, Dehahuit explained that "my words resemble the words my forefathers have told me they used to receive from the French in ancient times." This vision of the past ignored the lengthy but troublesome period of Spanish rule, referring instead to the era when French governance had brought with it relative autonomy for the Caddo. Using this selective memory as a foundation, Dehahuit proclaimed, "If your nation has purchased what the French formerly possessed, you have purchased the country that we occupy, and we regard you in the same light as we did them."[10]

It was, in some ways, a vague promise. Dehahuit asserted Caddo independence even as he gave tacit acknowledgement to American sovereignty. But this apparent conflict was entirely in keeping with his own experience in dealing with Europeans. Indians refused to abandon claims to the land that they occupied, but they acknowledged a need for some arrangement that addressed European territorial pretensions. Dehahuit soon provided more tangible proof of his willingness to acknowledge a Louisiana Purchase in keeping with American territorial ambitions. He did so by flying the flag of the United States in his own village.[11]

In the years that followed, the diplomatic disputes unleashed by the Louisiana Purchase continued to create opportunities for the Caddo. When Spain and the United States seemed likely to go to war over the western boundary of Louisiana in 1806, both powers resolved the matter by agreeing to create what they called the Neutral Ground. This zone was a strip of land that was off limits to troops from either side until the boundary could be settled by international negotiation. The Neutral Ground just happened to include most of the Caddo villages. The Neutral Ground preserved the very independence that the Caddo sought, with the benefits of unity that sustained Dehahuit's power.

These opportunities always came with risks. Chapter 4 emphasized the dangers that Thomas Jefferson faced as he attempted to exploit Eu-ropean circumstances to serve American aims. The Caddo were no less strategic in their outlook, nor were the dangers they faced any less real. The Neutral Ground only came into being because of the risk of war, a war that would have been devastating for the Caddo. Likewise, the Caddo found that runaway slaves and white squatters took advantage of the Neutral Ground to seek their own independence in the West. It was only by threatening Spain and the United States with violence that the Caddo were able to coerce an agreement by which troops from both powers made brief incursions to the Neutral Ground to evict the intruders.

"We Hope that He Does Love Your New Children"

A decade after 1803 the Caddo and Dehahuit still enjoyed the benefits of the Louisiana Purchase. They remained actively engaged with the United States. Meanwhile, their ties with Spain only became more distant when the Napoleonic invasion of the Iberian Peninsula in 1808 brought the governments of Spanish America to the verge of collapse. But the Caddo were unusual. Few other Indians saw such benefits through contact with the United States. Either the United States remained irrelevant, or its relevance was anything but positive.

The 1806 dispute that led to the creation of the Neutral Ground came about when Jefferson dispatched a scientific expedition up the Red River under the leadership of Thomas Freeman and Peter Custis. The Spanish saw the expedition as an effort to undermine their relations with the Indians. As Freeman and Custis approached the Caddo villages, the

Spanish dispatched troops who forced the explorers to return to New Orleans. In sharp contrast, a more famous expedition farther north introduced other Indians to the Louisiana Purchase.

As Freeman and Custis began their journey in the summer of 1806, Meriwether Lewis and William Clark were on their way home, concluding a two-year expedition traversing North America from the Mississippi to the Pacific. Jefferson had numerous goals for the "Corps of Discovery," as Lewis and Clark coined their expedition. Jefferson's scientific interests remain the most attractive aspect of the expedition, for they were both noble and visionary. More important at the time were commercial and diplomatic objectives. Jefferson actually began planning the expedition *before* the Louisiana Purchase, when he had no immediate plans to acquire land *west* of the Mississippi. Instead, he sought commercial opportunities that would enable Americans *east* of the Mississippi to trade through the North American interior and west to the Pacific. At the heart of his scientific and commercial aspirations was the goal of locating the Northwest Passage, a fabled waterway that Lewis and Clark eventually proved did not exist. With Indians commanding the shores of the Missouri and the Columbia, establishing peaceful relationships would be vital to any future American commerce. By acting in this way, the United States was only the latest empire to conclude that commerce could be the mechanism for extending sovereignty over the Indians of North America.

The Louisiana Purchase changed the Lewis and Clark expedition from a passage through foreign land to one establishing sovereignty over American soil. This task meant convincing the Indians of Louisiana that they lived on American property. Even if the Indians continued to wield day-to-day authority over the land, acknowledgments from them would nonetheless make federal sovereignty of the Louisiana Purchase a reality. So with each encounter, Lewis and Clark began by proclaiming that land that had been French or Spanish was now American. Implicit in their assertions was the notion that the Indians themselves had no viable claim to the land. The Indian response was primarily one of indifference or bemusement, in large part because the federal imprint was so small. Aside from the winters of 1804–1805 and 1805–1806, when the Mandan and Clatsop Indians, respectively, hosted the Corps of Discovery, the American expedition had only brief encounters with Indians. Although Lewis and Clark wrote confidently of their success, Indians showed few signs of surrendering their sovereignty to the United States. Instead, they would preserve the Indian vision of federalism, one which allowed for overlapping land claims.[12]

This did not mean that the Indians of the interior did not care about the United States. To the contrary, they were eager to establish friendly relations with the Americans, especially when that would bring alliances against local enemies. For example, in 1806—the same year that Dehahuit made his speech to William C. C. Claiborne—a gathering of chiefs, mostly from the lower Missouri, articulated a similar vision of the political order of North America that included the United States as well as Indian villages. On a visit to Washington, the chiefs opened with warm greetings. Addressing their speeches to men the Indians called their "fathers," the chiefs proclaimed that "it is with an open heart that we recieve your hands, friendship streches ours in yours & unites them together." They closed by stating, "You told us to go now & then to see our father the great chief of War (the secretary at war), that he would Communicate your word to us, we have visited him we have been wellcome. We hope that he does love your new Children Worthy of pity, & Consider us as Your white Children."[13]

This is a familiar sort of Indian language, employing a familial metaphor and striking a subservient pose. Yet in 1806 these Indians had no reason to be subservient, for the United States lacked the power to assert supremacy over the Indians of the eastern Plains. It was the Indians who controlled that landscape, not the United States. So why the vague language? Why the inherent subordination of referring to fathers and children? Why the promises of loyalty? The answers emerge from the doubts and uncertainties the Indians brought with them, not doubts about themselves, but doubts about language and the United States. Working through a variety of translators, unable to know exactly what could make a literal translation to English, Indians used the most basic language they could to convey their goals. By invoking the language of fathers and children, they flattered the United States. Finally, they could draw on their experience with European empires, where language of familial subordination had been the way Indians made demands on the Europeans.

The Indians of the North American interior hoped that the United States would be a distant ally against other villages that were commercial rivals and diplomatic opponents. Between the promises at the beginning and end of the speech was, in fact, a lengthy list of demands for the United States. In self-deprecating tones, the Indians attempted to determine regional trade in the North American West. "We Believe that you wish to pity us & to prevent our wants by sending us supplies of goods," they said, "but look sharp & tell to your men to take not too much fur for a little of goods, should they act in that way we would not be better off than we are now with our actual traders." The Indian delegates instructed the United States government to rein in its citizens, chastising the United States for telling "us that your children of this side of the Mississipi hear your Word, you are Mistaken, Since every day they Rise their tomahawks Over our heads, but we believe it be Contrary to your orders & inclination, & that, before long, should they be deaf to your voice, you will chastise them." And in the end, the delegates from the Plains spoke like Dehahuit, building their own historical context for the Louisiana Purchase and placing the United States within that context. "You say that the French, English & Spanish nations have left the waters of the Missouri & Missisipi," they said; "we are all glad of it, & we believe that the day they will leave us the weather will be Clear, the paths Clean, & our ears will be no more affected with the disagreable sounds of the bad Birds who wish us to relinquish the words of our Good fathers whose words we keep in our hearts."[14]

Jefferson and Secretary of War Henry Dearborn were solicitous toward the Indians, promising them both alliances and gifts. Like their European predecessors, they had learned that Indians considered gifts an essential part of the negotiating process. These gifts were all the more important given that several of the visiting chiefs died from illness during their extended journey to the federal capital. Dehahuit's efforts also came home in these negotiations, for Dearborn concluded that "the Osages should be informed that their depredations on the Caddos . . . are known by the president" and that the Osages should "take effectual measures for preventing any further hostilities on our particular friends."[15]

What else could the administration do? Securing friendly relations with the Indians of the North American interior was essential to making the Louisiana Purchase a reality. This was true whether that meant establishing federal sovereignty or preventing the sort of European intervention that would come from Indians who sought assistance overseas.

Conflict

The first indication of the long-term effects of the Louisiana Purchase came not in the West but in the East, and not in 1803 but a decade after the Louisiana Purchase, when the United States showed what federal sovereignty meant. In addition, as settlers began clamoring for land, even the loudest or most reasoned complaints from Indians could not reach the Jefferson administration. As federal power increased, the Indian vision of federalism in North America gave way to U.S. interpretations that created equality and unprecedented opportunity for white settlers, but at the cost of the Indians' freedom and eventually their lives.

Federal policymakers were already worried about Indians. Throughout eastern North America unification movements among Indian tribes arose that were based on resistance to

the United States. The most famous of these was in the Northwest (now the Midwest), under the military leadership of Tecumseh and the spiritual leadership of his brother, Tenskwetawa. But Tecumseh was all the more frightening because he negotiated with Indians in the Deep South. By the time the United States declared war on Great Britain in 1812, it was already engaged in a series of Indian wars stretching from the eastern Plains to the Deep South.

Among the first Indians to feel the pinch were the Choctaw and the Creek. When the United States purchased Louisiana, the Choctaw were spread across portions of the Territory of Orleans, the Territory of Mississippi, and the Spanish Gulf Coast. After a century of disease, attacks by other Indians, and periodic warfare with Europeans, the Choctaw had lost most of the power that had once made them dominant in the region. The problems with the United States and its citizens began almost immediately, and there was little the Choctaw could do. In the summer of 1807, for example, settlers in the Territory of Orleans killed a Choctaw Indian and seemed likely to stage additional attacks on neighboring villages. Claiborne issued an apologetic statement to the Indians, stating: "I have heard news which much grieves me. Some Blood has been shed and a warrior of your tribe dangerously wounded. . . . [I]f he should die, all I can promise is, that the white man who did the Mischief, shall be tried and punished agreeable to the Laws of this Territory."[16] Despite these promises, Claiborne conceded to other American officials that "my own opinion, is that differences between the frontier settlers, and the small tribes West of the Mississippi, will frequently arise, until Treaties are entered into with them." The United States had a long history of negotiating treaties with Indians. But it had an equally long history of breaking those treaties, especially when white settlers fomented interracial violence.[17]

Unlike the Caddo, the Choctaw could not successfully build leverage with the United States or with Spain. As a result, the federal Indian agent for the Choctaw, Henry Bry, could afford to be unsympathetic. He wrote to Secretary of War Dearborn that the Choctaw "are very numerous & troublesome neighbours. They commit depredations on the property of the industrious planters; Complaints of that kind are daily brought before me."[18]

The Creek Indians proved equally "troublesome" to the United States, and for a while they were more successful preserving their own autonomy against the United States. Located on the Gulf Coast, they occupied the very region the Jefferson administration had so eagerly sought in 1803. They also moved about. Claiming much of the land as their own, the Creek Indians ignored the disputed boundary between the United States and Spanish Florida. A number of Creek chiefs had grown increasingly militant in their opposition to the United States, threatening to kill American emissaries or chiefs friendly toward Americans. These militant Creeks also attempted to build broader alliances with other Indians in the Deep South—whether the Seminole Indians to the east in the Florida Peninsula, or the Choctaw to the West—or with other militants in the North. This was as much an internal dispute among Creeks as it was a move against the United States. The Creeks had their own divisions; some Creeks came to challenge the chiefs who, through changing notions of property, had ac-

cumulated tremendous power and wealth.[19] When federal officials tried to rebuild alliances with the Creeks, their own interpreter, a black slave named Tony, informed Indians that the Americans intended to steal their land: "[T]he old people will be put to sweep the yards of the white people, the young men to work for them and the young females to spin and weave for them."[20]

Even after Tecumseh's death in 1813, the danger of Indian unification and its implicit threat of resistance to federal sovereignty made the acquisition of the Floridas all the more important to federal policymakers.[21] Although the reasons why President Jefferson and Secretary of State Madison so desperately sought the Floridas in 1803 arose from their fears of European interference, a decade later President Madison was equally worried about Indian wars. As the War of 1812 dragged on, Indians hoped to take advantage of the beleaguered federal government. At the same time, the administration concluded that the numerous dangers on its frontiers demanded a cohesive policy targeting the British, the Spanish, and Indians. After a series of skirmishes between Indians and white settlers on the border between Georgia and Spanish Florida, Andrew Jackson launched a full-scale assault on the Creeks.

Like so many other Indians, the Creeks hoped to exploit diplomatic tensions among whites. They retreated to the Spanish fortress at Pensacola. When the Spanish governor refused Jackson's demand that he evict the Creeks, thus forcing them to do battle with the United States, Jackson responded with a letter that expressed the sort of unflinching opinion that was typical of the Tennessean's correspondence: "you have heaped insult, upon insult to my government, and the greatest disrespect for myself," he wrote. "You have thrown the gauntlet, and I take it up."[22] Jackson seized and destroyed the Pensacola fortress. In the process, he realized two American goals. He made it clear that he would ignore international boundaries to pursue his war with the Creeks. In so doing, he further eroded Spain's crumbling hold on the Floridas. Meanwhile, Jackson eventually routed the Creek forces.

The Creek War of 1813–1814 was only the first in a series of federal incursions into the Floridas precipitated by conflict with Indians. Andrew Jackson was usually the instrument behind those assaults. Conflicts between white settlers and Seminoles similar to those between settlers and the Creeks led Jackson to launch an invasion of Florida in 1817. The Monroe administration renounced Jackson's activities. Jackson's Indian war was upsetting negotiations with Spain, a nation the administration believed would deliver Florida to the United States anyway. But in the end, the administration showed little concern for the Seminoles because they knew that a successful resolution of the Louisiana Purchase, with Spain surrendering Florida to the United States, would be meaningless if Indians remained independent in the territory.

This story is partly one of Andrew Jackson, who cast such a large shadow over national events. But it is also a story of Indians. To the Creeks, the Seminoles, and other Indians of that vaguely defined area known as the Floridas, all of the opportunities that came with the ambiguity of the Louisiana Purchase began to collapse as the United States secured its territorial claims during the 1810s. And once the

United States claimed that the Transcontinental Treaty acknowledged American "ownership" of the Floridas, the Indians who had lived there for generations faced a new onslaught of white settlers and federal troops.

The Red River Valley has a low elevation. However, in metaphorical terms it provided Dehahuit with a good vantage point from which to observe the troubling events in the East. As the Creeks, the Choctaws, and the Seminoles faced new challenges, Dehahuit remained safe largely because he could continue to exploit the administration's desire for allies on its western frontier during the War of 1812. In October 1814, when a British invasion of Louisiana was imminent, the United States eagerly solicited Caddo membership in an alliance against Great Britain. Jackson wrote to James Monroe, then serving a brief but unprecedented tenure as secretary of state and secretary of war, that "the Caddo chief, with the neighbouring tribes . . . has made a tender of his services to the United States. . . . I have accepted the tender. . . . This measure will give security to that point at the present."[23] Claiborne (by then the elected governor of the state of Louisiana) confirmed Jackson's sentiments, adding: "The chief of the Caddoes, is a man of great merit, he is brave, sensible and prudent. But I advise, that you address a talk immediately to the chief, he is the most influential Indian on this side of the River Grande, and his friendship sir, will give much security to the western frontier of Louisiana."[24] Local officials like Claiborne and Jackson saw distinct advantages to Caddo power. Meanwhile, the Madison and Monroe administrations continued to focus on consolidating their holdings east of the Mississippi rather than claiming more land to the west. This set of priorities preserved the status quo and, in turn, the Neutral Ground.

Although the Caddo enjoyed relative security during these years, this hardly indicated that alliance with the United States would be an effective strategy for Indians. To the contrary, once the United States and Spain finally set to work hammering out an agreeable western boundary, Dehahuit's leverage instantly began to weaken. Unlike the eastern Indians, the greatest threat to Dehahuit and the Caddo was not war but peace. By 1818 Secretary of War John C. Calhoun proclaimed that the Caddo "must be made to yield the exercise of their barbarous custom of retaliation upon murderers, to the milder influence of our laws."[25] The Neutral Ground ceased to exist when the Transcontinental Treaty established a clear boundary between the United States and Spanish North America, a border that Mexico continued to respect after securing its independence in 1821. Surrounded on all sides by an antagonistic white government, the Caddos struggled to preserve their autonomy. After a generation for whom the Louisiana Purchase had created new opportunities, the Caddo once again faced considerable threats.

Dehahuit's political power did not immediately disappear with the loss of the Neutral Ground. In 1820, George Gray, the federal Indian agent assigned to western Louisiana, concluded that Dehahuit still "has more influence with those small tribes residing on Red River and the Province of Texas than any Indian within the limits of the Agency. In fact they are controlled by him entirely."[26] Dehahuit also hoped to exploit the often tense relations between the United States and Mexico. But there was little that Dehahuit could do as Gray and his successors attempted to enforce Calhoun's injunction that all Indians "be made to yield."

By 1835 Dehahuit retained his power among his fellow Caddos but had lost his power with the United States. He accepted an agreement through which the Caddo sold their land and agreed to leave the United States.[27] The Caddo left, only to face a new enemy in the Anglo-Americans who assumed power in the newly independent Republic of Texas. Worse still, the cordial relations between Texas and the United States prevented the Caddo from resurrecting the diplomatic policies that had worked so effectively for them in the past. When the United States formally annexed Texas in 1845, the Caddo once again found themselves surrounded by territory claimed by the federal government. By 1859 the remaining Caddo moved to Oklahoma, where they joined a growing number of Indians who had endured forced removal at the hands of the military and civil authorities of the American empire.

The experience of the Caddos was consistent with that of other eastern Indians. No alliance would protect them from a federal government that was increasingly antagonistic to Indian claims to land or to independence. Nobody was a more effective agent of this policy than Andrew Jackson. He concluded that western settlers were entitled to land, that Indian claims to that land were unfounded, and that the government was deluding itself by reaching any other conclusions. So Jackson set out to clear out all Indians east of the Mississippi. He looked to the lands of the Louisiana Purchase, specifically the southern Plains west of the new states and territories that fronted the Mississippi. As Jackson explained in his second an- nual message in 1830, "the consequences of a speedy removal will be important to the United States, to individual States, and to the Indians themselves. . . . It puts an end to all possible danger of collision between the authorities of the General and State Governments on account of the Indians. The pecuniary advantages which it Promises to the Government are the least of its recommendations." Jackson's mes- sage was a cornerstone in the removal policy by which the United States forced Indians to move. The policy initially targeted only those Indians living east of the Mississippi. Later, however, the federal government applied it al- most every place where white settlers collided with Indians.[28]

For the first half-century after independence, Jackson's predecessors had expressed sympathy for Indians even as they endorsed policies that led to their death and relocation. Consider the case of Meriwether Lewis and William Clark, who had written of Indians with growing re- spect during the expedition from 1804 to 1806. By 1809 Lewis was governor of the Territory of Louisiana, the massive stretch of land carved from the Louisiana Purchase and made up of everything north of what is now the state of Louisiana. So soon after swearing to Indians that the United States would respect their inde- pendence, Lewis concluded: "The Indian na- tions do not appear to have been considered by our Government as Citizens of, or as making any constituent part of the United States; nor indeed as being within their limits, except as re- gards the preservation of peace, & a kind of pre-emptive right which has been assisted to the lands within the Indian boundaries & within the limits of the United States."[29]

Meanwhile, William Clark served as an In- dian agent and militia commander, a joint ap- pointment made necessary by the militia's role in subjugating Indians. During the War of 1812, Clark was himself governor of the Mis- souri Territory (the successor to the Louisiana Territory), fashioning alliances with some In- dians while pursuing reprisals against others. After the War of 1812, white settlers clamored for land, leaving the Mississippi Valley that had been the traditional home of white settle- ments for lands farther West.[30] Once Missouri became a state in 1821, Clark once again be- came a federal Indian agent. He remained em- pathetic toward Indians even when he was not sympathetic toward their cause. Clark under- stood their concerns, but he also concluded that his primary responsibility was toward white settlers. As a result, Clark eventually en- dorsed a federal policy of removing Indians from U.S. territory and became one of this pol- icy's instruments on the eastern Plains. Once again, the expanse of the Louisiana Purchase seemed to present the United States with solu- tions to the very problems that came from gov- erning so much land.

Conclusion

News of these developments certainly reached the Indians farther west, but the changes in the East must have seemed abstract to them. Throughout much of the first half of the nine- teenth century, Indians continued to govern the northern Plains, the Rockies, and the Pacific Northwest. Although the United States con- solidated its claim to that land and battled Eu- ropean challenges, the federal government had neither the means nor the intention to make that sovereignty a fact. Instead, the federal government and private citizens built inroads through commerce. Only in the second half of the nineteenth century would the Indians of the West reach the same conclusion as Indians of the East: that American expansion in general and the Louisiana Purchase in particular would create the greatest threat they ever faced. In the decades that followed, many Indians shifted their diplomatic strategies from commerce to confrontation. In the end, however, despite their efforts to adapt to changing circumstances, the Indians' efforts proved no more successful at preventing the federal government or American settlers from completing the Louisiana Purchase.

It was not until the second half of the nineteenth century that the United States truly asserted its sovereignty over the North American interior. White settlement created a mandate for federal intervention; the United States Army as well as technologies like the railroad and the telegraph created the means. Throughout these decades, the United States also saved some of the least hospitable land acquired through the Louisiana Purchase and set it aside for Indian removal and resettlement.

Dehahuit did not live to see the removal of the Caddo from their land, let alone the other Indians of the North American West. He died in 1838—two years after James Madison, seven years after James Monroe, and twelve years after Thomas Jefferson. In a variety of government offices, those three men had acquired Louisiana and consolidated the hold of the United States west of the Mississippi. Madison, Monroe, and Jefferson knew full well that Louisiana was not uninhabited, and

they struggled to find effective ways to deal with the various peoples of the Mississippi Valley, the Gulf Coast, and the North American interior.

Of course, it was neither the United States nor the Louisiana Purchase alone that determined the fate of North American Indians. But the United States—whether through its federal leaders or its white settlers—and the Louisiana Purchase it engineered did shape the contours of the racial conflict that consumed western North America throughout much of the nineteenth century. In February 1803, five months before receiving news of the Louisiana Purchase, Jefferson wrote that Indians "will in time either incorporate with us as citizens of the United States, or remove beyond the Mississippi."[31] Once the United States extended past the Mississippi, Dehahuit attempted that sort of incorporation, only to find that the Louisiana Purchase would create changes that, in the end, would prove insurmountably destructive for the Indians of North America.

Notes

1. A note on terminology: the words that people use to describe the people who preceded Europeans to the Americas are the subject of unending—and I believe justifiable—debate. I use the word "Indian" primarily out of conformity. After a generation of using the term "Native Americans," most historians have returned to using the word "Indian."
2. For examples, see Gregory Dowd, *A Spirited Resistance: The North American Indian Struggle for Unity* (Baltimore: Johns Hopkins University Press, 1992); Anthony F. C. Wallace, *The Death and Rebirth of the Seneca* (New York: Knopf, 1970); R. David Edmunds, *Tecumseh and the Quest for Indian Leadership* (Boston: Little, Brown, 1984).

3. Richard White, *The Middle Ground: Indians, Empires, and Republics in the Great Lakes Region, 1650–1815* (Cambridge: Cambridge University Press, 1991), 16.

4. Dowd, *A Spirited Resistance;* Cladio Saunt, *A New Order of Things: Property, Power, and the Transformation of the Creek Indians, 1733–1816* (Cambridge: Cambridge University Press, 1999); John Sugden, *Blue Jacket: Warrior of the Shawnees* (Lincoln: University of Nebraska Press, 2000); White, *The Middle Ground,* 413–468.

5. Richard H. Kohn, *Eagle and Sword: The Federalists and the Creation of the Military Establishment in America, 1783–1802* (New York: Free Press, 1975), 100–104; Francis Paul Prucha, *The Sword of the Republic: The United States Army on the Frontier, 1783–1846* (New York: Macmillan, 1969).

6. Andrew C. Isenberg, *The Destruction of the Bison: An Environmental History, 1750–1920* (Cambridge: Cambridge University Press, 2000), 31–92; Tanis C. Thorne, *The Many Hands of My Relations: French and Indians on the Lower Missouri* (Columbia: University of Missouri Press, 1996), 17–20, 65–68.

7. The most concise yet thorough analysis of the early history of the Caddos is F. Todd Smith, *The Caddo Indians: Tribes at the Convergence of Empires, 1542–1854* (College Station: Texas A&M Press, 1995), a book that has also influenced much of my own analysis.

8. Smith, *The Caddo Indians,* 63–83.

9. John Sibley, *A Report from Natchitoches in 1807,* ed. Annie Heloise Abel (New York: Museum of the American Indian, 1922); John Sibley to William Eustis, 30 January 1810, *Letters Received by the Secretary of War: Registered Series* (Washington, D.C.: National Archives Record Group 107, Microfilm Copy M22), 40: S-71; Sibley to Eustis, 20 March 1810, Carter, IX: 878–879.

10. Dehahuit, speech to William C. C. Claiborne, 5 September 1806, *Claiborne Letterbooks,* vol. 3: 4.

11. Claiborne to Henry Dearborn, 29 July 1806, *Claiborne Letterbooks,* vol. 3: 374–375.

12. For the reaction of Indians to the Lewis and Clark expedition, see James P. Ronda, *Lewis and Clark Among the Indians* (Lincoln: University of Nebraska Press, 1988); James P. Ronda, "Coboway's Tale: A Story of Power and Places Along the Columbia," in *Power and Place in the North American West,* ed. Richard White and John Findlay (Seattle: University of Washington Press, 1999), 1–30.

13. Indian Speech to Thomas Jefferson and Dearborn, 4 January 1806, Donald Jackson, ed., *Letters of the Lewis and Clark Expedition, with Related Documents 1783–1854* (Urbana: University of Illinois Press, 1978), vol. 1: 284–289.

14. Indian Speech to Jefferson and Dearborn, 4 January 1806, *Letters of the Lewis and Clark Expedition,* vol. 1: 285–286.

15. Dearborn to James Wilkinson, 9 April 1806, *Letters of the Lewis and Clark Expedition,* vol. 1: 304.

16. Claiborne address to Indians, 28 September 1806, *Claiborne Letterbooks,* vol. 4: 21; Claiborne to John Collins, 28 September 1806, *Claiborne Letterbooks,* vol. 4: 21.

17. Claiborne to Dearborn and Sibley (two letters), 25 July 1807, *Letters Received, Registered Series,* vol. 5: C-317.; Dearborn to Jefferson, 26 December 1807, *Jefferson Papers.*

18. Henry Bry to Dearborn, 1 September 1807, *Letters Received, Registered Series,* vol. 4: B-295.

19. Pathkiller to Andrew Jackson, 22 October 1813, Sam B. Smith and Harriet Chappell Owsley et al., eds., *The Papers of Andrew Jackson* (Knoxville: University of Tennessee Press, 1980–), vol. 2: 439.

20. Quoted in Saunt, *A New Order of Things,* 237.

21. Dowd, *A Spirited Resistance,* 12–166.

22. Jackson to Gonzales Manrique, 9 September 1814, *Jackson Papers,* vol. 3: 130.

23. Jackson to James Monroe, 23 October 1814, *Jackson Papers,* vol. 3: 174.

24. Claiborne to Jackson, 28 October 1814, *Claiborne Letterbooks,* vol. 6: 293–294.

25. John C. Calhoun to John Jamison, 8 January 1818, *Calhoun Papers,* vol. 3: 476.

26. George Gray to Calhoun, 14 October 1820, *J. Fair Hardin Collection,* LSU, Box II: Folder 5.

27. Smith, *The Caddo Indians,* 121–122.

28. James D. Richardson, ed., *A Compilation of the*

Messages and Papers of the Presidents, 1789–1897 (Washington: Government Printing Office, 1896–1899), vol. 2: 519–520.

29. Meriwether Lewis to Silas Dinsmore, 26 January 1809, *Letters Received, Registered Series,* Reel 36: D-69.

30. William E. Foley, *The Genesis of Missouri: From Wilderness Outpost to Statehood* (Columbia: University of Missouri Press, 1989), 223–239.

31. Jefferson to William Henry Harrison, 27 February 1803, Merrill D. Peterson, ed., *Jefferson Writings* (New York: Library of America, 1984), vol. 1, 118.

7

Edward Livingston and the Problem of Law

MARK FERNANDEZ

Edward Livingston loved a fight. The New Yorker grew up in the snake pit of Tammany New York politics, honed his skills in the Federalist–Democratic-Republican controversies of the 1790s, and in 1804 took his talents and his malleable principles to the Louisiana frontier. In New Orleans, Livingston found ample controversy to boost his fortunes and to launch him on a career that would make him one of the most powerful Americans of the nineteenth century.

What was it about early Louisiana that made it a perfect laboratory for people like Livingston to realize the American dream? For Livingston, a talented and ambitious lawyer and politician, the answer lies in the most important legal and constitutional question raised by the Louisiana Purchase. How could the United States, a nation under rule of common law, superimpose its legal system on a territory dominated by the civilian legal traditions of continental Europe?

Such an imposition could not take place without a fight. Edward Livingston's older brother was none other than Robert R. Livingston—the American minister to France who, along with James Monroe, negotiated the Louisiana Purchase for the United States. Al-

though the purchase proved vitally important to both Livingstons, their relationships to the treaty could not have been more different. For Robert, Louisiana itself was a distant place, the subject of discussion within the rarefied atmosphere of diplomatic affairs. Robert R. Livingston's thoughts on the subject were similar to what many Americans considered Louisiana to be before April 1803: an abstract conception connected to the union east of the Mississippi—rather than the world to the West. For Edward, however, Louisiana would become real—and the stuff of dreams. His own experience reflected the problems and the challenges that came with the Louisiana Purchase, as private citizens and public officials alike wondered what the United States would actually do with all that land and all of its residents.

Edward Livingston's story is a case study on so many of the issues that surrounded the Louisiana Purchase. During the last quarter of the eighteenth century, the disputes within the young republic provided the ideal circumstances for his rise in national politics. When his fortunes—both political and monetary—collapsed in 1803, the Louisiana Purchase created new opportunities, and Livingston joined a throng of Americans seeking riches of all kinds west of the Mississippi. He soon found himself enmeshed in the tense ethnic relations that came with an English-speaking government's acquisition of land with a French-speaking population. Even the international disputes—most notably the War of 1812—that helped determine the fate of the Louisiana Purchase provided means for Livingston to seek his goals. He would do so through the law; and in tackling the law, he would confront the most complicated problems posed by the Louisiana Purchase.

A Young Lawyer in a New Nation

Livingston's early career proved a perfect apprenticeship for him to blossom amid the legal and political maelstrom of early Louisiana. Born in 1764 to one of New York's most privileged families, Livingston enjoyed a pampered childhood. On the family estates at Cleremont and Albany, private tutors carefully prepared young Edward for professional life. At an early age, he entered grammar school in the little village of Esopus in Ulster County and studied there until the British captured it in 1777. The thirteen-year-old then fled to nearby Hurley, where he continued his education until he enrolled in the College of New Jersey (later Princeton University) in 1779.

Princeton was an exciting place at the time of the American Revolution. Students lived in the stunning Nassau Hall. The faculty was equally impressive. Staffed by "New Light" Presbyterian disciples of Jonathan Edwards and orthodox Anglicans who were excluded from academic positions at Oxford and Cambridge, Princeton became one of the great intellectual centers of the early modern world. Its

rigid curriculum began with a solid foundation in the classics, followed by a grueling set of courses in the arts and sciences. Livingston sharpened his grasp of Latin and Greek and completed his mastery of the liberal arts. After graduation from Princeton, he decided to study law with John Lansing, one of the young nation's premier lawyers.

Legal education in the early republic differed greatly from the professionalism of such training today. George Wythe founded the first law school at the College of William and Mary the year that Livingston entered Nassau Hall. By 1800 only a handful of such institutions existed. In Livingston's day, most students read law with an able practitioner to prepare for the bar exam, usually administered by members of the state's supreme court. Admission to the bar came easily; examinations typically lasted fifteen to thirty minutes. The real test of a lawyer came when he represented clients. If he won cases, then he prospered; if not, there were other activities to keep ambitious young men occupied. John Lansing's students were among the best.

An able lawyer, and a scholar himself, Lansing attracted some of the nation's most brilliant young men to his parlor. Among Livingston's fellow students were Aaron Burr, Alexander Hamilton, and James Kent. It was only the beginning of a long and complex relationship between Burr and Livingston in which Burr's shadow determined Livingston's career. In the next century, Kent and Livingston would emerge as two of America's most distinguished legal thinkers in their own right. While Kent embraced the common law and wrote a seminal commentary on the American Constitution, Livingston developed a fascination with

Roman law under Lansing's tutelage. Early in his career he launched an attack on common law, especially in the realm of criminal law. For the rest of his life, Livingston lobbied his fellow Americans to abandon the medieval practices inherited from England and to adopt a civilian approach to jurisprudence and codification. He also became an expert common lawyer. In gaining expertise in both systems of law—the civil law, with its adherence to strict codes, and the common law, with its reliance on judicial precedent—Livingston established a solid foundation for his legal knowledge that would make him one of the world's leading scholars of law by the end of his career. By the time he completed his studies with Lansing and was accepted to practice before the New York bar, Livingston had acquired a legal training that would allow him to flourish in the complicated world of Louisiana at the time of the purchase.

Livingston's superb training and family connections (his uncle, William Livingston, was one of the founders of the New York bar) allowed him easy entry to the avenues of success. He quickly established himself as a leading New York citizen. In 1786 he joined the state militia. During the next two years, he campaigned unsuccessfully for the state assembly. Finally, in 1794, he won a seat in the U.S. House of Representatives.

As a junior member of the House, Livingston learned that he could thrive on controversy. Although he came from the Federalist stronghold in the Northeast, Livingston owed his allegiance to the Democratic-Republicans who had backed him in the congressional race. Almost immediately after he arrived in Philadelphia, Livingston served as chief interrogator on the Committee on Privileges so he could

clear the name of his old college chum and Republican firebrand William Branch Giles, who had been implicated in a bribery scheme. Landing such an important assignment demonstrated to the young member of Congress that turmoil could spawn opportunity.

Over the next several years in Congress, Livingston dove into the Federalist-Republican battles with gusto. The emerging disputes over foreign and domestic policy that Andrew Trees describes in Chapter 1 of this book provided the ideal circumstances for Edward Livingston to establish a career in national politics. He joined in the Republican critique of Federalist foreign policy, denouncing the Washington and Adams administrations' role in negotiating the Jay Treaty and their actions in the Quasi-War with France and the embarrassing XYZ affair. Livingston's role in the Republican opposition to the Jay Treaty offers an instructive glimpse into his contentious nature. In 1800 Livingston abandoned support for his fellow New Yorker, Aaron Burr, in favor of Thomas Jefferson during the hotly contested congressional debate that decided the presidential election.

Despite vigorous Republican opposition, the Jay Treaty won ratification in the Federalist Senate. House Republicans, however, had gained a majority. Livingston drafted a resolution forcing the executive branch to submit all treaty-related documents for House concurrence. James Madison disapproved of the grasping language in Livingston's resolution but supported it after tacking on an amendment to exclude any documents that might threaten ongoing treaty negotiations. George Washington shot back angrily, pointing out that House concurrence had no constitutional standing and that the framers had never intended the House to play such a role. Madison, though livid over Livingston's prose, was even more outraged by Washington's attempt to use the original intent of the framers as a justification for opposing the resolution. Madison denounced the president's response in resolutions cosponsored by William Blount. The Madison-Blount resolutions proved to be a public relations disaster. The party actually saw its House majority diminish in the midterm elections. The resulting equilibrium in the House precipitated even more sordid partisan battles as the decade drew to a close.

Even though Livingston had angered the Republican leadership, he continued to battle the Adams administration in the coming years. When the Federalists passed the Alien and Sedition Acts to silence their critics, the Republicans seethed in righteous indignation. Livingston led the attack. In a passionate speech against the acts, he sanctioned domestic insurrection as an acceptable response to tyranny. Such ferocity characterized the partisan struggles of the 1790s; however, inciting rebellion against the government was a bit extreme, even for the Republicans. Although opposition to the Alien and Sedition Acts involved Livingston in the most notable partisan fight of the decade, his most memorable moment as a Republican wrecking ball came during the controversy spawned by the extraordinary case of Jonathan Robbins.

In 1799 Robbins was accused of participating in a mutiny on a British vessel. Robbins sought refuge in the United States, and the British government demanded his extradition, invoking specific provisions from the Jay Treaty. Robbins claimed that he was a U.S. citizen who had been forcibly pressed into the

Royal Navy. When Adams ordered a federal judge to release Robbins, Livingston, ignoring the evidence, denounced Adams on the House floor and called on his colleagues to censure the president for interfering in judicial affairs. For a month during February and March 1800, the House debated the censure. Only an impassioned defense of the president by John Marshall saved Adams from disgrace. Ten years later, Adams remembered Livingston's role in the "fabulous, fictious case of a Jonathan Robbins [the mutineer] who never existed" and referred to his former denouncer as "a naughty lad as well as a saucy one," describing Livingston's actions as "lying villany."[1]

As Livingston's second term in Congress wound to an end, he decided not to seek a third. His part in the disastrous Madison-Blount resolutions angered party leaders. Without their strong support, Livingston won only a narrow victory in 1798. Rather than risk losing a fourth election, he retired after his third term ended in March 1801. During his time in the cockpit that was the early Congress, Livingston acquired tremendous experience in partisan combat. And the Jeffersonians weathered the controversy and emerged even more powerful after the election of 1800, reinforcing Livingston's views on the power of minority politics.

With the Jeffersonians in control, Livingston returned to New York to claim the plum prizes of United States Attorney for the District of New York and mayor of the city. This was a coup at the state and federal levels, for the New York State government selected the mayor of New York City, while the federal government chose U.S. attorneys. This unique opportunity afforded the thirty-seven-year-old

Livingston a chance to expand his legal expertise and gain valuable experience in municipal government. As United States Attorney, he not only honed his prosecutorial skills but also administered a large legal office with a $100,000 annual budget. As mayor of New York, Livingston also served as judge on the "Mayor's Court," penning twenty-nine opinions and drafting the court's rules of procedure. The knowledge he gleaned from both of these roles would serve him well in the Crescent City.

His New York interlude also instructed Livingston on the power of opposition politics—although this time the opposition came from his own party. One of Livingston's underlings in the U.S. attorney's office in New York who was in charge of collecting federal taxes had exercised his privilege to use those public funds to his own benefit between scheduled federal audits. The clerk abused his access to this "honest graft" and in 1803 found himself unable to replace the funds he had taken before the auditors arrived. As the clerk's superior, Livingston was personally liable for these missing funds. Since the indiscretion occurred in a federal office, the subsequent investigation fell to the secretary of the Treasury. Albert Gallatin ordinarily would have supported Livingston, but he had begun regarding him with suspicion since early 1801, when the notorious Aaron Burr referred to Livingston as his "confidential friend" in an unsuccessful bid to usurp Jefferson's power by inflating the office of president pro tempore of the Senate. Despite the fact that Livingston had supported Jefferson against Burr in the contested election of 1800, the administration began to doubt Livingston's loyalty. Friendless and under federal scrutiny, Liv-

ingston found he could not defend himself against his critics. Federalist newspapers, of course, covered the affair widely, caring as little about the facts as Livingston had in the Robbins case.

Worse still, Livingston contracted yellow fever as an epidemic swept the city of New York in the summer of 1803. While recuperating, he decided to move to New Orleans to avoid the press and to capitalize on the bonanza of the Louisiana Purchase. He pled no contest to the charges and agreed to settle the case for a $100,000 judgment. Livingston could have expunged the debt with a prompt $50,000 payment but could only raise $44,000 in cash. Securing the rest of the penalty with property, he departed for New Orleans. The Federalists deemed the property worthless and charged Livingston with defaulting on the judgment. Neither claim was true, but that both were made nonetheless indicated the viciousness of the political arena.

A New Life in New Orleans

In late December 1803 Livingston escaped his critics and booked passage to New Orleans. His arrival coincided with the French surrender of Louisiana to the United States, and Livingston hoped that the purchase would create the means for him to resuscitate his prospects. He was soon disappointed, as his crumbling reputation in the East prevented him from securing the public office he hoped to hold in the new American province. His dispute with Gallatin and Burr's unfortunate characterization of him as a "confidential friend" made it impossible for Livingston to garner any spoils from the Republican governor, William C. C. Claiborne. But Livingston had other assets worth more than political patronage. A brilliant lawyer as well as a seasoned politician, Livingston soon found that he could dominate the lesser lights that illuminated the city after the Louisiana Purchase. Much of Livingston's political skill emanated from his expert handling of his roles as an opposition bulldog, so being on the wrong side of Claiborne actually worked to his advantage.

New Orleans exploded in 1804. The attractions of new land and riches drew hordes of American settlers to the city, as well as other white newcomers from Saint Domingue and France. Recent emigrés vied with the entrenched Creole elite for control of the city. Shortly after the Louisiana Purchase, all parties recognized that many of the important battles to come would be fought in the legal arena. Livingston, the best lawyer in the territory, realized that disaffected white Louisianians needed a defender skilled in the new Anglo-American tradition. He happily proffered his services.

Claiborne, though, could not afford to fight every battle. As governor of the Territory of Orleans (consisting of most of present-day Louisiana), he had few to turn to for support. At Jefferson's request, Evan Jones compiled a list of New Orleanians suitable for available government positions. Jones identified 119 characters but found almost none of them suitable for public service. Among such luminaries, Livingston could not be ignored.

Of all the problems facing Claiborne, the most significant concerned how to impose common law on a territory with a tradition of civil (often called "civilian") law. Even the common law itself militated against Claiborne.

Common law is an English invention and rests on the notion that, over the centuries, the law will evolve and eventually approach the ideal of justice. This process of legal evolution, however, must build on tradition, custom, and accepted local usage. Truly, then, how could the common law replace the civilian legal heritage of Louisiana?

Although few Americans grasped the significance of this abstraction, Thomas Jefferson understood its very real implications. Taking possession of a colony is a tricky business. The Spanish found out as much in 1768 when, after acquiring Louisiana, its French citizens deposed Spanish governor Antonio de Ulloa. One of the chief complaints against Ulloa arose from the Louisianians' fear of his proposed legal reforms. They believed that he intended to replace French laws with Spanish ones that they were less familiar with so as to eventually dispossess them of their property. And Spain's system of law was civil!

Jefferson realized that Louisiana's transition from French colony to United States territory presented even more difficult obstacles. He instructed Claiborne accordingly, telling him to implement the common-law system cautiously and to allow the Orleanians to preserve as much of their civil law heritage (especially with regard to inheritance and property) as was necessary to keep the peace. In the area of criminal law, however, Jefferson believed there could be no alternative to the American system, since the constitutional protections of individual rights to *habeas corpus* and the presumption of innocence were totally alien to civil law.

Claiborne followed Jefferson's instructions closely when he organized the new territory's institutions. He quickly established a series of common-law courts: a Governor's Court (which heard civil appeals and had original jurisdiction in criminal matters, including capital cases), a Court of Common Pleas (similar to the Mayor's Court in New York), and the Superior Court for the Territory of Orleans. Livingston would not only practice in those courts but would also play an important role in their creation. Courts need rules. No other territorial notable had the kind of experience in establishing court rules that Livingston had. He had already issued and published a fine series of rules for the Mayor's Court. When Claiborne organized the Superior Court, he asked Livingston to chair a committee to draft the court's rules. Livingston complied. Although no records survive to chronicle the committee's activities, the rules themselves reflect Livingston's influence.

In seventeen concise rules, Livingston outlined the practices and procedures of the Superior Court. Although this might have been a seemingly mundane task, in writing the court's rules Livingston influenced the ways in which cases would be heard and decided in the new territory. For Louisiana, this undertaking was especially significant because Livingston's rules ensured that common-law procedures would dictate the court's operations. Forms of pleading and writs would follow Anglo-American patterns. The introduction of trial by jury in the rules marked an especially important development. Mandated by the Constitution of the United States and drawn from the common-law tradition, its institution marked a legal revolution of sorts for the territory. Livingston's rules then helped to construct an Anglo-American framework for the new judicial system.

Figuring out what laws would be enforced in the common-law courts, however, raised a unique problem for the public officials and private citizens in the Territory of Orleans. The outgoing French prefect, or chief magistrate, Pierre Clément Laussat, was the main source of the chaos. Laussat viewed the position of prefect as his big chance to rise in the French colonial administration. When he received his appointment, he drafted an extensive plan to reform the French colony after the retrocession from Spain. En route to New Orleans, however, he received notification of the Louisiana Purchase, along with amended instructions that required him simply to take control of Louisiana, then cede it to the United States immediately. Undaunted by this turn of events, and perhaps even hopeful of creating confusion, Laussat began his reforms anyway. In the two weeks that he led the colony, however, he could only proceed so far. Laussat closed the Cabildo (the municipal government of New Orleans) and suspended the laws-in-force. Unfortunately, Laussat never got around to replacing these laws with new ones, or with a new administrative office. So the Americans inherited a blank slate.

Although Claiborne, with Livingston's help, quickly enacted a judicial system, reestablishing the laws-in-force represented one of the major obstacles of his early administration. And Edward Livingston was a source of much obstruction. Jefferson had instructed Claiborne to create a common-law jurisdiction with a good bit of sensitivity and flexibility toward people whom he still regarded as quasi-foreign, despite the guarantees of citizenship granted them through the Louisiana Purchase. At first glance, the *tabula rasa* created by Laussat seemed to offer a great opportunity to put into effect an entirely new common-law system. Jefferson wisely counseled Claiborne to be cautious. But Livingston's interests had worked in exactly the opposite direction. A good controversy could open the door to new opportunities for him. Moreover, intellectually Livingston was drawn to the superior components of the civil law.

For Livingston, the most suspect characteristic of the common law stemmed from the role of judges. In the Anglo-American system, judges played an important part in the creation of law. Statutes and ordinances provided a substantial foundation for written law, but judicial decisions created precedents that were also part of the law. Livingston distrusted "judge made" law because judges made mistakes. Civil law judges, on the other hand, possessed no such power. They merely applied and interpreted written law. The common law's dependence on tradition and custom also allowed for the inclusion of medieval principles that seemed out of place in the modern world, especially with common law's emphasis on retaliation or retribution as a punishment for crimes.

Livingston's Political Agenda

Livingston also recognized a political opportunity in the chaotic legal arena in Louisiana. His estrangement from the Republicans prohibited an alliance with Claiborne; but by capitalizing on the distrust of the Americans, white Louisianians felt, he could still build a constituency. And there was ample opportunity to profit from that distrust. Not only did white Louisianians distrust the common law, they also disliked the provisions of the Governance Act of

1804. Livingston, along with another political outsider, the wealthy Daniel Clark (an Irish-born U.S. citizen who had become a successful merchant and American consul in New Orleans at the end of European rule), cast his lot with the emerging opposition among white Louisianians. In this role, with his superior talent and nimble intellect, Edward Livingston proved to be a dangerous man. His agitation led to a formal protest against Claiborne through the Remonstrance of 1804, which denounced the slavery prohibition. Livingston also persuaded several prominent Louisianians as well as Clark to refuse appointments to territorial offices as a way of embarrassing Claiborne.

These shenanigans, however, pale in both comparison and significance to Livingston's campaign against the common law in Louisiana. Again, the Governance Act of 1804 (which imposed the territorial system on the Louisiana Purchase) and Laussat's actions provide the source of the controversy. The Governance Act was modeled after the famous Northwest Ordinance of 1787 (which established the principles of the territorial system in the United States), which in turn was patterned after the Quebec Act of 1774 (which created a permanent British government in Canada following the Seven Years' War). All three laws dealt with the crucial question of how a country could superimpose its legal system on a settled territory.

Although both the Northwest Ordinance and the Quebec Act allowed for alien residents to maintain their legal conventions, the Governance Act of 1804 ordered the introduction of the common law to the territory. The vague wording of the Governance Act of 1804, however, raised a question: By "common law," did

Congress intend to institute the common-law tradition of England, or was it referring to the common law of the territory? American lawyers, dozens of whom had recently immigrated to Louisiana, favored English common law. Disaffected white Louisianians, however, disagreed. The argument was debated on several different planes.

One of the first disputes revolved around the official legal language of the new territory. Would it be French or English? American lawyers favored English and brought the matter before the Superior Court. Their main argument was financial—publication of laws and court decisions in English and French was a costly and unnecessary provision. White Louisianians, many of whom feared that legal innovations would lead to dispossession of their property, complained noisily. Livingston championed their cause. Judge John Prevost, a multilingual transplant from New York who presided over the Superior Court, agreed with Livingston, and both languages remained in use. In fact, the Livingston rules required all court papers to be drawn up in both English and French. This effort endeared Livingston to the *ancienne population* of Louisiana, who began to consider him as something of a protector. His status rose even higher in 1805, when he married Madame Louise Moreau de Lassy, a recent refugee from Saint Domingue. With a Louisianian for his bride, unparalleled legal expertise, and the skill of a seasoned partisan, Livingston was well prepared to carry on the fight for his political and social eminence.

The next related battle dealt with the laws-in-force. The American side argued that Congress clearly meant to institute English common law, as embraced in the other American states. Livingston argued that the term referred to the common law of the territory. John Prevost, who had the unsavory task of deciding cases in the Superior Court, again sided with Livingston. Without a clear indication of the laws-in-force, he had been referring to a hodgepodge of Roman, French, Spanish, and Anglo-American legal authorities on a case-by-case basis. As the lone judge of the Superior Court, this proved to be a herculean task. Nonetheless, Prevost muddled through. But neither the Americans nor the Louisianians were satisfied with the situation. Even those who favored Livingston and Prevost's interpretation recognized the absurdity of the mess. And for once, Claiborne and Livingston actually agreed. For a brilliant lawyer like Livingston, the situation worked out quite well, since his expertise in both traditions put him in demand as a lawyer. But Livingston's disdain for the inconsistencies of common law and his desire to cultivate influence among white Louisianians made him one of the most vocal critics of the situation.

Ultimately, Claiborne asked the territorial legislature to compile and publish a compendium of the laws-in-force. The legislature appointed three jurisconsults (jurists learned in international and public law) to complete the task. James Brown and Louis Moreau Lislet would compile a digest of the civil laws, while Lewis Kerr (once a Claiborne protégé but by 1806 a confidant of Claiborne's enemies), James Workman, and New Orleans mayor John Watkins assembled the criminal laws-in-force. Kerr had a much easier task, because the Constitution of the United States clearly prescribed that the criminal laws had to follow Anglo-American patterns. He completed his work (translated into French by Moreau Lislet), *Exposition of the Criminal Laws of the Territory of Orleans,* in 1806. Kerr also benefited from the extensive Crimes Act of 1805 that had recently been drafted by James Workman. In the end, Kerr's *Exposition* relied on Anglo-American traditions. His collection included the Crimes Act, constitutional provisions on trial by jury, presumption of innocence, and *habeas corpus.* England's premier authorities on the criminal law—Sir Matthew Hale, Sir William Blackstone, and Sir Edward Coke—figured prominently in the *Exposition.* Virginian William Waller Hening's *New Virginia Justice* (published in 1797) figured prominently in the *Exposition.* In fact, the writ of *habeas corpus* is nearly an exact copy of the one suggested in Hening's work.

For the civil laws, however, Brown and Moreau Lislet had to comb Roman, Spanish, French, English, and American authorities to compile a full list of civil procedures. In 1808 they presented their long-awaited and greatly appreciated *Digest of the Civil Laws Now in Force in the Territory of Orleans, with Alterations and Amendments Adapted to its Present System of Government.* The publication of the *Digest* is often misinterpreted as a victory for Livingston and his allies among the Louisianians. But it was nothing of the sort, even though lawyers of the period frequently referred to the *Digest* as the "Civil Code." Both the Superior Court of the Territory of Orleans and its successor, the Supreme Court of Louisiana, employed the *Digest* as a compendium of Louisiana's common law, to be used in concert with court decisions. The American-style judicial system that Claiborne imposed on the territory ensured that it could be construed in no other

way. Even Livingston and Moreau Lislet believed that the *Digest* fell short of Louisianian expectations. Too many English and Spanish authorities got in the way of what the authors perceived as the superior French alternative. The sections on land and inheritance did rely on civilian authorities; but a truly French solution was what the Louisianians had had in mind. From 1808 until 1825 the Louisianians, led often by Livingston, lobbied for frenchification of their legal system.

Opportunities Lost

In these early years following the purchase, Livingston's position in New Orleans society rose. He had endeared himself to the Louisianians by marrying well and by supporting their goals. His law practice thrived. Politically, he joined fellow Americans Daniel Clark and Evan Jones in creating a powerful opposition junto. Claiborne distrusted them but often had to depend on their talent and ingenuity to order the government. By 1806 it seemed that Livingston had resurrected his career. But his fortunes soon changed for the worse.

On the political front, Livingston's activities during the Burr controversy in 1807 dealt a crushing blow to the Livingston-Clark-Jones alliance. From a legal standpoint, his litigation over the right to use the batture lands along the Mississippi, a battle that began in 1807 and lasted until his death in 1836, alienated his friends among the Louisianians and fueled one of the most celebrated controversies associated with the Louisiana Purchase. (Battures are formed from the deposit of alluvial soil along riverfront lots.) Yet neither the Burr conspiracy nor the batture fight doomed Livingston to failure. In fact, the turmoil prodded him to rely ever more closely on his skill and legal brilliance—qualities that usually gave him the upper hand.

Aaron Burr plagued Livingston throughout his early career. His unfortunate reference to Livingston as a "confidential friend" in 1801 had caused the rift between Livingston and his political patrons just as the embezzlement scandal broke in New York. The fallout led to Livingston's political downfall and swift relocation to New Orleans.

After his indictment for the 1804 murder of Alexander Hamilton, Vice President Burr left office in disgrace in March 1805. As Chapter 5 explains, by 1806 Americans were following his activities with great concern, convinced that Burr's trek to the backcountry was an effort to form a separatist conspiracy. Whatever Burr intended, his hopes rested squarely on the support of the shadowy governor of Upper Louisiana and commander of the United States Army in the Mississippi Valley, James Wilkinson. Before Burr could realize his vague hopes, Wilkinson withdrew his support and went to New Orleans to crush the conspiracy. When he arrived in the Crescent City, Wilkinson embarked on his infamous "reign of terror" by arresting a wide array of alleged co-conspirators. All of the prisoners were Americans. Most of them, such as James Workman and Lewis Kerr, were Claiborne's enemies. Wilkinson also implicated Daniel Clark, who was in Washington serving as the nonvoting delegate from the Territory of Orleans. Wilkinson failed to implicate Livingston in the conspiracy, but Livingston's vigorous legal defense of the accused placed him squarely in the Burrite camp.

Before Burr even reached New Orleans, he surrendered. After a daring escape, he finally stood trial in Richmond, Virginia, in 1807. The chief justice of the United States, John Marshall, a Federalist and staunch enemy of President Jefferson, presided over the proceedings. After his acquittal, officials in Kentucky, Ohio, and Mississippi indicted Burr, inducing him to flee the country in June 1808. Burr's departure defused the tense situation. Without Burr as the big fish caught in the net, the little ones swam free. Those implicated in the Burr conspiracy carried the taint of treason for the rest of their lives. Even James Wilkinson, who proved instrumental in crushing the conspiracy, suffered from the accusations.

The Burr conspiracy transformed New Orleans politics. Daniel Clark was ruined. Claiborne's opponents—Workman, Kerr, and Watkins—were destroyed. And Edward Livingston lost his American allies. Livingston also fell from grace among the Louisianians, who remained steadfastly loyal to the United States during the treasonous affair. Claiborne emerged stronger than ever and began recruiting prominent Louisianians to his side, a development that destroyed Livingston's long-term designs. The Burr conspiracy was a disaster, but Livingston still remained convinced that he could survive the turmoil and emerge triumphant. Yet the road to his political and social resurrection would be a bumpy one fraught with legal battles.

Livingston versus the United States: The Imposition of Law

Livingston's most celebrated legal controversy of the post–Louisiana Purchase era grew out of a private matter that involved him in a lawsuit against the United States government. The fight began in 1807 and continued for the rest of Livingston's life. Again, the controversy centered on questions raised by the imposition of common law on Louisiana.

In 1726 the Society of Jesus acquired the Batture St. Mary on the Mississippi River in a royal land grant. When the French suppressed the Jesuits in 1763, the government confiscated and then sold the Batture St. Mary to Jean Pradel. The property changed hands several times until Jean Gravier acquired it in 1797. Before 1800, the land that had never been developed was open to New Orleanians, who freely used the soil for various purposes. In 1803 Gravier began to move the levee closer to the river so he could increase the size of his holdings. This step cut off public access to the batture. New Orleanians complained, and the municipal government tried to prevent the enclosure. Gravier sued and in 1807 won a judgment in the Superior Court for the Territory of Orleans in *John Gravier v. the Mayor, Alderman, and Inhabitants of the City of New Orleans.*

Livingston served as Gravier's attorney. After the trial he received a 33 percent share of the batture land. When Livingston set about improving the land for commercial use, he faced considerable public opposition. Claiming that Livingston had usurped their ancient rights to use the land, an angry mob gathered on the batture on September 15, 1807. Claiborne was caught on the horns of a dilemma. He could appease the crowd (a tempting idea, given his enmity toward Livingston), or he could uphold the judgment of the Superior Court. Both options were perilous. On the one hand, no governor of a territory could afford to give in to mob rule, no matter how valid the disputed claim. (Claiborne, still convinced that many white Louisianians were politically naïve, was particularly uncomfortable bending to popular whim.) On the other hand, supporting Livingston, beyond being a bitter pill to swallow, would cost Claiborne what little public support he had managed to acquire over the past four years. Claiborne had become increasingly adept at judging the political circumstances surrounding him. In this case, he opted to kick the matter up the line to his superiors. He promised the crowd and Livingston that President Jefferson would settle the matter. Claiborne's promises appeased the mob, but not the city of New Orleans, which formally asked the government to evict Livingston and to seize the land in the name of the United States. Jefferson, after a hasty cabinet meeting, complied and ordered United States Marshal Breton D'Orgenois to act on January 25, 1808.

Jefferson's actions precipitated one of the longest and most complicated American legal actions of the nineteenth century. In the territory, a pamphlet war began. For over a decade, some of the best legal minds in America weighed in on the controversy. New Orleanians Pierre Derbigny, Louis Moreau Lislet, and Livingston himself all published opinions on the matter. The renowned litigator Peter S. Duponceau of Philadelphia defended Livingston. Virginian John Wickham and Jefferson himself also published treatises on the complex questions of ownership of the batture lands; the rights of the United States; and, of course, whether the definitive answer to the question would be found in civil or common law. Livingston even sued Jefferson in federal court over the matter. The whole affair became so heated and personal that Jefferson nicknamed Livingston "the Spadassin," a term at the time synonymous with "desperado" or "assassin."[2]

For years the controversy continued even after public interest waned. Finally, in 1823, the case was settled in Livingston's favor. After that, the batture finally began to yield the lucrative political plums Livingston had hoped to enjoy in the territorial period. By then, however, Livingston had not only survived the setbacks caused by the Burr conspiracy and his initial dispute with the citizens over the batture lands but he had also begun to regain the kind of power he once wielded in New York.

Opportunities Found

Livingston's experiences during these years reveal much about the confused and unsettled issues raised by the imposition of American law in Louisiana. Clearly, the matter cannot be boiled down to a simple conflict of civil versus common law, or of Louisianians versus Americans. Shifting political and personal alliances also played a significant role. Livingston's early support for civil law won admirers among the suspicious Louisianians. But as Claiborne applied the common law cautiously and upheld important civil principles in the private law, he gradually earned the confidence of the *ancienne population*. As a result, what developed in territorial Louisiana and served as the foundation for the state was a judicial system modeled exclusively on Anglo-American practices that presided over a mixed jurisdiction.

Livingston survived the controversies of the early territorial period, however, and remained

on the lookout for new opportunities to pre-sent themselves. During the 1810s he tried repeatedly to be elected to public office, always without success. He made two bids for the governorship of Louisiana, losing in 1812 to Claiborne (who made an easy transition from territorial to state politics) and in 1816 to Jacques Philippe Villeré (a Creole planter and hero of the Battle of New Orleans). Whatever turmoil Livingston's shenanigans might have created, his reputation as a brilliant lawyer continued to grow. In fact, each battle gave him an opportunity to demonstrate his legal acumen. No one could survive in such a pressure-packed environment without becoming a consummate opportunist, and Livingston was no exception. The War of 1812 offered him the chance to endear himself to Andrew Jackson. This union proved to be a great boon to Livingston. When Jackson rose to executive office, Livingston went with him and finally gained the national prominence he had been pursuing since the 1780s.

War brought Andrew Jackson to Louisiana. His tenure in the Crescent City revealed another implication of the attempt to superimpose American law on the region. Again, Edward Livingston played a crucial role.

Although Claiborne had become thoroughly convinced of the allegiance of the Louisianians to the United States by the time the War of 1812 broke out, the rest of the nation was not so sure. Major General Andrew Jackson was especially dubious. On December 16, 1814, shortly after his arrival in New Orleans, he placed the city under martial law. Jackson made the decision partly to keep order under threat of foreign attack and partly because he worried that disaffected Louisianians in the city might support the British.

On December 24, 1814, American and British officials signed the Treaty of Ghent, ending the War of 1812. No one in or around New Orleans, however, knew about the agreement. After brief skirmishes on December 28 and again on New Year's Day, on January 8, 1815, British general Sir Edward Packenham launched a major attack on Jackson's troops at the Chalmette battery just east of the city. Jackson won a spectacular victory.

Jackson decided to extend the state of martial law for several months after the British withdrew from the field, because their fleet remained stationed in the Gulf of Mexico. Although the Louisianians groused about Jackson's decree before the battle, they tolerated it as a military necessity. After proving their loyalty in combat, however, they grew increasingly resentful of the extension of the martial law provisions. Jackson's most vocal critic, Louis Louaillier, a French-born member of the state legislature, wrote a vicious pamphlet attacking the general's policies. Jackson arrested Louaillier. When Judge Dominick Hall of the First District Court of the United States issued a writ of *habeas corpus* for Louaillier, Jackson arrested him as well as District Attorney John Dick. On February 10, Edward Livingston, who had been serving as Jackson's *aide de camp,* was aboard the British sloop *Brazen* arranging a prisoner exchange when he received the news that the Treaty of Ghent had been signed. Livingston returned to the city with the joyous news, but Jackson refused to suspend martial law until official word arrived on March 13. Only then were the prisoners released. John Dick sued Jackson in federal court, and Judge Hall slapped the general with a $1,000 fine. Incensed by the indignity

of the suit, Livingston graciously paid Jackson's fine.

Edward Livingston, more than any other Louisianian, stood by Jackson's side during his lengthy stay in New Orleans. The two were old friends, having served together in the U.S. House of Representatives. Not only did he serve as Jackson's aide and secretary, but Livingston also provided crucial assistance in enlisting the aid of Jean Lafitte and the Baratarian pirates in the Battle of New Orleans. When John Dick hauled Jackson into Judge Hall's court, Livingston defended the general.

Andrew Jackson was on the rise, a fact that the politically astute Livingston could not fail to appreciate. By endearing himself to Jackson, Livingston created another opportunity for himself to rebuild his stumbling career. Despite Louisiana's resistance to martial law, Jackson emerged from the war not only a national hero, but also a friend of Louisiana. When he made his way to the White House in 1828, Jackson would ensure that his friends in Louisiana benefited from his patronage. Livingston received the greatest spoils. Riding Jackson's coattails, he won a seat in the state legislature in 1820. Building on that success, he returned to Washington to serve in the House of Representatives in 1823. After campaigning heavily for Jackson in 1828, he won Old Hickory's favor in securing a Senate post. When President Jackson reorganized his cabinet in 1831, he appointed his loyal friend Edward Livingston as secretary of state. Two years later, Edward became the second Livingston to represent the United States in Paris, leaving Washington for a two-year stint as minister plenipotentiary to France.

When Livingston died in 1836 at the family estate in New York, he did so with the contentment of an old campaigner. His geographic movements were hardly unique; other ambitious Americans sought their fortunes in the West, only to return to the East with new or rebuilt careers. Livingston's career seemed to wander from battle to battle, bringing him dazzling victories and humiliating defeats. Through all the tumult, Livingston thrived on the fight and used every setback as a step toward his next victory.

The Louisiana Purchase provided Livingston with his first chance at career rehabilitation. His part in the controversies over superimposing American law on a foreign territory led to its share of ups and downs. In the end, however, like so many Americans who rein- vented themselves on the frontier in the nineteenth century, the battles Livingston fought in Louisiana afforded him his own hard-bought share of the American dream.

Notes

1. Lester J. Cappon, ed., *The Adams-Jefferson Letters: The Complete Correspondence Between Thomas Jefferson and Abigail and John Adams* (Chapel Hill and London: The University of North Carolina Press, published for the Institute of Early American History and Culture, 1959, 1987), 300–301.
2. Dumas Malone, *Jefferson and His Time: The Sage of Monticello* (Boston: Little, Brown, 1981), 63. Originally cited in Thomas Jefferson to Albert Gallatin, 27 September 1810, in *The Works of Thomas Jefferson*, vol. 11, ed. Paul Leicester Ford (New York: G. P. Putnam's Sons, 1904–1905), n. 283.

8

The Louisiana Purchase as Seminal Constitutional Event

SANFORD LEVINSON

What was the most important constitutional event of 1803? Most American lawyers—and historians influenced by these lawyers—would give as their answer John Marshall's opinion in *Marbury v. Madison*.[1] There the chief justice of the United States, writing on behalf of the Supreme Court, invalidated an obscure provision of the Judiciary Act of 1789 that was of little practical import so he could explain why the Court could not exercise the jurisdiction in the case ostensibly provided by that provision.[2] Although earlier cases had presupposed the power of judicial review (and, therefore, possible invalidation) of federal statutes, *Marbury* was the first example of the actual exercise of this power to invalidate a federal statute. Given that law professors tend to focus almost exclusively on *judicial* interpretation of the Constitution (including, of course, the possibility of judicial negation of legislative statutes or executive actions), *Marbury* holds pride of place as the first major articulation by the Supreme Court of its own role.[3]

Without wishing to play down the importance of *Marbury* or of the judicial review that it illustrates, the purpose of this chapter is to persuade the reader that the correct answer to the question "what was the most important constitutional event of 1803?" is the Louisiana Purchase. There the United States gained not only the territory including the state that we call Louisiana but also, and far more importantly, vast new lands that doubled the size of the country and made the United States a truly continental nation. To explain the Louisiana Purchase, however, this chapter also offers an introduction to American constitutionalism. Many of the themes in this chapter—the party split of the 1790s, the congressional debates of 1803, and the sectional disputes of the antebellum period—are subjects that other chapters in this book address in various ways. Here the goal is to consider these topics a bit differently. This chapter argues for the importance of the Louisiana Purchase in defining—or redefining—the Constitution. In the process, however, this discussion will show how Americans thought and argued about their Constitution. Almost every historian recognizes the political importance of the purchase. What is far less discussed is its constitutional importance.

The importance of the Louisiana Purchase is both substantive and institutional. That is, it raises a variety of basic questions about *how* to interpret the Constitution, such as whether the Constitution allows the United States to expand beyond its original borders. But independently important is the question of *who* gets to answer such questions. As already suggested, one common interpretation of *Marbury* is that it is the Supreme Court to whom we automatically look for guidance. American political culture during the period of constitutional formation assumed that an aroused public would be the primary guarantors of constitutional fidelity, with courts playing a relatively minor role.[4] The last two hundred years have seen a vast transformation of the theoretical role of the Supreme Court, in which it often proclaims its status as "ultimate interpreter" of constitutional norms. But even this remarkably invigorated Court scarcely acts to decide *all* major constitutional issues. Indeed, an active branch of contemporary constitutional scholarship is devoted to examining the process of constitutional decision making outside the courts.[5] The Louisiana Purchase is the best possible illustration of the proposition that the Supreme Court is often entirely irrelevant to the process of constitutional interpretation, and that it is Congress and the president (and, ultimately, the American people as represented in the electorate) who define constitutional possibilities in the United States.

Debating the Boundaries of "Necessary and Proper"

The United States Constitution of 1787, ratified in 1788, was in fact America's second "constitution." The first was the Articles of Confederation, by which the thirteen original colonies joined in uneasy collaboration to fight the Revolutionary War and gain their independence from Great Britain. By 1787 there

was widespread (though certainly not unanimous) agreement that the Articles established a national government that was far too weak. One meaning of the 1787 displacement of the Articles, shared by both proponents and opponents of ratification, was the establishment of a considerably more powerful national government. The central question, of course, was, "how powerful?"

Chapter 1 shows how Americans argued about the kind of political culture appropriate for their nation. But Americans—including those who had helped write the Constitution—also immediately disagreed over how to interpret it. One of the first major debates, for example, concerned Congress's power to charter a national bank. The three men who would prove so critical in defining the Constitution—Alexander Hamilton, James Madison, and Thomas Jefferson—all held powerful offices in the new government. Hamilton, the young (and brilliant) secretary of the Treasury in the Washington administration, argued forcefully that the "necessary and proper clause" found in Article I, Section 8 of the Constitution, at the conclusion of the listing of powers granted the new Congress, easily licensed the chartering. Madison, who had been the coauthor, with Hamilton (and John Jay) of the *Federalist,* which proved so influential to future generations of constitutional interpreters, vigorously disagreed with his former ally. A member of the House of Representatives from Virginia, Madison argued that the Congress had no such power and that Hamilton's reading of the "necessary and proper" clause was far too latitudinarian. This reading, he thought, would (if fully embraced) allow the national government to do basically whatever it wished. This would violate the fundamental maxim that the national government was a "limited government of assigned powers."

Meanwhile, President George Washington asked Jefferson, his secretary of state, to assess the constitutionality of the Bank of the United States. Like his close friend and associate Madison, Jefferson attacked the Bank's constitutionality. "To take a single step beyond the boundaries . . . specially drawn around the powers of congress is to take possession of a boundless field of power, no longer susceptible of any definition."[6] (This did not stop Washington from agreeing with Hamilton and signing the legislation.)

Expanding the Union and Interpreting the Constitution

In debating the Bank, Americans articulated principles that would later prove critical in their consideration of the Louisiana Purchase. Jefferson, of course, became president himself in the bitterly disputed election of 1800, sometimes described as the "Revolution of 1800" since it indeed brought to power a man widely regarded as fundamentally at odds with the expansive nationalism linked with Washington and Hamilton. Under Jefferson, one might therefore expect a far more limited notion of governmental power than that seen in the Washington and Adams administrations.

Like most prominent Americans, though, Jefferson had long entertained visions of an expanded American nation. It required no breach of his basic principles to negotiate with Napoleon about the terms of transferring new territory to the young nation. But the initial terms of Jefferson's charge to American diplo-

mats was to gain New Orleans. Instead, the French emperor offered a vast domain beginning with that important seaport, but extending at least to the Rocky Mountains. Jefferson obviously was not repelled by this possibility. Nevertheless, it *did* raise significant questions for those committed to the notion of limited national power, a notion itself generated by suspicion and fear about the possibility of federal overreaching.

From one perspective, the expansion of the United States by treaty seemed unexceptional. This was the view adopted, for example, by Jefferson's secretary of the Treasury, Albert Gallatin. After all, the Constitution allowed the United States to enter into treaties, subject only to ratification by two-thirds of the Senate after submission of the treaty by the president. No limits were listed in the Constitution as to what those treaties could do. Exchanges of territory, often as the aftermath of war, had been a traditional feature of the international system that the United States was now joining since attaining its independence. Moreover, Article IV, Section 3 of the Constitution explicitly provided both that "[t]he Congress shall have Power to dispose of and make all needful Rules and Regulations respecting the Territory . . . belonging to the United States," and the power of Congress to admit "[n]ew States" into the Union.

So why did Thomas Jefferson, whose negotiation of the Louisiana Purchase would be viewed by later historians as one of the triumphs of his checkered presidency, express constitutional doubts about it? Jefferson suggested an answer when he wrote to John Dickinson, whose political ties as a colleague of Jefferson's extended back to Philadelphia's

Independence Hall, where Dickinson had signed the Declaration of Independence. "Our Confederation is certainly confined," Jefferson wrote Dickinson, "to the limits established by the revolution. The general government has no powers but such as the constitution has given it; and it has not given it a power of holding foreign territory, and still less of incorporating it into the Union. An amendment of the constitution seems necessary for this."[7]

It is useful to analyze each part of Jefferson's argument. Note his use of the term "our Confederation" in the first sentence. This hearkens back to the period before the Constitution, when the Articles of Confederation could well be viewed as a kind of treaty among separate states jealous to preserve their own power and wary of entering into a truly strong American "union." Most nationalists (including, of course, those politicians linked with the Jeffersonian opposition in the Federalist Party) would disdain the word "confederation" and would indeed speak of "union."

What is the nature of this confederation/union? It is, according to Jefferson, "certainly confined to the [territorial] limits established by the revolution." This does not mean that it can *never* be expanded; Jefferson certainly did not oppose expansion. Rather, the question is how such expansion would take place. A more recent example actually helps make sense of Jefferson's reasoning. Consider in this context the expansion of NATO, the North Atlantic Treaty Organization formed by the West in 1948 that has been dramatically expanded over the last several decades. As a matter of legal fact, all such expansion required the approval of *all* of the constituent members, not least because (to take one example) the addi-

tion of the former Warsaw Pact countries of Hungary, Poland, and the Czech Republic was correctly viewed as fundamentally transforming NATO. This requirement for unanimity, though, is ultimately just what it means to be a "treaty organization" rather than a genuine union subject to rule by a majority of its members. It is this limited understanding of the nature of the United States of America—a decidedly ambiguous name for a country, taking on a dramatically different meaning depending on whether emphasis is placed on "United" or on "States"[8]—that allows us to understand the thrust of Jefferson's point: "the general government has no powers but such as the constitution has given it; and it has not given it a power of holding foreign territory, and still less of incorporating it into the Union."[9]

At least two clauses in the Constitution—the Treaty Clause (Article II, Section 2) and the Territories Clause (Article IV, Section 3)—might be viewed as just such powers "given" by the Constitution. For Jefferson and many other Republicans, though, reliance on the Treaty Clause seemed to suggest the president and two-thirds of the Senate in effect had limitless power to transform the nature of the union. To interpret the Treaty Clause in such a sweeping fashion was the same kind of bad faith (or so Jefferson might well have believed) as the earlier interpretation of the Necessary and Proper Clause (Article I, Section 8) by his opponents to justify the Bank of the United States or the suppression of civil liberties by the national government in the Alien and Sedition Acts of 1798. Indeed, Jefferson, even though he served as vice president under the Federalist John Adams, opposed the Federalist-sponsored Alien and Sedition Acts so strongly that he even suggested that the states had the power to nullify offending national legislation. Jefferson detailed this constitutional principle by secretly helping to draft the Kentucky Resolutions opposing those acts.[10] Surely treaties had to honor implicit constitutional limits. Otherwise, they could in effect serve as an alternative mode of constitutional amendment. Such a result would be contrary to the rigorous procedures established by Article V of the Constitution, which required not only the participation of state legislatures but also, just as importantly, the acquiescence of a full three-quarters of the states.[11]

And what of the Territories Clause, which, by definition, contemplates that the United States will possess territories? Here again Jefferson's insistence that "[o]ur Confederation is certainly confined to the limits established by the revolution" is crucial. He even appears to anticipate an argument that would be made a half-century later by Chief Justice Roger B. Taney in *Dred Scott v. Sandford,*[12]—a case that turned substantially on the reach of Congress's power to regulate the territories. Taney argued that the Territories Clause referred only to the *preexisting* territories possessed by the United States at the time of ratification, such as the Northwest Territories. These lands included the present states of Ohio, Michigan, Illinois, Indiana, and Wisconsin and were the subject of the famous Northwest Ordinance that banned slavery in them.

Similarly, Jefferson's rejection of the "power of holding foreign territory, and still less of incorporating it into the Union" is best understood as a distinctly limited view of the reach of the Territories Clause.[13] As Jefferson wrote Sen. Wilson Cary Nicholas, R-Va., who had a more expansive view of the Constitution, "I do not believe it was meant that [Congress] might receive England, Ireland, Holland, &c into" the Union, "which would be the case on your construction."[14] All of this added up to the proposition that the Treaty and Territories Clauses could not be used to turn "foreign territory" into "domestic territory" simply by having the Senate ratify a treaty by which a foreign owner would consent to its purchase by the new owner, the United States of America.

The significance of the sheer magnitude of the Louisiana Purchase cannot be overestimated. Through this acquisition, the reach of the fledgling government that had only recently been established in the new capital of Washington now extended from New Orleans to what is now Montana. Size matters, especially given certain basic conflicts inherent in American political thought of the time. After all, a basic controversy at the time of the ratification debates was whether the American goal of "republican" government could be successfully achieved in what political theorists then called an "extended republic." Baron de Montesquieu was the most famous among the political theorists who had suggested that republicanism required that a nation be quite small—one in which people (and their leaders) shared a basically homogeneous culture and set of political understandings. Consider, for example, the following statement from Montesquieu's book, *The Spirit of the Laws,* as quoted in one of the so-called Cato letters published in New York in 1787 by an opponent of ratification:[15]

It is natural to a republic to have only a small territory, otherwise, it cannot long subsist. In a large one, there are men of large fortunes, and consequently of less moderation. . . . In large republics, the public good is sacrificed to a thousand views; in a small one, the interests of the public is easily perceived, better understood, and more within the reach of every citizen, abuses have a less extent, and of course are less protected. . . .

Madison famously criticized this argument in *Federalist* Nos. 10 and 14, in effect by standing Montesquieu's argument on its head. To Madison, the size of the national union was an advantage rather than a disadvantage precisely because it diminished the potential power of what he called "factions," or groups committed to selfish, private concerns rather than to the public interest:

The smaller the society . . . the fewer probably will be the distinct parties and interests composing it; the fewer the distinct parties and interests, the more frequently will a majority be found of the same party; and the smaller the number of individuals composing a majority, and the smaller the compass within which they are placed, the more easily will they concert and execute their plans of oppression. [On the other hand, if one] extend[s] the sphere, [there will be] a greater variety of parties and interests; you make it less probable that a majority of the whole will have a common motive to invade the rights of other citizens; or if such a common motive exists, it will be more difficult for all who feel it to discover their own strength.[16]

Although Jefferson supported ratification, it is not clear how much he agreed with his friend about the virtues of what became known as the "extended republic."

It is important to realize, moreover, that the Union defended by Madison in 1788 was both significantly smaller and decidedly more homogeneous than that which would be created by the Louisiana Purchase. The overwhelming majority of the three million people in the thirteen original states—or, more to the point, the over-whelming majority of those permitted to participate in the polity—were white, Protestant, and English speaking (in addition, of course, to being male). It required a significant leap of faith to expand Madison's argument to embrace a far larger and more populous country created by the purchase. The new social reality was typified by New Orleans itself, a city dominated by French-speaking Catholics. The legal reality was underscored by the fact that New Orleans was ruled not by the arcane mysteries of the common law but by the rationalist promises of continental civil codes created in Spain and France. To this day, the state of Louisiana is unique within the United States because of the unusual legal system it adopted in the aftermath of the purchase. As Chapter 7 discussed, that system drew extensively on the French and Spanish colonial traditions that predated the introduction of American common law.

The treaty also promised certain rights to French shipping and, far more importantly, the inhabitants of the territory.[17] Thus, Article III of the treaty provided that

[t]he inhabitants of the ceded territory shall be incorporated in the Union of the United States, and admitted as soon as possible, according to the principles of the Federal constitution, to the enjoyment of all the rights, advantages and immunities of citizens of the United States; and in the mean time they shall be maintained and protected in the free enjoyment of their liberty, their property, and the religion which they profess.[18]

The religion "profess[ed]" by most New Orleanians (and white residents of what is today known as Louisiana) was Roman Catholicism, which was not easily tolerated by the dominantly Protestant (and sometimes virulently anti-Catholic) majority of the original states.

Adding Louisiana to the Union, with its inhabitants entitled to the "free enjoyment" of what many deemed a distinctly "un-American" religion, was scarcely uncontroversial.

To be sure, almost all Americans wanted New Orleans, insofar as the city would give the United States effective control of trade down the Mississippi River. But a desire for New Orleans did not entail similar support among stunned Americans for partaking of the entire landmass offered by Napoleon. Many believed that their task was simply to persuade the French emperor to part with his crown jewel of the Crescent City. But Napoleon, for his own particular reasons, offered the Americans a deal that was literally too good to refuse, and they accepted.

Constitutional Amendment or Use of Constitutional Clauses?

Despite his endorsement of the purchase, Jefferson believed that a constitutional amendment would be necessary to validate the sea changes generated by the Louisiana Purchase. The "constructions" allowing the purchase he deemed "dangerous." "I had," he wrote, "rather ask an enlargment of power from the nation where it is found necessary, than to assume it by a construction which would make our powers boundless. Our peculiar security is in possession of a written Constitution. Let us not make it a blank paper by construction." Instead, Jefferson emphasized the importance of "set[ting] an example against broad construction by appealing for new power to the people."[19]

There was, however, a fundamental problem with going the route of a formal amendment through Article V, which prescribed the rather detailed process for altering the text of the Constitution. Jefferson was not long in recognizing that the U.S. Constitution is extremely difficult to amend. Proposal of an amendment requires the approval of two-thirds of each house of Congress; then the proposed amendment must be ratified by the legislatures of three-quarters of the states. The United States in 1803 had seventeen states—the last of which, Ohio, was admitted in March 1803—all of which had bicameral legislatures (only Nebraska, admitted far later to the Union in 1867, has a unicameral one). This means, as a practical matter, that any proposal to amend the Constitution to explicitly allow the Louisiana Purchase would have needed the approval of at least twenty-six legislative houses in thirteen states. This was the minimum necessary out of seventeen states to reach the required three-quarters. Under the best of circumstances, this kind of legislative effort is time consuming. This was true not only because of the irregular schedule of state legislative sessions in the early years of the republic, but also because a number of Federalists were skeptical about the purchase. At a more pragmatic level, they worried that adding states in the West would further erode New England's influence.[20] Many opponents also accurately perceived the purchase as freighted with profound implications for the expansion of slavery. As a result, there was good reason to doubt whether the desired amendment could have been added, even if Napoleon had been kind enough to leave the offer open long enough to bear the inevitable delays in finding the minimum number of legislatures in session. It seemed then that Jefferson's idealized wish for a legitimating amendment could not be realized.

Gallatin, who disagreed with Jefferson's qualms, saw no problem with using the Treaty Clause to expand the United States. As he wrote Jefferson, "the existence of the United States as a nation presupposes the power enjoyed by every nation of extending their territory by treaties, and the general power given to the President and Senate of making treaties designates the organs through which the acquisition may be made."[21] As to the objection based on the Tenth Amendment, which declares "reserved" to the states (or to "the people") those powers not delegated to the national government by the sovereign people, Gallatin had this to say:

As the States are expressly prohibited from making treaties, it is evident that, if the power of acquiring territory by treaty is not considered within the meaning of the Amendment as delegated to the United States, it must be reserved to the people. If that be the true construction of the Constitution, it substantially amounts to this: that the United States are precluded from, and renounce altogether, the enlargement of territory, a provision sufficiently important and singular to have deserved to be expressly enacted. Is it not a more natural construction to say that the power of acquiring territory is delegated to the United States by the several provisions which authorize the several branches of government to make war, to make treaties, and to govern the territory of the Union.[22]

The last sentence in particular suggests that Gallatin had little patience with the restricted reading of the Territories Clause. He noted that Article IV referred to "the *Territory or other property belonging to the United States.*" Gallatin argued that "other property" could easily be interpreted to refer to new territories added afterward to "the territory" already possessed at the time of ratification.

Gallatin's arguments did not still Jefferson's doubts. As he wrote to his ally, Senator Nicholas, "[W]hatever congress shall think it necessary to do, should be done with as little debate as possible, & particularly so far as respects the constitutional difficulty."[23] In case this was too subtle, he forthrightly told another correspondent, Attorney General Levi Lincoln, that "the less that is said about the constitutional difficulties, the better."[24] The Louisiana Purchase was quite literally a deal too good to refuse. And because many believed that Napoleon might withdraw his offer should the United States linger over its decision, let alone insist on taking the time necessary for formal amendment, any constitutional doubts had to be suppressed instead of fully aired. The Senate ratified the treaty with France in October. France formally delivered the territory to the United States in December 1803. And America was never the same.

Jefferson's most famous defense of the purchase came seven years later, in an 1810 letter to John Colvin: "A strict observance of the written law is doubtless *one* of the high duties of a good citizen, but is not the *highest*. The laws of necessity, of self-preservation, of saving our country when in danger, are of higher obligation."[25] The end does indeed justify the means. Jefferson obviously believed that the Louisiana Purchase was sufficiently important to the flourishing of the Union—perhaps even to "self-preservation," if he feared that the territory in hostile hands might serve as a base for future attacks on a truncated United States—to justify shelving a professed commitment to "strict observance of the written law."

Ongoing Constitutional Controversy

These are some of the constitutional issues that were obvious to many Americans at the time, and they alone easily establish the Louisiana Purchase as the banner constitutional event of the era. But, as a matter of fact, they provide only some of the reasons for assigning the purchase this exalted role. The purchase might be regarded, for example, as a major cause of the later conflagration that would almost destroy the Union in 1861. The reason is simple: It was the purchase that established the extension of slavery into the territories as the central issue of American politics. The framers of 1787–1788 had in fact agreed to a compromise on slavery. They respected the Northwest Ordinance's prohibition on slavery, while acknowledging that more Southern states (beginning with Kentucky and Tennessee, but including what became Alabama and Mississippi) would enter the Union as slave states. This development would not threaten the Union, since it would provide each region with a veto over any untoward ambitions of the other.

But the Louisiana Purchase was a gigantic wild card in the game of American political poker. Each region reasonably feared that the entrance of new states, each electing two senators as well as new members of the House of Representatives (and electing presidents through the electoral college and affecting the politics of constitutional amendment), might tip the balance so carefully achieved in 1787. It might be lamentable that the initial compromise was entered into at all; there were, after all, those who advocated rejection of the Constitution precisely because it did collaborate with slaveholders. But the dominant opinion was that achieving the end (union) justified the means (compromising on slavery). Yet another part rested on an intensely practical point: The purchase, including its promise that the terri-

tories would eventually become members of the Union—Louisiana would lead the way in 1812—meant that the character of the American nation would change quite drastically, in all sorts of ways.

It cannot be said with confidence: "No Purchase, No Civil War," though, as Chapter 10 shows, the Louisiana Purchase helped to shape arguments that structured the sectional disputes thereafter. It is also possible, of course, that failure to absorb the lands of the Louisiana Purchase would have led to later warfare with the colonial powers that would continue to dominate those areas. Obviously, historians would require truly supernatural abilities in reading a counterfactual crystal ball to know exactly what the consequences of the purchase were. That being admitted, it is difficult indeed to avoid concluding that it was the political energies unleashed by white settlement of the new territories that ultimately destroyed the Whig Party in the 1850s, stimulated the formation of the Republican Party in 1856 (which was dedicated to prohibiting the expansion of slavery), and then led the southern states to secede after the Republican victory in 1860 of Abraham Lincoln. The Supreme Court, of course, had done its part to limit the force of the Republican victory by effectively declaring the party's platform unconstitutional in the 1857 *Dred Scott* case. *Dred Scott* offered an extremely limited reading of Congress's power under the Territories Clause—and a remarkably capacious reading of the rights of slaveowners to bring any of their slaves into American territories.

Given all of the fundamental constitutional issues linked with the Louisiana Purchase, one might well ask why it languishes in the shadow of *Marbury*. The answer is depressingly simple: Most American lawyers, and most historians who write on American constitutional development, are infatuated with the U.S. Supreme Court. They accept as a descriptive proposition the famous comment of Charles Evans Hughes, then governor of New York and later chief justice of the United States, that "the Constitution is what the judges say it is." Among other things, this leads too many people to ignore that fundamental constitutional decisions are made by people other than judges, and that presidents and members of Congress have played a role every bit as important as judges in defining the meaning of the Constitution.

There is no better proof of this point than the Louisiana Purchase. Political actors of the time recognized that its acquisition presented a variety of complex constitutional difficulties. It is equally evident that the Supreme Court played absolutely no role in resolving them. To be sure, in a notably obscure 1828 case,[26] decided a full quarter-century after the purchase, Chief Justice Marshall held that the United States had power to acquire new territory either by war or treaty, but no one seriously treated the issue as undecided. As a matter of fact, it was resolved entirely by members of the executive and legislative branches, who argued with one another and then concluded, for whatever reasons, that adding the Louisiana Territory through treaty was not barred by the Constitution. The Supreme Court was, in effect, recognizing the new constitutional reality achieved in 1803. As if underscoring the point that Congress felt fully empowered to decide basic constitutional questions on its own, it admitted the then-independent country of Texas directly into the union in 1844, citing its pow-

ers under the Admission Clause of the Constitution (Article IV, Section 3) and ignoring Marshall's limitation to "war" or "treaty" as the two modes by which the Union could be expanded.[27] As with the Louisiana Purchase itself, the judiciary played no role at all in resolving the intense constitutional debates of the time.

Conclusion

The United States began in 1789 as a country of eleven states along the Atlantic seaboard.[28] By 1803 it had grown to seventeen states; of course, today it comprises fifty states from the Atlantic to the Pacific, from just north of the Tropic of Cancer to well north of the Arctic Circle. To put it mildly, this remarkable expansion was not without significant constitutional consequences. Books could easily be written about the constitutional issues involved in the annexation of Texas, the absorption of the American Southwest, the purchase of Alaska from Russia in 1867, and the annexation of Hawaii in 1898. This does not even address the territories that continue to be part of the American empire—the most important by far of which is Puerto Rico, the world's largest remaining colony. Perhaps this brief overview of the constitutional dimensions of the Louisiana Purchase illustrates the richness of the issues open to anyone interested in American constitutional development.

Notes

1. 5 U.S. (1 Cranch) 137 (1803). See Mark A. Graber and Michael Perhac, *Marbury v. Madison: Documents and Commentary* (Washington, D.C.: CQ Press, 2002).

2. Except in *Marbury* itself insofar as the provision, which Marshall read in a controversial manner to give the Supreme Court jurisdiction in the case, put the Court in a potentially uncomfortable political position vis-à-vis its Jeffersonian adversaries. Thus the pressure on Marshall to avoid the discomfort by declaring it unconstitutional. See Robert McCloskey, *The American Supreme Court* (Chicago: University of Chicago Press, 2000), 23–30.

3. It should be emphasized that *Marbury*'s defense of "judicial review" in no way is the same as a defense of "judicial supremacy." The former justifies a definite judicial place in any institutional discussion of what the Constitution, rightly interpreted, means. The latter, however, labels the Court as the "definitive" interpreter of constitutional meaning, with other institutions being reduced to the role of supplicants offering the Court "suggestions" as to how to interpret the Constitution.

4. Larry Kramer, "Forward: We the Court," *Harvard Law Review* 115 (2001): 4.

5. Stephen Griffin, *American Constitutionalism: From Theory to Politics* (Princeton: Princeton University Press, 1996); Keith E. Whittington, *Constitutional Construction: Divided Powers and Constitutional Meaning* (Cambridge: Harvard University Press, 1999).

6. "Opinion on the Constitutionality of the Bill for Establishing a National Bank," quoted in Paul Brest et al., *Processes of Constitutional Decisionmaking: Cases and Materials* (Gaithersburg, Md.: Aspen Law and Business, 2000), 13.

7. David N. Mayer, *The Constitutional Thought of Thomas Jefferson* (University of Virginia Press, 1994), 247.

8. See Sebastian De Grazia, *A Country with No Name: Tales from the Constitution* (New York: Pantheon Books, 1997), a fascinating meditation on the essential tensions generated by the name of the United States (and an explanation of the opposition to proposals that the country be named something else, such as "Columbia." Another way of establishing the point is by noting that the term "United States" took the plural "are" before 1865 and the singular "is" following the defense of Union between 1861 and 1865.

9. Mayer, *The Constitutional Thought of Thomas Jefferson*, 247.

10. Jefferson had no principled objection to the *states'* suppressing the civil liberties of their citizens; he believed, though, that the citizenry had less to fear from their own state governments, composed of their neighbors, than from a distant national government dominated by strangers.

11. The issue of limits on the treaty power continues to be much discussed by constitutional theorists, especially in the aftermath of *Missouri v. Holland*, 252 U.S. 416 (1920), in which the Court, through Justice Holmes, appeared to tolerate a measure of congressional regulation that would not then have been thought proper under any of the powers assigned to Congress by Article I. See Curtis Bradley, "The Treaty Power and American Federalism," *Michigan Law Review* 97 (1998): 390, which summarizes much of the extant literature on the subject, even as he suggests that there are indeed limits to the scope of the treaty power.

12. 60 U.S. (19 How.) 393 (1857).

13. To be sure, Jefferson's (and Taney's) reading of the clause is hardly compelled (some might even say hardly plausible). For example, the Constitutional Convention in Philadelphia explicitly debated and then rejected a draft of the constitutional text that would have limited the creation of new states only "within the [present] limits of the United States." Thus, as David P. Currie writes, "some delegates thought such a limitation desirable, but surely [this does not demonstrate] that this was the view of the Convention as a whole." See David P. Currie, *The Constitution in Congress: The Jeffersonians, 1801–1829* (Chicago: University of Chicago Press, 2001), 103 n.116.

14. Quoted in Currie, *The Constitution in Congress,* 102. David P. Currie's discussion of the debate over the Louisiana Purchase is indispensable to anyone interested in the constitutional issues it presented.

15. *The Federalist,* ed. Benjamin Fletcher Wright (New York: Barnes and Noble, 1961), 4–5.

16. *Federalist* No. 10, *The Federalist,* 135.

17. As a matter of fact, the relevant "inhabitants" protected by the treaty's guarantees were the

white residents. The treaty's provisions certainly did not extend to black slaves or to Indians.

18. Currie, *The Constitution in Congress,* 97.
19. Jefferson to Wilson Cary Nicholas, 7 September 1803, quoted in David N. Mayer, *The Constitutional Thought of Thomas Jefferson,* 249.
20. E. James Ferguson, ed., *Selected Writings of Albert Gallatin* (Indianapolis: Bobbs-Merrill, 1967), 211.
21. Gallatin to Jefferson, 13 January 1803, *Selected Writings of Gallatin,* 213.
22. Ibid., 217.
23. Quoted in Mayer, *The Constitutional Thought of Thomas Jefferson,* 250.
24. Ibid.
25. Quoted in Brest, *Process of Constitutional Decisionmaking,* 75.
26. *American Insurance Co. v. Canter,* 26 U.S. (1 Pet.) 511 (1828).
27. To be sure, President John Tyler had first submitted a treaty between the Lone Star Republic of Texas and the United States to the Senate, but it failed to even garner a majority of the vote, let alone the constitutionally required two-thirds. His response was, in effect, to change the rules in the middle of the game and to decide that no treaty was required at all—that Texas could be admitted directly to the Union by a majority vote of each house of Congress, which was procured. The annexation would, of course, lead to the Mexican War, which would in turn substantially expand the Union by bringing into the United States the American Southwest, including California.
28. At the time George Washington was inaugurated, on April 30, 1789, North Carolina and Rhode Island had not yet ratified the Constitution, though each would do so within a year. But their status before ratification was a kind of juridical limbo; it seems impossible to argue that they were members of the United States of America before ratification unless in effect one treats them as part of "the Territory" over which Congress had power—an understanding that no North Carolinian or Rhode Islander was likely to accept.

The Louisiana Purchase and American Federalism

PETER S. ONUF

The United States began as a loose union of thirteen Anglo-American colonies that declared their independence from Britain in 1776. This first union was a kind of diplomatic and military alliance, as suggested by the use of the term "congress" to describe successive assemblies of delegates from the colony-states. Revolutionary-era Americans understood the crucial importance of sustaining and perfecting that union to make good on their claims of independence. Effective interstate cooperation was predicated on an "energetic" central government that could take the place of the former imperial British government, mobilizing the resources of the North American continent on behalf of the common cause and presenting a single face to the "powers of the world."[1] As a result, the United States took on a novel, hybrid character that defied the logic of contemporary political science. The goal of most revolutionary patriots was to establish a reformed, republican *empire*, purged of corruption from old regimes, that preserved the separate existence of its far-flung members. Yet the founders also recognized the necessity of constituting themselves into a single *nation* when dealing with the larger world. The potential conflict between these conceptions of union, the logical conun-drum of *imperium in imperio* (an empire within an empire), was played out in the subsequent history of American federalism.

Within this system, the separate states never aspired to full sovereignty and independence with respect to one another. To the contrary— the most compelling argument against the break with Britain was that these former provinces would be left in a "state of nature" that would inevitably degenerate into anarchy. When the states declared independence, they therefore simultaneously pledged *not* to exercise the full array of powers sovereignties could claim. Yet that pledge implied a threat: that fealty to the union of states was conditional on its success in securing the essential rights and interests of its respective members. If those conditions were violated, the individual states would resume a sovereignty they had never actually exercised, which would fulfill the direst prophecies of the imperial loyalists who had balked at independence in the first place. Disunion would unleash the dogs of war, leaving the states far worse off than they had ever been under British rule.

No good American could countenance the collapse of a union that was the sole guarantee of a prosperous and peaceful future for the

American people collectively. President Thomas Jefferson eloquently articulated that promise in his First Inaugural Address: the new nation was "kindly separated by nature and a wide ocean from the exterminating havoc of one quarter of the globe; too high-minded to endure the degradations of the others; possessing a chosen country, with room enough for our descendants to the thousandth and thousandth generation."[2] Jefferson was inclined to take the long view in 1801, confident as he was that the union had been redeemed from the threat of High Federalism through his "Revolution of 1800." But the author of the Kentucky Resolutions had been less sanguine about the prospects of union in 1798. Three years before his first inauguration as president, Jefferson had been acutely sensitive to the danger that the government of the union—as it was actually constituted and administered—could work to the advantage of some American (Anglophile "aristocrats" and "monocrats") and to the disadvantage of others (the silent, or silenced, majority of Republicans).

Jefferson's flirtation with disunion set the stage for his elevation of the concept of union in the wake of his electoral "revolution" in 1800. For Jefferson and his contemporaries, union and disunion were in dialectical tension—one defined and even invited the other. If peace and prosperity were so all-important, then patriotic statesmen must be prepared to make any necessary compromise or concession to prevent states with grievances from following through on threats to withdraw from, and thus destroy, the union. Though no state crossed that fatal threshold (with the exception of South Carolina in its abortive efforts to "nullify" the tariff in 1832) until the mass exodus of eleven southern states in 1861, the possibility that a state or bloc of states could destroy the union always enhanced a state's bargaining power in the arena of federal politics.

The ratification of the federal Constitution did not preempt disunionist threats or establish a "more perfect union." At the time of the Louisiana Purchase in 1803 the character and prospects of the federal union seemed as indeterminate as they had been either in 1776 or 1787. The purchase itself exacerbated chronic tensions (most conspicuously in the growing alienation of Federalist New England over the next decade), even while seeming to resolve others. Controversy revolved around the great question of the nation's size: how much further could the "extended republic" Madison celebrated in *Federalist* No. 10 extend, without weakening the ties of union and unleashing dangerously separatist forces? Would a dynamic, expansive union jeopardize the complicated set of intersectional compromises incorporated in the federal Constitution? Or, to frame the same problem differently, would westward expansion ease or intensify the sectional conflicts that had periodically surfaced during the party battles of the 1790s? And, finally, how well could the government of the expanding union protect the collective interests of the American states and people against external threats? The danger in every case was that a fragile American peace that depended on sustaining an effective union would give way to escalating conflict and war.

Jefferson's Louisiana diplomacy has garnered poor reviews by most diplomatic historians, who are "realists" inclined to play down his active role in this epochal transaction. These commentators also emphasize Jefferson's (undeserved) good luck—and the heroic efforts of Haitian revolutionaries in thwarting Napoleon's design for western empire. By contrast, political historians, noting popular enthusiasm for the Louisiana Purchase throughout the union, are more inclined to grant the visionary Jefferson his due. Anti-expansionist Federalists were, like the anti-federalists during ratification, men of little faith who failed to grasp the dynamic genius of the federal system, reflected in a continuous process of new state creation that augmented national wealth and power. The two contrasting versions of Jeffersonian politics can be sustained because historians are too prone to distinguish between diplomacy and domestic politics. As a result, they tend to link the consideration of federalism to ongoing party conflicts over the distribution of power within the union. But the distinction between foreign and domestic issues is by no means an easy one to make, at least until the end of the Napoleonic wars in 1815 or the Treaty of Ghent in 1814 (which ended the War of 1812), and perhaps not even then.

The Louisiana Purchase needs to be seen as merely one aspect of a revolutionary realignment in American politics that began with the election of a Republican president and Congress in 1800. The Republican ascendancy strengthened the union in the short run, but it also exposed new threats to America's long-term prospects. High Federalists had been hostile to states' rights, seemingly intent on relegating the states to a clearly subordinate, dependent role in the federal system, if not on abolishing them altogether. But Republicans were receptive to new state formation, which began with Ohio (1803) and was promised to other territories under the terms of western land cessions to Congress and represented a

vindication of states' rights generally. This promise was then extended to citizens and settlers in the trans-Mississippi region under the terms of the Louisiana Treaty.

East-West

The paradoxical premise of Republican expansionism was that the union grew stronger as the federal government's territorial regime gave way to statehood and republican self-government. This was the western equivalent of the Jeffersonian claim that Federalist measures to strengthen the union by concentrating power in the central government were in fact the greatest threat to that union's survival. Only when the federal balance was restored—and states' rights secured—would the union be truly powerful. It was the broad consent of a patriotic and grateful people that made the government of the United States "the strongest Government on earth . . . , the only one where every man, at the call of the law, would fly to the standard of the law, and would meet invasions of the public order as his own personal concern." As long as frontier settlers were frustrated in their quest for statehood (and could not therefore consider the interests of the union as a whole as their "own personal concern") they remained potential enemies—allies of any foreign state that would respond more expeditiously to meet their legitimate demands.[3] Outside of the union, frontier separatists and speculators were all too willing to entertain overtures from America's imperial rivals. Future president Andrew Jackson was not even alone in taking a loyalty oath to the king of Spain.

The Republican policy of co-opting frontier dissidents through the formation of new states thus combined an equal measure of political realism with its lofty appeal to republican principles. Jefferson's party challenged and inverted the axiom in contemporary political science (and Federalist policy) that expansion required greater central governmental power that would offset its diminished effectiveness over increasing distances. Jeffersonians insisted instead that the rapid expansion of the union would transform potential enemies into patriots, lessening the need to resort to coercive force. The states would, in turn, be a solid buttress against any future effort to consolidate power in the central government. "The true barriers of our liberty in this country are our State governments," Jefferson explained to the Frenchman Destutt de Tracy in 1811 in one of his most sustained commentaries on federalism. In France, by contrast, "republican government . . . was lost without a struggle," and Napoleon rose to power "because the party of 'un et indivisible' had prevailed; no provincial organizations existed to which the people might rally under authority of the laws, the seats of the directory were virtually vacant, and a small force sufficed to turn the legislature out of their chamber, and to salute its leader chief of the nation."[4]

In the political thought of Jefferson's day, the question of a nation's size was dominated by the Baron de Montesquieu's famous dictum that republican government could only survive in a small state and that monarchy was better suited to a unitary regime of continental dimensions. Jefferson's colleague James Madison countered Montesquieu during the debate over ratification of the federal Constitution by arguing that the proliferation of "factions" or interests in an "extended republic" would pre-

vent any single interest from becoming dominant.[5] Jefferson's letter to Tracy built on Madison's pluralist analysis. But Jefferson gave prominence to the role of *states* rather than factions in maintaining an explicitly *federal* balance, rather than the more complicated and diffuse system of countervailing forces envisioned by Madison. A history of party conflict since ratification had taught both Madison and Jefferson that struggles over the nature of the federal union were the fundamental fault line of American politics. The challenge was to avoid a consolidation of authority at the center that would give rise to an American Napoleon, while curbing dangerous tendencies toward separatism at the periphery—thus securing a genuinely federal balance.

The extravagant language of Jefferson's First Inaugural seemed to suggest that the patriotic loyalties of a grateful people were enough to sustain the union, and that these loyalties would be strengthened by curbing the power of the central government. Jefferson did believe that the division and diffusion of authority could make it easier to mobilize political and military power at a time of national crisis, translating the theory of popular sovereignty into something approaching political reality. But Jeffersonian federalism was not predicated on a libertarian fantasy that there could be union without government. Jeffersonian policy toward the creation of new states reveals a much more complex, realistic understanding.

The key premise of Jefferson's approach was that settlers of the frontier regions were potential enemies of the union—and counterrevolutionary tools of America's imperial rivals—until they were organized into states and incorporated in the union. Far from eschewing the use of force in foreign affairs, Jefferson did not hesitate to exercise executive authority on behalf of vital national interests. The first law of nature, self-preservation, might require him to lead the nation into another war—or it might justify the purchase and annexation of a vast new territory. Within strict constitutional limits, the president's authority to conduct foreign policy—like a monarch's prerogative—was absolute. (The French had taken yet another wrong turn during the Directory period of 1796 to 1800, when they created a plural executive branch, even as they fatefully centralized authority and abolished lesser jurisdictions.)

Jeffersonian federalism depended on "unity of action and direction in all the branches of the [federal] government" under a strong, unitary executive branch. The several states remained "single and independent as to their internal administration" and stood ready to resist any encroachments on their legitimate rights, but were "amalgamated into one as to their foreign concerns." If the machinery of state government were ever turned against the union itself—if "certain States from local and occasional discontents, might attempt to secede from the Union" and thus make themselves "foreigners"—then the federal government could turn its full force against them. Or, as Jefferson told another correspondent in 1814, when secessionist sentiment was rampant in New England, "I see our safety in the extent of our confederacy, and in the probability that in the proportion of the sound parts will always be sufficient to crush local poisons."[6] The incorporation of new states would guarantee their "soundness," preempting any tendencies to align with foreign enemies, and increase the ratio of "sound parts" to potentially diseased ones in the federal body politic.

But why should new states be so eager to join the union? During the Revolution, frontier separatists epitomized the selfish, calculating impulses that threatened to undermine the territorial integrity of the respective states and destroy the new union. In later decades, a tawdry history of land speculation and political adventurism on the periphery of the union only served to reinforce anti-expansionist skepticism. Though Jefferson might wax eloquent about the virtuous yeomanry, he had no illusions about what he saw as their semisavage western cousins. As Chapter 5 discussed, Americans—Jefferson included—believed that Aaron Burr's effort to detach Louisiana was only the latest example of unchecked and dangerous ambitions on the western frontier. But Jefferson also understood that interest was the pivot of western loyalty. Westerners would *become* good patriots if they calculated that the prospective advantages of membership in the union outweighed the risks—including the possibility that the federal government of that union might one day wage war against them.

Because of this, preserving the peace proved to be a leading motive for both the federal government and for frontier settlers in promoting new state formation. Other incentives naturally followed. First, statehood would enable an emerging political elite to consolidate its authority locally. In this way it would shake off the taint of complicity in a territorial regime that kept the citizenry in a state of "colonial" subjection to congressional overlords while enhancing their access to dine at the federal trough. In the Northwest Territory, for instance, Republicans who had railed against the "corruption" and "despotism" of Federalist governor Arthur St. Clair used their partisan connections with the new Jefferson administration to accelerate statehood and secure control over both federal and state patronage.

Simple political arithmetic guaranteed that the national administration would carefully cultivate the new state leadership: sparsely populated Ohio (with a population of 45,365, according to the 1800 census) would send the same number of senators to Washington as Virginia, the most populous state (807,557 in 1800). With the progress of settlement, the disparity in population would quickly disappear (by 1840 Ohio had about 50 percent more residents than Virginia), but in the meantime Ohio and other new states would enjoy disproportionate influence in federal councils. That influence could be used to distribute concrete rewards to the political elite, its clients, and its constituents. For most new states, the privatization of public (federal) lands was the most lucrative bonanza. But much was to be gained as well from political appointments, government contracts, internal improvements, and other forms of federal expenditure.

These appeals to self-interest proved a solid foundation for the patriotic sentiments Jefferson invoked in his First Inaugural. Jefferson understood that the same forces that had once jeopardized the survival of the states and the union could be redirected toward strengthening and perfecting it. Preserving a balance between states and union that would secure their distinct spheres of authority was the great goal of Jeffersonian federalism. But this balance could only be sustained by a dynamic and expansive political system that made states and union functionally interdependent and promoted the constant circulation of people and resources between them. The Republican Party mediated between theory and practice, linking political elites in the states to the central administration. The party therefore had to avoid divisions, Jefferson told disgruntled editor William Duane in 1811, for it alone could sustain the union: "if we schismatize . . . our *nation* will be undone. For the republicans are the *nation*."[7]

Jeffersonian federalism was most successful in containing and redirecting the separatist tendencies of westward expansion by drawing political elites on the frontier into a dynamic national political system. If the federal Constitution decentralized authority, making union dependent on the uncoerced consent of sovereign states, the Republican Party institutionalized that consent, directing political ambitions back toward the federal government. Yet the balance resulting from these offsetting tendencies-toward separatism in the formal Constitution, toward union in the informal—proved highly unstable. As Jefferson's letter to Duane indicated, the national party had to preserve a common front on "men and measures . . . resist its enemies within and without." Party unity was essential "during the *bellum omnium in omnia* of Europe," when a resurgent Federalist Party exploited escalating divisions over foreign policy to recoup its fortunes. But what would the state of the Republican Party be when the threat of foreign war waned, or when the Federalists were no longer effective as a national opposition party? Within only a few years, the end of the War of 1812 and the disgrace of the Federalists who had considered secession at the Hartford Convention in 1814 would test the durability of the national Republican Party—and of the union itself.

Jeffersonian federalism worked most effectively on an East-West axis by preempting separatist impulses through the creation of new states and the building of a national party. The ongoing struggle to secure the Republican experiment against counterrevolutionary forces at home (the Federalists) and abroad (the British, the Spanish, or even in the case of Louisiana, the French) gave a larger context for this dynamic, expansive concept of union. In his First Inaugural Address, Jefferson underscored the connections between the spirit of 1776 and its revival in 1800, between the Republican Party and the American nation. He also suggested that westward expansion itself constituted the logical continuation and culmination of the American Revolution. To later advocates of manifest destiny, Jefferson's language seemed visionary, anticipating and legitimizing vast annexations of territory. By 1815, however, the original context for Jefferson's paean to westward expansion—"the *bellum omnium in omnia*" in Europe and national partisan conflict in America—no longer existed. As party discipline eroded, new threats to vital state and sectional interests emerged. Opening up the West to rapid settlement and new state formation did not necessarily (or obviously) strengthen the union. A growing sense that slaveholding southern planters, the original core of the Republican Party, were the chief beneficiaries of westward expansion exposed a "geographical line" of distinction—a more fundamental North-South axis that would define the later history of American federalism.[8]

Federalist critics of Jefferson's Louisiana Purchase in 1803 presciently grasped this fundamental reorientation. The Federalists who later opposed Louisiana statehood in 1811 were powerless to resist the Republican juggernaut. In the process, they signaled instead their own disgrace and ultimate demise. But they also glimpsed the new fault line through the union that would eventually lead to its collapse.

North-South

Federalist anti-expansionists dissented from every premise of Jeffersonian federalism. Beginning with the controversial Jay Treaty in 1794, Federalists had long advocated closer relations with Britain. They thus rejected Jefferson's notion that American independence depended on a kind of permanent revolution against the former imperial power. Federalist advocacy of Anglo-American alliance reflected a realistic assessment both of the European balance of power and of America's relative weakness as a secondary power. But it also suggested that there was no fundamental difference between the new nation's republican regime and that of monarchical Britain—and that the power differential would be overcome in due time through nation-building policies that concentrated authority with the central government. These were all heresies to orthodox Republicans like Jefferson, evoking Montesquieu's discredited dictum that the preservation of a state of imperial dimensions depended on the consolidation of power in a vigorous, potentially despotic central government. If the new nation simply aspired to be another Britain, or if it submitted to the superior power of the mother country in a counterrevolutionary alliance against republican France, what was the point of American independence?

Jefferson's election in 1800, the temporary cessation of the French revolutionary wars that culminated in the Peace of Amiens in 1802, and the Louisiana Purchase in 1803 seemed to answer these questions definitively—at least for the time being. The United States, miraculously extricated from European politics, could fulfill its continental destiny without betraying its republican ideals. The American union, as one enthusiastic Republican orator exclaimed, soon would be recognized as "the wonder of the world, and more formidable to the irruptions of tyranny, than were Chinese walls to Tartar hordes."[9] But what sort of union did these Jeffersonians envision? Could it be entirely impartial—to all states, sections, or interests—in the benefits it distributed? Was isolation from external threat a sufficient condition for the progressive perfection of the republican regime? Federalists' skepticism on all these counts proved amply justified.

Federalist concerns about the implications of rapid westward expansion reflected a history of interstate and intersectional controversy in the United States while anticipating future conflicts. When the Constitution was drafted in Philadelphia, delegates negotiated an elaborate series of interdependent compromises that (at least temporarily) assuaged the most conspicuous conflicts of interest. The most notable among these compromises were between the staple-producing (and slaveholding) states of the South and the more diversified, commercially oriented states of the Northeast. The coincidental resolution of the long-standing controversy over the western land claims of the large "landed" states, which had jeopardized the union throughout the Confederation period, was yet another crucial compromise. States with claims in the trans-Ohio region—Massachusetts, Connecticut, New York, and

Virginia—ceded them to Congress. They did so under the condition that land sales in the new national domain generate revenue for the union as a whole while congressionally administered territories were being prepared for statehood and eventual incorporation into the union. Subsequent cessions from North Carolina and Georgia gave Congress jurisdiction over the Southwest as well as the Northwest. This set the stage for the spread of settlement and expansion of the union throughout the original limits of the United States as defined in the Paris peace treaty of 1783.

The creation of the national domain and the elaboration of Congress's western policy involved complicated calculations of their impact on state and regional interests. New Englanders could anticipate settlement opportunities for their surplus population in addition to the indirect benefits of national land sales revenue. Given the domination of Yankee settlers, the first new state formed in the Northwest Territory might well align itself with New England in the federal political arena. Virginians were equally persuaded that economic and geopolitical logic would draw all new states into their own expanding hinterland. These calculations were periodically recalibrated in the coming decades, particularly as westerners began to articulate their own distinct interests—namely in liberalizing land sales and promoting internal improvements. But the underlying concern over the impact of expansion on the existing balance of power in the union remained—and would remain—paramount. The Jeffersonian "Revolution of 1800" may have banished the specter of a high-toned, energetic national government. However, it did not diminish conventional calculations of relative advantage within the union. Americans would continue to calculate the value of the union until the union itself finally collapsed.

Critics of the Louisiana Purchase charged that the annexation of this vast new territory subverted the compromises that secured vital sectional interests in the federal Constitution. These compromises rested on the new nation's 1783 boundaries—limits that Jefferson conspicuously overlooked in his Inaugural Address. The intersectional balance negotiated at Philadelphia allowed for limited expansion of American territory: delegates understood that new states would be created in the national domain, and perhaps within the limits of some of the larger states. But expansion beyond the new nation's original boundaries was "unconstitutional," both from the perspective of the sort of "strict construction" Jefferson himself ordinarily favored and because the hard bargaining at Philadelphia that made union possible depended on respecting those limits. Would New Englanders have ever agreed to unlimited expansion, knowing that it would relegate them to an increasingly marginal place in the union?

Suppressing his own constitutional scruples, Jefferson insisted that the genius of American federalism was expansive. As he asked in his Second Inaugural Address, "Who can limit the extent to which the federative principle may operate effectively?" He answered, "The larger our association," echoing Madison's rejoinder to Montesquieu, "the less will it be shaken by local passions."[10] Jefferson did not derive his "federative principle" from the Constitution, but instead from the original "association" of revolutionary republics in 1776. Union came first, followed by the elaboration of constitutional provisions for its implementation. Strict construction of the Constitution was the means of securing states' rights and therefore preserving the union. Virginian John Page, one of Jefferson's dearest friends, summarized the Republican gospel in 1799 in this way: The federal Constitution "is the *Instrument* by which the people of the several *confederated states of America* meant to preserve to their respective states their *Independence*...."[11] The Constitution was the means, or "Instrument," of union, not an end in itself, particularly where strict adherence to the constitutional text jeopardized the rights of future states. "A strict observance of the written laws is doubtless one of the high duties of a good citizen," Jefferson explained in 1810, "but it is not the highest. The laws of necessity, of self-preservation, of saving our country when in danger, are of higher obligation."[12]

Federalist anti-expansionists embraced strict construction at precisely the point Jefferson abandoned it. Their disagreement hinged on the history and fundamental character of the union. For Jefferson's opponents, the ratification of the Constitution marked a fundamental break in American political history. The union itself was the product of specific, substantive constitutional compromises, and it ceased to exist when those original understandings were violated. Because the federal government—the institutional embodiment and *sine qua non* of union—also existed because of the Constitution, "loose" constructions of the text that enhanced the administration's effective power were "constitutional." The Constitution—and therefore the union—were only at risk when Republicans subverted the balance of power within the union that the Constitution was meant to secure. Jefferson invoked "reason of state" and the law of national self-preservation when dealing with external enemies; his opponents invoked the same logic in the new nation's domestic affairs. Anti-expansionists therefore insisted that the axioms of conventional political science continued to apply at home as well as abroad. Peace among the American states depended both on maintaining a vigorous central government and on securing the vital interests of the union's original partners.

Conflicting interpretations of American federalism were fully rehearsed in congressional debates over admitting Louisiana to the union, the first new state to be carved out of the Louisiana Purchase. With Louisiana's admission, Rep. Josiah Quincy, a Federalist from Massachusetts, warned, "the bonds of this Union are virtually dissolved." The balance that the founders had so carefully constructed would be "destroyed" if Congress should "throw the weight of Louisiana into the scale."[13] Quincy's controversial speech reflected and anticipated a growing sense of sectional grievance in New England that would culminate in separatist rumblings and opposition to the Madison administration during the War of 1812. The disgruntled Federalists who met at Hartford in 1814 sought to restore the union, and the balance of power that sustained it, to its original state. Yet they also criticized original constitutional provisions—notably the Three-fifths Clause (Article I, Section 3, Paragraph 3, and changed by Section 2 of the Fourteenth Amendment)—that gave slaveholders disproportionate power in Congress. Their action called into question the legitimacy of the union itself.

The Federalists' concerns about westward expansion and the waxing power of southern slaveholders survived the Federalists' demise as a national political party. Their heirs, the Antislavery Restrictionists who sought to bar Missouri's admission as a slave state in 1819, appealed to principle as well as self-interest in opposing the unfettered operation of Jefferson's "federative principle." The proliferation of new slave states made a mockery of the new nation's republican pretensions, even as it extended the influence and power of one section of the union—the slaveholding South—at the expense of the rest.

Conclusion

The history of American federalism at the time of the Louisiana Purchase can be illustrated using two geopolitical axes—East-West and North-South—and their ideological and interpretative correlates.

Jefferson and his Republican coadjutors focused on the East-West axis, celebrating a dynamic federal union's capacity to incorporate new members without dangerously concentrating power in an overbearing central government. Rapid expansion preempted separatist tendencies on the frontier, strengthening the union against external threats. The formation of new states (under the sanction of Article IV, Section 3 of the federal Constitution and the specific provisions of the Confederation Congress's Northwest Ordinance of 1787, and subsequent congressional organic acts) was a progressive, liberal alternative to the colonial rule of empires. Republican administrations would pursue this enlightened anticolonial policy in the vast region of the Louisiana Purchase.

Anti-expansionists instead focused on the North-South axis, emphasizing what the formation of new states implied for the balance of power in the original union. From their skeptical perspective, Jefferson's appeal to the "federative principle" disguised and mystified the concrete interests—of land speculators, Republican politicos, and slaveholding planters—that expansion really served. These interests were not equally distributed throughout the union, notwithstanding the hopes of New Englanders who first promoted settlement in the Ohio country. Jeffersonians may have de-emphasized the kind of strong central government Federalists favored, but they showed a genius for party and state building that successfully linked the nation's expanding periphery to the centers of power. In this way the Jeffersonians showed that control of the federal government was vitally important for promoting the coalition of interests aligned under their party's banner. While Republicans celebrated the triumph of principle, they were vigorously pursuing their own interests. As a result, union was not spontaneously consensual: the Republicans' success depended on their ability to mobilize consent by appealing to a wide array of interests. And the most important interest was always Jefferson's original core constituency—the staple-producing, slaveholding planters of the South.

Advocates of these opposing versions of federalism could easily see through their opponents' pretenses. Republicans argued persuasively that Federalists were out of step with history. They believed an ambitious, enterprising people would not be restrained in their expansive pursuits and would find ways of governing themselves that maintained order without concentrating power. But Federalists understood equally well that the new Republican order served some interests better than others. In their view, territorial expansion under Jeffersonian auspices expanded the empire of slavery as well as the "empire of liberty." The Federalists recognized that the principles of federalism could never be fully separated from the underlying issue of the actual balance of power in the union.

Northern Federalists anticipated the ultimate rupture of the union between North and South in their early opposition to the Louisiana Purchase and westward expansion. After the War of 1812, New Englanders and northerners generally overcame their misgivings about expansion, recognizing new ways they could enjoy its benefits and perhaps even direct its course. In an ironic reversal, southern Old Republicans who had rejected any active role for the federal government in promoting economic development now embraced the separatist logic of northern High Federalists. Increasingly concerned about their diminishing power in Congress and their status as an endangered minority section of America, these southerners began to question the value of the union. Parting company with Jefferson, they no longer envisioned limitless expansion in a dynamic, harmonious United States. They looked north, not west.

Notes

1. "A Declaration by the Representatives of the United States of America, in General Congress Assembled," *Jefferson Writings*, ed. Merrill D. Peterson (New York: Library of America, 1984), 19.
2. Jefferson's First Inaugural Address, 4 March 1801, *Jefferson Writings*, 494.
3. Ibid.
4. Jefferson to A. L. C. Destutt de Tracy, 26 January 1811, *Jefferson Writings*, 1245–1246.

5. *Federalist* No. 10 (Madison), in *The Federalist*, ed. Jacob E. Cooke (Middletown, Conn.: Wesleyan University Press, 1961), 56–65.

6. Thomas Jefferson to Horatio G. Spafford, 17 March 1814, in *The Writings of Thomas Jefferson*, Definitive Edition, vol. 14, ed. Andrew A. Lipscomb and Albert Ellery Bergh (Washington, D.C.: Thomas Jefferson Memorial Association, 1905), 120.

7. Jefferson to William Duane, 28 March 1811, *The Writings of Thomas Jefferson*, 13: 28–29.

8. Jefferson to Mark Landon Hill, 5 April 1820, *The Writings of Thomas Jefferson*, 15: 243.

9. Orasmus Cook Merrill, "The Happiness of America: An Oration Delivered at Shaftsbury, on the Fourth of July" (Bennington, Vt.: Anthony Haswell, 1804), 20.

10. Jefferson's Second Inaugural Address, 4 March 1805, *Jefferson Writings*, 519.

11. John Page, *Address to the Freeholders of Gloucester County, at their Election of a Member of Congress . . . April 24, 1799* (Richmond: 1799), 19.

12. Jefferson to John B. Colvin, 20 September 1810, *Jefferson Writings*, 1231.

13. U.S. Congress, House, *Annals of Congress*, 11th Congress, 3rd Session, 525, 540.

10

Empire of Liberty, Empire of Slavery: The Louisiana Territories and the Fate of American Bondage

ROBERT E. BONNER

It was fitting that Thomas Jefferson announced the Louisiana Purchase on the national anniversary of July 4, 1803, thereby linking America's revolutionary past to his own hopes for a glorious continental future. The new lands west of the Mississippi River gave the president faith in the destiny of a republic suddenly free of foreign intrigue and newly equipped to remain a boundless "empire of liberty" for centuries. But even after the initial problems that accompanied the purchase were resolved, other challenges remained to bedevil the next generation of political leaders. The most important question—could the union survive as it expanded?—would not change. In the quarter-century before the Louisiana Purchase and in the year immediately after it, Americans feared that foreign threats or domestic disputes—especially disputes in the West—would undermine the union. After 1820 this question took a more specific form. Could the union survive the debate over slavery that came with expansion? Concerns about slavery were not new, but they would only begin to dominate the political landscape in the 1820s, after plantation slavery was firmly fixed west of the Mississippi.

The destiny that Jefferson imagined for the Louisiana Purchase would be achieved in many respects during his own lifetime. The War of 1812, conducted by his successor, James Madison, secured the United States' hold on the Mississippi Valley and ensured that this region would indeed become the country's agricultural heartland. Yet the first major expansion of American territory also encapsulated the darker side of Jefferson's legacy, extending an empire of liberty for whites through the creation of a vast empire of slavery for African Americans. The liberty and opportunity achieved in the Louisiana territories came to depend on a system of plantation slavery that by the 1830s had become far more vibrant than it had been under French and Spanish rule. The first state to be carved from the territories of the purchase nurtured a particularly crushing form of bondage in its sugar industry. New Orleans, the territory's only major city, became the hub of a domestic slave trade that serviced an even more dynamic cotton kingdom on both sides of the Mississippi. As tobacco and hemp farms flourished in Arkansas and Missouri, the Louisiana Purchase territories gave imperial scope to America's great contradiction, spreading into the heart of the continent the racially specific blend of freedom and slavery that had first taken shape in Jefferson's own colonial Chesapeake.

In the long run, American acquisition of the Louisiana territories led not just to the extension of slavery, however, but to its final overthrow. Controversies over slavery in lands north of the state of Louisiana fueled sectional tensions that provoked slaveholders to rebellion. During the war to quell this revolt, the federal commitment to an undivided Mississippi Valley helped link the causes of Union and emancipation. The seeds of this development were planted in 1820, when a sectional split over western territories brought the United States to the brink of disunion. Although compromise alleviated that crisis by dividing the Louisiana territories at the line of 36°30′, there was no similarly effective formula to follow during the next major period of territorial expansion in the 1840s. In 1854 Congress overturned the original restriction on slavery throughout most of the Louisiana territories. The result was a political cataclysm, leading in rapid succession to the rise of a free-soil Republican Party, the outbreak of armed conflict in Kansas, and one of the most notorious decisions ever issued by the Supreme Court. No other series of events was more important than this in bringing about the American Civil War and its ultimate consequence of emancipation.

Black slaves had been in the Louisiana territories for nearly a century and a half before slavery, plantation agriculture, and empire brought the union to its greatest crisis. Over this span, these issues shifted in relative importance. An institution considered with some skepticism by European powers in the eighteenth century became fully incorporated in the global economy during the first thirty years of American occupation. The increased number of slaves that fueled this transition remained a controversial presence. However, the potential for black insurrection, which had been the most pressing issue during the colonial and early national periods, gradually became less important than the competition that these black slaves posed to free white farmers. As a result, the pervasive fear of racial conflict that had initially influenced Jefferson's diplomacy during the negotiations for the Louisiana Purchase was displaced by the fear (which would come to haunt even Jefferson himself) that America would face its greatest crisis in a dispute between North and South.

The Perils and Promise of Louisiana Slavery, 1720–1820

Slavery played an ambiguous role in the earliest struggles between rival European empires over the Mississippi Valley borderlands.[1] Though Africans had been part of Hernando de Soto's expedition in the early sixteenth century, black slaves were not brought to North America in significant numbers until two centuries later, when, in the 1720s, French promoters began to consider cultivating tobacco in Louisiana. It soon became evident, however, that introducing bound labor into these territories put larger imperial objectives at risk, especially after an alliance between fugitive slaves and the Natchez Indians led to a bloody war in 1729. The volatility likely to accompany large-scale plantation agriculture threatened the fragile imperial hold on the Mississippi Valley, which was too great a price to pay for uncertain profits. The French scaled back plans for staple crop production accordingly—plans that might have made Louisiana a rival of the Chesapeake or the Caribbean islands. Slavery increased in importance after Spain took possession of Louisiana, especially in the area around New Orleans; but the economic significance of the institution was still relatively limited. That would only change with the introduction of sugar production, first undertaken in the 1790s, when the revolutionary disruption in the cane fields of Saint Domingue initiated a scramble among Caribbean planters for new lands.[2]

The revolutionary turmoil of the 1790s was a seminal moment in Louisiana history, both in initiating an economic transformation to sugar production and in reorienting the territories' strategic importance. The rebellion led by free people of color and slaves in Saint Domingue eventually transformed the wealthiest French colony into the Western Hemisphere's second independent republic. This result was still uncertain in 1800, however, when Napoleon Bonaparte first began to consider how he might revitalize the French empire by reintroducing slavery to its colonial possessions. Napoleon looked to Louisiana as a possible outpost for those French troops charged with crushing the Haitian rebellion. Meanwhile, he also considered making this area a penal colony for those black rebels responsible for the uprising. Although Jefferson was already haunted by the events in the Caribbean, this plan would have been particularly disturbing to him, since it threatened to reverse his own vision of a North American mainland gradually drained of its black population by the colonization of African Americans in the West Indies and in Africa.[3]

American policymakers had a number of reasons to fear a powerful French presence in Louisiana. Perhaps the main concern was the reawakening of alliances between the French and Mississippi Valley Indians, which had threatened British settlers a half-century earlier. The shifting loyalties of backcountry whites also were a factor—especially since Spain, a comparatively weak power, had used its control of the New Orleans trade to gain support from Tennessee and Kentucky settlers. In addition to these anxieties, officials at the highest levels worried about the effect that French occupation of the lower Mississippi might have on American slaves hundreds of miles away. Secretary of State James Madison warned in 1801 that masters "would be excited in the Southern States" about Napoleonic intrigue in Louisiana, because their "numerous slaves have been taught to regard the French as the patrons of their cause." A literate slave named Gabriel had recently led a failed uprising of slaves in Virginia that bore the trace of French influence. The likelihood of further Chesapeake disturbances weighed heavily on Virginia Jeffersonians. Their sense of feeling insecure in their own backyard seemed to resonate in Madison's vague, if pregnant, complaint in 1802 that a French Louisiana would "plant in our neighborhood troubles of different kinds" that would "prepare the way for very serious events."[4]

The most apocalyptic fears about slavery on America's western border were quieted by the Louisiana Purchase, which incorporated Americans' chief objective, New Orleans, as well as an additional 800,000 square miles of territory. Some white Americans had already imagined that the United States might free itself of slavery by colonizing free blacks west of the Mississippi, a program that American ownership of these lands might have bolstered. Yet the Jefferson administration devoted most of its energies to the challenges presented by those African Americans already in the West. Sporadic fears of insurrection continued into James Madison's presidency, when the largest slave revolt in American history erupted north of New Orleans. This 1811 uprising, which involved perhaps several hundred armed slaves (the limited amount of documentary evidence makes an exact number impossible to ascertain), was crushed only by the action of U.S. troops, whose display of force was intended to discourage any further attempt at black revolt. For at least the next decade, Madison and his successor, James Monroe, realized that the Southwest was the country's most vulnerable flank. This perception guided their policies on a range of issues, including the continuing attempt to isolate Haiti, the move to annex Florida to the United States, and early attempts to clear southwestern lands of their Indian inhabitants.[5]

The threat of black rebellion led Congress to place a series of restrictions on Louisiana slavery. The most important of these focused on the Territory of Orleans, the southernmost area of the purchase, which in 1812 became the state of Louisiana. Sen. James Hillhouse of Connecticut successfully led an effort in 1804 to ban the importation of foreign slaves to this area, though his more sweeping attempt to provide for gradual emancipation failed. The restriction on entry was modified the following year so that slaves from within the United States, but not those from either the Caribbean or Africa, could be brought to the Territory of Orleans. Migration into the lower Mississippi Valley remained a federal concern throughout the territorial period, especially in a series of appeals by Caribbean refugees who sought to relocate to Louisiana.[6]

The eastward flow of white settlers into the area proved to be the most effective means of stabilizing Louisiana society. This migration included both free farmers and slaveholders, who, along with other frontier settlers, increasingly turned to growing short-staple cotton. The South's cotton explosion, ignited by late-eighteenth-century advances in ginning technology, served to "release the plantation from the narrow confines of the coastlines and the tobacco belt, and stamp it as the reigning power on all the country," as W. J. Cash memorably put it in his classic work, *The Mind of the South*. The spread of the plantation was especially important in the Mississippi Valley. It was there that, just a short time after the cotton gin's power had been realized, cotton worked to

end stagnation, beat back the wilderness, mow the forest, pour black men and plows and mules along the Yazoo and the Arkansas, spin out the railroad, freight the yellow waters of the Mississippi with panting stern-wheelers, in brief, create the great South.[7]

Within two decades of its acquisition, Lower Louisiana had been incorporated as the western hinterland of an expanding nation. What had been a circuit between the continent and the Gulf of Mexico became a gateway to the continental West. In the process, Louisiana settlers weathered their transition to plantation slavery without the revolutionary disturbances that some had feared. But forced labor still held dangerous implications for the nation, as would be apparent in a different sort of imperial controversy over slavery that broke out in 1820.

Missouri Slavery: Crisis and Compromise

Jefferson expressed renewed concern about the trans-Mississippi empire in 1820, turning his attention to the "firebell in the night" that he heard ringing in Missouri. His famous response to the congressional impasse over Missouri's admission to the union gave the sense that a national emergency had flared up without warning. This was partly true, since the unexpectedly heated debates over the Louisiana territories involved the most wide-ranging debate over slavery yet witnessed in the U.S. Congress. It would be a mistake to see this controversy as the first time that westward expansion had produced sectional tension involving the issue of slavery, however. Earlier incidents influenced the perspective of both sides and caused both to harbor deep suspicions about the motives of their opponents.[8]

It was hard for Jefferson and many of his southern associates to take opposition to slavery in Missouri seriously. From their point of view, the "agitation" of this question was a political ploy to revive the Federalist Party at the expense of the country's western empire. President James Monroe identified the leading advocates of Missouri restriction with their historical indifference toward American rights on the Mississippi River in the 1780s. Sen. William Smith, R-S.C., invoked a more recent parallel, linking the opponents of Missouri slavery with those who had threatened disunion during the debate on Louisiana statehood in 1811. Southerners were quick to associate the northern campaign against Missouri with a sectional agenda that bordered on treason. One of the most common themes in their speeches was the recent opposition

by New England to the War of 1812 that had culminated in the Hartford Convention of 1814.[9]

Northern advocates of a free Missouri had their own set of grievances that mounted up and spilled out during the extended congressional debate. Particularly upsetting to them was the series of Virginians who had assumed the presidency. This was especially irksome since this Jeffersonian ascendancy, which was just entering its third decade, had depended on the three-fifths representation of nonvoting slaves engineered at the Constitutional Convention (Article I, Section 2, Paragraph 3). Several New England leaders had opposed statehood for a slaveholding Louisiana for fear that this power would be further consolidated just as slave rebellion threatened national security. The War of 1812 did not quell these fears, nor did the attempts made afterwards to push into Florida and Texas, and even to spread black bondage to Illinois and Indiana, where the Northwest Ordinance had prohibited slavery since 1787. Although in 1820 there was no recognizable tradition of condemning the southern "slave power," some of the ingredients for such a critique were clearly in place. Hints of this appeared immediately before Congress turned to Missouri in the lengthy review of Gen. Andrew Jackson's execution of two British officers in Florida.[10]

The debate over Missouri drew much of its urgency from the continuing association of the continental heartland with the country's destiny. New York representative James Tallmadge Jr., whose free-soil measures initiated the debate, asked listeners to "extend your view across the Mississippi, over your newly acquired territory" and to "look down the long vista of futurity" and "see your empire, in extent unparalleled" and "occupying all the valuable part of this continent." If these lands were reserved for the "hardy sons of American freemen," then the United States would surpass any country in the world. But if Americans chose to "people this fair dominion with the slaves of your planters," they would "prepare its dissolution" by turning "its accumulated strength into a positive weakness" by putting "poison in your bosom."[11] Faced with a steady assault from other free-soil congressional representatives, southerners responded as best they could by arguing that diffusing slavery over a larger territory would be the best way to accomplish removing it altogether.[12]

After months of heated debates that touched on issues of morality, expediency, security, and national destiny, Congress resolved the 1820 crisis by pairing the admission of Missouri with that of the free state of Maine and then by adding the restriction of slavery in most of the remaining U.S. territory. This legislation, which was followed by a less familiar compromise that allowed Missouri to abridge the rights of free blacks the next year, provided for Missouri's entry into the union. The crisis also established a set of important precedents. From their failure to end Missouri slavery, free-soil advocates learned the practical importance of committing a region for freedom before it was settled extensively and residents applied for statehood. Their subsequent model would be the Northwest Ordinance, which carved "free soil" territory out of thinly settled land. On the other hand, southerners learned that the best way to assure the admission of a slave state was to pair it with a free one. In this way they would mitigate sectional tensions by continu-

ing a political balance of power between North and South. The dual admission of Maine and Missouri became the basis for linking Arkansas, the third state created from the Louisiana territories, with Michigan in 1835. Congress invoked the precedent for a final time in the 1840s when Iowa and Wisconsin, the first free states created from the Louisiana Purchase lands, entered the union along with Florida and Texas.[13]

The most important legacy of the 1820 compromise was the imaginary line drawn across the Louisiana territories at 36°30′. This part of the legislation garnered the least amount of attention at the time and as a result left basic aspects of its legitimacy and implications unexplored. Sen. Jesse Thomas of Illinois offered the measure as an incentive to opponents of slavery, successfully persuading a handful of free-soil advocates in the House of Representatives to change their vote and to permit Missouri to enter the union. Over time, this relic of hard negotiations became an important basis for intersectional trust. It served to remind white Americans of a tradition of sectional compromise that had begun with the disputes between North and South in framing the federal Constitution. In this way, an arbitrary line of latitude took on a talismanic quality that made it a touchstone for future compromise. Some hoped that the extension of this imaginary line to the Pacific would solve the territorial disputes of the 1840s and 1850s, when the future of slavery in the lands acquired during the Mexican-American War transformed national politics. Later, the unsuccessful Crittenden compromise of 1861 tried the same approach, suggesting use of the old geographic line as the best basis for averting civil war.[14] No one offered more effective praise for the "Missouri line" and its place in the American imagination than did Sen. Stephen A. Douglas, D-Ill. In 1849, five years before he would sanction the repeal of the line in the Kansas-Nebraska act, Douglas effusively described how this measure "had become canonized in the hearts of the American people, as a sacred thing, which no ruthless hand would ever be reckless enough to disturb."[15]

Despite his best efforts, Douglas could not persuade other northern members of Congress to accept the "Missouri line" that divided the West between slavery and freedom as a solution for the territorial crisis of the late 1840s. Basic geographic differences between the Louisiana Purchase and the lands acquired from Mexico in 1847 explain this failure. The ban on slavery above 36°30′ had been a clear northern gain in 1820, since the Transcontinental Treaty made it likely that only a single additional slave state, Arkansas, would emerge from the Louisiana territories. Though losing Missouri to slavery, opponents of western slavery could still find solace in the fact that a half-dozen or more free states might be carved from the area set aside in the settlement to this state's immediate west and north. The more southern center of gravity in the lands acquired from Mexico yielded a much different result from the same formula, however. One or more slave states could be expected in the area of New Mexico that lay below 36°30′; slavery would also be permitted to spread to the Pacific and would likely force a division of California between slavery and freedom. Free-soil advocates were unlikely to accept this outcome. This was especially true because their strength in the House of Representatives, as

seen in votes for the free-soil Wilmot Proviso, seemed less conducive to compromise than the Tallmadge restriction on slavery in Missouri had been in 1820.[16]

Proslavery southerners faced this new crisis with a sense of uncertainty. They vacillated between a preference for the extension of the Missouri line, which would have been a practical victory, and a growing sense that the restriction of 1820 had been politically unwise and constitutionally impermissible. Sen. John C. Calhoun, R-S.C., formulated the constitutional case against federal power. In doing so, Calhoun established some of the theoretical groundwork for the Supreme Court's 1857 decision in the case of *Dred Scott v. Sandford*.[17] Southern attitudes toward the territories went beyond questions of constitutional legitimacy, however. This was clear in the observations of South Carolinian William Henry Trescot in 1850. The presence of a line at 36°30′, Trescot argued, should not be considered a national triumph but a "broad declaration that in the American Union there are two people, differing in institutions, feelings, and in the basis of their political faith." Americans in 1820 had realized "that the government could not legislate for both on the same principles and on the same subject, and therefore that as to certain matters of political interest, they must, by an imaginary line, be separated." From Trescot's perspective, there was only one real question left to answer—"Shall this imaginary line become a real boundary?" A disunionist himself, Trescot considered it only a matter of time before this would happen and "the two people, bidding each other a friendly but firm farewell" would "enter upon their paths as separate and independent nations."[18]

The Return and Resolution of Controversy, 1854–1865

Jefferson concluded his warning of 1820 about the Missouri "firebell in the night" on an especially bitter note. The creation of "geographical line, coinciding with a marked principle moral and political," he wrote, threatened to ruin those revolutionary accomplishments associated with the "generation of 1776." These victories, he warned, would soon "be thrown away by the unwise and unworthy passions of their sons." Jefferson's "only consolation," was that "I will not live to weep over it."[19]

Jefferson had been dead for nearly thirty years and the Louisiana territories had been a part of the United States for more than half a century when a new round of debate over slavery in these territories brought the union to a crisis that would be resolved by force rather than through compromise. This turn of events did not occur exactly as Jefferson had imagined. It would be the grandsons of the revolutionaries, not their sons, who would witness the nation's failure. And it would be the decision to strip a line of sectional significance in 1854, not the act of creating one between North and South in 1820, that initiated this renewed period of sectional turmoil. Advocates of slavery initiated the crisis with a bold move. They shifted from a sectional to a national defense of slavery, removing earlier limits on what they thought might become a proslavery American empire in the country's heartland. Their actions led first to disunion and then to a war in which the Mississippi Valley would be reunited on the basis of freedom.

Sen. Stephen Douglas was a key participant in these events, defending the repeal of the "Missouri line" in 1854 as consistent with the failure of Congress to extend it all the way to the Pacific. Most in the North rejected this logic, believing that the agreement had been a fundamental and perpetual pact over a specific territory in 1820, not over the entire national domain. The sense of betrayal was more acute given that these lands were considered a free agricultural paradise for more than thirty years. One New York paper characteristically denounced the repeal as a selfish, diabolical act, in which "the wall . . . erected to guard the domain of Liberty," had been "flung down by the Lords of an American Congress" who now allowed slavery to crawl "like a slimey reptile over the ruins, to defile a second Eden." Such northern outrage spelled political disaster for those directly involved in the decision. Douglas ruined his chance to become president. Meanwhile, his northern Democratic colleagues paid an even higher price at the next election. Southern advocates of slavery also suffered a serious setback, since the uproar over Kansas doomed attempts then under way for the United States to bring slaveholding Cuba into the union.[20]

Western lands had a different effect on political antislavery, rehabilitating its fortunes and giving it a new focus for political action. After the political betrayal of 1854, more acts of proslavery aggression followed in attempting to spread slavery to Kansas. The increasingly violent struggles over these territories eclipsed all other issues in congressional politics by the late 1850s, producing a deadlock between North and South. In 1857 the Supreme Court also entered the fray, deciding in the case of *Dred Scott* that the earlier restriction on slavery had been unconstitutional. This decision, handed down by Chief Justice

Roger B. Taney, deepened the crisis by handing the emerging Republican Party evidence of a concerted conspiracy against freedom at the highest levels of federal power.[21]

It was in this political context that Abraham Lincoln rose to prominence, with his powerful argument that only the Republican Party could save Jefferson's Empire of Liberty from the designs of slavery expansionists. Though Lincoln had little experience in elected office, he gained national stature in challenging Douglas's Senate seat in 1858 and, in a series of famous debates, confronting the future of the Louisiana territories, particularly that of Kansas. Lincoln had some personal knowledge of the Mississippi Valley, having traveled the river to New Orleans as a young man. He combined a deep commitment to the political integrity of this area with a vision of its future as a land of free labor. Though Lincoln lost the Illinois contest with Douglas over this issue, he effectively presented himself as the true heir of the revolutionary founders' vision of a West preserved from the stain of slavery. Lincoln's invocation of Jefferson's promise of an empire of liberty was rhetorically powerful, even if it skirted the concessions to slavery that had been made by the Jeffersonians in administering the Louisiana territories.[22]

Slavery in the Mississippi Valley ended much faster than it had developed. The decision of southern senators to resign their seats after Lincoln's election allowed Kansas to be admitted to the union as a free state in 1861. Then, during the first year of civil war, Lincoln concentrated his attention as commander in chief on wresting control of New Orleans from the Confederacy. As slaveholding Confederates fled before Union troops, many slaves were effectively liberated even before the Emancipation Proclamation was issued on January 1, 1863. This act, though limited in its scope to slaves who lay beyond federal control, changed the basis of the Union effort. The new state constitutions adopted by Arkansas and Louisiana during 1864 officially abolished slavery, and Missouri did the same early in 1865. Although the Louisiana Purchase had divided whites among themselves in the 1850s, African Americans would become important actors during the war, seizing the opportunities of the disruption at slavery's end to flee their masters and then to fight for the Union army.[23]

African Americans' role in their country's imperial battle between slavery and freedom in the Louisiana territories extended long past emancipation into a postwar quest for economic independence. During the Exodusters' movement of the late 1870s, thousands of African Americans helped to complete the transformation of this continental heartland into a land capable of nourishing a Jeffersonian existence for them as well as for whites. Seventy years after an empire of white liberty had been planted at the heart of the North American continent, black migrants from the Deep South crossed the Mississippi River to St. Louis and then trekked across Kansas to establish self-governing farming communities. Settling in yeomen enclaves on the Great Plains, these men and women had arrived at what was quite literally a promised land. In the process, they committed themselves to sharing as fully as they could in the blessings of a United States that spanned a continent.[24]

Notes

1. D. W. Meinig, *The Shaping of America: A Geographical Perspective on 500 years of History*, Vol. 1: *Atlantic America, 1492–1800* (New

Haven: Yale University Press, 1986), 193–202; David J. Weber, *The Spanish Frontier in North America* (New Haven: Yale University Press: 1992), 198–203.

2. Ira Berlin, *Many Thousands Gone: The First Two Centuries of Slavery in North America* (Cambridge: Belknap Press of Harvard University Press, 1999), 77–90.

3. Robert L. Paquette, "Revolutionary Saint Domingue in the Making of Territorial Louisiana," in *A Turbulent Time: The French Revolution and the Greater Caribbean,* ed. David B. Gaspar and David Patrick Geggus (Bloomington: Indiana University Press, 1997); Tim Matthewson, "Thomas Jefferson and Haiti," *Journal of Southern History* 61 (1995): 209–248.

4. Madison to Livingston, 28 September 1801, and Madison to Rufus King, 1 May 1802, in *State Papers and Correspondence Bearing Upon the Purchase of the Territory of Louisiana* (Washington, D.C.: U.S. Government Printing Office, 1903), 6–8, 25; James Sidbury, "Saint Domingue in Virginia: Ideology, Local Meanings, and Resistance to Slavery, 1790–1800," *Journal of Southern History* 53 (1997): 531–553.

5. Robin Blackbourne, *The Overthrow of Colonial Slavery, 1776–1848* (London: Verso, 1988).

6. Don E. Fehrenbacher, *The Slaveholding Republic: An Account of the United States Government's Relations to Slavery* (New York and Oxford: Oxford University Press, 2001), 259–263.

7. W. J. Cash, *The Mind of the South* (New York: Knopf, 1940), 110.

8. Jefferson to John Holmes, Glover Moore, *The Missouri Controversy, 1819–1821* (Lexington: University of Kentucky Press, 1954); Andrew A. Lipscomb and Albert Ellery Bergh, eds., *The Writings of Thomas Jefferson,* Definitive Edition, vol. 10 (Washington, D.C.: Thomas Jefferson Memorial Association, 1905), 157–158.

9. James E. Lewis Jr., *The American Union and the Problem of Neighborhood: The United States and the Collapse of the Spanish Empire, 1783–1829* (Chapel Hill: University of North Carolina Press, 1998), 131–132; Moore, *The Missouri Controversy, 1819–1821.*

10. David W. Blight, "Perceptions of Southern Intransigence and the Rise of Radical Antislavery Thought, 1816–1830," *Journal of the Early Republic* 3 (1983): 139–163.

11. James Tallmadge Jr. in U.S. Congress, *Annals of Congress,* 15th Congress, 2nd Session, 1206; Robert P. Forbes, "Slavery and the Meaning of America" (Ph.D. diss., Yale University, 1994).

12. William H. Freehling, *The Road to Disunion,* Vol. 1: *Secessionists at Bay* (New York and Oxford: Oxford University Press, 1992).

13. Meinig, *The Shaping of America,* 449–456.

14. Peter Knupfer, *The Union as It Is: Constitutional Unionism and Sectional Compromise, 1787–1861* (Chapel Hill: University of North Carolina Press, 1991); David Potter, "The Impending Crisis, 1848–1861," in *The Impending Crisis 1848–1861,* ed. Don E. Ferhenbacher (New York: Harper and Row, 1976).

15. Quotation in Robert W. Johannsen, *Stephen A. Douglas* (New York and Oxford: Oxford University Press, 1973), 255.

16. Don Fehrenbacher, *The Dred Scott Case: Its Significance in American Law and Politics* (New York and Oxford: Oxford University Press, 1978).

17. 60 U.S. (19 How.) 393 (1857).

18. William Henry Trescot, "Oration Delivered Before the Beaufort Volunteer Artillery" (Charleston: Walker and James, 1850), 7.

19. Jefferson to Holmes, *The Writings of Thomas Jefferson,* 10: 157–158.

20. *Albany Evening Journal,* quoted in Michael A. Morrison, *Slavery and the American West: The Eclipse of Manifest Destiny and the Coming of the Civil War* (Chapel Hill: University of North Carolina Press, 1997), 154.

21. John Fiske, *The Mississippi Valley in the Civil War* (Boston and New York: Houghton Mifflin, 1900).

22. Donald Fehrenbacher, *Prelude to Greatness: Lincoln in the 1850s* (Stanford: Stanford University Press, 1962).

23. William H. Freehling, *The South vs. the South: How Anti-Confederate Southerners Shaped the Course of the Civil War* (New York and Oxford: Oxford University Press, 2001).

24. Nell Painter, *Exodusters: Black Migration to Kansas after Reconstruction,* (New York: Knopf, 1976).

Documents

Introduction to the Documents

The documents appear in six sections with the sections (as well as the documents within each section) organized chronologically. There is one logical exception: the first section (comprising documents 1–3), which concerns the Louisiana Purchase itself, enjoys top billing.

The documents include many of the archival materials referred to by the authors in this collection—materials that the authors considered essential to their work and that, reproduced here, help illustrate the factors that shaped the Louisiana Purchase. These documents also stand on their own. They chronicle the workings of the American government at a time of constitutional uncertainty and international dispute and show the fears of policymakers as well as their dreams and goals. These documents also show how the Louisiana Purchase changed over time, beginning with an abstract set of commercial goals during the American Revolution and ending with an agreement that commentators later would consider one of the crowning achievements of American statecraft.

Section I (Documents 1-3): The Louisiana Purchase

"The Louisiana Purchase" is a vague term that actually refers to three separate agreements between the United States and France. The first document in this section, the treaty of cession, is what most people refer to as the Louisiana Purchase (document 1). In this document, France ceded to the United States its holdings on the North American mainland. The subsequent conventions (documents 2 and 3) established specific terms for the sale of Louisiana and provisions for the diplomatic relationship between the United States and France. Even the dates can be confusing. Although the negotiators signed the documents on May 2, 1803, they finalized the agreement on April 30, the date that appears on these documents and the date that Americans associated with the "signing" of the Louisiana Purchase. The signatures are those of Robert R. Livingston, the American minister to France; James Monroe, the American minister plenipotentiary; and Francois Barbé-Marbois, the French minister of the treasury. A former French diplomat in the United States and a personal acquaintance of Monroe, Barbé-Marbois served as Napoleon's representative to the Americans during the Louisiana negotiations.

1

Treaty Between the United States of America and the French Republic

The President of the United States of America and the First Consul of the French Republic in the name of the French People desiring to remove all Source of misunderstanding relative to objects of discussion mentioned in the Second and fifth articles of the Convention of the 8th Vendémiaire an 9 [30 September 1800] relative to the rights claimed by the United States in virtue of the Treaty concluded at Madrid the 27 of October 1795, between His Catholic Majesty & the Said United States, & willing to Strengthen the union and friendship which at the time of the Said Convention was happily reestablished between the two nations have respectively named their Plenipotentiaries to wit The President of the United States, by and with the advice and consent of the Senate of the Said States; Robert R. Livingston Minister Plenipotentiary of the United States and James Monroe Minister Plenipotentiary and Envoy extraordinary of the Said States near the Government of the French Republic; And the First Consul in the name of the French people, Citizen Francis Barbé Marbois Minister of the public treasury who after having respectively exchanged their full powers have agreed to the following Articles.

ARTICLE I

Whereas by the Article the third of the Treaty concluded at St Ildefonso the 9th Vendémiaire an 9 [1st October 1800] between the First Consul of the French Republic and his Catholic Majesty it was agreed as follows.

"His Catholic Majesty promises and engages on his part to cede to the French Republic six months after the full and entire execution of the conditions and Stipulations herein relative to his Royal Highness the Duke of Parma, the Colony or Province of Louisiana with the Same extent that it now has in the hand of Spain, & that it

had when France possessed it; and Such as it Should be after the Treaties subsequently entered into between Spain and other States."

And whereas in pursuance of the Treaty and particularly of the third article the French Republic has an incontestible title to the domain and to the possession of the said Territory—The First Consul of the French Republic desiring to give to the United States a strong proof of his friendship doth hereby cede to the United States in the name of the French Republic for ever and in full Sovereignty the said territory with all its rights and appurtenances as fully and in the Same manner as they have been acquired by the French Republic in virtue of the above mentioned Treaty concluded with his Catholic Majesty.

ART: II

In the cession made by the preceeding article are included the adjacent Islands belonging to Louisiana all public lots and Squares, vacant lands and all public buildings, fortifications, barracks and other edifices which are not private property.— The Archives, papers & documents relative to the domain and Sovereignty of Louisiana and its dependances will be left in the possession of the Commissaries of the United States, and copies will be afterwards given in due form to the Magistrates and Municipal officers of such of the said papers and documents as may be necessary to them.

ART: III

The inhabitants of the ceded territory shall be incorporated in the Union of the United States and admitted as soon as possible according to the principles of the federal Constitution to the enjoyment of all these rights, advantages and immunities of citizens of the United States, and in the mean time they shall be maintained and protected in the free enjoyment of their liberty, property and the Religion which they profess.

ART: IV

There Shall be Sent by the Government of France a Commissary to Louisiana to the end that he do every act necessary as well to receive from the Officers of his Catholic Majesty the Said country and its dependances in the name of the French Republic if it has not been already done as to transmit it in the name of the French Republic to the Commissary or agent of the United States.

ART: V

Immediately after the ratification of the present Treaty by the President of the United States and in case that of the first Consul's shall have been previously obtained, the commissary of the French Republic shall remit all military posts of New Orleans and other parts of the ceded territory to the Commissary or Commissaries named by the President to take possession—the troops whether of France or Spain who may be there shall cease to occupy any military post from the time of taking possession and shall be embarked as soon as possible in the course of three months after the ratification of this treaty.

ART: VI

The United States promise to execute Such treaties and articles as may have been agreed between Spain and the tribes and nations of Indians until by mutual consent of the United States and the said tribes or nations other Suitable articles Shall have been agreed upon.

ART: VII

As it is reciprocally advantageous to the commerce of France and the United States to encourage the communication of both nations for a limited time in the country ceded by the present treaty until general arrangements relative to commerce of both nations may be agreed on; it has been agreed between the contracting parties that the French Ships coming directly from France or any of her colonies loaded only with the produce and manufactures of France or her Said Colonies; and the Ships of Spain coming directly from Spain or any of her colonies loaded only with the produce or manufactures of Spain or her Colonies shall be admitted during the Space of twelve years in the Port of New-Orleans and in all other legal ports-of-entry within the ceded territory in the Same manner as the Ships of the United States coming directly from France or Spain or any of their Colonies without being Subject to any other or greater duty on merchandize or other or greater tonnage than that paid by the citizens of the United. States.

During that Space of time above mentioned no other nation Shall have a right to the Same privileges in the Ports of the ceded territory—the twelve years Shall commence three months after the exchange of ratifications if it Shall take place in France or three months after it Shall have been notified at Paris to the French Government if it Shall take place in the United States; It is however well understood that the object of the above article is to favour the manufactures, Commerce, freight and navigation of France and of Spain So far as relates to the importations that the French and Spanish Shall make into the Said Ports of the United States without in any Sort affecting the regulations that the United States may make concerning the exportation of the produce and merchandize of the United States, or any right they may have to make Such regulations.

ART: VIII

In future and forever after the expiration of the twelve years, the Ships of France shall be treated upon the footing of the most favoured nations in the ports above mentioned.

ART: IX

The particular Convention Signed this day by the respective Ministers, having for its object to provide for the payment of debts due to the Citizens of the United States by the French Republic prior to the 30th Sept. 1800 (8th Vendémiaire an 9) is approved and to have its execution in the Same manner as if it had been inserted in this present treaty, and it Shall be ratified in the same form and in the Same time So that the one Shall not be ratified distinct from the other.

Another particular Convention Signed at the Same date as the present treaty relative to a definitive rule between the contracting parties is in the like manner approved and will be ratified in the Same form, and in the Same time and jointly.

ART: X

The present treaty Shall be ratified in good and due form and the ratifications Shall be exchanged in the Space of Six months after the date of the Signature by the Ministers Plenipotentiary or Sooner if possible.

In faith whereof the respective Plenipotentiaries have Signed these articles in the French and English languages; declaring nevertheless that the present Treaty was originally agreed to in the French language; and have thereunto affixed their Seals.

Done at Paris the tenth day of Floréal in the eleventh year of the French Republic; and the 30th of April 1803.

2

Convention Between the United States of America and the French Republic

The President of the United States of America and the First Consul of the French Republic in the name of the French people, in consequence of the treaty of cession of Louisiana which has been Signed this day; wishing to regulate definitively every thing which has relation to the Said cession have authorized to this effect the Plenipotentiaries, that is to say the President of the United States has, by and with the advice and consent of the Senate of the Said States, nominated for their Plenipotentiaries, Robert R. Livingston, Minister Plenipotentiary of the United States, and James Monroe, Minister Plenipotentiary and Envoy-Extraordinary of the Said United States, near the Government of the French Republic; and the First Consul of the French Republic, in the name of the French people, has named as Pleniopotentiary of the Said Republic the citizen Francis Barbé Marbois: who, in virtue of their full powers, which have been exchanged this day, have agreed to the followings articles:

ART: 1

The Government of the United States engages to pay to the French government in the manner Specified in the following article the sum of Sixty millions of francs independant of the Sum which Shall be fixed by another Convention for the payment of the debts due by France to citizens of the United States.

ART: 2

For the payment of the Sum of Sixty millions of francs mentioned in the preceeding article the United States shall create a Stock of eleven millions, two hundred and fifty thousand Dollars bearing an interest of Six per cent: per annum payable half yearly in London Amsterdam or Paris amounting by the half year to three hundred and thirty Seven thousand five hundred Dollars, according to the proportions which Shall be determined by the french Government to be paid at either place: The principal of the Said Stock to be reimbursed at the treasury of the United States in annual payments of not less than three millions of Dollars each; of which the first payment Shall commence fifteen years after the date of the exchange of ratifications:—this Stock Shall be transferred to the government of France or to Such person or persons as Shall be authorized to receive it in three months at most after the exchange of ratifications of this treaty and after Louisiana Shall be taken possession of the name of the Government of the United States.

It is further agreed that if the french Government Should be desirous of disposing of the Said Stock to receive the capital in Europe at Shorter terms that its measures for that purpose Shall be taken So as to favour in the greatest degree possible the credit of the United States, and to raise to the highest price the Said Stock.

ART: 3

It is agreed that the Dollar of the United States Specified in the present Convention shall be fixed at five francs 3333/100000 or five livres eight Soustournois.

The present Convention Shall be ratified in good and due form, and the ratifications Shall be exchanged the Space of Six months to date from this day or Sooner it possible.

In faith of which the respective Plenipotentiaries have Signed the above articles both in the french and english languages, declaring nevertheless that the present treaty has been originally agreed on and written in the french language; to which they have hereunto affixed their Seals.

Done at Paris the tenth of Floréal eleventh year of the french Republic [30th April 1803].

Robt R Livingston
Jas. Monroe
Barbé Marbois

---

3   Convention Between the United States of America and the French Republic

The President of the United States of America and the First Consul of the French Republic in the name of the French People having by a Treaty of this date terminated all difficulties relative to Louisiana, and established on a Solid foundation the friendship which unites the two nations and being desirous in complyance with the Second and fifth Articles of the Convention of the 8th Vendémiaire ninth year of the French Republic (30th September 1800) to Secure the payment of the Sums due by France to the citizens of the United States have respectively nominated as Plenipotentiaries that is to Say The President of the United States of America by and with the advise and consent of their Senate Robert R. Livingston Minister Plenipotentiary and James Monroe Minister Plenipotentiary and

Envoy Extraordinary of the Said States near the Government of the French Republic: and the First Consul in the name of the French People the Citizen Francis Barbé Marbois Minister of the public treasury; who after having exchanged their full powers have agreed to the following articles.

ART: 1

The debts due by France to citizens of the United States contracted before the 8th Vendémiaire ninth year of the French Republic [30th September 1800] Shall be paid according to the following regulations with interest at Six per Cent; to commence from the period when the accounts and vouchers were presented to the French Government.

ART: 2

The debts provided for by the preceeding Article are those whose result is comprised in the conjectural note annexed to the present Convention and which, with the interest cannot exceed the Sum of twenty millions of Francs. The claims comprised in the Said note which fall within the exceptions of the following articles, Shall not be admitted to the benefit of this provision.

ART: 3

The principal and interests of the Said debts Shall be discharged by the United States, by orders drawn by their Minister Plenipotentiary on their treasury, these orders Shall be payable Sixty days after the exchange of ratifications of the Treaty and the Conventions Signed this day, and after possession Shall be given of Louisiana by the Commissaries of France to those of the United States.

ART: 4

It is expressly agreed that the preceding articles Shall comprehend no debts but Such as are due to citizens of the United States who have been and are yet creditors of France for Supplies for embargoes and prizes made at Sea, in which the appeal has been properly lodged within the time mentioned in the Said Convention 8th Vendémiaire ninth year, [30th Sept 1800].

ART: 5

The preceding Articles Shall apply only, First: to captures of which the council of prizes Shall have ordered restitution, it being well understood that the claimant cannot have recourse to the United States otherwise than he might have had to the Government of the French republic, and only in case of insufficiency of the captors—2d the debts mentioned in the Said fifth Article of the Convention contracted before the 8th Vendémiaire an 9 [30th September 1800] the payment of which has been heretofore claimed of the actual Government of France and for which the creditors have a right to the protection of the United States;—the Said 5th Article does not comprehend prizes whose condemnation has been or Shall be confirmed: it is the express intention of the contracting parties not to extend the benefit of the present Convention to reclamations of American citizens who Shall have established houses of Commerce in France, England or other countries than the United States in partnership with foreigners, and who by that reason and the nature of their commerce ought to be regarded as domiciliated in the places where Such house exist.—All agreements and bargains concerning merchandize, which Shall not be the property of American citizens, are equally excepted from the benefit of the said Conventions, Saving however to Such persons their claims in like manner as if this Treaty had not been made.

ART: 6

And that the different questions which may arise under the preceding article may be fairly investigated, the Ministers Plenipotentiary of the United States Shall name three persons, who Shall act from the present and provisionally, and who shall have full power to examine, without removing the documents, all the accounts of the different claims already liquidated by the Bureaus established for this purpose by the French Republic, and to ascertain whether they belong to the classes designated by the present Convention and the principles established in it or if they are not in one of its exceptions and on their Certificate, declaring that the debt is due to an American Citizen or his representative and that it existed before the 8th Vendémiaire 9th year [30 September 1800] the debtor shall be entitled to an order on the Treasury of the United States in the manner prescribed by the 3d Article.

ART: 7

The Same agents Shall likewise have power, without removing the documents, to examine the claims which are prepared for verification, and to certify those which ought to be admitted by uniting the necessary qualifications, and not being comprised in the exceptions contained in the present Convention.

ART: 8

The Same agents Shall likewise examine the claims which are not prepared for liquidation, and certify in writing those which in their judgement ought to be admitted to liquidation.

ART: 9

In proportion as the debts mentioned in these articles Shall be admitted they Shall be discharged with interest at Six per Cent: by the Treasury of the United States.

ART: 10

And that no debt shall not have the qualifications above mentioned and that no unjust or exorbitant demand may be admitted, the Commercial agent of the United States at Paris or such other agent as the Minister Plenipotentiary or the United States Shall think proper to nominate shall assist at the operations of the Bureaus and cooperate in the examinations of the claims; and if this agent Shall be of the opinion that any debt is not completely proved, or if he shall judge that it is not comprised in the principles of the fifth article above mentioned, and if notwithstanding his opinion the Bureaus established by the french Government should think that it ought to be liquidated, he shall transmit his observations to the board established by the United States, who, without removing documents, shall make a complete examination of the debt and vouchers which Support it, and report the result to the Minister of the United States.—The Minister of the United States Shall transmit his observations in all Such cases to the Minister of the treasury of the French Repub-

lic, on whose report the French Government Shall decide definitively in every case.

The rejection of any claim Shall have no other effect than to exempt the United States from the payment of it, the French Government reserving to itself, the right to decide definitively on Such claim So far as it concerns itself.

ART: 11

Every necessary decision Shall be made in the course of a year to commence from the exchange of ratifications, and no reclamation Shall be admitted afterwards.

ART: 12

In case of claims for debts contracted by the Government of France with citizens of the United States Since the 8th Vendémiaire 9th year [30 September 1800] not being comprised in this Convention may be pursued, and the payment demanded in the Same manner as if it had not been made.

ART: 13

The present convention Shall be ratified in good and due form and the ratifications Shall be exchanged in Six months from the date of the Signature of the Ministers Plenipotentiary, or Sooner if possible.

In faith of which, the respective Ministers Plenipotentiary have signed the above Articles both in the french and english languages, declaring nevertheless that the present treaty has been originally agreed on and written in the french language, to which they have hereunto affixed their Seals.

Done at Paris, the tenth of Floréal, eleventh year of the French Republic. [30th April 1803]

Robt R Livingston
Jas. Monroe
Barbé Marbois

Section II (Documents 4–23): Building a Consensus

As Chapter 1 shows, the reasons why the United States purchased Louisiana arose from various factors as old as American independence. In the quarter-century following the Declaration of Independence, Americans concluded that control of the Mississippi was essential to a prosperous union. This consensus was in part planned, in part coincidental. The documents in this section chronicle that emerging consensus, showing how concerns about the Mississippi fit within broader considerations. In private conversations and correspondence, people extolled the importance of unobstructed trade down the length of the Mississippi and discussed the ongoing problems of European control of the region. From American independence until 1801 (when news of the retrocession reached the United States), the nation controlling that region was Spain. But many Americans concluded that Louisiana had changed hands so many times that it was entirely likely that Spain might yet turn over Louisiana to France or—worst of all in the eyes of American observers—Great Britain.

Documents 4–6: Louisiana, the World Order, and the Challenges Facing the New Republic

Thomas Jefferson and James Madison—the U.S. policymakers who proved most important in shaping the Louisiana Purchase—were among the first Americans to worry about the Mississippi. They had good reason. In 1776 Virginia claimed much of what is now the Midwest. As Virginia settlers moved farther west, Virginia leaders like Jefferson and Madison wondered how they could promote both commerce and security on the Mississippi. In documents 4–6, which date from the 1780s, Jefferson and Madison expressed concerns that were still valid in 1803.

Documents 7–10: The Mississippi in the New Constitutional Order

When Americans like Jefferson and Madison lamented the flaws of the system of government imposed by the Articles of Confederation, among their complaints was the inability of the Articles to create a diplomatic structure that would allow the United States to secure trade down the Mississippi. But Americans were equally afraid that the Mississippi could be the spark that would set off a war between the United States and Spain. The question was how to prevent that sort of war while still supplying the diplomatic muscle that many Americans found so painfully absent in the Articles. These challenges proved difficult as the authors of the Constitution set to work in the summer of 1787. But those same problems also provided powerful ammunition for advocates of the Constitution. The authors of The Federalist repeatedly referred to the Mississippi as they extolled the benefits of the Constitution, claiming that the new federal structure would provide the specific means to serve the nation's interests in the West.

Documents 7–10 show how the Mississippi figured in the process of building the Constitution. The first two passages from the federal convention are the work of James Madison, who kept copious notes of the proceedings even as he emerged as its leading figure. The last two passages are from *The Federalist* (often inaccurately called *The Federalist Papers*), the collection of essays advocating the new federal Constitution. Madison himself contributed to that collection, but the selections here are from the other two contributors, John Jay and Alexander Hamilton.

Documents 11–23: The Mississippi Crisis

As advocates of the Constitution predicted, the new federal system seemed to solve the problems that Americans associated with Louisiana and with the Mississippi. Not only was the federal government able to secure the Treaty of San Lorenzo, which established American trading rights for the length of the Mississippi, but federal control over new territories in the West seemed to guarantee peaceful settlement on the river's eastern banks. Confidence shifted to alarm in 1801, when Americans learned that France had restored its possession of Louisiana through the Treaty of San Ildefonso. The retrocession not only convinced Americans that they faced ongoing dangers from the mercurial European powers, but it also led them to wonder how their own constitutional structure would provide the means to resolve these disputes.

Documents 11–23 illustrate these concerns while showcasing the different venues in which American politicians engaged these issues. The letters from within the Jefferson administration are characteristic examples of private correspondence on diplomatic affairs. Similar letters were even written in rudimentary numeric codes. Meanwhile, official letters between diplomats of different nations were quasi-public efforts by one government to express its position. Finally, a pamphlet like William Duane's was an explicitly public statement, published at a time when pamphlets were among the most important forms of political engagement.

4

Virginia as a Model for an Emerging Nation

Notes on the State of Virginia *was Jefferson's only full-length book. Organized by a set of queries about the commonwealth's geography and population, Jefferson hoped to respond to European critics who derided the potential of the North American landscape and its population. Virginia still held its western reserve when Jefferson began this project in 1781. Not only was it an expansive state, but Jefferson believed that Virginia could provide models for the nation. As a result, this book on one particular state often reads like a commentary on the whole of the United States.*

The Shenandoah branch interlocks with James river about the Blue Ridge, and may perhaps in future be opened. The Mississippi will be one of the principal channels of future commerce for the country westward of the Alleghany. From the mouth of this river to where it receives the Ohio, is one thousand miles by water, but only five hundred by land, passing through the Chickasaw country. From the mouth of the Ohio to that of the Missouri, is two hundred and thirty miles by water, and one hundred and forty by land, from thence to the mouth of the Illinois river, is about twenty-five miles. The Mississippi, below the mouth of the Missouri, is always muddy, and abounding with sand bars, which frequently change their places. However, it carries fifteen feet water to the mouth of the Ohio, to which place it is from one and a half to two miles wide, and thence to Kaskaskia from one mile to a mile and a quarter wide. Its current is so rapid, that it never can be stemmed by the force of the wind alone acting on sails. Any vessel however, navigated with oars, may come up at any time, and receive much aid from the wind. A batteau passes from the mouth of Ohio to the mouth of Mississippi in three weeks, and is from two to three months getting up again.

Source: Thomas Jefferson, from "Query II: A notice of its rivers, rivulets, and how far they are navigable?" in *Notes on the State of Virginia.*

5

Letter from James Madison to Thomas Jefferson, August 20, 1784

In the summer of 1784, thirty-three-year-old James Madison was serving in the Continental Congress and forty-one-year-old Thomas Jefferson had left the United States only a month before for Paris, there to begin his five-year tenure as American minister to France. Meanwhile, Virginia was losing its Mississippi frontier. The state legislature had concluded that it could not effectively govern its western reserve, and both Madison and Jefferson had eagerly advocated that the commonwealth cede the territory to the national government. Jefferson had drafted a preliminary plan for governing that land. This plan was codified in 1787 as the Northwest Ordinance, which in turn served as the model for the territorial system that eventually encompassed the Louisiana Purchase. In this letter, Madison revealed his ongoing attention to matters on the Mississippi, as well as his own understanding of how foreign and domestic factors could work together to endanger the infant republic.

Dear Sir,

Your favor of the lst July, written on the eve of your embarcation from Boston was safely delivered by your servant Bob about the 20th of the same month. Along with it I received the pamphlet on the West India trade . . .

Nothing can delay such a revolution with regard to our staple but an impolitic and perverse attempt in Spain to shut the mouth of the Mississippi against the inhabitants above. I say *delay*, because she can no more finally stop the current of trade down the river than she can that of the river itself. The importance of this matter is in almost every mouth. I am frequently asked what progress has been made towards a treaty with Spain, and what may be expected from her liberality on this point, the querists all counting on an early ability in the western settlements to apply to other motives, if necessary. My answers have, both from ignorance and prudence, been evasive. I have not thought fit, however, to cherish unfavorable impressions, being more and more led by revolving the subject to conclude that Spain will never be so mad as to persist in her present ideas. For want of better matter for correspondence, I will state the grounds on which I build my expectations.

First. Apt as the policy of nations is to disregard justice and the general rights of mankind, I deem it no small advantage that these considerations are in our favour. They must be felt in some degree by the most corrupt councils on a question whether the interest of millions shall be sacrificed to views concerning a distant and paltry settlement; they are every day acquiring weight from the progress of philosophy and civilization, and they must operate on those nations of Europe who have given us a title to their friendly offices, or who may wish to gain a title to ours.

Secondly. May not something be hoped from the respect which Spain may feel for consistency of character on an appeal to the doctrine maintained by herself in the year 1609, touching the Scheld, or at least from the use which may be made of that fact by the powers disposed to favor our views?

Thirdly. The interest of Spain at least ought to claim her attention. 1. A free trade down the Mississippi would make New Orleans one of the most flourishing emporiums in the world, and deriving its happiness from the benevolence of Spain, it would feel a firm loyalty to her government. At present it is an expensive establishment, settled chiefly by French, who hate the government which oppresses them, who already covet a trade with the upper country, will be-

come every day more sensible of the rigor which denies it to them, and will join in any attempt which may be made against their *masters*. 2d. A generous policy on the part of Spain towards the United States will be the cement of friendship and lasting peace with them. A contrary one will produce immediate heart burnings, and sow the *seeds* of inevitable hostility. The United States are already a power not to be despised by Spain; the time cannot be distant when, in spite of all precautions, the safety of her possessions in this quarter of the Globe must depend more on our peaceableness than her own power. 3. In another view, it is against the interest of Spain to throw obstacles in the way of our Western settlements. The part she took during the late war shews that she apprehended less from the power growing up in her neighborhood in a state of independence than as an instrument in the hands of Great Britain. If in this she calculated on the impotence of the United States, when dismembered from the British empire, she saw but little way into futurity; if on the pacific temper of republics, unjust irritations on her part will soon prove to her that these have like passions with other governments. Her *permanent* security seems to lie in the complexity of our federal government, and the diversity of interests among the members of it, which render offensive measures improbable in council and difficult in execution. If such be the case, when thirteen States compose the system, ought she not to wish to see the number enlarged to three and twenty? A source of temporary security to her is our want of naval strength; ought she not, then, to favor those emigrations to the Western land which, as long as they continue, will leave no supernumerary hands for the sea?

Fourthly. Should none of these circumstances affect her councils, she cannot surely so far disregard the usage of nations as to contend that her possessions at the mouth of the Mississippi justify a total denial of the use of it to the inhabitants above, when possessions much less disproportionate at the mouth of other rivers have been admitted only as a title to a moderate toll. The case of the Rhine, the Maese, and the Scheld, as well as the Elbe and Oder, are, if I mistake not, in point here. How far other Rivers may afford parallel cases, I cannot say. That of the Mississippi is probably the strongest in the world.

Fifthly. Must not the general interest of Europe in all cases influence the determinations of any particular nation in Europe, and does not that interest in the present case clearly lie on our side? 1. All the principal powers have, in a general view, more to gain than to lose by denying a right of those who hold the mouths of rivers to intercept a communication with them above. France, Great Britain, and Sweden, have no opportunity of exerting such a right, and must wish a free passage for their merchandize in every country. Spain herself has no such opportunity, and has, besides, three of her principal rivers, one of them the seat of her metropolis, running through Portugal. Russia can have nothing to lose by denying this pretension, and is bound to do so in favor of her great rivers, the Neiper, the Niester, and the Don, which mouth in the Black sea, and of the passage thro' the Dardanelles, which she extorted from the Turks. The Emperor, in common with the inland States of Germany, and, moreover, by his possessions on the Maese and the Scheld, has a similar interest. The possessions of the King of Prussia on the Rhine, the Elbe, and the Oder, are pledges for his orthodoxy . . .

2. In a more important view, the settlement of the Western country, which will much depend on the free use of the Mississippi, will be beneficial to all nations who either directly or indirectly trade with the United States. By a free expansion of our people the establishment of internal manufactures will not only be long delayed, but the consumption of foreign manufactures long continue increasing; and at the same time, all the productions of the American soil, required by Europe in return for her manufactures, will proportionably increase. The vacant land of the United States lying on the waters of the Mississippi is, perhaps, equal in extent to the land actually settled. If no check be given to the emigrations from the latter to the former, they will probably keep pace at least with the increase of our people, till the population of both becomes nearly equal. For twenty or twenty-five years we shall consequently have as few internal manufactures in proportion to our numbers as at present, and at the end of that period our imported manufactures will be doubled. It may be observed, too, that as the market for their manufactures will first increase, and the provision for supplying it will follow, the price of supplies will naturally rise in favor of those who manufacture them. On the other hand, as the demand for the tobacco, indigo, rice, corn, &c., produced by America for exportation, will neither precede nor keep pace with their increase, the price must naturally sink in favor also of those who consume them.

Reverse the case by supposing the use of the Mississippi denied to us, and the consequence is, that many of our supernumerary hands who, in the former case, would be husbandmen on the waters of the Mississippi, will, on the latter supposition, be manufacturers on those of the Atlantic, and even those who may not be discouraged from seating the vacant lands will be obliged, by the want of vent for the produce of the soil, and of the means of purchasing foreign manufactures, to manufacture in a great measure for themselves.

Should Spain yield the point of the navigation of the Mississippi, but at the same time refuse us the use of her shores, the benefit will be ideal only. I have conversed with several persons who have a practical knowledge of the subject, all of whom assure me that not only the right of fastening to the Spanish shore, but that of holding an entrepot in our own, or of using New Orleans as a free port, is essential to a free trade through that channel. It has been said that sea vessels can get up as high as latitude thirty-two to meet the river craft, but it will be with so much difficulty and disadvantage as to amount to a prohibition.

The most intelligent of those with whom I have conversed think that, on whatever footing our trade may be allowed, very judicious provision will be necessary for a fair adjustment of disputes between the Spaniards and the Americans—

disputes which must be not only noxious to trade, but tend to embroil the two nations. Perhaps a joint tribunal, under some modification or other, might answer the purpose. There is a precedent, I see, for such an establishment, in the twenty-first article of the treaty of Munster, in 1648, between Spain and the United Netherlands.

I am informed that, sometime after New Orleans passed into the hands of Spain, her Governor forbid all British vessels navigating under the treaty of Paris to fasten to the shore, and caused such as did so to be cut loose. In consequence of this practice a British frigate went up near the Town, fastened to the shore, and set out guards to fire on any who might attempt to cut her loose. The Governor, after trying in vain to remove the frigate by menaces, acquiesced, after which British vessels indiscriminately used the shore; and even the residence of British Merchants in the town of New Orleans, trading clandestinely with the Spaniards, as well as openly with their own people, was winked at. The Treaty of 1763 stipulated to British subjects, as well as I recollect, no more than the right of navigating the river; and if that of using was admitted under that stipulation, the latter right must have been admitted to be included in the former. . . .

Source: William T. Hutchison et al., eds., *The Papers of James Madison* (Charlottesville and Chicago: University Press of Virginia and the University of Chicago Press), vol. 8: 1–4.

---

6   **Letter from Thomas Jefferson to James Madison, January 30, 1787**

Jefferson and Madison remained active correspondents throughout the former's sojourn in Paris, largely because they continued to share common beliefs. By January 1787 both had concluded that the constitutional order created during the Revolution was incapable of meeting the demands that came with independence. In this letter Jefferson addressed themes that would prove critical that summer at the Constitutional Convention. He attempted to resolve the tensions between liberty and power, between popular involvement and orderly government. But, like Madison three years before, he also addressed the issue of the Mississippi. And like Madison, he believed that development in the West was inseparable from the broader development of the nation.

DEAR SIR,

My last to you was of the 16th of Dec, since which I have received yours of Nov 25, & Dec 4, which afforded me, as your letters always do, a treat on matters public, individual & oeconomical. I am impatient to learn your sentiments on the late troubles in the Eastern states. So far as I have yet seen, they do not appear to threaten serious consequences. Those states have suffered by the stoppage of the channels of their commerce, which have not yet found other issues. This must render money scarce, and make the people uneasy. This uneasiness has produced acts absolutely unjustifiable; but I hope they will provoke no severities from their governments. A consciousness of those in power that their administration of the public affairs has been honest, may perhaps produce too great a degree of indignation: and those characters wherein fear predominates over hope may apprehend too much from these instances of irregularity. They may conclude too hastily that nature has formed man insusceptible of any other government but that of force, a conclusion not founded in truth, nor experience. Societies exist under three forms sufficiently distinguishable. 1. Without government, as among our Indians. 2. Under governments wherein the will of every one has a just influence, as is the case in England in a slight degree, and in our states, in a great one. 3. Under governments of force: as is the case in all other monarchies and in most of the other republics. To have an idea of the curse of existence under these last, they must be seen. It is a government of wolves over sheep. It is a problem, not clear in my mind, that the 1st condition is not the best. But I believe it to be inconsistent with any great degree of population. The second state has a great deal of good in it. The mass of mankind under that enjoys a precious degree of liberty & happiness. It has it's evils too: the principal of which is the turbulence to which it is subject. But weigh this against the oppressions of monarchy, and it becomes nothing. *Malo peiculosam libertatem quam quietam servitutem.* Even this evil is productive of good. It prevents the degeneracy of government, and nourishes a general attention to the public affairs. I hold it that a little rebellion now and then is a good thing, & as necessary in the political world as storms in the physical. Unsuccessful rebellions indeed generally establish the encroachments on the rights of the people which have produced them. An observation of this truth should render honest republican governors so mild in their punishment of rebellions, as not to discourage them too much. It is a medicine necessary for the sound health of government. If these transactions give me no uneasiness, I feel very differently at another piece of intelligence, to wit, the possibility that the navigation of the Mississippi may be abandoned to Spain. I never had any interest Westward of the Alleghaney; & I never will have any. But I have had great opportunities of knowing the character of the people who inhabit that country. And I will venture to say that the act which abandons the navigation of the Mississippi is an act of separation between the Eastern & Western country. It is a relinquishment of five parts out of eight of the territory of the United States, an abandonment of the fairest subject for the paiment of our public debts, & the chaining those debts on our own necks *in perpetuum*. I have the utmost confidence in the honest intentions of those who concur in this measure; but I lament their want of acquaintance with the character & physical advantages of the people who, right or wrong, will suppose their interests sacrificed on this occasion to the contrary interests of that part of the confederacy in possession of present power. If they declare themselves a separate people, we are incapable of a single effort to retain them. Our citizens can never be induced, either as militia or as souldiers, to go there to cut the throats of their own brothers & sons, or rather to be themselves the subjects instead of the perpetraors of the parricide. Nor would that country requite the cost of being retained against the will of it's inhabitants, could it be done. But it cannot be done. They are able already to rescue the navigation of the Mississippi out of the hands of Spain, & to add New Orleans to their own territory. They will be joined by the inhabitants of Louisiana. This will bring on a war between them & Spain; and that will produce the question with us whether it will not be worth our while to become parties with them in the war, in order to reunite them with us, & thus correct our error? & were I to permit my forebodings to go one step further, I should predict that the inhabitants of the U S would force their rulers to take the affirmative of that question. I wish I may be mistaken in all these opinions. . . .

Source: William T. Hutchison et al., eds., *The Papers of James Madison* (Charlottesville and Chicago: University Press of Virginia and the University of Chicago Press), vol. 9: 247–252.

7

Comments of Gouverneur Morris at the Constitutional Convention, July 13, 1787

A distinction had been set up & urged, between the Nn. & Southn. States. He had hitherto considered this doctrine as heretical. He still thought the distinction groundless. He sees however that it is persisted in; and that the Southn. Gentlemen will not be satisfied unless they see the way open to their gaining a majority in the public Councils. The consequence of such a transfer of power from the maritime to the interior & landed interest will he foresees be such an oppression of commerce, that he shall be obliged to vote for ye. vicious principle of equality in the ed. branch in order to provide some defence for the N. States agst. it. But to come now more to the point, either this distinction is fictitious or real: if fictitious let it be dismissed & let us proceed with due confidence. If it be real, instead of attempting to blend incompatible things, let us at once take a friendly leave of each other. There can be no end of demands for security if every particular interest is to be entitled to it. The Eastern States may claim it for their fishery, and for other objects, as the Southn. States claim it for their peculiar objects. In this struggle between the two ends of the Union, what part ought the Middle States in point of policy to take: to join their Eastern brethren according to his ideas. If the Southn. States get the power into their hands, and be joined as they will be with the interior Country they will inevitably bring on a war with Spain for the Mississippi. This language is already held. The interior Country having no property nor interest exposed on the sea, will be little affected by such a war. He wished to know what security the Northn. & middle States will have agst. this danger. It has been said that N.C.S.C. and Georgia only will in a little time have a majority of the people of America. They must in that case include the great interior Country, and every thing was to be apprehended from their getting the power into their hands.

Source: Max Farrand, ed., *Notes of the Debates in the Federal Convention of 1787* (New Haven: Yale University Press, 1911), 604–605.

8

From Proceedings at the Constitutional Convention, August 28, 1787

Mr. Sherman from the Committee to whom were referred several propositions on the 25th. instant, made the following report—

That there be inserted after the 4 clause of 7th. section

"Nor shall any regulation of commerce or revenue give" preference to the ports of one State over those of another, "or oblige vessels bound to or from any State to enter, clear or pay duties in another and all tonnage, duties, imposts" & excises laid by the Legislature shall be uniform throughout "the U. S." Ordered to lie on the table. . . .

Mr. Govr. Morris thought the regulation necessary to prevent the Atlantic States from endeavouring to tax the Western States—& promote their interest by opposing the navigation of the Mississippi which would drive the Western people into the arms of G. Britain.

Source: Max Farrand, ed., *Notes of the Debates in the Federal Convention of 1787* (New Haven: Yale University Press, 1911), 441–442.

9

Federalist No. 3

To the People of the State of New York: MY LAST paper assigned several reasons why the safety of the people would be best secured by union against the danger it may be exposed to by JUST causes of war given to other nations; and those reasons show that such causes would not only be more rarely given, but would also be more easily accommodated, by a national government than either by the State governments or the proposed little confederacies.

But the safety of the people of America against dangers from FOREIGN force depends not only on their forbearing to give JUST causes of war to other nations, but also on their placing and continuing themselves in such a situation as not to INVITE hostility or insult; for it need not be observed that there are PRETENDED as well as just causes of war.

It is too true, however disgraceful it may be to human nature, that nations in general will make war whenever they have a prospect of getting anything by it; nay, absolute monarchs will often make war when their nations are to get nothing by it, but for the purposes and objects merely personal, such as thirst for military glory, revenge for personal affronts, ambition, or private compacts to aggrandize or support their particular families or partisans. These and a variety of other motives, which affect only the mind of the sovereign, often lead him to engage in wars not sanctified by justice or the voice and interests of his people. But, independent of these inducements to war, which are more prevalent in absolute monarchies, but which well deserve our attention, there are others which affect nations as often as kings; and some of them will on examination be found to grow out of our relative situation and circumstances.

With France and with Britain we are rivals in the fisheries, and can supply their markets cheaper than they can themselves, notwithstanding any efforts to prevent it by bounties on their own or duties on foreign fish.

With them and with most other European nations we are rivals in navigation and the carrying trade; and we shall deceive ourselves if we suppose that any of them will rejoice to see it flourish; for, as our carrying trade cannot increase without in some degree diminishing theirs, it is more their interest, and will be more their policy, to restrain than to promote it.

In the trade to China and India, we interfere with more than one nation, inasmuch as it enables us to partake in advantages which they had in a manner monopolized, and as we thereby supply ourselves with commodities which we used to purchase from them.

The extension of our own commerce in our own vessels cannot give pleasure to any nations who possess territories on or near this continent, because the cheapness and excellence of our productions, added to the circumstance of vicinity, and the enterprise and address of our merchants and navigators, will give us a greater share in the advantages which those territories afford, than consists with the wishes or policy of their respective sovereigns.

Spain thinks it convenient to shut the Mississippi against us on the one side, and Britain excludes us from the Saint Lawrence on the other; nor will either of them permit the other waters which are between them and us to become the means of mutual intercourse and traffic.

From these and such like considerations, which might, if consistent with prudence, be more amplified and detailed, it is easy to see that jealousies and uneasinesses may gradually slide into the minds and cabinets of other nations, and that we are not to expect that they should regard our advancement in union, in power and consequence by land and by sea, with an eye of indifference and composure.

The people of America are aware that inducements to war may arise out of these circumstances, as well as from others not so obvious at present, and that whenever such inducements may find fit time and opportunity for operation, pretenses to color and justify them will not be wanting. Wisely, therefore, do they consider union and a good national government as necessary to put and keep them in SUCH A SITUATION as, instead of INVITING war, will tend to repress and discourage it. That situation consists in the best possible state of defense, and necessarily depends on the government, the arms, and the resources of the country.

As the safety of the whole is the interest of the whole, and cannot be provided for without government, either one or more or many, let us inquire whether one good government is not, relative to the object in question, more competent than any other given number whatever.

One government can collect and avail itself of the talents and experience of the ablest men, in whatever part of the Union they may be found. It can move on uniform principles of policy. It can harmonize, assimilate, and protect the several parts and members, and extend the benefit of its foresight and precautions to each. In the formation of treaties, it will regard the interest of the whole, and the particular interests of the parts as connected with that of the whole. It can apply the resources and power of the whole to the defense of any particular part, and that more easily and expeditiously than State governments or separate confederacies can possibly do, for want of concert and unity of system. It can place the militia under one plan of discipline, and, by putting their officers in a proper line of subordination to the Chief Magistrate, will, as it were, consolidate them into one corps, and thereby render them more efficient than if divided into thirteen or into three or four distinct independent companies.

What would the militia of Britain be if the English militia obeyed the government of England, if the Scotch militia obeyed the government of Scotland, and if the Welsh militia obeyed the government of Wales? Suppose an invasion; would those three governments (if they agreed at all) be able, with all their respective forces, to operate against the enemy so effectually as the single government

of Great Britain would? We have heard much of the fleets of Britain, and the time may come, if we are wise, when the fleets of America may engage attention. But if one national government, had not so regulated the navigation of Britain as to make it a nursery for seamen—if one national government had not called forth all the national means and materials for forming fleets, their prowess and their thunder would never have been celebrated. Let England have its navigation and fleet—let Scotland have its navigation and fleet—let Wales have its navigation and fleet—let Ireland have its navigation and fleet—let those four of the constituent parts of the British empire be under four independent governments, and it is easy to perceive how soon they would each dwindle into comparative insignificance.

Apply these facts to our own case. Leave America divided into thirteen or, if you please, into three or four independent governments—what armies could they raise and pay—what fleets could they ever hope to have? If one was attacked, would the others fly to its succor, and spend their blood and money in its defense? Would there be no danger of their being flattered into neutrality by its specious promises, or seduced by a too great fondness for peace to decline hazarding their tranquillity and present safety for the sake of neighbors, of whom perhaps they have been jealous, and whose importance they are content to see diminished? Although such conduct would not be wise, it would, nevertheless, be natural. The history of the states of Greece, and of other countries, abounds with such instances, and it is not improbable that what has so often happened would, under similar circumstances, happen again.

But admit that they might be willing to help the invaded State or confederacy. How, and when, and in what proportion shall aids of men and money be afforded? Who shall command the allied armies, and from which of them shall he receive his orders? Who shall settle the terms of peace, and in case of disputes what umpire shall decide between them and compel acquiescence? Various difficulties and inconveniences would be inseparable from such a situation; whereas one government, watching over the general and common interests, and combining and directing the powers and resources of the whole, would be free from all these embarrassments, and conduce far more to the safety of the people.

But whatever may be our situation, whether firmly united under one national government, or split into a number of confederacies, certain it is, that foreign nations will know and view it exactly as it is; and they will act toward us accordingly. If they see that our national government is efficient and well administered, our trade prudently regulated, our militia properly organized and disciplined, our resources and finances discreetly managed, our credit re-established, our people free, contented, and united, they will be much more disposed to cultivate our friendship than provoke our resentment. If, on the other hand, they find us either destitute of an effectual government (each State doing right or wrong, as to its rulers may seem convenient), or split into three or four independent and probably discordant republics or confederacies, one inclining to Britain, another to France, and a third to Spain, and perhaps played off against each other by the three, what a poor, pitiful figure will America make in their eyes! How liable would she become not only to their contempt but to their outrage, and how soon would dear-bought experience proclaim that when a people or family so divide, it never fails to be against themselves.

Source: Publius (John Jay), "The Same Subject Continued (Concerning Dangers From Foreign Force and Influence) for the *Independent Journal.*"

10   *Federalist* No. 15

. . . We may indeed with propriety be said to have reached almost the last stage of national humiliation. There is scarcely anything that can wound the pride or degrade the character of an independent nation which we do not experience. Are there engagements to the performance of which we are held by every tie respectable among men? These are the subjects of constant and unblushing violation. Do we owe debts to foreigners and to our own citizens contracted in a time of imminent peril for the preservation of our political existence? These remain without any proper or satisfactory provision for their discharge. Have we valuable territories and important posts in the possession of a foreign power which, by express stipulations, ought long since to have been surrendered? These are still retained, to the prejudice of our interests, not less than of our rights. Are we in a condition to resent or to repel the aggression? We have neither troops, nor treasury, nor government. Are we even in a condition to remonstrate with dignity? The just imputations on our own faith, in respect to the same treaty, ought first to be removed. Are we entitled by nature and compact to a free participation in the navigation of the Mississippi? Spain excludes us from it. . . .

It is true, as has been before observed that facts, too stubborn to be resisted, have produced a species of general assent to the abstract proposition that there exist material defects in our national system; but the usefulness of the concession, on the part of the old adversaries of federal measures, is destroyed by a strenuous opposition to a remedy, upon the only principles that can give it a chance of success. While they admit that the government of the United States is destitute of energy, they contend against conferring upon it those powers which are requisite to supply that energy. They seem still to aim at things repugnant and irreconcilable; at an augmentation of federal authority, without a diminution of State authority; at sovereignty in the Union, and complete independence in the members. They still, in fine, seem to cherish with blind devotion the political monster of an imperium in imperio. This renders a full display of the principal defects of the Confederation necessary, in order to show that the evils we experience do not proceed from minute or partial imperfections, but from fundamental errors in the structure of the building, which cannot be amended otherwise than by an alteration in the first principles and main pillars of the fabric.

Source: Publius (Alexander Hamilton), "The Insufficiency of the Present Confederation to Preserve the Union for the *Independent Journal.*"

11 Letter from Rufus King to James Madison, March 29, 1801

Rufus King was one of the few Federalists to remain in office after the Republican Party won the presidency in 1800. Appointed the American minister to Great Britain in 1796, he served the Jefferson administration faithfully until 1803, when he left London just as Americans were debating the Louisiana Purchase.

In confirmation of the rumours of the day, Carnot's answer to Bailleul, published during the Exile of the former, states the Project which had been discussed in the Directory to obtain from Spain a cession of Louisiana and the Floridas. A reference to that performance, copies of which I at the time sent to the Department of State, will shew the manner in which it was expected to obtain the consent of Spain, as well as afford a clue to the views of France in seeking this establishment. What was then meditated, has in all probability since been executed: the cession of Tuscany to the infant Duke of Parma, by the Treaty between France and Austria, forms a more compact and valuable compensation to this Branch of the House of Spain than was formerly thought of, and adds very great credit to the opinion which at this time prevails both at Paris and London that Spain has in return actually ceded Louisiana and the Floridas to France. There is reason to know that it is the opinion of certain influential Persons in France that nature has marked a line of Separation between the People of the United States living upon the two sides of the range of Mountains which divides their Territory. Without discussing the considerations which are suggested in support of this Opinion, or the false consequences, as I wish to believe them, deduced from it, I am apprehensive that this cession is intended to have, and may actually produce, Effects injurious to the Union and consequent happiness of the People of the United States. Louisiana and the Floridas may be given to the French Emigrants, as England once thought of giving them to the American Tories; or they may constitute the Reward of some of the Armies which can be spared at the end of the War.

I hear that General Collot, who was a few years ago in America, and a Traveller in the Western Country, and who for sometime has been in disgrace and confinement in France, has been lately set at liberty; and that he, with a considerable number of disaffected and exiled Englishmen, Scotchmen and Irishmen, is soon to proceed from France to the United States. Whether their voyage has any relation to the cession of Louisiana is matter of mere conjecture, but having heard of it in connection with that Project, I think proper to mention it to you.

What effect a plain and judicious representation upon this Subject, made to the French Government by a Minister of Talents and entitled to confidence, would be likely to have is quite beyond any means of judging which I possess; but on this account, as well as others of importance, it is a subject of regret that we have not such a character at this time at Paris. . . .

Source: Robert J. Brugger et al., eds., *The Papers of James Madison: Secretary of State Series* (Charlottesville: University Press of Virginia), vol. 1: 55–56.

12   **Letter from Thomas Jefferson to Robert R. Livingston, April 18, 1802**

Among Thomas Jefferson's most bellicose statements on Louisiana, this letter is extremely important but often misunderstood. Here Jefferson expressed his growing frustration with the Europeans and his conviction that the United States needed a speedy resolution of the Mississippi crisis. He dispatched this letter with his friend, Pierre Samuel Du Pont de Nemours, who was traveling to France. Jefferson's covering letter to Du Pont expressed equal frustration. Together, the two letters suggest that Jefferson was considering a war or a foreign alliance. These were brief flirtations, however, and Jefferson soon concluded that only a diplomatic resolution would be possible or acceptable.

. . . The cession of Louisiana and the Floridas by Spain to France works most sorely on the U.S. On this subject the Secretary of State has written to you fully. Yet cannot forbear recurring to it personally, so deep is the impression it makes in my mind. It compleatly reverses all the political relations of the U.S. and will form a new epoch in our political course. Of all nations of any consideration France is the one which hitherto has offered the fewest points on which we could have any conflict of right, and the most points of a communion of interests. From these causes we have ever looked to her as our natural friend, as one with which we never could have an occasion of difference. Her growth therefore we viewed as our own, her misfortunes ours. There is on the globe one single spot, the possessor of which is our natural and habitual enemy. It is New Orleans, through which the produce of three-eighths of our territory must pass to market, and from its fertility it will ere long yield more than half of our whole produce and contain more than half our inhabitants. France placing herself in that door assumes to us the attitude of defiance. Spain might have retained it quietly for years. Her pacific dispositions, her feeble state, would induce her to increase our facilities there, so that her possession of the place would be hardly felt by us, and it would not perhaps be very long before some circumstance might arise which might make the cession of it to us the price of something of more worth to her. Not so can it ever be in the hands of France. The impetuosity of her temper,

the energy and restlessness of her character, placed in a point of eternal friction with us, and our character, which though quiet, and loving peace and the pursuit of wealth, is high-minded, despising wealth in competition with insult or injury, enterprising and energetic as any nation on earth, these circumstances render it impossible that France and the U.S. can continue long friends when they meet in so irritable aposition. They as well as we must be blind if they do not see this; and we must be very improvident if we do not begin to make arrangements on that hypothesis. The day that France takes possession of N. Orleans fixes the sentence which is to restrain her forever within her low water mark. It seals the union of two nations who in conjunction can maintain exclusive possession of the ocean. From that moment we must marry ourselves to the British fleet and nation. We must turn all our attentions to a maritime force, for which our resources place us on very high grounds: and having formed and cemented together a power which may render reinforcement of her settlements here impossible to France, make the first cannon, which shall be fired in Europe the signal for tearing up any settlement she may have made, and for holding the two continents of America in sequestration for the common purposes of the united British and American nations. This is not a state of things we seek or desire. It is one which this measure, if adopted by France, forces on us, as necessarily as any other cause, by the laws of nature, brings on its necessary effect. It is not from a fear of France that we deprecate this measure proposed by her. For however greater her force is than ours compared in the abstract, it is nothing in comparison of ours when to be exerted on our soil. But it is from a sincere love of peace, and a firm persuasion that bound to France by the interests and the strong sympathies still existing in the minds of our citizens, and holding relative positions which ensure their continuance we are secure of a long course of peace. Whereas the change of friends, which will be rendered necessary if France changes that position, embarks us necessarily as a belligerent power in the first war of Europe. In that case France will have held possession of New Orleans during the interval of a peace, long or short, at the end of which it will be wrested from her. Will this short-lived possession have been an equivalent to her for the transfer f such a weight into the scale of her enemy? Will not the amalgamation of a young, thriving, nation continue to that enemy the health and force which are at present so evidently on the decline? And will a few years possession of N. Orleans add equally to the strength of France? She may say she needs Louisiana for the supply of her West Indies. She does not need it in time of peace. And in war she could not depend on them because they would be so easily intercepted. I should suppose that all these considerations might in some proper form be brought into view of the government of France. Tho' stated by us, it ought not to give offence; because we do not bring them forward as a menace, but as consequences not controulable by us, but inevitable from the course of things. We mention them not as things which we desire by any means, but as things we deprecate; and we beseech a friend to look forward and to prevent them for our common interests.

If France considers Louisiana however as indispensable for her views she might perhaps be willing to look about for arrangements which might reconcile it to our interests. If anything could do this it would be the ceding to us the island of New Orleans and the Floridas. This would certainly in a great degree remove the causes of jarring and irritation between us, and perhaps for such a length of time as might produce other means of making the measure permanently conciliatory to our interests and friendships. It would at any rate relieve us from the necessity of taking immediate measures for countervailing such an operation by arrangements in another quarter. Still we should consider N. Orleans and the Floridas as equivalent for the risk of a quarrel with France produced by her vicinage. I have no doubt you have urged these considerations on every proper occasion with the government where you are. They are such as must have effect if you can find the means of producing thorough reflection on them by that government. The idea here is that the troops sent to St. Domingo, were to proceed to Louisiana after finishing their work in that island. If this were the arrangement, it will give you time to return again and again to the charge, for the conquest of St. Domingo will not be a short work. It will take considerable time to wear down a great number of souldiers. Every eye in the U.S. is now fixed on this affair of Louisiana. Perhaps nothing since the revolutionary war has produced more uneasy sensations through the body of the nation. Notwithstanding temporary bickerings have taken place with France, she has still a strong hold on the affections of our citizens generally. I have thought it not amiss, by way of supplement to the letters of the Secretary of State to write you this private one to impress you with the importance we affix to this transaction. I pray you to cherish Dupont. He has the best dispositions for the continuance of friendship between the two nations, and perhaps you may be able to make a good use of him. Accept assurances of my affectionate esteem and high consideration.

Source: Paul Leicester Ford, ed., *The Works of Thomas Jefferson* (New York: G.P. Putnam's Sons, 1904–1905), vol. 8: 142–145.

13   ## Letter from Thomas Jefferson to Pierre Samuel Du Pont de Nemours, April 25, 1802

Jefferson dispatched his April 18 letter (document 12) with a trusted fiend, Pierre Samuel Du Pont de Nemours, who came from the wealthy Delaware family whose company was making gunpowder in 1803 but which eventually diversified into manufacturing a broad range of chemicals. Although technically a cover letter, Jefferson could not resist the opportunity to repeat his frustrations with the state of European affairs.

. . . you may be able to impress on the government of France the inevitable consequences of their taking possession of Louisiana; and tho', as I here mention, the cession of N. Orleans & the Floridas to us would be palliative; yet I believe it would be no more; and that this measure will cost France, & perhaps not very long hence, a war which will annihilate her on the ocean, and place that element under the despotism of two nations, which I am not reconciled to the more because my own would be one of them. Add to this the exclusive appropriation of both continents of America as a consequence. I wish the present order of things to continue, and with a view to this I value highly a state of friendship between France & us. You know too well how sincere I have ever been in these dispositions to doubt them. You know too how much I value peace, and how unwillingly I should see any event take place which would render war a necessary resource; and that all our movements should change their character and object. I am thus open with you, because I trust that you will have it in your power to impress on that government considerations, in the scale against which the possession of Louisiana is nothing. In Europe, nothing but Europe is seen, or supposed to have any right in the affairs of nations. But this little event, of France's possessing herself of Louisiana, which is thrown in as nothing, as a mere make-weight, in the general settlement of accounts, this speck which now appears as an almost invisible point in the horizon, is the embryo of a tornado which will burst on the countries on both sides of the Atlantic and involve in it's effects their highest destinies. That it may yet be avoided is my sincere prayer, and if you can be the means of informing the wisdom of Buonaparte of all it's consequences, you [will] have deserved well of both countries. Peace and abstinence from European interferences are our objects, and so will continue while the present order of things in America remain uninterrupted. There is another service you can render. I am told that Talleyrand is personally hostile to us. This I suppose, has been occasioned by the XYZ history. [The XYZ Affair was an embarrassing attempt by Talleyrand in 1797 to extort money from the United States in exchange for negotiations to settle mounting French-American tensions.] But he should consider that that was the artifice of a party, willing to sacrifice him to the consolidation of their power: That this nation has done him justice by dismissing them; that those in power [now], are precisely those who disbelieved that story, and saw in it nothing but an attempt to deceive our country: that we entertain towards him personally the most friendly dispositions; that as to the government of France, we know too little of the state of things there, to understand what it is, and have no inclination to meddle in their settlement. Whatever government they establish, we wish to be well with it. . . .

Source: Dumas Malone, ed., *Correspondence Between Thomas Jefferson and Pierre Samuel Du Pont de Nemours 1798–1817* (Boston: Houghton Mifflin, 1930), 46–49.

14   Letter from James Madison to Carlos Martinez de Yrujo, November 25, 1802

This letter exemplifies the sort of not-so-subtle anger that could flow through seemingly cordial correspondence. In this communication with the Spanish minister to the United States, James Madison expressed the Jefferson administration's reaction to news that the Spanish intendant at New Orleans had restricted American merchants. Whether this was the act of a rogue official (as proved to be the case) or a concerted policy of the Spanish government was not yet clear to the administration, but Madison admitted to himself that the retrocession seemed to have nullified Spanish agreements with the United States.

Information has just been received that the Port of New Orleans has been shut against the Commerce of the U. States from the Ocean into the Mississippi; and that the right of American Citizens to deposit their Merchandizes and effects in that port has also been prohibited, without substitution of any equivalent establishment on the Banks of the Mississippi. An extract from the proclamation, by which the latter prohibitions made is herein inclosed. It is impossible to see in either of these measures any thing less than a direct and gross violation of the terms as well as spirit of the Treaty of 1795 between his Catholic Majesty and the United States and the Minister Plenipotentiary of the United States at Madrid will be instructed by the President to represent it to the Spanish Government that in the mean time it is thought proper to communicate to you the wrong which has been done, that you may have an opportunity of using such interpositions as the occasion may require. The President is persuaded Sir that you will endeavor to render them both as expeditious and as efficacious as possible, not only from your personal candor and regard for right, but from the further consideration of the indemnification which will justly accrue for american citizens, whose property to a very great amount will soon be exposed to the injurious consequences of this proceeding. . . .

Source: Robert J. Brugger et al., eds., *The Papers of James Madison: Secretary of State Series* (Charlottesville: University Press of Virginia), vol. 4: 139–140.

15   Letter from Robert R. Livingston to James Madison, November 10, 1802

If the Spanish were frustrating, the French could be frightening. Members of the Jefferson administration often described the Spanish government as corrupt and old-fashioned. By contrast, the Napoleonic regime seemed the harbinger of a new, violent extremism. Even as American policymakers attempted to secure a resolution to the Mississippi crisis through negotiations with France, they also worried that the French might eject the Spanish from Louisiana as a prelude to establishing a French empire on the American mainland. Robert Livingston certainly expected as much in the winter of 1802, when he heard that Napoleon was dispatching an armada across the Atlantic. Although most of these troops were intended to suppress the revolt in Saint Domingue, others were earmarked for Louisiana.

The urgency in Livingston's letter proved unnecessary. The expedition encountered considerable delays in Holland, and Napoleon had decided to abandon both Saint Domingue and Louisiana before the armada was ready to sail.

Note: *Passages in italic were originally encoded text. They were decoded by the editors of the* Papers of James Madison.

France has cut the knot. The difficulties relative to Parma and Placentia that stopped the expedition to Louisiana have ended by their taking possession of the first. As you see by the enclosed paper, orders are given for the immediate embarkation of troops (two demi briages) for Louisiana they will sail about twenty days from Holland. *The government here will give no answer to my notes on the subject. They will say nothing on that of their limit or of our rights under the Spanish treaty. Clerk* [Daniel Clark, an Irish-born merchant who served as deputy American consul in New Orleans] *has been presented to General Victoire* [Claude-Victor Perrin, who was supposed to command the expedition] *as a merchant from Louisiana taking him for a French citizen the general he says did not conceal their views which are nothing short of taking exactly what they find* convenient. When asked what they meant to do *as to our right of entrep he spoke of the treaty as wastepaper* & the préfet did not know that *we had such right tho* it had been the subject of many conversations with the minister & of three different notes. The sum

voted for this service is two millions & a half as to the rest they expect *to compel the people to support the expences of government which will be very heavy as the* number & suite of the officers civil & military are great, and they are not empowered *to draw so that the first act of the new government will be the oppression of their people and of our commerce.* I believe you may add to this early *attempted to corrupt our western people* & if I may judge by the temper that *the general will carry with him an early attempt upon the Natchez which they consider as the rival of New Orleans.* If you will look back to some of my letters on this subject you will see my opinion of the necessity *of strengthening ourselves* as soon as possible both *by forces and ships at home and by alliance abroad.* No prudence will I hear *prevent hostilities ere long and perhaps the sooner their plans develop themselves the better.* In a letter to the president sent by the way of England I mention a conversation with *Joseph Bonaparte* from which I derived some small hopes, but they are of no avail now that the expedition is determined upon. . . .

Source: Robert J. Brugger et al., eds., *The Papers of James Madison: Secretary of State Series* (Charlottesville: University Press of Virginia), vol. 4: 110–111.

---

16   William Duane on the Mississippi Question

William Duane helped found newspaper and pamphlet publishing in the United States. Born in Ireland in 1760, he immigrated to the United States, settling in Philadelphia. He published the Aurora, which set standards for journalism throughout the country. Like many newspaper publishers, Duane engaged in the equally important pamphlet trade. In this excerpt, he explains the options offered by Federalist senator James Ross of Pennsylvania to address and resolve the Spanish policy of restricting American trade on the Mississippi River.

. . . Mr. Ross said, that although he came from a part of the country where the late events upon the Mississippi had excited great alarm and solicitude; he had hitherto forborne the expression of his sentiments, or to bring forward any measure relative to the unjustifiable, oppressive

conduct of the officers of the Spanish government at New Orleans. . . . But seeing the session now drawing to a close . . . he could not reconcile a longer silence, either to his own sense of propriety, or to the duty he owed to his constituents. . . .

He was fully aware that the executive of the United States had acted: that he had sent an envoy extraordinary to Europe. This was the peculiar province, and perhaps the duty of the President. He would not say that it was unwise in this state of our affairs to prepare for remonstrance and negociation, much less was he then about to propose any measure that would thwart negociation, or embarrass the President. On the other hand, he was convinced that more than negociation was absolutely necessary, that more power and more means ought to be given to the President, in order to render his negociations efficacious. . . .

Mr. R. said he held in his hands certain resolutions . . . and before he offered them to the senate, he would very fully explain his reasons for bringing them forward and pressing them with earnestness, as the best system the United States could now pursue.

It was certainly unnecessary to waste the time of that body in stating that we had a solemn explicit treaty with Spain; that this treaty had been wantonly and unprovokedly violated, not only in what related to the Mississippi, but by the most flagrant, destructive spoliations of our commerce on every part of the ocean, where Spanish armed vessels met the American flag. These spoliations were of immense magnitude, and demanded the most serious notice of our government. They had been followed by an indignity and a direct infraction of our treaty relative to the Mississippi, which bore an aspect not to be dissembled or mistaken.

. . . Sir, said Mr. R. whom does this infraction of the treaty and the natural rights of this country most intimately affect? If the wound inflicted on national honor be not sensibly felt by the whole nation, is there not a large portion of your citizens exposed to immediate ruin by a continuance of this state of things? The calamity lights upon all those who live upon the western waters. More than half a million of your citizens are by this cut off from a market. What would be the language, what would be the feelings of gentlemen in this house, were such an indignity offered on the Atlantic coast? . . .

. . . It may be said that this is an overcharged description of the evil side of our affairs, without offering any remedy.

Mr. R. said, that was far from his intention, and he would now examine that subject, because to his mind the remedy was obvious.

. . . The treaty had been long in a state of execution. It was violated and denied without provocation or apology. The treaty then was no security. . . . He declared it therefore to be his firm and mature opinion, that so important a right would never be secure, while the mouth of the Mississippi was exclusively in the hands of the Spaniards. . . . From the very position of our country, from its geographical shape, from motives of complete independence, the command of the navigation of the river ought to be in our hands.

We are now wantonly provoked to take it. . . . why not seize then what is so essential to us as a nation? Why not expel the wrongdoers? . . . Paper contracts or treaties, have proved too feeble. Plant yourselves on the river, fortify the banks, invite those who have an interest at stake to defend it . . . do justice to yourselves when your adversaries deny it . . . and leave the event to him who controls the fate of nations.

Source: William Duane, *The Mississippi Question Fairly Stated* (Philadelphia: W. Duane, 1803), 1–5.

17 Letter from Charles Pinckney to James Madison, May 4, 1803

The scion of a wealthy South Carolina family whose members held state and federal offices, Charles Pinckney was the American minister to Madrid. He suddenly found himself scrambling to extract concessions from the Spanish government. This letter suggests just how little influence the United States actually wielded in European affairs.

Since closing the dispatches I delivered this morning to Mr: Wells I have recieved the inclosed letter from Mr Cevallos in answer to the different applications made to him on the subject of the purchase of the Floridas & such parts of Louisiana as was convenient to us & indemnification for the Damages sustained by our Citizens in consequence of the irregular conduct of the Intendant at New Orleans. By his answer you will see his Catholic Majesty declines selling the Floridas & has referred us to the French Government for such purchases of Louisiana or a part of it as we wish & has declared that our claims for indemnification which you will find by the papers transmitted I had pushed as far as "amicable decision" would permit, were unsupported by the Treaty of 1795. His manner of expressing himself on the subject of the navigation of the Misissipi— *the Favour* as he calls it of our being allowed a Deposit at New Orleans & its continuation after 1798 & of the revocation of the Edict of the Intendant, all serve to strengthen the Opinions that the French wished to recieve this country from the Spaniards at a time when doubts existed respecting the power to revoke our right to deposit & when the Spaniards themselves considered that & all our other rights as mere favours springing from the Generosity of the King & that it might possibly hereafter rest with the French Government to determine how far it might be convenient to them to continue these rights. This answer appeared to me to be so important that I sent it off immediately to Mr: Livingston & Mr Monroe at Paris with my opinions tending to shew the absolute necessity there is for their now definitively ar-

ranging every Question respecting the Misissipi before the French can take possession. To these gentlemen I have also communicated very fully every thing I have done or attempted here with my Opinions at large. Copies of my letters to them I now inclose you & I am waiting to hear from them not having recieved a line from you later than the *18 January nor one Word from Mr Monroe* so that at this moment nearly the middle of May I am entirely in the dark & uninformed of *What Congress* have done since the beginning of January. I have governed myself entirely by your instructions & I trust that if you recieve all the numerous Dispatches & their inclosure[s] I have sent you will see We have not been idle or left a single mode or thing unattempted to obtain what we wish from this Government. I am happy I obtained the restoration of the Deposit & hope the Order is arrived before this time. The Quarantine also is taken off, & on the subject of the indemnification for the Damages occasioned by the conduct of the Intendant at New Orleans, You find the Secretary says our claim is unsupported by the Treaty. Should it be possible for me to persuade them to reconsider this Opinion & agree to make compensation I shall do so but consider the inclosed answer as expressing the Opinion of the Government that they are not bound by treaty to do so I have taken the earliest Opportunity to transmit it to You for your information . . .

Should it be necessary for me to recieve further instructions on the subject of the indemnifications for the Damages sustained by our Citizenship occasioned by the irregular conduct of the Intendant at New Orleans, it will be proper to transmit the best account of what have been the Damages that have been sustained because should the Damages be not very considerable it may have great Weight with this Court in rather promising compensation than risquing the inconveniencies of a rupture.

Source: Robert J. Brugger et al., eds., *The Papers of James Madison: Secretary of State Series* (Charlottesville: University Press of Virginia), vol. 4: 571.

18   Alexander Hamilton on the Louisiana Purchase

These two documents, from the February 8 and July 5, 1803, issues, respectively, of the New York Evening Post, *show how one of the Jefferson administration's chief opponents responded to the Mississippi crisis. Through the* New York Evening Post, *a newspaper he helped create, Alexander Hamilton was among the commentators who recommended a military action to seize New Orleans. When news of the Louisiana Purchase reached the United States, he was forced to find a means of responding to a treaty that seemed to achieve all that the Jefferson administration's critics—including Hamilton—had demanded.*

In his July 5 commentary, Hamilton was among the few Americans to directly celebrate the slaves and free people of color on Saint Domingue. Although the victories of those nonwhite residents of Saint Domingue in 1802 and 1803 precipitated the Louisiana Purchase, members of the administration—especially Thomas Jefferson and James Madison, both slaveholders—were so fearful of a slave revolt spreading to the United States that they made few comments about the role of Caribbean events.

New York Evening Post,
February 8, 1803

Since the question of Independence, none has occurred more deeply interesting to the United States than the cession of Louisiana to France. This event threatens the early dismemberment of a large portion of our country: more immediately the safety of all the Southern States; and remotely the independence of the whole union. This is the portentous aspect which the affair presents to all men of sound and reflecting minds of whatever party, and it is not to be concealed that the only question which now offers itself, is, how is the evil to be averted?

The strict right to resort at once to WAR, if it should be deemed expedient cannot be doubted. *A manifest and great danger* to the nation: the nature of the cession to France, extending to ancient limits without respect to our rights by treaty; the direct infraction of an important-article of the treaty itself in withholding the deposit of New-Orleans; either of these affords justifiable cause of WAR and that they would authorize immediate hostilities, is not to be questioned by the most scrupulous mind.

The whole is then a question of expediency. Two courses only present. First, to negotiate and endeavour to purchase, and if this fails to go to war. Secondly, to seize at once on the Floridas and New-Orleans, and then negociate.

A strong objection offers itself to the first. There is not the most remote probability that the ambitious and aggrandizing views of Bonaparte will commute the territory for money. Its acquisition is of immense importance to France, and has long been an object of her extreme solicitude. The attempt therefore to purchase, in the first instance, will certainly fail, and in the end, war must be resorted to, under all the accumulation of difficulties caused by a previous and strongly fortified possession of the country by our adversary.

The second plan is, therefore, evidently the best. First, because effectual: the acquisition easy; the preservation afterwards easy: The evils of a war with France at this time are certainly not very formidable: Her fleet crippled and powerless, her treasury empty, her resources almost dried up, in short, gasping for breath after a tremendous conflict which, though it left her victorious, left her nearly exhausted under her extraordinary exertions. On the other hand, we might count with certainty on the aid of Great Britain with her powerful navy.

Secondly, this plan is preferable because it affords us the only chance of avoiding a long-continued war. When we have once taken possession, the business will present itself to France in a new aspect. She will then have to weigh the immense difficulties, if not the utter impracticability of wresting it from us. In this posture of affairs she will naturally conclude it is her interest to bargain. Now it may become expedient to terminate hostilities by a purchase, and a cheaper one may reasonably be expected.

To secure the better prospect of final success, the following auxiliary measures ought to be adopted.

The army should be increased to ten thousand men, for the purpose of insuring the preservation of the conquest. Preparations for increasing our naval force should be made. The militia should be classed, and effectual provision made for raising on an emergency, 40,000 men. Negociations should be pushed with Great-Britain, to induce her to hold herself in readiness to co-operate fully with us, at a moment's warning.

This plan should be adopted and proclaimed before the departure of our envoy.

Such measures would astonish and disconcert Bonaparte himself; our envoy would be enabled to speak and treat with effect; and all Europe would be taught to respect us.

These ideas have been long entertained by the writer, but he has never given himself the trouble to commit them to the public, because he despaired of their being adopted. They are now thrown out with very little hope of their producing any change in the conduct of administration, yet, with the encouragement that there is a strong current of public feeling in favour of decisive measures.

If the President would adopt this course, he might yet retrieve his character; induce the best part of the community to look favorably on his political career, exalt himself in the eyes of Europe, save the country, and secure a permanent fame. But for this, alas! Jefferson is not destined!

Alexander Hamilton, "The Purchase of Louisiana," *New York Evening Post,* July 5, 1803

At length the business of New-Orleans has terminated favourably to this country. Instead of being obliged to rely any longer on the force of treaties, for a place of deposit, the jurisdiction of the territory is now transferred to our hands and in future the navigation of the Mississippi will be ours unmolested. This, it will be allowed is an important acquisition, not, indeed, as territory, but as being essential to the peace and prosperity of our Western country, and as opening a free and valuable market to our commercial states. This purchase has been made during the period of Mr. Jefferson's presidency, and, will, doubtless, give eclat to his administration. Every man, however, possessed of the least candour and reflection will readily acknowledge that the acquisition has been solely owing to a fortuitous concurrence of unforseen and unexpected circumstances, and not to any wise or vigorous measures on the part of the American government.

As soon as we experienced from Spain a direct infraction of an important article of our treaty, in withholding the deposit of New-Orleans, it afforded us justifiable cause of war, and authorised immediate hostilities. Sound policy unquestionably demanded of us to begin with a prompt, bold and vigorous resistance against the injustice: to seize the object at once; and having this vantage ground, should we have thought it advisable to terminate hostilities by a purchase, we might then have done it on almost our own terms. This course, however, was not adopted, and we were about to experience the fruits of our folly, when another nation has found it her interest to place the French Government in a situation substantially as favourable to our views and interests as those recommended by the federal party here, excepting indeed that we should probably have obtained the same object on better terms.

On the part of France the short interval of peace had been wasted in repeated and fruitless efforts to subjugate St. Domingo; and those means which were originally destined to the colonization of Louisiana, had been gradually exhausted by the unexpected difficulties of this ill-starred enterprize.

To the deadly climate of St. Domingo, and to the courage and obstinate resistance made by its black inhabitants are we indebted for the obstacles which delayed the colonization of Louisiana, till the auspicious moment, when a rupture between England and France gave a new turn to the projects of the latter, and destroyed at once all her schemes as to this favourite object of her ambition.

It was made known to Bonaparte, that among the first objects of England would be the seizure of New-Orleans, and that preparations were even then in a state of forwardness for that purpose. The First Consul could not doubt, that if an English fleet was sent thither, the place must fall without resistance, it was obvious, therefore, that it would be in every shape preferable that it should be placed in the possession of a neutral power; and when, besides, some millions of money, of which he was extremely in want, were offered him, to part with what he could no longer hold it affords a moral certainty, that it was to an accidental state of circumstances, and not to wise plans, that this cession, at this time, has been owing. We shall venture to add, that neither of the ministers through whose instrumentality it was effected, will ever deny this, or even pretend that previous to the time when a rupture was believed to be inevitable, there was the smallest chance of inducing the First Consul, with his ambitious and aggrandizing views, to commute the territory for any sum of money in their power to

offer. The real truth is, Bonaparte found himself absolutely compelled by situation, to relinquish his darling plan of colonising the banks of the Mississippi: and thus have the Government of the United States, by the unforseen operation of events, gained what the feebleness and pusillanimity of its miserable system of measures could never have acquired. Let us then, with all due humility, acknowledge this as another of those signal instances of the kind interpositions of an over-ruling Providence, which we more especially experienced during our revolutionary war, & by which we have more than once, been saved from the consequences of our errors and perverseness.

We are certainly not disposed to lessen the importance of this acquisition to the country, but it is proper that the public should be correctly informed of its real value and extent as well as of the terms on which it has been acquired. We perceive by the newspapers that various & very vague opinions are entertained; and we shall therefore, venture to state our ideas with some precision as to the territory; but until the instrument of cession itself is published, we do not think it prudent to say much as to the conditions on which it has been obtained.

Prior to the treaty of Paris 1763 France claimed the country on both sides of the river under the name of Louisiana, and it was her encroachments on the rear of the British Colonies which gave rise to the war of 1755. By the conclusion of the treaty of 1763, the limits of the colonies of Great Britain and France were clearly and permanently fixed; and it is from that and subsequent treaties that we are to ascertain what territory is really comprehended under the name of Louisiana. France ceded to Great-Britain all the country east and south-east of a line drawn along the middle of the Mississippi from its source to the Iberville, and from thence along that river and the Lakes Maurepas and Pontchartrain to the sea; France retaining the country lying west of the river, besides the town and Island of New-Orleans on the east side. This she soon after ceded to Spain who acquiring also the Floridas by the treaty of 1783, France was entirely shut out from the continent of North America. Spain, at the instance of Bonaparte, ceded to him Louisiana, including the Town and Island (as it is commonly called) of New-Orleans. Bonaparte has now ceded the same tract of country, and this only, to the United States. The whole of East and West-Florida, lying south of Georgia and of the Mississippi Territory, and extending to the Gulf of Mexico, still remains to Spain, who will continue, therefore, to occupy, as formerly, the country along the southern frontier of the United States, and the east bank of the river, from the Iberville to the American line.

Those disposed to magnify its value will say, that this western region is important as keeping off a troublesome neighbour, and leaving us in the quiet possession of the Mississippi. Undoubtedly this has some force, but on the other hand it may be said, that the acquisition of New-Orleans is perfectly adequate to every purpose; for whoever is in possession of that, has the uncontrouled command of the river. Again, it may be said, and this probably is the most favourable point of view in which it can be placed, that although not valuable to the United States for settlement, it is so to Spain, and will become more so, and therefore at some distant period will form an object which we may barter with her for the Floridas, obviously of far greater value to us than all the immense, undefined region west of the river.

It has been usual for the American writers on this subject to include the Floridas in their ideas of Louisiana, as the French formerly did, and the acquisition has derived no inconsiderable portion of its value and importance with the public from this view of it. It may, however, be relied on, that no part of the Floridas, not a foot of land on the east of the Mississippi, excepting New-Orleans, falls within the present cession. As to the unbounded region west of the Mississippi, it is, with the exception of a very few settlements of Spaniards and Frenchmen bordering on the banks of the river, a wilderness through which wander numerous tribes of Indians. And when we consider the present extent of the United States, and that not one sixteenth part of its territory is yet under occupation, the advantage of the acquisition, as it relates to actual settlement, appears too distant and remote to strike the mind of a sober politician with much force. This, therefore, can only rest in speculation for many years, if not centuries to come, and consequently will not perhaps be allowed very great weight in the account by the majority of readers. But it may be added, that should our own citizens, more enterprising than wise, become desirous of settling this country, and emigrate thither, it must not only be attended with all the injuries of a too widely dispersed population, but by adding to the great weight of the western part of our territory, must hasten the dismemberment of a large portion of our country, or a dissolution of the Government. On the whole, we think it may with candor be said, that whether the possession at this time of any territory west of the river Mississippi will be advantageous, is at best extremely problematical. For ourselves, we are very much inclined to the opinion, that after all, it is the Island of N. Orleans by which the command of a free navigation of the Mississippi is secured, that gives to this interesting cession, its greatest value, and will render it in every view of immense benefit to our country. By this cession we hereafter shall hold within our own grasp, what we have heretofore enjoyed only by the uncertain tenure of a treaty, which might be broken at the pleasure of another, and (governed as we now are) with perfect impunity. Provided therefore we have not purchased it too dear, there is all the reason for exultation which the friends of the administration display, and which all Americans may be allowed to feel.

As to the pecuniary value of the bargain; we know not enough of the particulars to pronounce upon it. It is understood generally, that we are to assume *debts* of France to our own citizens not exceeding four millions of dollars; and that for the remainder, being a very large sum, 6 per cent stock to be created, and payment made in that. But should it contain no conditions or stipulations on our part, no "tangling alliances" of all things to be dreaded, we shall be very much inclined to regard it in a favorable point of view though it should turn out to be what may be called a costly purchase. By the way a question here presents itself of some little moment: Mr. Jefferson in that part of his famous electioneering message, where he took so much pains to present a flattering state of the Treasury in so few words that every man could carry it in his noddle and repeat it at the poll, tells us, that "experience too so far authorises us to believe, *if no extraordinary event supervenes, and the expences which will be actually incurred shall not be greater than was contemplated* by Congress at their last session, that we shall not be disappointed in the expectations formed" that the debt would soon be paid; &c. &c. But the first and only measure of the administration that has really been of any material service to the country (for they have hitherto gone on the strength of the provisions made by their predecessors) is really "an extraordinary event," and calls for more money than they have got. According to Mr. Gallatin's report, they had about 40,000 to spare for contingencies, and now the first "extraordinary event" that "supervenes" calls upon them for several millions. What a poor starvling system of administering a government! *But how is the money to be had? Not by taxing luxury and wealth and whiskey, but by increasing of the taxes on the necessaries of life.* Let this be remembered.

But we are exceeding our allowable limits. It may be satisfactory to our readers, that we should finish with a concise account of New-Orleans itself.

The Island of New-Orleans is in length about 150 miles; its breadth varies from 10 to 30 miles. Most of it is a marshy swamp, periodically inundated by the river. The town of New-Orleans, situated about 105 miles from the mouth of the river, contains near 1300 houses, and about 8000 inhabitants, chiefly Spanish and French. It is defended from the overflowings of the river, by an embankment, or *leveé,* which extends near 50 miles.

The rights of the present proprietors of real estate in New-Orleans and Louisiana, whether acquired by descent or by purchase, will, of course, remain undisturbed. How they are to be governed is another question; whether as a colony, or to be formed into an integral part of the United States, is a subject which will claim consideration hereafter. The probable consequences of this cession, and the ultimate effect it is likely to produce on the political state of our country, will furnish abundant matter of speculation to the American statesman.

If reliance can be placed on the history given of the negociation of Louisiana in private letters, from persons of respectability residing at Paris, and who speak with confidence, the merit of it, after making due allowance for the great events which have borne it along with them, is due to our ambassador, Chancellor Livingston, and not to the Envoy Extraordinary. "The cession was voted in the Council of State on the 8th of April, and Mr. Munro did not even arrive till the 12th." Judging from Mr. Munro's former communications to the French Government on this subject, we really cannot but regard it as fortunate, that the thing was concluded before he reached St. Cloud.

19   Letter from James Madison to Robert R. Livingston and James Monroe,
March 2, 1803

When James Monroe left for France in March 1803, Thomas Jefferson and James Madison had their final chance to shape negotiations before surrendering authority to their diplomats. In these lengthy, exquisitely detailed instructions to Monroe, Madison issued specific orders while acknowledging the latitude that Livingston and Monroe would inevitably need to employ. In addition, more than any other document in this anthology, these instructions crystallized the priorities and the concerns that reigned within the Jefferson administration in the winter and spring of 1803.

Department Of State March 2d 1803

Gentlemen,

You will herewith receive a Commission and letters of Credence, one of you as Minister Plenipotentiary, the other as Minister Extraordinary and Plenipotentiary, to treat with the Government of the French Republic, on the Subject of the Mississipi, and the Territories Eastward thereof, and without the limits of the United States. The object in view is to procure by just and satisfactory arrangements, a Cession to the United States, of New Orleans, and of West and East Florida, or as much thereof as the actual proprietor can be prevailed on to part with.

The French Republic is understood to have become the proprietor by a Cession from Spain in the Year [BLANK] of New Orleans, as part of Louisiana, if not of the Floridas also. If the Floridas should not have been then included in the Cession, it is not improbable that they will have been since added to it.

It is foreseen that you may have considerable difficulty in overcoming the repugnance and the prejudices of the French Government against a transfer to the United States of so important a part of the acquisition. The apparent solicitude and exertions amidst many embarrassing circumstances, to carry into effect the Cession made to the French Republic, the reserve so long used on this subject by the French Government in its communications with the Minister of the United States at Paris, and the declaration finally made

by the French Minister of foreign Relations, that it was meant to take possession, before any overtures from the United States would be discussed, shew the importance which is attached to the Territories in question. On the other hand, as the United States have the Strongest motives of interest, and of a pacific policy, to seek by just means the establishment of the Mississipi, down to its mouth as their boundary, so there are considerations which urge on france a concurrence in so natural and so convenient an arrangement.

Notwithstanding the circumstances which have been thought to indicate in the French Government designs of unjust encroachment, and even direct hostility on the United States, it is scarcely possible, to reconcile a policy of that sort, with any motives which can be presumed to sway either the Government or the Nation. To say nothing of the assurances given both by the French Minister at Paris, and by the Spanish Minister at Madrid, that the Cession by Spain to France was understood to carry with it all the conditions stipulated by the former to the United States, the manifest tendency of hostile measures against the United States, to connect their Councils and their Colossal growth with the great and formidable rival of France, can neither escape her discernment, nor be disregarded by her prudence; and might alone be expected to produce very different views in her Government.

On the supposition that the French Government does not mean to force, or to court war with the United States; but on the contrary, that it sees the interest which France has in cultivating their neutrality and amity, the dangers to so desirable a relation between the two Countries which lurk under a neighbourhood modified as is that of Spain at present, must have great weight in recommending the change which you will have to propose. These dangers have been always sufficiently evident; and have moreover been repeatedly suggested by collisions between the stipulated rights or reasonable expectations of the United States, and the Spanish jurisdiction at New Orleans. But they have been brought more strikingly into view by the late proceeding of the Intendant at that place. The sensibility and unanimity in our nation which have appeared on this occasion, must convince France, that friendship and peace with us must be precarious until the Mississipi shall be made the boundary between the United States and Louisiana; and consequently render the present moment favorable to the object with which you are charged.

The time chosen for this experiment is pointed out also by other important considerations: The instability of the peace of Europe, the attitude taken by Great Britain, the languishing state of the French finances, and the absolute necessity of either abandoning the West India Islands or of sending thither large armaments at great expence all contribute at the present crisis to prepare in the French Government a disposition to listen to an arrangement which will at once dry up one source of foreign controversy, and furnish some aid in struggling with internal embarrassments. It is to be added that the overtures committed to you coincide in great measure with the ideas of the person thro' whom the letter from the President of April 30th. 1802 was conveyed to Mr. Livingston, and who is presumed to have gained some insight into the present sentiments of the French cabinet.

Among the considerations which have led the French Government into the project of regaining from Spain the Province of Louisiana, and which you may find it necessary to meet in your discussions, the following suggests themselves as highly probable.

1st. A jealousy of the Atlantic States as leaning to a coalition with Great Britain not consistent with neutrality & amity towards France; and a belief that by holding the key to the commerce of the Mississipi, she will be able to command the interests and attachments of the Western portion of the United States; and thereby either controul the Atlantic portion also; or if that cannot be done, to seduce the former into a separate Government, and a close alliance with herself.

In each of these particulars the calculation is founded in error.

It is not true that the Atlantic States lean towards any connection with Great Britain inconsistent with their amicable relations to France. Their dispositions and their interests equally prescribe to them amity and impartiality to both of those Nations. If a departure from this simple and salutary line of policy should take place, the causes of it will be found in the unjust or unfriendly conduct experienced from one or other of them. In general it may be remarked, that there are as many points on which the interests and views of the United States and of Great Britain may not be thought to coincide as can be discovered in relation to France. If less harmony and confidence should therefore prevail between France and the United States than may be maintained between Great Britain and the United States, the difference will lie not in the want of motives drawn from the mutual advantage of the two Nations; but in the want of favorable dispositions in the Governments of one or other of them. That the blame in this respect will not justly fall on the Government of the United States, is sufficiently demonstrated by the Mission and the objects with which you are now charged.

The French Government is not less mistaken if it supposes that the Western part of the United States can be withdrawn from their present union with the Atlantic part, into a separate Government closely allied with France.

Our Western fellow Citizens are bound to the union not only by the ties of kindred and affection which for a long time will derive strength from the stream of emigration peopling that region; but by two considerations which flow from clear and essential interests.

One of these considerations is the passage thro' the Atlantic ports of the foreign Merchandize consumed by the Western Inhabitants, and the payments thence made to a Treasury in which they would lose their participation by erecting a separate Government. The bulky productions of the Western Country may continue to pass down the Mississipi; but the difficulties of the ascending Navigation of that river, however free it may be made, will cause the imports for consumption to pass through the Atlantic States. This is the course thro' which they are now received; nor will the impost to which they will be subject change the course, even if the passage up the Mississipi should be duty free. It will not equal the difference in the freight thro' the latter channel. It is true that mechanical and other improvements in the navigation of the Mississipi may lessen the labour and expence of ascending the stream; but it is not in the least probable, that savings of this sort will keep pace with the improvements in Canals and Roads, by which the present course of imports will be favored. Let it be added that the loss of the contributions thus made to a foreign Treasury would be accompanied with the necessity of providing by less convenient revenues for the expence of a separate Government, and of the defensive precautions required by the change of situation.

The other of these considerations results from the insecurity to which the trade from the Mississipi would be exposed, by such a revolution in the Western part of the United States. A connection of the Western People as a separate State with France, implies a connection between the Atlantic States and Great Britain. It is found from long experience, that France and Great Britain are nearly half their time at War. The case would be the same with their allies. During nearly one half the time, therefore, the trade of the Western Country from the Mississipi, would have no protection but that of France, and would suffer all the interruptions which Nations having the command of the sea could inflict on it.

It will be the more impossible for France to draw the Western Country under her influence, by conciliatory regulations of the trade thro' the Mississipi; because regulations which would be regarded by her as liberal, and claiming returns of gratitude, would be viewed on the other side as falling short of justice. If this should not be at first the case, it soon would be so. The Western people believe, as do their Atlantic brethren, that they have a natural and indefeasible right to trade freely thro' the Mississipi. They are conscious of their power to enfor[c]e this right against any Nation whatever. With these ideas in their minds, it is evident that France will not be able to excite either a sense of favor, or of fear, that would establish an ascendency over them. On the contrary, it is more than probable, that the different views of their respective rights, would quickly lead to disappointments and disgusts on both sides, and thence to collisions and controversies fatal to the harmony of the two Nations. To guard against these consequences, is a primary motive with the United States, in wishing the arrangement proposed. As France has equal reason to guard against them, she ought to feel an equal motive to concur in the arrangement.

2d. The advancement of the commerce of France by an establishment on the Mississipi, has doubtless great weight with her Government in espousing this project.

The commerce thro' the Mississipi will consist 1st. of that of the United States 2d. of that of the adjacent Territories to be acquired by France.

The first is now and must for ages continue the principal commerce. As far as the faculties of France will enable her to share in it, the article to be proposed to her on the part of the United States, on that subject promises every advantage she can desire. It is a fair calculation that under the proposed arrangement, her Commercial opportunities would be extended rather than diminished; inasmuch as our present right of deposit gives her the same competitors as she would then have, and the effect of the more rapid settlement of the Western Country consequent on that arrangement would proportionally augment the mass of Commerce to be shared by her. The other portion of Commerce, with the exception of the

Island of New Orleans and the contiguous ports of West Florida, depends on the Territory Westward of the Mississipi. With respect to this portion, it will be little affected by the cession desired by the United States. The footing proposed for her commerce on the shore to be ceded, gives it every advantage she could reasonably wish, during a period within which she will be able to provide every requisite establishment, on the right shore; which according to the best information, possesses the same facilities for such establishments as are found on the Island of New Orleans itself. These circumstances essentially distinguish the situation of the French Commerce in the Mississipi after a Cession of New Orleans to the United States, from the situation of the Commerce of the United States, without such a Cession; their right of deposit being so much more circumscribed and their Territory on the Mississipi not reaching low enough for a Commercial establishment on the shore, within their present limits.

There remains to be considered, the commerce of the ports in the Floridas. With respect to this branch, the advantages which will be secured to France by the proposed arrangement ought to be satisfactory. She will here also derive a greater share from the increase, which will be given by a more rapid settlement of a fertile Territory, to the exports and imports thro' those ports, than she would obtain from any restrictive use she could make of those ports as her own property. But this is not all. The United States have a just claim to the use of the Rivers which pass from their Territories thro' the Floridas. They found their claim on like principles with those which supported their claim to the use of the Mississipi. If the length of these Rivers be not in the same proportion with that of the Mississipi, the difference is balanced by the circumstance that both banks in the former case belong to the United States.

With a view to permanent harmony between the two Nations, a Cession of the Floridas, is particularly to be desired, as obviating serious controversies that might otherwise grow even out of the regulations however liberal in the opinion of France, which she may establish at the Mouths

of those rivers. One of the Rivers, the Mobille, is said to be at present navigable for 400 Miles above the 31° of Latitude, and the navigation may no doubt be opened still further. On all of them the Country within the boundary of the United States, tho' otherwise between that and the sea, is fertile. Settlements on it are beginning; and the people have already called on the Government to procure the proper outlets to foreign Markets. The President accordingly, gave some time ago, the proper instructions to the Minister of the United States at Madrid. In fact, our free communicat[i]on with the Sea, thro' those channels is so natural, so reasonable, and so essential, that eventually it must take place, and in prudence therefore ought to be amicably and effectually adjusted without delay.

3. A further object with France may be, to form a Colonial establishment having a convenient relation to her West India Islands and forming an independent Source of supplies for them.

This object ought to weigh but little against the Cession we wish to obtain for two reasons: 1st. because the Country which the Cession will leave in her hands on the right side of the Mississipi, is capable of employing more than all the faculties she can spare for such an object, and of yielding all the supplies, which she could expect or wish from such an establishment: 2d. because in times of general peace, she will be sure, of receiving whatever supplies her Islands may want, from the United States; and even thro' the Mississippi if more convenient to her; because in times of peace with the United States tho' of War with Great Britain, the same sources will be open to her, whilst her own would be interrupted; and, because in case of War with the United States, which is not likely to happen without a concurrent war with Great Britain (the only case in which she could need a distinct fund of supplies) the entire command of the Sea, and of the trade thro' the Mississipi, would be against her and would cut off the source in question. She would consequently never need the aid of her new Colony, but when she could make little or no use of it.

There may be other objects with France in the projected acquisition; but they are probably such as would be either satisfied by a reservation to herself of the Country on the right side of the Mississipi, or are of too subordinate a character to prevail against the plan of adjustment we have in view; in case other difficulties in the way of it can be overcome. The principles and outlines of this plan are as follows viz:

I. France cedes to the United States, for ever, the territory East of the River Mississippi, comprehending the two Floridas, the Island of New Orleans and the Islands lying to the North and East of that channel of the said River, which is commonly called the South-pass, together with all such other Islands as appertain to either West or East Florida; France reserving to herself all her territory on the West side of the Mississippi.

II. The boundary between the territory, ceded and reserved by France, shall be a continuation of that already defined above the thirty first degree of North Latitude, viz. the middle of the channel or bed of the River, thro' the said South Pass to the sea. The navigation of the River Mississippi in its whole breadth from its source to the Ocean, and in all its passages to and from the same shall be equally free and common to citizens of the United States and of the French Republic.

III. The vessels and citizens of the French Republic may exercise commerce to and at such places on their respective shores below the said thirty first degree of North Latitude as may be allowed for that use by the parties to their respective citizens and vessels. And it is agreed that no other nation shall be allowed to exercise commerce to or at the same or any other places on either shore, below the said thirty first degree of Latitude. For the term of ten years to be computed from the exchange of the ratifications hereof, the citizens, vessels and merchandizes of the United States and of France shall be subject to no other duties on their respective shores below the said thirty first degree of latitude than are imposed on their own citizens vessels and merchandizes. No duty whatever shall, after the expiration of ten years, be laid on articles the growth or manufacture of the United States or of the ceded territory exported thro' the Mississippi in French vessels; so long as such articles so exported in vessels of the United States shall be exempt from duty: nor shall French vessels exporting such articles, ever afterwards be subject to pay a higher duty than vessels of the United States.

IV. The citizens of France may, for the term of ten years, deposit their effects at New Orleans and at such other places on the ceded shore of the Mississippi, as are allowed for the commerce of the United States, without paying any other duty than a fair price for the hire of stores.

V. In the ports and commerce of West and East Florida, France shall never be on a worse footing than the most favoured nation; and for the term of ten years, her vessels and merchandize shall be subject therein to no higher duties than are paid by those of the United States. Articles of the growth and manufacture of the United States and of the ceded territory, exported in French vessels from any port in West or East Florida, shall be exempt from duty as long as vessels of the United States shall enjoy this exemption.

VI. The United States, in consideration of the cession of territory made by this treaty shall pay to France thirty (see cypher) millions of livres tournois, in the manner following, viz. They shall pay [BLANK] millions of livres tournois immediately on the exchange of the ratifications hereof: they shall assume, in such order of priority as the Government of the United States may approve, the payment of claims, which have been or may be acknowledged by the French Republic to be due to American citizens, or so much thereof as with the payment to be made on the exchange of ratifications will not exceed the sum of [BLANK] and in case a balance should remain due after such payment and assumption, the same shall be paid at the end of one year from the final liquidation of the claims hereby assumed, which shall be payable in three equal annual payments, the first of which is to take place one year after the exchange of ratifications; they shall bear interest at the rate of six per cent. per annum from the dates of such intended payments, until they shall be discharged. All the above mentioned payments shall be made at the Treasury of the United States, and at the rate of one dollar and ten cents for every six livres tournois.

VII. To incorporate the inhabitants of the hereby ceded territory with the citizens of the United States on an equal footing, being a provision, which cannot now be made, it is to be expected, from the character and policy of the United States, that such incorporation will take place without unnecessary delay. In the mean time, they shall be secure in their persons and property, and in the free enjoyment of their religion.

Observations on the plan.

1st. As the Cession to be made by France in this case must rest on the Cession made to her by

Spain, it might be proper that Spain should be a party to the transaction. The objections however to delay require that nothing more be asked on our part, than either an exhibition and recital of the Treaty between France and Spain; or an engagement on the part of France, that the accession of Spain will be given. Nor will it be advisable to insist even on this much, if attended with difficulty or delay, unless there be ground to suppose that Spain will contest the validity of the transaction.

2d The plan takes for granted also that the Treaty of 1795 between the United States and Spain is to lose none of its force in behalf of the former, by any transactions whatever between the latter and France. No change it is evident, will be, or can be admitted to be produced in that Treaty or in the arrangements carried into effect under it, further than it may be superceded by stipulations between the United States and France, who will stand in the place of Spain. It will not be amiss to insist on an express recognition of this by France as an effectual bar against pretexts of any sort not compatible with the stipulations of Spain.

3 The first of the articles proposed, in defining the Cession refers to the South pass of the Mississippi, and to the Islands North and East of that channel. As this is the most navigable of the several channels, as well as the most direct course to the sea, it is expected that it will not be objected to. It is of the greater importance to make it the boundary, because several Islands will be thereby acquired, one of which is said to command this channel, and to be already fortified. The article expressly includes also the Islands appertaining to the Floridas. To this there can be no objection. The Islands within six leagues of the shore are the subject of a British proclamation in the year 1763 subsequent to the Cession of the Floridas to Great Britain by France, which is not known to have been ever called in question by either France or Spain.

The 2d Article requires no particular observations. Art 3d is one whose import may be expected to undergo the severest scrutiny. The modification to be desired is that, which, whilst it provides for the interest of the United States will be acceptable to France, and will give no just ground of complaint, and the least of discontent to Great Britain.

The present form of the article ought and probably will be satisfactory to France; first because it secures to her all the commercial advantages in the river which she can well desire; secondly, because it leaves her free to contest the mere navigation of the river by Great Britain, without the consent of France.

The article also, in its present form violates no right of Great Britain, nor can she reasonably expect of the United States that they will contend beyond their obligation for her interest at the expence of their own. As far as Great Britain can claim the use of the river under her treaties with us, or by virtue of contiguous territory, the silence of the Article on that subject leaves the claim unaffected. As far again, as she is entitled under the treaty of 1794 to the use of our bank of the Mississippi above the 31st. degree of North latitude, her title will be equally entire. The article stipulates against her only in its exclusion of her commerce from the bank to be ceded below our present limits. To this she cannot of right object 1st because the territory not belonging to the United States at the date of our Treaty with her is not included in its stipulations 2d because the privileges to be enjoyed by France are for a consideration which Great Britain has not given and cannot give; 3dly because the exclusion in this case, being a condition on which the Territory will be ceded and accepted, the right to communicate the privilege to Great Britain will never have been vested in the United States.

But altho' these reasons fully justify the article in its relation to Great Britain, it will be advisable before it be proposed, to feel the pulse of the French Government with respect to a stipulation that each of the parties may without the consent of the other, admit whomsoever it pleases to navigate the river and trade with their respective Shores, on the same terms, as in other parts of France and the United States; and as far as the disposition of that Government will concur, to vary the proposition accordingly. It is not probable that this concurrence will be given; but the trial to obtain it, will not only manifest a friendly regard to the Wishes of Great Britain, and if successful furnish a future price for privileges within her grant; but is a just attention to the interests of our Western fellow citizens, whose commerce will not otherwise be on an equal footing with that of the Atlantic States.

Should France not only refuse any such change in the Article, but insist on a recognition of her right to exclude all nations other than the United States from navigating the Mississippi; it may be observed to her, that a positive stipulation to that effect might subject us to the charge of intermeddling with and prejudging questions existing merely between her and Great Britain; that the silence of the Article is sufficient; that as Great Britain never asserted a claim on this subject against Spain, it is not to be presumed that she will assert it against France on her taking the place of Spain; that if the claim should be asserted, the treaties between the United States and Great Britain will have no connection with it, the United States having in those treaties given their separate consent only to the use of the river by Great Britain, leaving her to seek whatever other consent may be necessary.

If, notwithstanding such expostulations as these, France shall inflexibly insist on an express recognition to the above effect, it will be better to acquiesce in it, than to lose the opportunity of fixing an arrangement in other respects satisfactory; taking care to put the recognition into a form not inconsistent with our treaties with Great Britain, or with an explanatory article that may not improbably be desired by her.

In truth it must be admitted, that France as holding one bank, may exclude from the use of the river any nation not more connected with it, by territory than Great Britain is understood to be. As a river where both its banks are owned by one nation, belongs exclusively to that nation; it is clear that when the territory on one side is owned by one nation, and on the other side by another nation, the river belongs equally to both,

in exclusion of all others. There are two modes by which an equal right may be exercised; the one by a negative in each on the use of the river, by any other nation execept the joint proprietor; the other by allowing each to grant the use of the river to other nations without the consent of the joint proprietor. The latter mode would be preferable to the United States. But if it be found absolutely inadmissible to France, the former must in point of expediency, since it may in point of right, be admitted by the United States. Great Britain will have the less reason to be dissatisfied on this account, as she has never asserted against Spain, a right of entering and navigating the Mississippi, nor has either she or the United States ever founded on the treaties between them, a claim to the interposition of the other party in any respect; altho' the river has been constantly shut against Great Britain from the year 1783 to the present moment, and was not opened to the United States, until 1795 the year of their treaty with Spain.

It is possible also that France may refuse to the United States, the same commercial use of her shores, as she will require for herself on these ceded to the United States. In this case it will be better to relinquish a reciprocity than to frustrate the negotiation. If the United States held in their own right, the shore to be ceded to them, the commercial use of it allowed to France, would render a reciprocal use of her shore, by the United States, an indispensible condition. But as France may if she chuses, reserve to herself the commercial use of the ceded shore as a condition of the cession, the claim of the United States to the like use of her shore, would not be supported by the principle of reciprocity, and may therefore without violating that principle, be waved in the transaction.

The article limits to ten years the equality of French citizens, vessels and Merchandizes, with those of the United States. Should a longer period be insisted on, it may be yielded. The limitation may even be struct out, if made essential by France, but a limitation in this case is so desirable, that it is to be particularly pressed, and the shorter the period the better.

Art IV—The right of deposit provided for in this article, will accommodate the commerce of France to and from her own side of the river, until an emporium shall be established on that side, which it is well known will admit of a convenient one. The right is limitted to ten years, because such an establishment may within that period be formed by her. Should a longer period be required, it may be allowed; especially as the use of such a deposit, would probably fall within the general regulations of our commerce there. At the same time, as it will be better that it should rest on our own regulations, than on a stipulation, it will be proper to insert a limitation of time, if France can be induced to acquiesce in it.

Art V. This article makes a reasonable provision for the commerce of France in the ports of West and East Florida. If the limitation to ten years, of its being on the same footing with that of the United States, should form an insuperable objection, the term may be enlarged. But it is much to be wished that the privilege may not in this case be made perpetual.

Art VI The pecuniary consideration, to be offered for the territories in question, is stated in article VI. You will of course favor the United States as much as possible, both in the amount and modifications of the payments. There is some reason to believe, that the gross sum, expressed in the article, has occurred to the French Government, and is as much as will be finally insisted on. It is possible that less may be accepted, and the negotiation ought to be adapted to that supposition. Should a greater sum be made an ultimatum on the part of France, the President has made up his mind to go as far as *fifty* millions of livres tournois, rather than lose the main object. Every struggle however is to be made against such an augmentation of the price, that will consist with an ultimate acquiescence in it.

The payment to be made immediately on the exchange of ratifications is left blank; because it cannot be foreseen either what the gross sum or the assumed debts will be; or how far a reduction of the gross sum may be influenced by the antici-

pated payments provided for by the act of Congress herewith communicated and by the authorization of the President and Secretary of the Treasury endorsed thereon. This provision has been made with a view to enable you to take advantage of the urgency of the French government for money, which may be such as to overcome their repugnance to part with what we want, and to induce them to part with it on lower terms, in case a payment can be made before the exchange of ratifications. The letter from the Secretary of the Treasury to the Secretary of State, of which a copy is herewith enclosed, will explain the manner in which this advance of the ten millions of livres, or so much thereof as may be necessary, will be raised most conveniently for the United States. It only remains here to point out the condition or event on which the advance may be made. It will be essential, that the Convention be ratified by the French Government, before any such advance be made; and it may be further required, in addition to the stipulation to transfer possession of the ceded territory as soon as possible, that the orders for the purpose, from the competent source, be actually and immediately put into your hands. It will be proper also to provide for the repayment of the advance, in the event of a refusal of the United States to ratify the Convention.

It is apprehended that the French Government will feel no repugnance to our designating the classes of claims and debts, which, embracing more equitable considerations than the rest, we may believe entitled to a priority of payment. It is probable therefore that the clause of the VI article, referring it to our discretion may be safely insisted upon. We think the following classification such as ought to be adopted by ourselves:

1st. Claims under the fourth article of the Convention of Septr. 1800.

2nd. Forced contracts or sales imposed upon our citizens by French authorities; and

3rd. Voluntary contracts, which have been suffered to remain unfulfilled by them.

Where our citizens have become creditors of the French Government, in consequence of agencies or appointments derived from it, the United

States are under no particular obligation to patronise their claims, and therefore no sacrifice of any sort, in their behalf ought to be made in the arrangement. As far as this class of claimants can be embraced, without embarrassing the negotiation, or influencing in any respect the demands or expectations of the French Government, it will not be improper to admit them into the provision. It is not probable however, that such a deduction from the sum ultimately to be received by the French government will be permitted, without some equivalent accommodation to its interests, at the expense of the United States.

The claims of Mr. Beaumarchais and several other French individuals on our government, founded upon antiquated or irrelevant grounds, altho' they may be attempted to be included in this negotiation, have no connection with it. The American Government is distinguished for its just regard to the rights of Foreigners, and does not require those of individuals to become subjects of treaty in order to be admitted. Besides, their discussion involves a variety of minute topics, with which you may fairly declare yourselves to be unacquainted. Should it appear, however, in the course of the negotiation, that so much stress is laid on this point, that without some accommodation, your success will be endangered, it will be allowable to bind the United States for the payment of one million of livres tournois to the representatives of Beaumarchais, heretofore deducted from his accounts against them; the French government declaring the same never to have been advanced to him on account of the United States.

Art. VII is suggested by the respect due to the rights of the people inhabiting the ceded territory, and by the delay which may be found in constituting them a regular and integral portion of the union. A full respect for their rights might require their consent to the Act of Cession; and if the French Government should be disposed to concur in any proper mode of obtaining it, the provision would be honorable to both nations. There is no doubt that the inhabitants would readily agree to the proposed transfer of their allegiance.

It is hoped that the idea of a guarantee of the country reserved to France, may not be brought into the negotiation. Should France propose such a stipulation it will be expedient to evade it if possible, as more likely to be a source of disagreeable questions, between the parties concerning the actual casus foederis, than of real advantage to France. It is not in the least probable that Louisiana, in the hands of that nation, will be attacked by any other, whilst it is in the relations to the United States, on which the guarantee would be founded; whereas nothing is more probable than some difference of opinion as to the circumstances and the degree of danger necessary to put the stipulation in force. There will be the less reason in the demand of such an article, as the United States would set little value on a guarantee of any part of their territory, and consequently there would be no just reciprocity in it. Should France notwithstanding these considerations, make a guarantee an essential point, it will be better to accede to it, than to abandon the object of the negotiation; mitigating the evil as much as possible, by requiring for the casus foederis a great and manifest danger threatened to the territory guaranteed, and by substituting for an indefinite succour, or even a definite succour in military force, a fixed sum of money, payable at the Treasury of the United States. It is difficult to name the precise sum which is in no posture of the business to be exceeded, but it can scarcely be presumed that more than about *two million* dollars, to be paid annually during the existence of the danger, will be insisted on. Should it be unavoidable to stipulate troops in place of money, it will be prudent to settle the details with as much precision as possible, that there may be no room for controversy either with France or with her enemy, on the fulfilment of the stipulation.

The instructions thus far given suppose that France may be willing to cede to the United States, the whole of the Island of New Orleans and both the Floridas. As she may be inclined to dispose of a part or parts, and of such only, it is proper for you to know that the Floridas together are estimated at ¼ the value of the whole Island of New Orleans, and East Florida at ½ that of West Florida.

In case of a partial Cession, it is expected, that the regulations of every other kind, so far as they are onerous to the United States, will be more favourably modified.

Should France refuse to cede the whole of the Island, as large a portion as she can be prevailed on to part with, may be accepted; should no considerable portion of it be attainable, it will still be of vast importance to get a jurisdiction over space enough for a large commercial town and its appurtenances, on the banks of the river, and as little remote from the Mouth of the river as may be. A right to chuse the place, would be better than a designation of it in the Treaty. Should it be impossible to procure a complete jurisdiction over any convenient spot whatever, it will only remain to explain and improve the present right of deposit, by adding thereto the express privilege of holding real estate for commercial purposes, of providing hospitals, of having Consuls residing there, and other Agents who may be authorized to authenticate and deliver all documents requisite for Vessels belonging to and engaged in the trade of the United States to and from the place of deposit. The United States cannot remain satisfied, nor the Western people be kept patient under the restrictions which the existing Treaty with Spain authorizes.

Should a Cession of the Floridas not be attainable your attention will also be due to the establishment of suitable deposits at the mouths of the Rivers passing from the United States thro' the Floridas, as well as of the free navigation of those rivers by Citizens of the United States. What has been above suggested in relation to the Mississipi and the deposit on its banks is applicable to the other rivers: and additional hints relative to them all may be derived from the letter of which a copy is enclosed, from the Consul at New Orleans.

It has been long manifest, that whilst the injuries to the United States so frequently occurring from the Colonial Officers scattered over our hemisphere and in our neighborhood can only be repaired by a resort to their respective Governments in Europe, that it will be impossible to guard against the most serious inconveniences. The late events at New Orleans strongly manifest the necessity of placing a power somewhere nearer to us, capable of correcting and controuling the mischievous proceedings of such Officers towards our Citizens, without which a few individuals not always among the wisest or best of men may at any time threaten the good understanding of the two Nations. The distance between the United States and the old Continent, and the mortifying delays of explanations and negotiations across the Atlantic on emergencies in our neighborhood render such a provision indispensable, and it cannot be long before all the Governments of Europe having American Colonies must see the necessity of making it. This object therefore will likewise claim your special attention.

It only remains to suggest, that considering the possibility of some intermediate violences between Citizens of the United States, and the French or Spaniards in consequence of the interruption of our right of deposit, and the probability that considerable damages will have been occasioned by that measure to Citizens of the United States, it will be proper that indemnification in the latter case be provided for, and that in the former, it shall not be taken on either side as a ground or pretext for hostilities.

These instructions, tho as full as they could be conveniently made, will necessarily leave much to your discretion. For the proper exercise of it, the President relies on your information, your judgment, and your fidelity to the rights, the interests and the dignity of your Country. With great Respect and Consideration, I have the Honor to be, Gentlemen, Your Obedt huble. servant,

James Madison

Source: Robert J. Brugger et al., eds., *The Papers of James Madison: Secretary of State Series* (Charlottesville: University Press of Virginia), vol. 4: 364–378.

20   Letter from Thomas Jefferson to James Madison, March 19, 1803

Just why Thomas Jefferson sent James Monroe to France soon became clear. In this excerpt from a brief letter, Jefferson revealed his own doubts about Robert R. Livingston, his minister to Paris. But Jefferson also made broader statements about how he saw the United States fitting into the community of nations. Jefferson had long attacked the balance-of-power system that reigned in Europe. But, as Chapter 4 shows, Jefferson's attitude was rooted in his evaluation of American strengths and weakness as much as it was based on any philosophical objection to balance-of-power politics. Jefferson was convinced that in direct negotiations the Europeans would usually be able to outmaneuver their less experienced American counterparts. Add to this the fact that Jefferson already questioned Livingston's talents, and his decision to send Monroe—whom he considered both more intelligent and more realistic than Livingston—makes all the more sense.

Jefferson's decision did not sit well with Livingston, who already suspected a lack of support from within the administration. When Monroe arrived, the egos of both men led them to an immediate dislike for one another. And once the negotiations were over, both men immediately sought credit for the Louisiana Purchase.

I wrote you on the 17th. since which yours of the 14th. is received, and I now return the letters of Mr. Livingston & O'Brien. I hope the game Mr. Livingston says he is playing is a candid & honourable one. Besides an unwillingness to accept any advantage which should have been obtained by other means, no other means can probably succeed there. An American contending by stratagem against those exercised in it from their cradle would undoubtedly be outwitted by them. In such a field and for such an actor nothing but plain direct honesty can be either honourable or advantageous. . . .

Source: Robert J. Brugger et al., eds., *The Papers of James Madison: Secretary of State Series* (Charlottesville: University Press of Virginia), vol. 4: 434.

21   Letter from Robert R. Livingston and James Monroe to James Madison, May 13, 1803

In their first major letter to Washington after completing the negotiations, Robert R. Livingston and James Monroe introduced the Jefferson administration to the Louisiana Purchase. They announced the resolution of the Mississippi crisis through the execution of a treaty profoundly different from the one that Madison had ordered them to secure in his March 2 instructions.

PARIS, May 13 1803.

SIR,

We have the pleasure to transmit to you by Mr d'Erieux a Treaty which we have concluded with the french Republic for the Purchase & Cession of Louisiana. The negociation of this important object was committed on the part of France to Mr. Marbois, Minister of the Treasury, whose conduct therein has already received the Sanction of his Government, as appears by the Ratification of the first Consul, which we have also the pleasure to forward to you.

An acquisition of so great an extent was, we well Know, not contemplated by our appointment; but we are persuaded that the Circumstances and Considerations which induced us to make it, will justify us, in the measure, to our Government and Country.

Before the negociation commenced, we were apprised that the first Consul had decided to offer to the U. States by sale the whole of Louisiana, & not a part of it. We found in the outset that this information was correct; so that we had to decide as a previous question whether we would treat for the whole, or jeopardize, if not abandon the hope of acquiring any part. On that point, we did not long hesitate, but proceeded to treat for the whole. We were persuaded that by so doing, it might be possible, if more desirable to conclude eventually a Treaty for a part, since being thus possessed of the subject, it might be easy in discussion at least, to lead from a view of the whole to that of a part, and with some advantages peculiar to a negotiation on so great a scale. By treating for the whole, whereby we should be enabled to ascertain the idea which was entertained by this Government of its value; we should also be able to form some estimate of that which was affixed to the value of its parts. It was too, probable that a less sum would be asked for the whole, if sold entire to a single Purchaser, a friendly Power who was able to pay for it, and whom it might be disposed to accomodate at the present juncture, than if it should be sold in parcels, either to several Powers or Companies of Individuals: it was equally so, if this Government should be finally prevailed on to sell us a part, that some regard would be paid in the price asked for it, to that which was demanded for the whole lastly, by treating for the whole, whereby the attention of this Government would be drawn to the U. States, as the sole Purchasers, we might prevent the interference of other Powers, as also that of Individuals, which might prove equally injurious in regard to the price asked for it, whether we acquired the whole or any part of the Territory. We found, however, as we advanced in the negociation, that Mr. Marbois was absolutely restricted to the disposition of the whole; that he would treat for no less portion, and of Course that it was useless to urge it. On mature consideration therefore, we finally concluded a Treaty on the best terms we could obtain for the whole.

By this measure, we have sought to carry into effect to the utmost of our power the wise and benevolent Policy of our Government, on the Principles laid down in our instructions. The possession of the left bank of the River, had it been attainable alone, would, it is true, have accomplished much in that Respect; but it is equally true that it would have left much still to accomplish. By it our People would have had an outlet to the Ocean, in which no power would have a right to disturb them; but while the other bank remained in the possession of a foreign Power, circumstances might occur to make the neighbourhood of such Power highly injurious to us in many of our most important concerns. A divided Jurisdiction over the River might beget jealousies, discontents and dissensions which the wisest policy on our part could not prevent or controul. With a train of Colonial Governments established along the western bank, from the entrance of the river far into the interior, under the command of military men, it would be difficult to preserve that state of things which would be necessary to the Peace and tranquillity of our Country. A single act of a capricious, unfriendly or unprincipled subaltern might wound our best interests, violate our most unquestionable Rights, and involve us in war. But by this acquisition, which comprizes within our limits this great River and all the streams that empty into it, from their sources to the ocean, the apprehension of these disasters is banished for ages from the U. states. We adjust to it the only remaining Known cause of variance with this very powerful nation: we anticipate the discontent of the great rival of France, who would probably have been wounded at any stipulation of a permanent nature which favored the latter, and which it would have been difficult to avoid had she retained the right bank. We cease to have a motive of urgency at least for inclining to one power, to avert the unjust pressure of another. We separate ourselves in a great measure from the European World & its concerns, especially its wars & intrigues. We make in fine a great stride to real and substantial independence, the good effect whereof will, we trust, be felt essentially and extensively in all our foreign & domestic Relations. Without exciting the apprehensions of any Power, we take a more imposing attitude, with respect to all. The Bond of our Union will be strengthened, and its movements become more harmonious by the encreased parity of interest which it will communicate to the several Parts which compose it.

In deliberating on this subject in a financial view, we were strongly impressed with the idea that while we had only a right of deposit, or indeed while the right bank remained in the possession of a foreign power, it was always to be expected that we should, at some time or other, be involved in war on questions resulting from that cause. We were well satisfied that any war would cost us more than hereby is stipulated to be given for this Territory; that none could produce a more favorable result while it might, especially in the present disturbed state of the world, prove the ruin of our affairs.

There were other considerations which, tho' of minor importance, had nevertheless their due weight in our decision on this great question. If france, or any other Power holding the right bank of the River, imposed lighter duties than comported with the revenue system of the United States, supposing even that we had acquired the left bank, all the supplies destined for our extensive & populous settlements on the other side, would be smuggled in thro' that Channel, and our revenue thereby considerably diminished. Should such Power open offices for the sale of lands on the western bank, our Population might be drained to the advantage of that Power, the price of our lands be diminished, and their sale prevented. But, by the possession of both banks, these evils are averted.

The terms on which we have made this acquisition, when compared with the objects obtained by it will, we flatter ourselves, be deemed advantageous to our Country. We have stipulated, as you will see by the Treaty and Conventions, that the United States shall pay to the french Government sixty millions of francs, in stock, bearing an interest of six per Cent., and a sum not exceeding twenty millions more to our citizens, in discharge of the debts due to them by France, under the Convention of 1800; and also to exempt the manufactures, Productions & Vessels of France and Spain, in the direct trade from those Countries respectively, in the ports of the ceded territory, from foreign duties, for the term of twelve years. The stock is to be created irredimable for fifteen years, and discharged afterwards in three, in equal annual instalments; the interest on it is to be paid in Europe, and the Principal, in case this Government thinks proper to sell it, disposed of in such manner as will be most conducive to the credit of the american funds. The Debts due to our citizens are to be discharged by Drafts on our Treasury. We omit a more minute view of the stipulations on these Instruments, since, as you will possess them, it is unnecessary.

Louisiana was acquired of Spain by France, in exchange for Tuscany, which latter is settled by Treaty on the son-in-law of the King of Spain, with the title of King of Etruria, and was estimated in the Exchange, in consideration of its revenue, at 100,000,000 francs. The first Consul thought he had made an advantageous bargain in that exchange, as appears by the high idea which he entertained of its value, as shewn on many occasions. Louisiana was the Territory which he promised in his proclamation at the Peace, as an asylum to those who had become unfortunate by the Revolution, and which he spoke of as vast & fertile. When he made up his mind to offer the Cession of it to the United States, it was contemplated to ask for it 100,000,000 francs exclusive of the debts they owed to our citizens, which they proposed we should also pay, with a perpetual exemption from foreign duties on the manufactures, Productions and Vessels of France and Spain, in the Ports of the ceded Territory. From that demand however, in respect to the sum, he receded, under the deliberation of his own Cabinet; for the first Proposition which Mr. Marbois made to us was that we should pay 80 millions, sixty of which in cash, the balance to our citizens, the whole in one year in Paris, with a perpetual exemption from foreign duties, as above. The modification in the mode of payment, that is by stock, for from the quantum he never would depart, and the limitation of the term of the duties to twelve years, with the proviso annexed to it, which was introduced into the Treaty, with every other change from his project, was the effect of negociation, and accomodation, in which we experienced on his part and that of his Government a promptitude & Candour which were highly grateful to us.

In estimating the real value of this Country to the United States, a variety of considerations occur, all of which merit due attention. Of these we have already noticed many of a general nature, to which however it may be difficult to fix a precise value. Others present themselves of a nature more definite, to which it will be more practicable to fix some standard. By possessing both Banks, the whole revenue or duty on imports will accrue to the United states, which must be considerable. The value of the exports, we have understood, was last year four millions of Dollars. If a portion only of the Imports pass thro' that Channel as under our Government we presume they will, the amount of the revenue will be considerable. This will annually encrease in proportion as the Population and Productions in that quarter do. The value of the Lands in the province of Louisiana, amounting to some hundred millions of acres of the best quality, and in the best Climate, is perhaps incalculable. From either of these sources it is not doubted that the sum stipulated may be raised in time to discharge the debt.

We hope to be able to forward you herewith the order of this Government for the Delivery of the Possession of the ceded Territory to the U. States, or to communicate its arrangements for that Purpose, as also its views relative to the sale of the stock, since it is understood that their intention is to sell it. It has been intimated to us that the house of Baring, in London, connected with that of Hope in Holland, will take the whole at their risk, at the current price in England, on a Commission to be agreed on, paying to France a stipulated sum by the month. Their object is said to be, exclusive of that of making profit by it, to Keep up the Credit of our stock, they being much interested in it. Considering the great Capital of these houses, it is presumable that they would be able to comply with any engagement they might make to that effect. And it cannot be doubted that it would be more advantageous to us that the whole should be disposed of, than remain in the hands of France, who, under the pressure of difficulties, might have it less in her power to preserve or regard our Credit, in the disposition of it. We shall communicate with Mr. Marbois fully on this subject, and apprize you of the result.

We received some days past a Letter from Mr. King, in which he says that in case of war, which he deemed inevitable, the British Government contemplated taking possession of the Island of New-Orleans. He desired information to be communicated to that Government, whether it had been ceded to the U. States, as he presumed a Knowledge thereof would prevent the measure. We gave an immediate Reply to his Letter, in which we informed him that the whole of Louisiana had been ceded to the United States, which he was at liberty to communicate to the British Government. We likewise made the same Communication to Lord Whitworth, the British Ambassador here, who expressed himself to be well satisfied with the event.

These Countries, France & England, have been on the point of a rupture for some time past. At present, the Prospect of an accomodation is more remote, as the English Ambassador left Paris, at 10 o'clock last night. Still some hope of it is entertained by some Persons in power here. This nation is desirous of peace, and it is believed that its government is similarly disposed.

Permit us to express an earnest wish that the President and Senate may decide with the least possible delay on the Treaty & Conventions which we have concluded, & have the pleasure to transmit you. If it is the sense of our Governt. to ratify them, the sooner that fact is Known to this Government, the better its effect will be.

The list of the debts due by France to American Citizens not being yet prepared owing to Mr. Marbois absence from Paris to day, & the previous delays of the Offices, in which the evidencies [sic] were, cannot be sent by this Conveyance. In consequence we retain the original of the Convention to which it should be annexed & send a Copy of it. We shall forward in a day or two the Original. By the list it may be infer'd that the debts amount to a greater sum than they really do. They will be subject according to the Convention to the revision of our Board, by whom it is expected they will be reduced considerably. We have full confidence that including the Interest they will not exceed the sum of 20 Millions of francs, which is much to be desired, as in that case all our Citizens whose claims are entitled to the support of our Government, will be provided for and paid by it. You will observe that in the mode adopted considerable indulgence is given to our Treasury. The whole sum is to be paid there which will free it from embarrassment. We have the honor to be with great respect and esteem, Your very Hume Servants

Robt R Livingston
Jas. Monroe

Source: Robert J. Brugger et al., eds., *The Papers of James Madison: Secretary of State Series* (Charlottesville: University Press of Virginia), vol. 4: 601–606.

---

22   Letter from James Madison to Robert R. Livingston and James Monroe, July 29, 1803

For more than three months, Robert R. Livingston and James Monroe could only wait and worry. James Madison did little to end the suspense. He waited more than three weeks after receiving the Louisiana Purchase agreement before composing a formal reply, and that letter required the same lengthy trip across the Atlantic as all other correspondence. In this letter, Madison told the American diplomats exactly what they wanted to read: that the Jefferson administration approved of their actions.

Department of State July 29th—1803.

Gentlemen,

Your dispatches, including the Treaty and two conventions signed with a French Plenipotentiary on the 30th of April, were safely delivered on the 14th by Mr. Hughes, to whose care you had committed them.

In concurring with the disposition of the French Government to treat for the whole of Louisiana, alto' the western part of it was not embraced by your powers, you were justified by the solid reasons which you give for it, and I am charged by the President to express to you his entire approbation of your so doing.

This approbation is in no respect precluded by the silence of your Commission and instructions. When these were made out, the object of the most sanguine was limited to the establishment of the Mississippi as our boundary. It was not presumed that more could be sought by the United States either with a chance of success, or perhaps without being suspected of a greedy ambition, than the Island of New Orleans and the two Floridas, it being little doubted that the latter was or would be comprehended in the Cession from Spain to France. To the acquisition of New Orleans and the Floridas, the provision was therefore accommodated. Nor was it to be supposed that in case the French Government should be willing to part with more than the Territory on our side of the Mississippi, an arrangement with Spain for restoring to her the territory on the other side would not be preferred to a sale of it to the United States. It might be added, that the ample views of the subject carried with him by Mr. Monroe and the confidence felt that your judicious management would make the most of favorable occurrences, lessened the necessity of multiplying provisions for every turn which your negotiations might possibly take.

The effect of such considerations was diminished by no information or just presumptions whatever. The note of Mr. Livingston in particular stating to the French Government the idea of ceding the Western Country above the Arkansa and communicated to this Department in his letter of the 29th January, was not received here till April 5 more than a month after the Commission and instructions had been forwarded. And besides that this project not only left with France the possession and jurisdiction of one bank of the Mississippi from its mouth to the Arkansa, but a part of West Florida, the whole of East Florida, and the harbours for ships of war in the Gulph of Mexico, the letter inclosing the note intimated that it had been treated by the French Government with a decided neglect. In truth the communications in general between Mr. Livingston and the French Government, both of prior and subsequent date, manifested a repugnance to our views of purchase which left no expectation of any arrangement with France by which an extensive acquisition was to be made, unless in a favorable crisis of which advantage should be taken. Such was thought to be the crisis which gave birth to the extraordinary commission in which you are joined. It consisted of the state of things produced by the breach of our deposit at New Orleans, the situation of the French Islands, particularly the important Island of St. Domingo; the distress of the French finances, the unsettled posture of Europe, the increasing jealousy between G Britain and France, and the known aversion of the former to see the mouth of the Mississippi in the hands of the latter. These considerations it was hoped, might so far open the eyes of France to her real interest and her ears to the monitory truths which

were conveyed to her thro' different channels, as to reconcile her to the establishment of the Mississippi as a natural boundary to the United States; or at least to some concessions which would justify our patiently waiting for a fuller accomplishment of our wishes under auspicious events. The crisis relied on has derived peculiar force from the rapidity with which the complaints and questions between France and Great Britain ripened towards a rupture, and it is just ground for mutual and general felicitation, that it has issued under your zealous exertions, in the extensive acquisition beyond the Mississippi.

With respect to the terms on which the acquisition is made, there can be no doubt that the bargain will be regarded as on the whole highly advantageous. The pecuniary stipulations would have been more satisfactory, if they had departed less from the plan prescribed; and particularly if the two millions of dollars in cash, intended to reduce the price or hasten the delivery of possession had been so applied, and the assumed payments to American claimants on the footing specified in the instructions. The unexpected weight of the draught now to be made on the Treasury will be sensibly felt by it, and may possibly be inconvenient in relation to other important objects.

The President has issued his proclamation convening Congress on the 17th of October, in order that the exchange of the ratifications may be made within the time limitted. It is obvious that the exchange, to be within the time, must be made here and not at Paris; and we infer from your letter of [blank] that the ratifications of the Chief Consul are to be transmitted hither with that view.

I only add the wish of the President to know from you the understanding which prevailed in the negotiation with respect to the Boundaries of Louisiana, and particularly the pretensions and proofs for carrying it to the River Perdigo, or for including any lesser portion of West Florida.

With high respect, &c.

Source: Jack N. Rakove, ed., *James Madison: Writings* (New York: Library of America), 671–673.

23   Letter from Thomas Jefferson to Joseph Priestley, January 29, 1804

Joseph Priestly was exactly the sort of man Thomas Jefferson wanted as a friend. Priestley's inquisitive mind and diverse interests made him the very embodiment of an Enlightenment thinker that Jefferson also aspired to be. An English-born clergyman, Priestly eventually became a scientist whose most important discovery was to isolate and define the element oxygen. But Priestly was also an unapologetic political commentator, and when his support for the French Revolution made him a pariah in Britain, he immigrated to the United States in 1794. The regular correspondence between Jefferson and Priestley ended with this letter, written eight days before Priestley died.

. . . I very early saw that Louisiana was indeed a speck in our horizon which was to burst in a tornado; and the public are unapprized how near this catastrophe was. Nothing but a frank & friendly development of causes & effects on our part, and good sense enough in Bonaparte to see that the train was unavoidable, and would change the face of the world, saved us from that storm. I did not expect he would yield till a war took place between France and England, and my hope was to palliate and endure, if Messrs. Ross, Morris, &c. did not force a premature rupture, until that event. I believed the event not very distant, but acknolege it came on sooner than I had expected. Whether, however, the good sense of Bonaparte might not see the course predicted to be necessary & unavoidable, even before a war should be imminent, was a chance which we thought it our duty to try; but the immediate prospect of rupture brought the case to immediate decision. The dénoument has been happy; and confess I look to this duplication of area for the extending a government so free and economical as ours, as a great achievement to the mass of happiness which is to ensue. Whether we remain in one confederacy, or form into Atlantic and Mississippi confederacies, I believe not very important to the happiness of either part. Those of the western confederacy will be as much our children & descendants as those of the eastern, and I feel myself as much identified with that country, in future time, as with this; and did I now foresee a separation at some future day, yet I should feel the duty & the desire to promote the western interests as zealously as the eastern, doing all the good for both portions of our future family which should fall within my power. . . .

Source: Merrill D. Peterson, ed., *Jefferson Writings* (New York: Library of America, 1984), 1142–1143.

Section III (Documents 24-31): Building a Coalition

Although Americans of all political stripes wanted a resolution to the Mississippi crisis, many were uncomfortable with the stipulations of the Louisiana Purchase. Even Jefferson and Madison acknowledged the challenges that it brought. But they also recognized the utter necessity of securing ratification of the treaty, since they were convinced that failing to do so would lead Napoleon to reject any future settlement. So, in the months following the Louisiana Purchase, the Jefferson administration attempted to gain support for the treaty within Congress. Meanwhile, public speakers and pamphleteers launched an uncoordinated but nonetheless far-flung effort to build public support.

Documents 24–27:
Jefferson's Constitutional Concerns

In the summer of 1803 Jefferson worried about the constitutionality of the Louisiana Purchase. As Chapter 8 shows, many worried that executing the agreement with France might reconfigure power within the federal government. For Jefferson, these were political as well as ethical concerns. He acknowledged that opposition to the treaty might be more than mere political interference by the Federalists. And rightly so, for Republicans had their own ambivalence about the treaty.

In documents 24–27, Jefferson began formulating strategies for situating the Louisiana Purchase within the federal Constitution. First, he selected John Breckinridge of Kentucky as his agent within the U.S. Senate. A close friend and political ally of the president, Breckinridge not only helped shepherd the Louisiana Purchase through the Senate, but in the following year he also became the dominant figure on the committee that crafted the territorial government for Louisiana. In the meantime, however, Jefferson toyed with the prospect that a constitutional amendment was both politically and constitutionally necessary to implement the Louisiana Purchase. In two drafts of such a proposed amendment, Jefferson did more than respond to the particular circumstances of the Louisiana Purchase. He also attempted to alter the text of the purchase—especially Article III—in ways that he considered more consistent with the rules governing citizenship for whites and exclusion for all others. By the fall of 1803, however, Jefferson had changed his mind on both counts. Not only did he decide that the Louisiana Purchase was constitutional; he also concluded that his administration had sufficient support within the Senate to secure ratification of the treaty and within Congress as a whole to gain permission for the United States to take possession of Louisiana. By contrast, he knew how long and difficult the amendment process could be, and he abandoned any official alterations to the Constitution.

Documents 28–29:
Explaining the Purchase

As Congress debated the Louisiana Purchase, advocates of the treaty were hard at work building public support. Public statements from the Jefferson administration were, in fact, overshadowed by the public pronouncements by private citizens in venues ranging from newspaper articles to pamphlets and short books. All of these printed comments reflected strong opinions on the matter, and all served obvious political aims. Documents 28 and 29, among others of the time, only reflected the highly politicized nature of journalism and publishing in the early American republic.

Documents 30–31:
Announcing the Purchase

The Louisiana Purchase dominated American newspapers for the better part of a year. As Chapter 3 explains, newspapers tended to divide on partisan lines when it came to the purchase. Documents 30 and 31, two selections from the *National Intelligencer,* show how early American newspapers reported events and editorialized about them. The July 4, 1803, selection was among the first articles to announce the purchase. The second selection appeared soon after news finally reached Washington that the peaceful transfer of power in New Orleans had taken place on December 20, 1803, more than a month earlier.

24 Letter from Thomas Jefferson to John Breckinridge, August 12, 1803

Dear Sir—

The enclosed letter, tho' directed to you, was intended to me also, and was left open with a request, that when perused, I would forward it to you. It gives me occasion to write a word to you on the subject of Louisiana, which being a new one, an interchange of sentiments may produce correct ideas before we are to act on them.

Our information as to the country is very incompleat; we have taken measures to obtain it in full as to the settled part, which I hope to receive in time for Congress. The boundaries, which I deem not admitting question, are the high lands on the western side of the Missisipi enclosing all it's waters, the Missouri of course, and terminating in the line drawn from the northwestern point of the Lake of the Woods to the nearest source of the Missipi, as lately settled between Gr Britain and the U S. We have some claims, to extend on the sea coast Westwardly to the Rio Norte or Bravo, and better, to go Eastwardly to the Rio Perdido, between Mobile & Pensacola, the antient boundary of Louisiana. These claims will be a subject of negociation with Spain, and if, as soon as she is at war, we push them strongly with one hand, holding out a price in the other, we shall certainly obtain the Floridas, and all in good time. In the meanwhile, without waiting for permission, we shall enter into the exercise of the natural right we have always insisted on with Spain, to wit, that of a nation holding the upper part of streams, having a right of innocent passage thro' them to the ocean. We shall prepare her to see us practise on this, & she will not oppose it by force.

Objections are raising to the Eastward against the vast extent of our boundaries, and propositions are made to exchange Louisiana, or a part of it, for the Floridas. But, as I have said, we shall get the Floridas without, and I would not give

one inch of the waters of the Mississippi to any nation, because I see in a light very important to our peace the exclusive right to it's navigation, & the admission of no nation into it, but as into the Potomak or Delaware, with our consent & under our police. These federalists see in this acquisition the formation of a new confederacy, embracing all the waters of the Missipi, on both sides of it, and a separation of it's Eastern waters from us. These combinations depend on so many circumstances which we cannot foresee, that I place little reliance on them. We have seldom seen neighborhood produce affection among nations. The reverse is almost the universal truth. Besides, if it should become the great interest of those nations to separate from this, if their happiness should depend on it so strongly as to induce them to go through that convulsion, why should the Atlantic States dread it? But especially why should we, their present inhabitants, take side in such a question? When I view the Atlantic States, procuring for those on the Eastern waters of the Missipi friendly instead of hostile neighbors on it's Western waters, I do not view it as an Englishman would the procuring future blessings for the French nation, with whom he has no relations of blood or affection. The future inhabitants of the Atlantic & Missipi States will be our sons. We leave them in distinct but bordering establishments. We think we see their happiness in their union, & we wish it. Events may prove it otherwise; and if they see their interest in separation, why should we take side with our Atlantic rather than our Missipi descendants? It is the elder and the younger son differing. God bless them both, & keep them in union, if it be for their good, but separate them, if it be better. The inhabited part of Louisiana, from Point Coupée to the sea, will of course be immediately a territorial government, and soon a State. But above that, the best use we can make of the country for some time, will be to give establishments in it to the Indians on the East side of the Missipi, in exchange for their present country, and open land offices in the last, & thus make this acquisition the means of filling up the Eastern side, instead of drawing off it's population. When we shall be full on this side, we may lay off a range of States on the Western bank from the head to the mouth, & so, range after range, advancing compactly as we multiply.

This treaty must of course be laid before both Houses, because both have important functions to exercise respecting it. They, I presume, will see their duty to their country in ratifying & paying for it, so as to secure a good which would otherwise probably be never again in their power. But I suppose they must then appeal to the nation for an additional article to the Constitution, approving & confirming an act which the nation had not previously authorized. The constitution has made no provision for our holding foreign territory, still less for incorporating foreign nations into our Union. The Executive in seizing the fugitive occurrence which so much advances the good of their country, have done an act beyond the Constitution. The Legislature in casting behind them metaphysical subtleties, and risking themselves like faithful servants, must ratify & pay for it, and throw themselves on their country for doing for them unauthorized what we know they would have done for themselves had they been in a situation to do it. It is the case of a guardian, investing the money of his ward in purchasing an important adjacent territory; & saying to him when of age, I did this for your good; I pretend to no right to bind you: you may disavow me, and I must get out of the scrape as can: I thought it my duty to risk myself for you. But we shall not be disavowed by the nation, and their act of indemnity will confirm & not weaken the Constitution, by more strongly marking out its lines.

We have nothing later from Europe than the public papers give. I hope yourself and all the Western members will make a sacred point of being at the first day of the meeting of Congress; for vestra res agitur.

Source: *Thomas Jefferson Papers* (Washington, D.C.: Library of Congress Microfilm Collection).

25 Jefferson, Draft Constitutional Amendments, 1803

Amendment to the Constitution

Louisiana as ceded by France to the US. is made a part of the US. ~~it's [sic] white inhabitants shall be citizens, and stand, as to their rights & delegations, on the same footing with other citizens of the US in analogous situations. Save only~~ But that as to the portion thereof lying North of an East & West line drawn through the mouth of Arkansa river, no new state shall be established, nor any grants of land made, other than to Indians in exchange for equivalent portions of land occupied by them, until authorized by subsequent amendment to the Constitution. ~~shall be made for these purposes.~~

Florida also, wheresoever it may be rightfully obtained, shall become a part of the US. ~~it's [sic] white inhabitants shall thereupon be citizens, & shall stand, as to their rights & obligations, on the same footing with other citizens of the US. in analogous situations."~~

Amendment to the Constitution

The province of Louisiana is incorporated with the US. and made a part thereof. The rights of occupying in the soil, and of self government, are confirmed to the Indian inhabitants, as they now exist. Preemption only of the portions rightfully occupied by them, & a succession to the occupancy of such as they may abandon, with the full rights of possession as well as of property & sovereignty, in whatever is not or shall cease to be so rightfully occupied by them, shall belong to the US.

The legislature of the union shall have authority to exchange the right of occupancy in portions where the US have full right for lands possessed by Indians within the US. to exchange lands on the East side of the river for those White inhabitants on the West side thereof and along the eastside of W 31 degrees: to maintain in any part of the Province such military posts as may be requisite for peace or safety: to exercise police over all persons therein, not being Indian inhabitants: to work salt springs, or mines of coal, metals & other minerals within the possession of the US, or in any other with the consent of the possessors: to regulate trade & intercourse between the Indian inhabitants and all other persons: to

explore and ascertain the geography of the province, its productions and other interesting circumstances: to open roads & navigation therein where necessary for beneficial communication; and to establish agencies & factories therein for the cultivation of commerce, peace & good understanding with the Indians residing there.

The legislature shall have no authority to dispose of the lands of the prince otherwise than is herein before permitted, until a new amendment of the constitutions shall give that authority. Except as to that portion thereof which lies South of the latitude of 31. degrees; which whenever they deem expedient, they may erect into a territorial government, either separate, or as making part of one on the Eastern side of the river, vesting the inhabitants thereof with all the rights possessed by other territorial citizens of the US.

Source: Thomas Jefferson Papers (Washington, D.C.: Library of Congress Microfilm Collection).

---

26   Congressional Debate over the Louisiana Purchase and the Governance Act of 1804

The debate over the Louisiana Purchase was, in fact, quite brief. By the end of October the Senate was prepared to ratify the treaty, while members of both chambers of Congress were set to authorize the administration to accept the land from France. This did not mean the subject was without debate, however. Even those members who endorsed the purchase had serious qualms about its constitutionality. Like President Thomas Jefferson, they welcomed the agreement but worried about the effect it might have on the federal system.

These concerns became even more prevalent during the winter of 1803–1804, when Congress turned to the difficult task of creating a government for Louisiana. The matter here had less to do with executive power than with the provisions of the purchase. In debates over the treaty and over governance, members of Congress worried how—or even if—the United States could ever convert the seemingly foreign population of Louisiana into something "American." The chief participants were Sens. John Breckinridge, R-Ky., Timothy Pickering, F-Mass., John Taylor, R-Va., and Samuel White, F-Del., and Reps. William Eustis, R-Mass., Gaylord Griswold, F-N.Y., Samuel Mitchill, R-N.Y., and Joseph Nicholson, R-Md.

The source of these debates deserves some explanation. Annals of Congress published the most thorough record of congressional activity from 1789 to 1824, but they were not an exact duplication of what happened in Congress. Gales and Seaton, the publishers of Annals of Congress, had also been publishers of the National Intelligencer, a Washington, D.C., newspaper with strong Republican ties. More important, the Intelligencer provided regular reports on Congress. Beginning in the 1830s, those reports provided the basis for Annals of Congress.

This excerpt comes from the U.S. Senate debate of November 3, 1803. A month earlier a similar debate was conducted in the U.S. House of Representatives.

LOUISIANA TREATY.

The Senate resumed the second reading of the bill, entitled "An act authorizing the creation of a stock to the amount of eleven millions two hundred and fifty thousand dollars, for the purpose of carrying into effect the convention of the 30th of April, 1803, between the United States of America and the French Republic, and making provision for the payment of the same;" and having amended the bill—

. . . Mr. WHITE rose and made the following remarks:

. . . Gentlemen may say this money is to be paid upon the responsibility of the President of the United States, and not until after the delivery of possession to us of the territory; but why cast from ourselves all the responsibility upon this subject and impose the whole weight upon the President, which may hereafter prove dangerous and embarrassing to him? Why make the President the sole and absolute judge of what shall be a faithful delivery of possession under the treaty? What he may think a delivery of possession sufficient to justify the payment of this money, we might not; and I have no hesitation in saying that if, in acquiring this territory under the treaty, we have to fire a single musket, to charge a bayonet, or to lose a drop of blood, it will not be such a cession on the part of France as should justify to the people of this country the payment of any, and much less so enormous a sum of money. What would the case be, sir? It would be buying of France authority to make war upon Spain; it would be giving the First Consul fifteen millions of dollars to stand aloof until we can settle our differences with His Catholic Majesty. Would honorable gentlemen submit to the degradation of purchasing even his neutrality at so inconvenient a price? . . .

. . . But as to Louisiana, this new, immense, unbounded world, if it should ever be incorporated into this Union, which I have no idea can be done but by altering the Constitution. I believe it will be the greatest curse that could at present befall us; it may be productive of innumerable evils, and especially of one that I fear even to look upon. Gentlemen on all sides, with very few exceptions, agree that the settlement of this country will be highly injurious and dangerous to the United States. . . . The gentleman from Tennessee (Mr. COCKE) has shown his usual candor on this subject, and I believe with him, to use his strong language, that you had as well pretend to inhibit the fish from swimming in the sea as to prevent the population of that country after its sovereignty shall become ours. . . . Louisiana must and will become settled, if we hold it, and with the very population that would otherwise occupy part of our present territory. Thus our citizens will be removed to the immense distance of two or three thousand miles from the capital of the Union, where they will scarcely ever feel the rays of the General Government; their affections will become alienated; they will gradually begin to view us as strangers; they will form other commercial connexions, and our interests will become distinct.

These, with other causes that human wisdom may not now foresee, will in time effect a separation, and I fear our bounds will be fixed nearer to our houses than the waters of the Mississippi. We have already territory enough, and when I contemplate the evils that may arise to these States, from this intended incorporation of Louisiana into the Union, I would rather see it given to France, to Spain, or to any other nation of the earth, upon the mere condition that no citizen of the United States should ever settle within its limits, than to see the territory sold for an hundred millions of dollars, and we retain the sovereignty. . . .

Mr. WELLS said: Mr. President, having always held to the opinion that, when a treaty was duly made under the constituted authorities of the United States, Congress was bound to pass the laws necessary to carry it into effect; and as the vote which I am about to give may not at first seem to conform itself to this opinion, I feel an obligation imposed upon me to state, in as concise a manner as I can, the reasons why I withhold my assent from the passage of this bill.

There are two acts necessary to be performed to carry the present treaty into effect—one by the

French Government, the other by our own. They are to deliver us a fair and effectual possession of the ceded territory; and then, and not till then, are we to pay the purchase money. We have already authorized the President to receive possession. This co-operation on our part was requisite to enable the French to comply with the stipulation they had made; they could not deliver unless somebody was appointed to receive. In this view of the subject, the question which presents itself to my mind is, who shall judge whether the French Government does, or does not, faithfully comply with the previous condition? The bill . . . gives to the President this power. I am for our retaining and exercising it ourselves. I may be asked, why not delegate this power to the President? Sir, I answer by inquiring why we should delegate it? To us it properly belongs; and, unless some advantage will be derived to the United States, it should not be transferred with my consent. . . .

Mr. JACKSON.—

. . . Mr. President, the honorable gentleman appears to be extremely apprehensive of vesting the powers delegated by the bill, now on its passage, in the President, and wishes to retain it in the Legislature. Is this a Legislative or an Executive business? Assuredly, in my mind, of the latter nature. The President gave instruction for, and, with our consent, ratified the treaty. We have given him the power to take possession, which his officers are, perhaps, at this moment doing; and surely, as the ostensible party, the representative of the sovereignty to whom France will alone look, he ought to possess the power of fulfilling our part of the contract. Gentlemen, indeed, had doubted, on a former occasion, the propriety of giving the President the power of taking possession and organizing a temporary government. . . . For my part, sir, I have none of those fears. I believe the President will be as cautious as ourselves, and the bill is as carefully worded as possible; for the money is not to be paid until after Louisiana shall be placed in our possession. . . .

Mr. WRIGHT.—

. . . Can it be supposed that the Louisianians, who so lately gave so demonstrative proof of their loyalty in their answer to the address of the Prefect of France, will be less disposed to loyalty to the United States, when they recollect that we have treated them as our children, and ourselves, by securing them in their property and in their civil and religious liberty, agreeably to the principles of our own Constitution? Can they be so unwise as to prefer being the colonists of a distant European Power, to being members of this immense Empire, with all the privileges of American citizens? Can any gentleman seriously entertain such an unauthorized opinion—that that people, whom we have seen so lately, with so much respect to their late King, submit cheerfully to be citizens of the French Republic, will now, in direct violation to the royal order, refuse to obey it, and treasonably take up arms to resist its execution? It is cruel as it is unfounded! But should an infatuation so treasonable beget in them insurgent principles of resistance, I hope and trust that our troops on the spot may be permitted to aid the officers of His Catholic Majesty to reduce them to reason and submission to the royal order of their King; that they may be delivered up to be brought to condign punishment, and that their treasonable project may be nipped in the bud. . . .

Mr. TAYLOR.—

. . . Recollect, sir, that it has been proved that the United States may acquire territory. Territory, so acquired, becomes from the acquisition itself a portion of the territories of the United States, or may be united with their territories without being erected into a State. An union of territory is one thing; of States another. Both are exemplified by an actual existence. The United States possess territory, comprised in the union of territory, and not in the union of States. Congress is empowered to regulate or dispose of territorial sections of the Union, and have exercised the power; but it is not empowered to regulate or dispose of State sections of the Union. The citizens of these territorial sections are citizens of the United S[t]ates, and they have all the rights of citizens of the United States; but such rights do not include those political rights arising from State compacts or governments, which are dissimilar in different

States. Supposing the General Government or treaty-making power have no right to add or unite States and State citizens to the Union, yet they have a power of adding or uniting to it territory and territorial citizens of the United States.

. . . The Constitution recognises and the practice warrants an incorporation of a Territory and its inhabitants into the Union, without admitting either as a State. . . .

. . . I had hoped . . . that the gentleman from Connecticut, (Mr. TRACY) from the trouble he was so good as to give himself yesterday in assisting to amend this bill, would have voted for it; but it seems he is constrained to vote to-day against it. He asks, if the United States have power to acquire and add new States to the Union, can they not also cede States? . . . I answer they cannot; but for none of the reasons assigned by him. The Government of the United States cannot . . . because, first, it would be annihilating part of that sovereignty of the nation which is whole and entire, and upon which the Government of the United States is dependant for its existence; and secondly, because the fourth section of the fourth article of the Constitution forbids it. But how does it follow as a consequence, that because the United States cannot cede an existing State, they cannot acquire a new State? He admits explicitly that Congress may acquire territory and hold it as a territory, but cannot incorporate it into the Union. By this construction he admits the power to acquire territory, a modification infinitely more dangerous than the unconditional admission of a new State; for by his construction, territories and citizens are considered and held as the property of Government of the United States, and may consequently be used as dangerous engines in the hands of the Government against the States and people.

Could we not, says the same gentleman, incorporate in the Union some foreign nation containing ten millions of inhabitants—Africa, for instance—and thereby destroy our Government? Certainly the thing would be possible if Congress would do it, and the people consent to it; but it is supposing so extreme a case and is so barely pos-

sible, that it does not merit serious refutation. It is also possible and equally probable that republicanism itself may one day or other become unfashionable, (for I believe it is not without its enemies,) and that the people of America may call for a King. . . .

The same gentleman . . . observes, that although Congress may admit new States, the President and Senate who are but a component part, cannot. Apply this doctrine to the case before us. How could Congress by any mode of legislation admit this country into the Union until it was acquired? And how can this acquisition be made except through the treaty-making power? Could the gentleman rise in his place and move for leave to bring in a bill for the purchase of Louisiana and its admission into the Union? I take it that no transaction of this or any other kind with a foreign Power can take place except through the Executive Department, and that in the form of a treaty, agreement, or convention. When the acquisition is made, Congress can then make such disposition of it as may be expedient.

. . . If you reject this treaty, with what face can you open another negotiation? What President would venture another mission, or what Minister could be prevailed on to be made the instrument of another negotiation? You adopt the treaty, direct possession to be taken of the country, and then refuse to pay for it!

What palliation can we offer to our Western citizens for a conduct like this? . . . Will it be satisfactory to them to be told that the title is good, the price low, the finances competent, and the authority, at least to purchase, Constitutional; but that the country is too extensive, and that the admission of these people to all the privileges we ourselves enjoy, is not permitted by the Constitution? It will not, sir.

. . . There is a point of endurance beyond which even the advocates for passive obedience and non-resistance cannot expect men to pass. That point is at once reached the moment you solemnly declare, by your vote, that a part of your citizens shall not enjoy those natural rights and advantages of which they are unjustly deprived, and which you have not the complete power to restore to them. Then it is that gentlemen may talk of danger to the Union; then it is I shall begin to tremble for my country; and then it is, and not till then, I shall agree with gentlemen that the Confederacy is in danger. . . .

Source: Annals of Congress: Debates and Proceedings of the Congress of the United States, 8th Cong., 2d sess. (Washington: Gales and Seaton, 1834–1856), 31–44, 49–51, 63–65.

27 Taking Possession of the Territories

Federal legislation approved in October and November 1803 formed a domestic counterpoint to the international agreements that together formed the Louisiana Purchase. Members of Congress and the administration agreed that the Louisiana Purchase had such profound implications for domestic governance that both houses of Congress would need to take any steps after the Senate ratified the treaty. In these documents Congress removed any limitations on the administration's ability to take charge west of the Mississippi. Any subsequent resistance from critics within Congress took the form of opposition to specific governance plans or the creation of new states.

STATUTE I.

CHAPTER I.—An Act to enable the President of the United States to take possession of the territories ceded by France to the United States, by the treaty concluded at Paris, on the thirtieth of April last; and for the temporary government thereof.
APPROVED, October 31, 1803

CHAP. II.—An Act authorizing the creation of a stock, to the amount of eleven millions two hundred and fifty thousand dollars, for the purpose of carrying into effect the convention . . . between the United States and the French Republic; and making provision for the payment of the same.
APPROVED, November 10, 1803.

CHAP. III.—An Act making provision for the payment of claims of citizens of the United States on the government of France, the payment of which has been assumed by the United States, by virtue of the convention . . . between the United States and the French Republic.
APPROVED, November 10, 1803.

Source: The Public Statutes at Large of the United States of America, (Boston: Charles C. Little and James Brown, 1845), vol. 2: 245–248.

28 Thomas Jefferson's Third Annual Message as President, October 17, 1803

By the fall of 1803 Thomas Jefferson had dispensed with any plans for constitutional revision. He had convinced himself of the constitutionality of the Louisiana Purchase, and he was certain of congressional approval. So it was a confident Jefferson who focused his third annual message as president on what he described as a diplomatic victory for the United States. But he celebrated the Louisiana Purchase because he knew an equally difficult struggle lay ahead. Taking possession of Louisiana would only begin the process of establishing American sovereignty west of the Mississippi.

In calling you together, fellow citizens, at an earlier day than was contemplated by the act of the last session of Congress, I have not been insensible to the personal inconveniences necessarily resulting from an unexpected change in your arrangements. But matters of great public concernment have rendered this call necessary, and the interest you feel in these will supersede in your minds all private considerations.

Congress witnessed, at their last session, the extraordinary agitation produced in the public mind by the suspension of our right of deposit at the port of New Orleans, no assignment of another place having been made according to treaty. They were sensible that the continuance of that privation would be more injurious to our nation than any consequences which could flow from any mode of redress, but reposing just confidence in the good faith of the government whose officer had committed the wrong, friendly and reasonable representations were resorted to, and the right of deposit was restored.

Previous, however, to this period, we had not been unaware of the danger to which our peace would be perpetually exposed while so important a key to the commerce of the western country remained under foreign power. Difficulties, too, were presenting themselves as to the navigation of other streams, which, arising within our territories, pass through those adjacent. Propositions had, therefore, been authorized for obtaining, on fair conditions, the sovereignty of New Orleans, and of other possessions in that quarter interesting to our quiet, to such extent as was deemed practicable; and the provisional appropriation of two millions of dollars, to be applied and accounted for by the president of the United States, intended as part of the price, was considered as conveying the sanction of Congress to the acquisition proposed. The enlightened government of France saw, with just discernment, the importance to both nations of such liberal arrangements as might best and permanently promote the peace, friendship, and interests of both; and the property and sovereignty of all Louisiana, which had been restored to them, have on certain conditions been transferred to the United States by instruments bearing date the 30th of April last. When these shall have received the constitutional sanction of the senate, they will without delay be communicated to the representatives also, for the exercise of their functions, as to those conditions which are within the powers vested by the constitution in Congress. While the property and sovereignty of the Mississippi and its waters secure an independent outlet for the produce of the western States, and an uncontrolled navigation through their whole course, free from collision with other powers and the dangers to our peace from that source, the fertility of the country, its climate and extent, promise in due season important aids to our treasury, an ample provision for our posterity, and a widespread field for the blessings of freedom and equal laws.

With the wisdom of Congress it will rest to take those ulterior measures which may be necessary for the immediate occupation and temporary government of the country; for its incorporation into our Union; for rendering the change of government a blessing to our newly-adopted brethren; for securing to them the rights of conscience and of property: for confirming to the Indian inhabitants their occupancy and self-government, establishing friendly and commercial relations with them, and for ascertaining the geography of the country acquired. Such materials for your information, relative to its affairs in general, as the short space of time has permitted me to collect, will be laid before you when the subject shall be in a state for your consideration. . . .

A further knowledge of the ground in the north-eastern and north-western angles of the United States has evinced that the boundaries established by the treaty of Paris, between the British territories and ours in those parts, were too imperfectly described to be susceptible of execution. It has therefore been thought worthy of attention, for preserving and cherishing the harmony and useful intercourse subsisting between the two nations, to remove by timely arrangements what unfavorable incidents might otherwise render a ground of future misunderstanding. A convention has therefore been entered into, which provides for a practicable demarkation of those limits to the satisfaction of both parties.

An account of the receipts and expenditures of the year ending 30th September last, with the estimates for the service of the ensuing year, will be laid before you by the secretary of the treasury so soon as the receipts of the last quarter shall be returned from the more distant States. It is already ascertained that the amount paid into the treasury for that year has been between eleven and twelve millions of dollars, and that the revenue accrued during the same term exceeds the sum counted on as sufficient for our current expenses, and to extinguish the public debt within the period heretofore proposed.

The amount of debt paid for the same year is about three millions one hundred thousand dollars, exclusive of interest, and making, with the payment of the preceding year, a discharge of more than eight millions and a half of dollars of the principal of that debt, besides the accruing interest; and there remain in the treasury nearly six millions of dollars. Of these, eight hundred and eighty thousand have been reserved for payment of the first installment due under the British convention of January 8th, 1802, and two millions are what have been before mentioned as placed by Congress under the power and accountability of the president, toward the price of New Orleans and other territories acquired, which, remaining untouched, are still applicable to that object, and go in diminution of the sum to be funded for it.

Should the acquisition of Louisiana be constitutionally confirmed and carried into effect, a sum of nearly thirteen millions of dollars will then be added to our public debt, most of which is payable after fifteen years; before which term the present existing debts will all be discharged by the established operation of the sinking fund. When we contemplate the ordinary annual augmentation of imposts from increasing population and wealth, the augmentation of the same revenue by its extension to the new acquisition, and the economies which may still be introduced into our public expenditures, I cannot but hope that Congress in reviewing their resources will find means to meet the intermediate interests of this additional debt without recurring to new taxes, and applying to this object only the ordinary progression of our revenue. Its extraordinary increase in times of foreign war will be the proper and sufficient fund for any measures of safety or precaution which that state of things may render necessary in our neutral position. . . .

29 **Samuel Brazer's Pamphlet Commemorating the Cession of Louisiana to the United States, May 12, 1804**

Samuel Brazer's pamphlet was typical of the publications that celebrated the Louisiana Purchase. These pamphlets appeared throughout the U.S. from the summer of 1803 through the spring of 1804. There was a specific political objective to most of these pamphlets. Brazer, like other pamphleteers, hoped to build public support for the purchase. Like others, he did so less by emphasizing the acquisition of new land than by calling attention to the administration's ability to find a peaceful resolution to the Mississippi crisis.

. . . THE event we celebrate, whether we regard merely its intrinsic consequence, or the mode in which it was produced, will well justify our joy and gratulation. The acquisition of the vast territory of *Louisiana,* in itself was a great, a wonderful achievement of wisdom and policy. The means, by which it was obtained, afford an honorable, an unprecedented example of magnanimity and justice.

THE value of the acquisition is beyond doubt or dispute. The high estimation, in which it was once held by those, whom the spirit of party now induces to underrate and belittle it, furnishes unequivocal evidence of its magnitude. Before the object had been compassed, before success had given a sanction to the project, when the most sanguine of the votaries of hope were startled at the boldness of the enterprize; at this time, the enemies of the government were loud in their assertions, that the attainment was of the first and greatest moment. . . . That the *United States* MUST possess the control of the navigation of the *Mississippi*, was stated as a settled and established point. To prevent the colonization of the country by the *French,* was declared an object of great and momentous concern. The Northern States were told, by these careful guardians of their rights and interest, that if the proposed colonization should be effected, their *Commerce* to the *West-Indies* would be materially injured, if not utterly destroyed. The dangers consequent on the vicinity of a great and enterprising colony, were depicted in dark and frowning characters. . . . In a word, we were told, that an adequate compensation for such an acquirement could scarce be conceived, that it was a prize worthy the loftiest ambition,—that the horrors of war were not to be shunned, when such an object was at stake. . . .

. . . the Administration pursued the path of policy, with deliberate, determined and considerate energy. Disregarding the puny censure of disappointed partizans, despising the little malice of the slaves of faction, they consulted only the interest and honor of the nation.

. . . BUT it is not merely the selfish consideration, that we have obtained possession of a city or a country, or the navigation of a river, that warrants our festive rejoicings. Our hearts dilate with nobler rapture and with new enjoyment, when we recollect, that, by this event, is opened a "WIDER SPREAD FOR THE BLESSINGS OF FREEDOM AND EQUAL LAWS!"

. . . FELLOW-CITIZENS! In the occasion of our joy, we anticipate neither the excesses of Liberty, nor the horrors of Tyranny. We rejoice, that an Empire of Laws is about to be established; that mild, social, rational *Freedom* is about to pervade a widely-extended territory; that *Despotism* and his minions are expelled from this fair *American Eden*. . . .

AND while we offer to our Rulers our tribute of applause, for this instance of their wisdom and patriotism, let us not forget, that this is but one of a series of meritorious services, that they have labored incessantly, honestly and successfully for the public good; that they have thus justly acquired the praise, the esteem, the support of every friend to his country. . . .

NEVER had a cause nobler inducements to offer;—never had a cause better or more brilliant prospects. The *Sun* of *Republicanism* has grown brighter and brighter, almost unto a perfect day! Already it shines with full-orb'd splendor, on the mountains of *Hampshire*. Already has it "tipt, with its rising beams," the hundred hills of *Massachusetts*. Soon may every portion of our Fellow-Citizens and our Fellow-Men bask in its meridian rays! Soon may that glorious political Millennium arrive, when every knee shall bow to the MAJESTY of the PEOPLE, and every tongue confess their SOVEREIGNTY!!

Source: Samuel Brazer, Address, Pronounced at Worcester, May 12, 1804, in commemoration of the cession of Louisiana to the United States (Worcester: Sewall Goodridge, 1804), 5–15.

30 Defining Louisiana

This simple announcement from the National Intelligencer was the first news that most people in Washington received of the Louisiana Purchase. More extensive coverage appeared throughout the United States in the months that followed. But the simplicity of this one article does more than show the workings of American journalism. It also gives an immediate indication of what would become the most important—and most controversial—aspects of the purchase: the agreement delivered far more land than Americans expected or wanted, and the land had no fixed boundaries. The very vagueness of this article reflected just how difficult it was to define "Louisiana."

The Executive have received official information that a treaty was signed on the 30th of April between the Ministers Plenipotentiary and Extraordinary of the United States and the Minister Plenipotentiary of the French government; by which the United States have obtained full right to an sovereignty over New Orleans and the whole of Louisiana, as Spain possessed the same.

Source: National Intelligencer, July 4, 1803.

31 Poetic Explanation of the Louisiana Purchase

Most newspapers rarely departed from standard prose. Nonetheless, they would on occasion include rhyme, usually explained as the work of some writer who felt moved to express himself in this way on some important matter. Whether intended as a poem or a song, this passage was a rather uncomplicated effort to use the Louisiana Purchase to distinguish the United States from Europe.

Whilst England and France madly fight for a rock
Or an April chimera produced by foul weather
By prudence we've gained, fighting war's shock
A land more extensive than both put together.

Chorus:
Tho' we've shown to our foes
When exchanging of blows
That our flag is triumphant whenever unfurl'd
Yet as happiness springs
From exchange of good things
We earnestly seek it all over the world.

What thousands of lives, what millions of money
Have been spent to acquire by belligerent powers

Louisiana overflowing with milk and with honey
By open, plain policy honestly ours.

Chorus

No widows, no orphans bedew with their tears
The spot where our banner exaltingly flies
By Spaniards and Frenchmen we're held without fear
And songs of thanksgiving ascend to the skies.

Chorus

Prosperity, harmony offspring of peace
Objects cherished with by the man of our choice

And [sanctioned] by Providence shall still encrease
Whilst we join hand to hand and unite in one voice.

Chorus

Source: *National Intelligencer,* January 25, 1804.

May freedom still wider and wider extend
May nations no longer each other destroy
May they only be rival now most so befriend
And like us all the blessings of union enjoy

Chorus

Section IV (Documents 32–54):
Building a Government

Approving the Louisiana Purchase gave American policymakers only a brief respite. Members of Congress and the administration scrambled to create a government for a land that was infinitely larger than what they expected to acquire from France. Working through legislators like Kentucky senator John Breckinridge, Jefferson and Madison hoped to be active players in this process. And, regardless of the outcome, they knew that the United States would implement some form of territorial government. Before any final plan was ready, members of the administration and a few chosen delegates on the frontier set to work extending the federal government to encompass the people and the land acquired by the Louisiana Purchase. On December 20, 1803, the French surrendered Lower Louisiana to the United States in an elaborate ceremony in New Orleans. In March 1804 a much smaller event marked the passage of Upper Louisiana from Spanish to French to American rule. The men who arrived to govern these new provinces were not elected officials; they were federal appointees who reported to the secretary of state. Although Congress might have settled the constitutionality of the Louisiana Purchase, these territorial officials found that governing a land that seemed so definitively foreign posed tremendous challenges to the federal policymaking apparatus.

Documents 32–35: Congress Acts

After the debates over the constitutionality of the Louisiana Purchase, Congress passed the 1804 Governance Act, designed to extend the territorial system of the United States to the land acquired through the Louisiana Purchase. It was an ungainly fit. Where the territorial system had originally been developed to govern lands sparsely populated by whites until settlers arrived from the East, the 1804 act served a very different purpose. It would instruct the existing white population in the principles of American governance. In the process, the act would provide a solution to the problem many members of Congress associated with the Louisiana Purchase: the absence of any period of naturalization for the Louisianians. But when local residents complained about what they considered the limitations of the 1804 Governance Act, Congress responded in 1805 with a second act that expanded opportunities for political participation and representation for the residents of Louisiana.

Documents 36–41:
Reaching the Residents

Crafting systems of government proved to be only half the job facing the Jefferson administration—they also had to select men to fill those posts. In more general terms, the administration was eager to build effective linkages to people living west of the Mississippi. Jefferson and Madison dispatched a broad range of emissaries to the territory. They included civil officials who would govern the new territories created by the Governance Act of 1804, military personnel whose job it was to establish and preserve American sovereignty, and private individuals who shared some personal connection with the administration.

Regardless of who the messenger was, the message was the same: that the Louisiana Purchase would bring unprecedented benefits to those who lived in the West. Those residents responded in various ways. In general, however, they were pragmatic, asking what this new regime would mean for them. Official communication with two very different constituencies—white settlers and Indians—show just how quickly the residents of Louisiana began pressing their claims on the United States. Members of Congress and the Jefferson administration were hardly alone in arguing about the meaning of the Louisiana Purchase. Residents of Louisiana believed that they too knew how things should work in an expanded United States.

Document 42–50: Statehood

Although fourteen states eventually were carved from the Louisiana Purchase (either in whole or in part), the first two states that emerged are particularly telling, both about the political order of the early American republic and about the disputes that would hold sway in later decades. In 1812 Congress created the state of Louisiana. Nine years later, the state of Missouri came into being. Documents 42–50 tell the story of how local residents appealed for changes in their government and how officials in Washington responded. This long-distance conversation marked a counterpoint to the initial contact between Washington and the West in the immediate aftermath of the Louisiana Purchase. Within a few years, both ends

of this continuum had learned one another's languages. The residents of Louisiana were particularly effective at describing themselves as the most loyal Americans, whether they were expressing their loyalty to the union as a whole or to the Jeffersonian majority in Washington. Of course, to the Jeffersonians there wasn't much difference between the two.

Documents 42–50 include selections from congressional debate and the legislative acts authorizing the state-building process. In the case of Louisiana, the debate over statehood was brief. More vociferous was the argument over permitting the Territory of Orleans to form a state constitutional convention. Once advocates of statehood had won that battle, their critics had little to say in return. Besides, when the Territory of Orleans submitted its constitution for final approval in January 1812, Congress was too busy planning for war to engage in much consideration about Louisiana. Chapters 9 and 10 show just how different things were before and after 1820. When Congress considered Missouri statehood, international peace and the emerging domestic dispute over the expansion of slavery created a far more divisive debate.

Documents 51–54:
Politics and Diplomacy

As the administrations of Jefferson, Madison, and Monroe sought to resolve the domestic challenges that came with the Louisiana Purchase, they were equally troubled by ongoing diplomatic problems. Foremost among these was the lack of any clear boundaries to Louisiana that included the Floridas. This remained the case for almost a decade, even as the United States successfully annexed portions of West

Florida. Then, months after the end of the War of 1812, rumors reached the United States that Spain might cede the Floridas to Great Britain, Spain's new ally after the Napoleonic invasion of 1808. Even with peace restored in Europe and the Spanish losing their grip on their American colonies, American policymakers feared that a final resolution of the Louisiana Purchase might yet elude them.

Scattered over more than a decade and a half, documents 51–54 reveal the continuities within the administrations. James Madison and James Monroe felt these problems particularly acutely. For sixteen years as secretary of state and then as president, Madison struggled to promote American security, with mixed results. Meanwhile, in the years following the Louisiana Purchase, Monroe became a jour-neyman diplomat, holding senior posts throughout Europe while trying without success to realize American goals. Madison acknowledged Monroe's failings in the 1805 letter to William C. C. Claiborne (document 51). These men continued to worry about the frontiers of North America (and about European intervention) into the 1820s. But the most pertinent threat—the international disputes that came from the ambiguous boundaries of the Louisiana Purchase—finally came to an end in 1819 with the signing of the Transcontinental Treaty. If the treaty did not solve all the problems that American statesmen saw on the diplomatic horizon, it did at least mark a clean break from decades spent worrying about the Mississippi and then about the treaty that was supposed to end those fears.

32   The 1804 Governance Act

An Act erecting Louisiana into two territories, and providing for the temporary government thereof

Be it enacted by the Senate and House of Representatives of the United States of America in Congress Assembled, That all that portion of country ceded by France to the United States, under the name of Louisiana, which lies south of the Mississippi territory, and of an east and west line to commence on the Mississippi river, at the thirty third degree of North Latitude, and to extend west to the western boundary of the said cession, shall constitute a territory of the United States, under the name of the territory of Orleans, the government whereof shall be organized and administered as follows:

SEC. 2. The executive power shall be vested in a governor, who shall reside in the said territory, and hold his office during the term of three years, unless sooner removed by the President of the United States. He shall be commander in chief of the militia of the said territory, shall have power to grant pardons for offences against the said territory, and reprieves for those against the United States, until the decision of the President of the United States thereon, shall be made known, and to appoint and commission all officers civil and of the militia, whose appointments are not herein otherwise provided for, and which shall be established by law. He shall take care that the laws be faithfully executed.

SEC. 3. A secretary of the territory shall also be appointed, who shall hold his office during the term of four years, unless sooner removed by the President of the United States, whose duty it shall be, under the direction of the governor, to record and preserve all the papers and proceedings of the executive, and all the acts of the governor and legislative council, and transmit authentic copies of the proceedings of the governor in his executive department, every six months, to the President of the United States. In case of the vacancy of the office of governor, the government of the said territory shall devolve on the secretary.

SEC. 4. The legislative powers shall be vested in the governor, and in thirteen of the most fit and discreet persons of the territory, to be called the legislative council, who shall be appointed annually by the President of the United States 11 from among those holding real estate therein, and who shall have resided one year at least, in the said territory, and hold no office of profit under the territory or the United States. The governor, by and with advice and consent of the said legislative council, or of a majority of them, shall have power to alter, modify, or repeal the laws which may be in force at the commencement of this act. Their legislative powers shall also extend to all the rightful subjects of legislation; but no law shall be valid which is inconsistent with the constitution and laws of the United States, or which shall lay any person under restraint, burden, or disability, on account of his religious opinions, professions, or worship; in all which he shall be free to maintain his own, and not burdened for those of another. The governor shall publish throughout the said territory, all the laws which shall be made, and shall from time to time report the same to the President of the United States to be laid before Congress; which if disapproved of by Congress, shall thenceforth be of no force. The governor or legislative council shall have no power over the primary disposal of the soil, nor to tax the lands of the United States, nor to interfere with the claims to land within the said territory. The governor shall convene and prorogue the legislative council, whenever he may deem it expedient. It shall be his duty to obtain all the information in his power, in relation to the customs, habits, and dispositions of the inhabitants of the said territory, and communicate the same from time to time, to the President of the United States.

SEC. 5. The judicial power shall be vested in a superior court, and in such inferior courts, and justices of the peace, as the legislature of the territory may from time to time establish. The judges of the superior court and the justices of the peace, shall hold their offices for the term of four years. The superior court shall consist of three judges, any one of whom shall constitute a court; they shall have jurisdiction in all criminal cases, and exclusive jurisdiction in all three which are capital; and original and appellate jurisdiction in all civil cases of the value of one hundred dollars. Its sessions shall commence on the first Monday of every month, and continue till all the business depending before them shall be disposed of. They shall appoint their own clerk. In all criminal prosecutions which are capital, the trial shall be by a jury of twelve good and lawful men of the vicinage; and in all cases criminal and civil in the superior court, the trial shall be by a jury, if either of the parties require it. The inhabitants of the said territory shall be entitled to the benefits of the writ of habeas corpus; they shall be bailable, unless for capital offences where the proof shall be evident, or the presumption great; and no cruel and unusual punishments shall be inflicted.

SEC. 6. The governor, secretary, judges, district attorney, marshal, and all general officers of the militia, shall be appointed by the President of the United States, in the recess of the Senate; but shall be nominated at their next meeting for their advice and consent. The governor, secretary, judges, members of the legislative council, justices of the peace, and all other officers civil, and of the militia, before they enter upon the duties of their respective offices, shall take an oath or affirmation to support the constitution of the United States, and for the faithful discharge of the duties of their office; the governor, before the President of the United States, or before a judge of the supreme or district court of the United States, or before such other person as the President of the United States shall authorize to administer the same; the secretary, judges, and members of the legislative council, before the governor, and all

other officers before such persons as the governor shall direct. The governor shall receive an annual salary of five thousand dollars; The secretary of two thousand dollars; and the judges of two thousand dollars each; to be paid quarter-yearly out of the revenues of impost and tonnage accruing within the said territory. The members of the legislative council shall receive four dollars each per day, during their attendance in council.

SEC. 7. *And be it further enacted,* That the following acts, that is to say:

An act for the punishment of certain crimes against the United States.

An act, in addition to an act, for the punishment of certain crimes against the United States.

An act to prevent citizens of the United States from privateering against nations in amity with, or against citizens of the United States.

An act for the punishment of certain crimes therein specified.

An act respecting fugitives from justice, and persons escaping from service of their masters.

An act to prohibit the carrying on the slave trade from the United States to any foreign place or country.

An act to prevent the importation of certain persons into certain states, when by the laws thereof, their admission is prohibited.

An act to establish the post office of the United States.

An act further to alter and establish certain post roads, and for the more secure carriage of the mail of the United States.

An act for the more general promulgation of the laws of the United States.

An act, in addition to an act, entitled An act for the more general promulgation of the laws of the United States.

An act to promote the progress of useful arts, and to repeal the act heretofore made for that purpose.

An act to extend the privilege of obtaining patents for useful discoveries and inventions to certain persons therein mentioned, and to enlarge and define the penalties for violating the rights of patentees.

An act for the encouragement of learning, by securing the copies of maps, charts, and books, to the authors and proprietors of such copies, during the time therein mentioned.

An act supplementary to an act, entitled An act for the encouragement of learning, by securing the copies of maps, charts, and books, to the authors and proprietors of such copies, during the time therein mentioned; and extending the benefits thereof to the arts of designing, engraving, and etching historical and other prints.

An act providing for salvage in cases of recapture.

An act respecting alien enemies.

An act to prescribe the mode in which the public acts, records, and judicial proceedings in each state shall be authenticated, so as to take effect in every other state.

An act for establishing trading houses with the Indian tribes.

An act for continuing in force a law, entitled An act for establishing trading houses with the Indian tribes; and

An act making provision relative to rations for Indians, and to their visits to the seat of Government, shall extend to, and have full force and effect in the above mentioned territories.

SEC. 8. There shall be established in the said territory a district court, to consist of one judge, who shall reside therein, and be called the district judge, and who shall hold, in the city of Orleans, four sessions annually; the first to commence on the third Monday in October next, and the three other sessions, progressively, on the third Monday of every third calendar month thereafter. He shall in all things, have and exercise the same jurisdiction and powers, which are by law given to, or may be exercised by the judge of Kentucky district; and shall be allowed an annual compensation of two thousand dollars, to be paid quarter-yearly out of the revenues of impost and tonnage accruing within the said territory. He shall appoint a clerk for the said district, who shall reside, and keep the records of the court, in the city of Orleans, and shall receive for the services performed by him, the same fees to which the clerk of Kentucky district is entitled for similar services.

There shall be appointed in the said district, a person learned in the law, to act as attorney for the United States, who shall, in addition to his stated fees, be paid six hundred dollars, annually, as a full compensation for all extra services. There shall also be appointed a marshal for the said district, who shall perform the same duties, be subject to the same regulations and penalties, and be entitled to the same fees to which marshals in other districts are entitled for similar services; and shall moreover be paid two hundred dollars, annually, as a compensation for all extra services.

SEC. 9. All free male white persons, who are house-keepers, and who shall have resided one year, at least, in the said territory, shall be qualified to serve as grand or petit jurors, in the courts of the said territory; and they shall, until the legislature thereof shall otherwise direct, be selected in such manner as the judges of the said courts, respectively shall prescribe, so as to be most conducive to an impartial trial, and to be least burdensome to the inhabitants of the said territory.

SEC. 10. It shall not be lawful for any person or persons to import or bring into the said territory, from any port or place without the limits of the United States, or cause or procure to be so imported or brought, or knowingly to aid or assist in so importing or bringing any slave or slaves. And every person so offending, and being thereof convicted before any court within said territory, having competent jurisdiction, shall forfeit and pay for each and every slave so imported or brought, the sum of three hundred dollars; one moiety for the use of the United States, and the other moiety for the use of the person or persons who shall sue for the same; and every slave so imported or brought, shall thereupon become entitled to, and receive his or her freedom. It shall not be lawful for any person or persons to import or bring into the said territory, from any port or place within the limits of the United States, or to cause or procure to be so imported or brought, or knowingly to aid or assist in so importing or bringing any slave or slaves, which shall have been imported since the first day of May, one thousand seven hundred and ninety eight, into any port or place within the limits of the United States, or which may hereafter be so imported, from any port or place without the limits of the United States; and every person so offending, and being thereof convicted before any court within said territory, having competent jurisdiction, shall forfeit and pay for each and every slave so imported or brought the sum of three hundred dollars, one moiety for the use of the United States, and the other moiety for the use of the person or persons who shall sue for the same; and no slave or slaves shall directly or indirectly be introduced into said territory, except by a citizen of the United States, removing into said territory for actual settlement, and being at the time of such removal bona fide owner of such slave or slaves; and every slave imported or brought into the said territory, contrary to the provisions of this act, shall thereupon be entitled to, and receive his or her freedom.

SEC. 11. The laws in force in the said territory, at the commencement of this act, and not inconsistent with the provisions thereof, shall continue in force, until altered, modified, or repealed by the legislature.

SEC. 12. The residue of the province of Louisiana, ceded to the United States, shall be called the District of Louisiana, the government whereof shall be organized and administered as follows: The executive power now vested in the governor of the Indiana territory, shall extend to, and be exercised in the said District of Louisiana. The governor and judges of the Indiana territory shall have power to establish, in the said District of Louisiana, inferior courts, and prescribe their jurisdiction and duties, and to make all laws which they may deem conducive to the good government of the inhabitants thereof: *Provided however,* That no law shall be valid which is inconsistent with the constitution and laws of the United States, or which shall lay any person under restraint or disability on account of his religious opinions, profession, or worship; in all which he shall be free to maintain his own, and

not burdened for those of another; *And provided also,* That in all criminal prosecutions, the trial shall be by a jury of twelve good and lawful men of the vicinage, and in all civil cases of the value of one hundred dollars, the trial shall be by jury, if either of the parties require it. The judges of the Indiana territory, or any two of them, shall hold annually two courts within the said district, at such place as will be most convenient to the inhabitants thereof in general, shall possess the same jurisdiction they now possess in the Indiana territory, and shall continue in session until all the business depending before them shall be disposed of. It shall be the duty of the secretary of the Indiana territory to record and preserve all the papers and proceedings of the governor, of an executive nature, relative to the district of Louisiana, and transmit authentic copies thereof every six months to the President of the United States. The governor shall publish throughout the said district, all the laws which may be made as aforesaid and shall, from time to time report the same to the President of the Uited States, to be laid before Congress, which, if disapproved of by Congress, shall thenceforth cease, and be of no effect.

The said district of Louisiana shall be divided into districts by the governor, under the direction of the President, as the convenience of the settlements shall require, subject to such alterations hereafter as experience may prove more convenient. The inhabitants of each district, between the ages of eighteen and forty five shall be formed into a militia, with proper officers, according to their numbers, to be appointed by the governor, except the commanding officer, who shall be appointed by the President, and who whether a captain, a major or a colonel, shall be the commanding officer of the district, and as such shall, under the governor, have command of the regular officers and troops in his district, as well as of the militia, for which he shall have a brevet commission, giving him such command, and the pay and emoluments of an officer of the same grade in the regular army; he shall be specially charged with the employment of the military and militia of his district, in cases of sudden invasion or insurrection, and until the orders of the governor can be received, and at all times with the duty of ordering a military patrol, aided by militia if necessary, to arrest unauthorized settlers in any part of his district, and to commit such offenders to jail to be dealt with according law.

SEC. 13. The laws in force in the said district of Louisiana, at the commencement of this act, and not inconsistent with any of the provisions thereof, shall continue in force until altered, modified or repealed by the governor and judges of the Indiana territory, as aforesaid.

SEC. 14. *And be it further enacted,* That all grants for lands within the territories ceded by the French republic to the United States, by the treaty of the thirtieth of April, in the year one thousand eight hundred and three the title whereof was, at the date of the treaty of St. Ildefonso, in the crown, government or nation of Spain, and every act and proceeding subsequent thereto, of whatsoever nature, towards the obtaining any grant, title, or claim to such lands, and under whatsoever authority transacted, or pretended, be, and the same are hereby declared to be, and to have been from the beginning, null, void, and of no effect in law or equity. *Provided nevertheless,* that any thing in this section contained shall not be construed to make null and void any bona fide grant, made agreeably to the laws usages and customs of the Spanish government to an actual settler on the lands so granted, for himself, and for his wife and family; or to made null and void any bona fide act or proceeding done by an actual settler agreeably to the laws, usages and customs of the Spanish government to obtain a grant for lands actually settled on by the person or persons claiming title thereto, if such settlement in either case was actually made prior to the twentieth day of December, one thousand eight hundred and three; *And provided further* that such grant shall not secure to the grantee or his assigns more than one mile square of land together with such other and further quantity as heretofore hath been allowed for the wife and family of such actual settler, agreeably to the laws usages and customs of the Spanish

government. And that if any citizen of the United States, or other person, shall make a settlement on any lands belonging to the United States, within the limits of Louisiana, or shall survey, or attempt to survey, such lands, or to designate boundaries by marking trees, or otherwise, such offender shall, on conviction thereof, in any court of record of the United States, or the territories of the United States, forfeit a sum not exceeding one thousand dollars, and suffer imprisonment not exceeding twelve months; and it shall, moreover, be lawful for the President of the United States to employ such military force as he may judge necessary to remove from lands belonging to the United States any such citizen or other person, who shall attempt a settlement thereon.

SEC. 15. The President of the United States is hereby authorized to stipulate with any Indian tribes owning lands on the east side of the Mississippi, and residing thereon, for an exchange of lands, the property of the United States, on the west side of the Mississippi, in case the said tribes shall remove and settle thereon; but in such stipulation, the said tribes shall acknowledge themselves to be under the protection of the United States, and shall agree that they will not hold any treaty with any foreign power, individual state, or with the individuals of any state or power; and that they will not sell or dispose of the said lands, or any part thereof, to any sovereign power, except the United States, nor to the subjects or citizens of any other sovereign power, nor to the citizens of the United States. And in order to maintain peace and tranquility with the Indian tribes who reside within the limits of Louisiana, as ceded by France to the United States, the act of Congress, passed on the thirtieth day of March, one thousand eight hundred and two, entitled "An act to regulate trade and intercourse with the Indian tribes, and to preserve peace on the frontiers," is hereby extended to the territories erected and established by this act; and the sum of fifteen thousand dollars of any money in the treasury not otherwise appropriated by law is hereby appropriated to enable the President of the United States to effect the object expressed in this section.

SEC. 16. The act passed on the thirty-first day of October, one thousand eight hundred and three, entitled "An act to enable the President of the United States to take possession of the territories ceded by France to the United States, by the treaty concluded at Paris, on the thirtieth day of April last, and for the temporary government thereof," shall continue in force until the first day of October next, any thing therein to the contrary notwithstanding; on which said first day of October, this act shall commence, and have full force, and shall continue in force for and during the term of one year, and to the end of the next session of Congress which may happen thereafter.

APPROVED, March 26, 1804

Source: Francis Newton Thorpe, ed., *The Federal and State Constitutions, Colonial Charters, and Other Organic Laws of the States, Territories, and Colonies Now or Heretofore Forming the United States of America* (Washington, D.C.: Government Printing Office), vol. 3: 1364–1371.

33 Remonstrance of the People of Louisiana Against the Political System Adopted by Congress for Them, May 1804

We the subscribers, planters, merchants and other inhabitants of Louisiana, respectfully approach the Legislature of the United States with a memorial of our rights, a remonstrance against certain laws which contravene them, and a petition for that redress to which the laws of nature, sanctioned by positive stipulation, have entitled us.

Without any agency in the events which have annexed our country to the United States, we yet considered them as fortunate, and thought our liberties secured even before we knew the terms of the cession. Persuaded that a free people would acquire territory only to extend the blessings of freedom; that an enlightened nation would never destroy those principles on which its government was founded, and that their Representatives would disdain to become the instruments of oppression, we calculated with certainty that their first act of sovereignty would be a communication of all the blessings they enjoyed. . . . It was early understood that we were to be American citizens: this satisfied our wishes, it implied every thing we could desire, and filled us with that happiness which arises from the anticipated enjoyment of a right long withheld. We knew that it was impossible to be citizens of the United States without enjoying personal freedom, protection for property, and above all the privileges of free representative government, and did not therefore imagine that we could be deprived of these rights even if there should have existed no promise to impart them; yet it was with some satisfaction we found these objects secured to use by the stipulations of treaty, and the faith of Congress pledged for their uninterrupted enjoyment. We expected them from your magnanimity, but were not displeased to see them guarantied by solemn engagements. . . .

With a firm persuasion that these engagements would be soon fulfilled, we passed under your jurisdiction with a joy bordering on enthusiasm, submitted to the inconveniences of an intermediate dominion without a murmur, and saw the last tie that attached us to our mother country severed with less regret. . . . We could not bring ourselves to believe that we had so far mistaken the stipulations in our favor, or that Congress could so little regard us, and we waited the result with anxiety which distance only prevented our expressing before the passing of the bill. After a suspense which continued to the last moment of the session, after debates which only tended to show how little our true situation was known, after the rejection of every amendment declaratory of our rights, it at length became a law, and, before this petition can be presented, will take effect in our country.

Disavowing any language but that of respectful remonstrance, disdaining any other but that which befits a manly assertion of our rights, we pray leave to examine the law for erecting Louisiana into two Territories and providing for the temporary government thereof, to compare its provisions with our rights, and its whole scope with the letter and spirit of the treaty which binds us to the United States.

. . . Uninformed as we are supposed to be of our acquired rights, is it necessary for us to demonstrate that this act does not "incorporate us in the Union," that it vests us with none of the "rights," gives us no advances and deprives us of all the "immunities" of American citizens. . . .

Source: American State Papers: Documents, Legislative and Executive, of the Congress of the United States (Washington, D.C.: Gales and Seaton), Miscellaneous, vol. I: 396–405.

34 The 1805 Governance Act

An Act further providing for the government of the territory of Orleans.

Be It Enacted, by the Senate and House of Representatives of the United States of America, in Congress assembled, That the President of the United States be, and he is hereby authorized to establish within the territory of Orleans, a government in all respects similar, (except as is herein otherwise provided) to that now exercised in the Mississippi territory; and shall, in the recess of the Senate, but to be nominated at their next meeting, for their advice and consent, appoint all the officers necessary therein, in conformity with the ordinance of Congress, made on the thirteenth day of July, one thousand seven hundred and eighty-seven, and that from and after the establishment of the said government, the inhabitants of the territory of Orleans, shall be entitled to and enjoy all the rights, privileges, and advantages secured by the said ordinance, and now enjoyed by the people of the Mississippi territory.

SEC. 2. *And be it further enacted,* That so much of the said ordinance of Congress, as relates to the organization of a general assembly, and prescribes the powers thereof, shall, from and after the fourth day of July next, be in force in the said territory of Orleans; and in order to carry the same into operation, the governor of the said territory shall cause to be elected twenty-five representatives, for which purpose he shall lay off the said territory into convenient election districts, on or before the first Monday of October next, and give due notice thereof throughout the same; and shall appoint the most convenient time and place within each of the said districts, for holding the elections; and shall nominate a proper officer or officers to preside at and conduct the same, and to return to him the names of the persons who may have been duly elected. All subsequent elections shall be regulated by the legislature; and the number of representatives shall be determined, and the apportionment made in the manner prescribed by the said ordinance.

SEC. 3. *And be it further enacted,* That the representatives to be chosen as aforesaid shall be convened by the governor, in the city of Orleans, on the first Monday in November next; and the first general assembly shall be convened by the governor as soon as may be convenient, at the city of Orleans, after the members of the legislative council shall be appointed and commissioned; and the general assembly shall meet, at least, once in every year, and such meeting shall be on the first Monday in December, annually, unless they shall, by law, appoint a different day. Neither house, during the session, shall, without the consent of the other, adjourn for more than three days, nor to any other place than that, in which the two branches are sitting.

SEC. 4. *And be it further enacted,* That the laws in force in the said territory, at the commencement of this act, and not inconsistent with the provisions thereof, shall continue in force, until altered, modified, or repealed by the legislature.

SEC. 5. *And be it further enacted,* That the second paragraph of the said ordinance, which regulates the descent and distribution of estates; and also the sixth article of compact which is annexed to, and makes part of said ordinance, are hereby declared not to extend to, but are excluded from all operation within the said territory of Orleans.

SEC. 6. *And be it further enacted,* That the governor, secretary, and judges, to be appointed by virtue of this act, shall be severally allowed the same compensation which is now allowed to the governor, secretary, and judges, of the territory of Orleans. And all the additional officers authorized by this act, shall respectively receive the same compensations for their services, as are by law established for similar offices in the Mississippi territory, to be paid quarter-yearly out of the revenues of impost and tonnage, accruing within the said territory of Orleans.

SEC. 7. *And be it further enacted,* That whenever it shall be ascertained by an actual census, or enumeration of the inhabitants of the territory of Orleans, taken by proper authority, that the number of free inhabitants included therein shall amount to sixty thousand, they shall thereupon be authorized to form for themselves a constitu-

tion and state government, and be admitted into the Union upon the footing of the original states, in all respects whatever, conformably to the provisions of the third article of the treaty, concluded at Paris, on the thirtieth of April, one thousand eight hundred and three, between the United States and the French republic: Provided, that the constitution so to be established shall be republican, and not inconsistent with the constitution of the United States, nor inconsistent with the ordinance of the late Congress, passed the thirteenth day of July, one thousand seven hundred and eighty-seven, so far as the same is made applicable to the territorial government hereby authorized to be established: Provided however, that Congress shall be at liberty, at any time prior to the admission of the inhabitants of the said territory to the right of a separate state, to alter the boundaries thereof as they may judge proper: *Except only,* that no alteration shall be made which shall procrastinate the period for the admission of the inhabitants thereof to the rights of a state government according to the provision of this act.

SEC. 8. *And be it further enacted,* That so much of an act, entitled "An act erecting Louisiana into two territories, and providing for the temporary government thereof," as is repugnant with this act, shall, from and after the first Monday of November next, be repealed. And the residue of the said act shall continue in full force, until repealed, any thing in the sixteenth section of the said act to the contrary notwithstanding.

Approved, March 2, 1805.

Source: Francis Newton Thorpe, ed., *The Federal and State Constitutions, Colonial Charters, and Other Organic Laws of the States, Territories, and Colonies Now or Heretofore Forming the United States of America* (Washington, D.C.: Government Printing Office), vol. 3: 1371–1373.

35   The 1812 Governance Act for the Territory of Missouri

An Act providing for the government of the Territory of Missouri. Be it enacted by the Senate and House of Representatives of the United States of America in Congress assembled, That the Territory heretofore called Louisiana shall hereafter be called Missouri, and that the temporary government of the Territory of Missouri shall be organized and administered in the manner hereinafter prescribed.

SEC. 2. *And be it further enacted,* That the executive power shall be vested in a governor, who shall reside in the said Territory; he shall hold his office during the term of three years, unless sooner removed by the President of the United States; shall be commander-in-chief of the militia of the said Territory; shall have power to appoint and commission all officers, civil and of the militia, whose appointments are not herein otherwise provided for, which shall be established by law; shall take care that the laws be faithfully executed; shall have power to grant pardons for offences against the said Territory, and reprieves for those against the United States, until the decision of the President of the United States thereon shall be made known; shall have power on extraordinary occasions to convene the general assembly, and he shall *ex officio* be superintendent of Indian affairs. . . .

SEC. 4. *And be it further enacted,* That the legislative power shall be vested in a general assembly, which shall consist of the governor, a legislative council, and a house of representatives. The general assembly shall have power to make laws in all cases, both civil and criminal, for the good government of the people of the said Territory, not repugnant to or inconsistent with the Constitution and laws of the United States, and shall have power to establish inferior courts and to prescribe their jurisdiction and duties, to define the powers and duties of justices of the peace and other civil offices in the said Territory, and to reg-

ulate and fix the fees of office and to ascertain and provide for payment of the same, and for all other services rendered to the said Territory under the authority thereof. All bills having passed by a majority in the house of representatives and by a majority in the legislative council shall be referred to the governor for his assent, but no bill or legislative act whatever shall be of any force without his approbation. . . .

SEC. 9. *And be it further enacted,* That all and every free white male person, who, on the twentieth day of December, in the year one thousand eight hundred and three, was an inhabitant of the Territory of Louisiana, and all free white male citizens of the United States who, since the said twentieth day of December, in the year one thousand eight hundred and three, emigrated, or who hereafter may emigrate, to the said Territory, being otherwise qualified according to the provisions of this act, shall be capable to hold any office of honor, trust, or profit in the said Territory, under the United States, or under the said Territory, and to vote for members of the general assembly and a Delegate to Congress during the temporary government provided for by this act.

SEC. 10. *And be it further enacted,* That the judicial power shall be vested in a superior court, and in inferior courts and justices of the peace. The judges of the superior court and justices of the peace shall hold their offices for the term of four years, unless sooner removed; the superior court shall consist of three judges, who shall reside in the said Territory, any two of whom shall constitute a court; the superior court shall have jurisdiction in all criminal cases, and exclusive jurisdiction in all those that are capital; and original and appellate jurisdiction in all civil cases of the value of one hundred dollars; the said judges shall hold their courts at such times and places as shall be prescribed by the general assembly. The sessions of the superior and inferior courts shall continue until all the business depending shall be disposed of, or for such time as shall be prescribed by the general assembly. The superior and inferior courts shall respectively appoint their clerks, who shall be commissioned by the governor, and shall hold their offices during the temporary government of the said Territory, unless sooner removed by the court. . . .

SEC. 14. *And be it further enacted,* That the people of the said Territory shall always be entitled to a proportionate representation in the general assembly; to judicial proceedings according to the common law and the laws and usages in force in the said Territory; to the benefit of the writ of habeas corpus. In all criminal cases the trial shall be by jury of good and lawful men of the vicinage. All persons shall be bailable, unless for capital offences where the proof shall be evident or the presumption great. All fines shall be moderate, and no cruel or unusual punishment shall be inflicted. No man shall be deprived of his life, liberty, or property, but by the judgment of his peers and the law of the land. If the public exigencies make it necessary for the common preservation to take the property of any person, or to demand his particular services, full compensation shall be made for the same. No *ex post facto* law, or law impairing the obligation of contracts, shall be made. No law shall be made which shall lay any person under restraint, burden, or disability, on account of his religious opinions, professions, or mode of worship, in all which he shall be free to maintain his own, and not burdened for those of another. Religion, morality, and knowledge, being necessary to good government and the happiness of mankind, schools and the means of education shall be encouraged and provided for from the public lands of the United States in the said Territory, in such manner as Congress may deem expedient.

SEC. 15. *And be it further enacted,* That the general assembly shall never interfere with the primary disposal of the soil by the United States in Congress assembled, nor with any regulation Congress may find necessary to make for securing the title in the *bona-fide* purchasers. No tax shall ever be imposed on lands the property of the United States. The lands of non-resident proprietors shall never be taxed higher than those of residents. The Mississippi and Missouri Rivers, and the navigable waters flowing into them, and the carrying-places between the same, shall be common highways and forever free to the people of said Territory, and to the citizens of the United States, without any tax, duty, or impost therefor.

SEC. 16. *And be it further enacted,* That the laws and regulations in force in the Territory of Louisiana, at the commencement of this act, and not inconsistent with the provisions thereof, shall continue in force until altered, modified, or repealed by the general assembly. And it is hereby declared that this act shall not be construed to vacate the commission of any officer in the said Territory, acting under the authority of the United States, but that every such commission shall be and continue in full force as if this act had not been made. And so much of an act entitled "An act further providing for the government of the Territory of Louisiana," approved on the third day of March, one thousand eight hundred and five, and so much of an act entitled "An act for erecting Louisiana into two Territories and providing for the temporary government thereof," approved the twenty-sixth of March, one thousand eight hundred and four, as is repugnant to this act, shall, from and after the first Monday in December next, be repealed. On which first Monday in December next this act shall commence and have full force: *Provided,* So much of it as requires the governor of said Territory to perform certain duties, previous to the said first Monday in December next, shall be in force from the passage thereof.

APPROVED, June 4, 1812.

Source: The Public Statutes at Large of the United States of America, 8 vols. (Boston: Charles C. Little and James Brown, 1845), vol. 2: 743–747.

36   William C. C. Claiborne Proclamation, December 20, 1803

William C. C. Claiborne was the most prominent example of the sort of men the Jefferson administration selected to govern Louisiana. Most of their appointees in Louisiana were Virginians or Kentuckians of impeccable Republican credentials, proven loyalty to the administration and to the nation, and some degree of political or administrative experience. A Virginian by birth, Claiborne moved to Tennessee, eventually inheriting the congressional seat vacated by Andrew Jackson when the latter moved to the Senate. By 1803 the twenty-eight-year-old Claiborne was governor of the Mississippi Territory and the logical candidate to oversee the transfer of power in Louisiana. Although Thomas Jefferson and James Madison both initially doubted the man's abilities and occasionally considered replacements in the years immediately after the Louisiana Purchase, they eventually concluded that Claiborne was an effective administrator. Louisianians apparently agreed, electing him the first governor of the state of Louisiana. In this proclamation, Claiborne attempted to explain the purchase to the residents of Louisiana.

The following address was delivered by the Undersigned to a large Assemblage of Citizens in the Grand Salee of the City Hall, on the 20th day of December 1803.

Fellow Citizens of Louisiana!

On the great and interesting event which is now finally consummated;—An event so advantageous to yourselves, and so glorious to United America, I cannot forbear offering you my warmest congratulations.—The wise Policy of the Consul of France, has by the Cession of Louisiana to the United States secured to you a connection *beyond the reach of change,* and to your posterity the sure inheritance of Freedom. The American people receive you as Brothers, and will hasten to extend to you a participation in those invaluable rights which have formed the basis of their own unexampled prosperity. Under the Auspices of the American Government, you may confidently rely upon the security of your Liberty, your property and the religion of your choice;— You may with equal certainty rest assured that your commerce will be promoted, and your agriculture cherished; in a word that your interest will be among the principal cares of the National Legislature. In return for these benefits the United States will be amply renumerated, if your growing attachment to the *Constitution* of our Country, and your veneration for the principles on which it is founded, be duly proportioned to the blessings which they will confer.

Among your first duties therefore you should cultivate with assiduity among yourselves the advancement of Political information; you should guide the rising generation in the paths of republican economy and virtue: you should encourage Literature, for without the advantages of education, your descendants will be unable sufficiently to appreciate the intrinsic worth of the Government transmitted to them.

As for myself fellow Citizens, receive a sincere assurance that during my continuance in the situation in which the President of the United States has been pleased to place me, every exertion will be made on my part, to foster your internal happiness, and to promote your general welfare, for it is by such measures alone, that I can Secure to myself the approbation of those great and just men who preside in the Council of our nation.

Source: Dunbar Rowland, ed., *The Letter Books of William C. C. Claiborne, 1801–1816* (Jackson: Mississippi State Archive), vol. 1: 309–310.

37   **Letter from William C. C. Claiborne to James Madison, December 27, 1803**

Like most territorial officials, William C. C. Claiborne owed his office not to election but to his appointment from Washington. As a result, he went out of his way to curry favor within the Jefferson administration, calling attention to his own accomplishments and explaining his failings. In this letter Claiborne made some of his first observations on the realities of governing in Louisiana, implicitly assuring the secretary of state that he would make the utmost effort to secure American sovereignty.

Sir,

Since my last I have been as busily engaged as circumstances would admit, in making such arrangements for the temporary Government of the Province, as I esteemed most consonant to the intentions of the President, and the expectations of the inhabitants. The difficulties I meet with in this undertaking, are peculiarly embarrassing on account of the neglected State in which I found the Colony:— The functions of Government have been nearly at a stand for some time, and considerable arrears of business have accumulated in every department.

The French Prefect during the time he held the Country, exerted himself to remedy this evil and his efforts were so happily directed as to give pretty general Satisfaction. But he could feel only a temporary interest in the concerns of the Country, and his time was too short for extensive operations. There is one of his measures however, to which I feel myself not a little indebted: *He abolished the Cabildo, or City Council: This body was created on principles altogether incongruous with those of our Government;*— It was in part an Hereditary Council. In action feeble and arbitrary and supposed to be devoted to the views of the Spanish Government. In their place I found a Municipality established, consisting for the most part of approved Characters, and well disposed towards the expected change of Government, and I therefor, did not long hesitate to sanction the new arrangement.

Being a stranger in the Country, I of course stand in need of much local information as I proceed; and the suspicions which I have too much reason to apprehend from latent Interests in almost every quarter to which I can look, have often induced me to deliberate perhaps longer than is consistent with the promptitude expected from me. Among my other difficulties I have to mention the re-organization of the Militia. I have to regret that the Prefect was not so fortunate in his arrangements on this head as I could have wished. I have found several very young men holding rank above their years, and some others who are unpopular as officers and under whom the Militia will serve very reluctantly if at all. But my principal difficulty arises from two large Companies of people of Colour, who are attached to the Service, and were esteemed a very Serviceable Corps under the Spanish Government. On this particular Corps, I have reflected with much anxiety. To re-commission them might be considered as an outrage on the feelings of a part of the Nation, and as opposed to those principles of Policy which the Safety of the Southern States has necessarily established; on the other hand not to be re-commissioned, would disgust them, and might be productive of future mischief. To disband them would be to raise an armed enemy in the very heart of the Country, and to disarm them would savour too strongly of that desperate System of Government which Seldom Succeeds. Should therfore no necessity urge me to a hasty decision on this point, I shall await some opinions and instructions from the Department of State, and have therefore to beg, that I may be favoured with them as soon as possible. In my first proclamation I did not insert the Treaty as was intended by the draft forwarded to me some time since;— I omitted it because in the course of the week before my arrival, it appeared in the several New Orleans Papers, in the English and French Languages, and had already got into general circulation: The insertion of it in my proclamation, would moreover have considerably retarded the publication, and the lively anxiety of the people at that interesting crisis, forbad the delay of my proclamation.

I had formed very favourable expectations of the Country, but I have had the satisfaction to find them surpassed. The Banks of the River from Baton Rouge to the City exhibit almost uninterrupted Streets of comfortable, and frequently magnificent buildings, with every appearance of prosperity around them. The principal Streets of the City are well built, many of the Houses are elegant, and improvements seem to progress. New Orleans appears to me, to be, not unlike what Baltimore was four years ago, with every prospect of rapid advancement. The Governors House is large and I am told Commodious. I took an early opportunity of communicating to the late Governor, through his eldest son, that I wished him to consider that House as his own, until it was perfectly convenient to leave it. I however learn that he means to quit it in the course of a few days.

I yesterday paid a visit of Ceremony to the Convent here and returned I assure you deeply impressed with the importance of that establishment at the present period. There is an Abbess and eleven Nuns, the sole *object* of whose temporal cares *is,* the Education of Female youth;— they at present accomodate *seventy three Boarders* and a hundred day Scholars, each of whom contribute to the Support of the House, in proportion to the means and conditions of their respective parents, and many receive their tuition gratis.

In the name of the President of the United States I undertook to give the Nuns a Solemn assurance, that they would be protected in their persons, their property, and the Religion of their Choice; and they in return expressed the highest confidence in the Government. They even indulge an expectation, that several of the Nuns who, on the arrival of the French Officers retired to the Havanna would return, it being now certain that nothing is to be apprehended from the French, and that with us, they would enjoy the advantage of Just and Mild Laws. Our Army here is so small, that General Wilkinson has not yet thought it expedient to dismiss the Militia of the Mississippi Territory. I think it necessary to mention, that the General at my request furnished many of them at Fort Adams with clothing, Blankets &c as the men were too poor to provide themselves, and the weather was inclement and severe. For the sake of these Patriotic Men I have to intreat that the articles furnished, may be considered by the Government as a present. They deserve well of their Country, they turned out in the middle of Winter when a serious Campaign was apprehended. Their duty has been hard, and if at the expiration of their time, the price of the equipment be deducted from their pay, they will go home poorer than they came, with the fatigues of the expedition, the only reward of their Services.

Source: Dunbar Rowland, ed., *The Letter Books of William C. C. Claiborne, 1801–1816* (Jackson: Mississippi State Archive), vol. 1: 312–316.

38 Address from the Free People of Color, January 1804

New Orleans was home to North America's largest population of free people of color. All the more striking was how quickly this population had grown. Slaves found securing their freedom less difficult in the French colonial system than in the British, but the number of free people of color was still small when the Spanish took charge in 1768. Under the Spanish regime the numbers began to grow, in part as a reflection of the general increase in Louisiana's non-Indian population, in part because slaves effectively exploited Spanish law to secure their freedom, and in part because the growth in people of mixed-race ancestry led whites to help provide freedom for their children. Not only were they more numerous, but free people of color were also more prosperous in Spanish Louisiana than in the United States.

These free people of color saw that the Louisiana Purchase made no reference to race in the guarantees of freedom contained in Article III. They hoped to exploit this ambiguity to create new opportunities for themselves, and, like their white neighbors, they were eager to cultivate the goodwill of the new American government. The territorial regime saw things differently, as did the administration. Jefferson, Madison, and their delegates on the frontier uniformly sought tighter restrictions on free people of color. White Louisianians responded in kind. Although New Orleans remained the home to a large and prosperous community of free people of color, public officials soon enacted new restrictions on their behavior and imposed new limitations on the ability of slaves to purchase their freedom.

January, 1804

To His Excellency William C. C. Claiborne: Governor General and Intendant of Louisiana

We the Subscribers, free Citizens of Louisiana beg leave to approach your Excellency with Sentiments of respect & Esteem and sincere attachment to the Government of the United States.

We are Natives of this Province and our dearest Interests are connected with its welfare. We therefore feel a lively Joy that the Sovereignty of the Country is at length united with that of the American Republic. We are duly sensible that our personal and political freedom is thereby assured to us for ever, and we are also impressed with the fullest confidence in the Justice and Liberality of the Government towards every Class of Citizens which they have here taken under their Protection.

We were employed in the military service of the late Government, and we hope we may be permitted to say, that our Conduct in that Service has ever been distinguished by a ready attention to the duties required of us. Should we be in like manner honored by the American Government, to which every principle of Interest as well as affection attaches us, permit us to assure your Excellency that we shall serve with fidelity and Zeal. We therefore respectfully offer our Services to the Government as a Corps of Volunteers agreeable to any arrangement which may be thought expedient.

We request your Excellency to accept our congratulations on the happy event which has placed you at the Head of this Government, and promises so much real prosperity to the Country.

Source: Clarence Edward Carter, ed., *The Territorial Papers of the United States* (Washington: Government Printing Office), vol. 9: 174–175.

39

Indians' Speech to Thomas Jefferson and Henry Dearborn, January 4, 1806

The Jefferson administration was eager to establish contact with the Indians of the North American West, whether to develop commercial opportunities or to make federal sovereignty a reality. Meanwhile, those Indians attempted to come to terms with the new government claiming their land. In this message from a gathering of chiefs representing the Indians of the Eastern Plains, Indians articulated their priorities.

Speech of the Osages, Missouri, Otos, Panis, Cansas, Ayowais & Sioux Nations to the president of the U.S. & to the Secretary at War.

My Grandfather & My Father

It is with an open heart that we recieve your hands, friendship streches ours in yours & unites them together.

fathers

We feel entirely our happiness at this Day, since you tell us that we are wellcome in the Grand lodge of prosperity. We percieve that we are numbered among your Most Cherished Children.

fathers

You observe that we have undertaken a very long journey in order to see our fathers & Brethren; it is Most true: but fathers, we will tell you that we Did not look back for to measure the road, & our Sight streching to the rising Sun, discovered every New day the pleasure Rising with him, as we were reflecting our daily approach, our hearts were overjoy'd, for we were Soon to See our New good fathers who wish to pity us.

Fathers

There is a long While that we wish to be acquiainted with our fathers & Brothers of the rising Sun & we hope that, when will return back, where the sun sets, we will Dispell all the thick Clouds whose Darkness obscures the Light of the Day.

Fathers

That Great Spirit who disposes of every thing, & fixes into our Bosom the ardent Desire of seeing you, we thank him & we will thank him more when w'ill be at home amongst our Wives & children, for, then, our eyes Will be satisfied, our ears full with your words, & our hearts with joy.

But, fathers, we have to thank our interpreters who advis'd us to strengthen our hearts, & listen not to the sense of those men who wanted to prevent us from Coming to see you, alledging that we would be unwellcome & all of us should die. Our interpreters told us that our fathers were good & would pity us, that they wanted to be acquainted with their new red Children; & that we ought not to listen to the Crowing of Bad Birds.

fathers

You do not know yet your new red Children, & we see that you are as much worthy of pity as we are; flatterers Came Before you, made vast promises, but when far away, they Constitute themselves masters, decieve you & your Children Suffer.

fathers

Do pity your Children who wish to do Good & Behave well, if you say it [is] in their power, but, fathers trust them we know: we know them who love your new red Children who wish them to be happy, who hear your word, fill up our ears with it insinuate it in our hearts & spread it all over our fields; & fathers, that Spirit who took Care of us in Coming hither, here he is! He alone Can Carry your words together with us, to our Warriors wives & Children & they all will Call you then their fathers.

Fathers

We Believe that you wish to pity us & to prevent our wants by sending us supplies of goods, but look sharp & tell to your men to take not too much fur for a little of goods, should they act in that way we would not be better off than we are now with our actual traders.

Fathers

We have Seen the belov'd Man, we shook hands with him & we heard the words you put in his mouth. We wish him well, where he is, we have him in our hearts, & when he will return we believe that he will take Care of us prevent our wants & make us happy: he told us you wished us to Come to see you & our Brethren of the rising Sun: here we are: we are happy to see you & glad to hear the words of good fathers.

Fathers

You tell us to be in peace & amity with our Brethren: we wish to be So: Misunderstanding Sometimes Breaks Peace & Amity, because we listen too much to those men who live yet amongst us & who do not belong to your family, but when we will have but your own Children with us, then it will be easy for you to maintain the peace of your red children & we will all acknowledge that we have good fathers.

Fathers

Meditate what you say, you tell us that your children of this side of the Mississipi hear your Word,

you are Mistaken, Since every day they Rise their tomahawks Over our heads, but we believe it be Contrary to your orders & inclination, & that, before long, should they be deaf to your voice, you will chastise them.

Fathers

Though your forefathers were inhabiting the other side of the Big lake, we Consider you as ourselves, since, like us, you spring out of our land, for the Same reason, we believe you Consider us to be your Children, that you pity us & wish to make us happy should we follow your advices.

Fathers

You say that the french, English & Spanish nations have left the waters of the Missouri & Missisipi, we are all glad of it, & we believe that the day they will leave us the weather will be Clear, the paths Clean, & our ears will be no more affected with the disagreable sounds of the bad Birds who wish us to relinquish the words of our Good fathers whose words we keep in our hearts.

Although fathers

Do not believe that the number of our new Brethren would be able to frighten us, were we not inclined to acknowledge you for our fathers; but we wish to live like you & to be Men like you; we hope you will protect us from the wicked, you will punish them who wont hear your word, open their ears, & lead them in the good path.

Fathers

Since you wish to be acquainted with your new children of the other Side of the mississipi, you may Believe that they have the same desire, but if we Contempt your word as they do on this side of that River you will soon be Compell'd to Chastise the wicked, but, fathers, we shall not do as they do, for we wish to be numbered among your best Children, & we will try only to punish the wicked.

Fathers

You say that you are as numerous as the stars in the skies, & as strong as numerous. So much the better, fathers, tho', if you are so, we will see you ere long punishing all the wicked Red skins that you'll find amongst us, & you may tell to your white Children on our lands to follow your orders, & to do not as they please, for they do not keep your word. Our Brothers who Came here before told us you had ordered good things to be done & sent to our villages, but we have seen nothing, & your waged Men think that truth will not reach your ears, but we are Conscious that we must speak the truth, truth must be spoken to the ears of our fathers, & our fathers must open their ears to truth to get in. Fathers You tell us to Complain to the beloved man, should any one Commit injury & decline Compensation, but you Know fathers that the beloved man is gone far away, that he Can not do the justice which you want him to do; while he is absent we do better to Complain to his fathers, & when he will arrive we will Complain to him, then he will have justice done to the injured man & if he loves his fathers he will chastise the one who Broke the peace which our good fathers told us to make together & to maintain.

Fathers

We hear your word, we will Carry it into our villages, & spread it all over our fields, we will tell to our warriors, wives & Children that, ever since you became the fathers of all the red skins, like good fathers, you wish us to live like Children of but one family who have but one father, & that before we should go at war we have to take the advice of our good fathers & then we shall know what these latter will tell us.

Fathers

Our hearts are good, though we are powerfull & strong, & we know how to fight, we do not wish to fight but shut the mouth of your Children who

speak war, stop the arm of those who rise the tomahawk over our heads & Crush those who strike first, then we will Confess that we have good fathers who wish to make their red Children happy & peace maintained among them. For when we are at peace we hunt freely, our wives & Children Do not stand in want, we smoke & sleep easy.

Fathers

We left the place where the sun sets in order to see & hear you, fathers we see & hear you & we are happy; the skies are Clear where our fathers breathe & we wish it may be so where the sun sets. We wish our wives & children may be joy full when they think that we breathe where our fathers Breathe, for we are wellcome to Breathe with you, fathers.

fathers

Pity your own new Children, they wish to follow your advice, tell them what you wish them to do, they will do any thing that you wish them to do, they do not Belong any more to themselves but they are your own property, dispose of them as you please.

Fathers

As you spoke that we had brethren inhabiting the shores of the big Lake & that you offered us to visit them, we do wish to be acquainted with them, to shake hands with them & to tell them that we are their Brothers & if they are good Children we will tell them that we are so, for you know fathers we acknowledge you for our fathers.

Fathers

After shaking hands with all our new Brothers, being acquainted with them all, then we will tell to our warriors, our wives, our Children how many things we have seen, they all will listen to our sayings, they will gather around us, hear the words of their new fathers & Brethren, love them all & wonder at all things; yes fathers, we will speak the truth, you know the truth must Come out of the mouth of a father.

Fathers

We hope the more we will See our new Brethren the More we will love them for we hope they will wellcome us & recieve us as their Brethren.

Fathers

We wish to have this, your Warrior (major Rodger) for our leader in the journey that we will undertake to visit our Brethren: he will take good Care of us, for he does love us, he will hold the weather Clear, Clean & smooth the paths of his red Brethren. Our Brother (Capt. Stoddert) is a good man, but he is not acquainted with his Brethren, the red Skins, he can not take good Care of them for he is always Sick & leaves them to the Care of Careless people who are not acquainted with your new Children the red Skins.

Fathers

You Say, that, when we will Come back the ice will be broken, the snow Melted, & then we will return into our Villages:—yes, fathers, when we will see our Warriors, when we will see our Wives, when we will see our Children, our hearts will be overjoy'd, their hearts will be overjoyed they will hear the word you put in our Mouth, we will Carry it to them Deeply engraved in our hearts. Our Warriors will bury the tomahawk, the wicked will be good, when ever they will hear

the word of their fathers & know them to be good to all the red Skins.

Fathers

We will keep your Word in our Bosom; the stinking Cloud may Rise, it will melt away when We will remember the Word of our fathers, the bad birds may fly over our heads, & Crow Mischief, their flesh will be poor, their voice weak, they will hush & fly away when hearing the word of our fathers; we will be happy with your word, fathers, & never part with it.

Fathers

It is most true, there is some people amongst us, who wish us to be deaf to your word, they have a smooth lying tongue but they Can't be your Children, because a Child allways says the word of his father. They are unhappy for we will not listen to them, your sun will give them light, & shine heretofore over all your Children.

Grandfather (the President)

You told us to go now & then to see our father the great chief of War (the secretary at war), that he would Communicate your word to us, we have visited him & have been wellcome. We hope that he does love your new Children Worthy of pity, & Consider us as Your white Children.

fathers

We give you again the hand of friendship.

Source: Philadelphia: The Historical Society of Pennsylvania.

40   Dehahuit to William C. C. Claiborne, September 5, 1806

In September 1806 Dehahuit, the leading chief of the Caddo Indians, was at the height of his power. He had used the Louisiana Purchase to reinforce his own power over the Caddo villages, and he was about to see Spanish-American disputes create the Neutral Ground. He negotiated with Spanish and American officials, and in this speech to William C. C. Claiborne he explained his own vision of federalism on the borderlands.

I am highly gratified at meeting to day with your Excellency and so respectable a number of American officers, and shall forever remember the words you have spoken.

I have heard, before, the words of the President; though not from his own mouth:—his words are always the same; but what I have this day heard will cause me to sleep more in peace.

Your words resemble the words my forefathers have told me they used to receive from the French in ancient times. My ancestors from Chief to Chief were always well pleased with the French;

they were well received and well treated by them when they met to hold talks together, and we can now say the same of you, our new friends.

If your nation has purchased what the French formerly possessed, you have purchased the country that we occupy, and we regard you in the same light as we did them.

Your request that our wars in future may be against the . . .

[The rest of the manuscript, from William C. C. Claiborne's letterbooks, is torn, and the remainder of Dehahuit's letter is lost.]

Source: Dunbar Rowland, ed., *The Letter Books of William C. C. Claiborne, 1801–1816* (Jackson: Mississippi State Archive), vol. 4: 4–5.

41   Thomas Jefferson's Speech to the Wolf and People of the Mandan Nation, December 30, 1806

Although not a direct reply to the speech of the Indian chiefs (document 39), Thomas Jefferson's speech to the Wolf and the Mandans exemplified the message he sent to all Indians. Like the chiefs' speech, Jefferson also used simplistic terminology, in large part because both sides worried about translation—whether the literal translation of words or the potentially disputed symbolic meaning that Indians and Americans associated with them.

My children, the Wolf and people of the Mandan nation:—take you by the hand of friendship hearty welcome to the seat of the government of the United States. The journey which you have taken to visit your fathers on this side of our island is a long one, and your having undertaken it is a proof that you desired to become acquainted with us. I thank the Great Spirit that he has pro-

tected you through the journey and brought you safely to the residence of your friends, and I hope He will have you constantly in his safe keeping, and restore you in good health to your nations and families.

My friends and children, we are descended from the old nations which live beyond the great water, but we and our forefathers have been so long here that we seem like you to have grown out of this land. We consider ourselves no longer of the old nations beyond the great water, but as united in one family with our red brethren here. The French, the English, the Spaniards, have now agreed with us to retire from all the country which you and we hold between Canada and Mexico, and never more to return to it. And remember the words I now speak to you, my children, they are never to return again. We are now your fathers; and you shall not lose by the change. As soon as Spain had agreed to withdraw from all the waters of the Missouri and Mississippi, I felt the desire of becoming acquainted with all my red children beyond the Mississippi, and of uniting them with us as we have those on this side of that river, in the bonds of peace and friendship. I wished to learn what we could do to benefit them by furnishing them the necessaries they want in exchange for their furs and peltries. I therefore sent our beloved man, Captain Lewis, one of my own family, to go up the Missouri river to get acquainted with all the Indian nations in its neighborhood, to take them by the hand, deliver my talks to them, and to inform us in what way we could be useful to them. Your nation received him kindly, you have taken him by the hand and been friendly to him. My children, I thank you for the services you rendered him, and for your attention to his words. He will now tell us where we should establish trading houses to be convenient to you all, and what we must send to them.

My friends and children, I have now an important advice to give you. I have already told you that you and all the red men are my children, and I wish you to live in peace and friendship with one another as brethren of the same family ought to do. How much better is it for neighbors to help than to hurt one another; how much happier must it make them. If you will cease to make war on one another, if you will live in friendship with all mankind, you can employ all your time in providing food and clothing for yourselves and your families. Your men will not be destroyed in war, and your women and children will lie down to sleep in their cabins without fear of being sur-

prised by their enemies and killed or carried away. Your numbers will be increased instead of diminishing, and you will live in plenty and in quiet. My children, I have given this advice to all your red brethren on this side of the Mississippi; they are following it, they are increasing in their numbers, are learning to clothe and provide for their families as we do. Remember then my advice, my children, carry it home to your people, and tell them that from the day that they have become all of the same family, from the day that we became father to them all, we wish, as a true father should do, that we may all live together as one household, and that before they strike one another, they should go to their father and let him endeavor to make up the quarrel.

My children, you are come from the other side of our great island, from where the sun sets, to see your new friends at the sun rising. You have now arrived where the waters are constantly rising and falling every day, but you are still distant from the sea. very much desire that you should not stop here, but go and see your brethren as far as the edge of the great water. I am persuaded you have so far seen that every man by the way has received you as his brothers, and has been ready to do you all the kindness in his power. You will see the same thing quite to the sea shore; and wish you, therefore, to go and visit our great cities in that quarter, and see how many friends and brothers you have here. You will then have travelled a long line from west to east, and if you had time to go from north to south, from Canada to Florida, you would find it as long in that direction, and all the people as sincerely your friends. I wish you, my children, to see all you can, and to tell your people all you see; because I am sure the more they know of us, the more they will be our hearty friends. I invite you, therefore, to pay a visit to Baltimore, Philadelphia, New York, and the cities still beyond that, if you are willing to go further. We will provide carriages to convey you and a person to go with you to see that you want for nothing. By the time you come back the snows will be melted on the mountains, the ice in the rivers broken up, and you will be wishing to set out on your return home.

My children, I have long desired to see you; I have now opened my heart to you, let my words sink into your hearts and never be forgotten. If ever lying people or bad spirits should raise up clouds between us, call to mind what I have said, and what you have seen yourselves. Be sure there are some lying spirits between us; let us come together as friends and explain to each other what is misrepresented or misunderstood, the clouds will fly away like morning fog, and the sun of friendship appear and shine forever bright and clear between us.

My children, it may happen that while you are here occasion may arise to talk about many things which I do not now particularly mention. The Secretary at War will always be ready to talk with you, and you are to consider whatever he says as said by myself. He will also take care of you and see that you are furnished with all comforts here.

Source: Thomas Jefferson Papers (Washington, D.C.: Library of Congress Microfilm Collection).

42   Territorial Legislature to Congress, March 12, 1810

To the honorable the Senate and House of Representatives of the United States, in Congress assembled,

The inhabitants of the territory of Orleans, become your Country men by a Combination of political events, but as satisfied with the title of Citizens of the United States, as if they had acquired it from choice, raise up to you, through the organ of their Representatives, their respectful remontrances on the inconveniencies which, no doubt against your intentions have been the inevitable consequences of the system of Government which you have given them. They appear before your honorable assembly, full of confidence in your Justice, not to vent any complaints, but to claim their rights. They Bring you not testimony of their Discontent, but the expression of their wishes and of their hopes; and they pray you, before you listen to their representations, to accept the homage of the fidelity which they again swear to the Constitution of the United States and the tribute of admiration which they pay to that Sacred Charter, where the true principles of liberty are recorded in indelible characters. After this Solemn protestation of their sentiments they intreat you to lend an attentive ear to the object which they are going to submit to your consideration. Its importance claims that it interests the fate of a great number of men, whose happiness you have contracted the obligation to procure, when you adopted them for your fellow Citizens.

A Considerable portion of the inhabitants of this territory thought Some years ago that they had a right to sollicit the incorporation of this Country into the Union. They founded their claims on the Stipulations of the treaty of April 1803, and demanded that this territory should be erected into a state, not so much because of the Utility of the measure, than because they considered it as secured by the treaty.

Things are now materially altered. The Legislature of this territory come forward, several years after, to Sollicit that incorporation, not so much as a right than as a favor. Whatever may have been the political considerations which induced your honorable body to reject the application which was made to you in 1804, those reasons exist no longer. The loyalty of the whole population of this Territory has since then been put to the trial in circumstances sufficiently critical for you to be Now convinced that the inhabitants of Lower Louisiana are not undeserving the Confidence of the federal Government. The devoted spirit of our militia, when war with Spain was on the eve of breaking out. Our unshaken fidelity in the midst of treasons and conspiracies, are irrefragable proofs of the incorruptibility of our honor and of the sincerity of our affection to our common Country.

But not only there is no longer any reason to oppose the wish of the citizens of this territory, there exists powerful motives to induce to your honorable assembly to see it in a favorable point of view. The System of Government which you have given them, because you thought it would be convenient, does not suit either their physical nor their political situation. To use the expressions of the person who is at the head of our executive, when speaking of a particular branch of our government: "The ordinance of 1787 Originally intended, for a small agricultural Society was of hazardous experiment in a territory like ours, populous, wealthy and commercial, where the landed property is holden by titles so various and complex, and where the principles of the common and Civil law, the Statutes of the United States and the municipal regulations of France and of Spain" mingle together to render the administration of our affairs more complicated and more embarrassing. Since the introduction of that ordinance a sad experience has shewn us its imperfection and its insufficiency. As we have been endeavouring to conciliate it with our wants and our localities, the difficulties multiplied themselves so much that we now think it impossible to establish harmony amidst the incoherent materials of which our present government is composed.

We live, however at the distance of six hundred leagues from your honorable assembly who gave us those laws, and who alone has the right of remedying the evils which they may have created. Convened, moreover for the general good of the Union, occupied with great political subjects, on which depends the safety of the whole nation, you cannot, nay you ought not to stop to the details of our local administration; and although you should consent to enter into the ex-

amination of those details; you are not sufficiently acquainted with our situation to have in your power to ameliorate it.

Such were undoubtedly the reasons which determined your honorable Body to give us an elective Legislature. You thought that by granting us the privilege of making our own laws, you furnished us with the means of securing our Happiness. No doubts, Legislators, such were your benevolent intentions. But how far that institution fell short of the end for which it was established! From the bosom of that ordinance, which you had given us as a favor, inconveniencies and difficulties have sprung which made our situation worse than it was before.

In almost all the measures which we attempt to take for the amelioration of the Government of the territory, the provisions of the ordinance shackle our efforts. It would be preposterous to entertain your honorable assembly with the particulars that form the mass of our grievances, and to conduct you through the windings of the labyrinth of our administration. Higher objects call your attention, and bid us to spare the precious time which you are bound to employ for the general good of the nation. But without tiring your patience with useless details, if you will deign to cast an eye on the most striking inconveniencies of our present situation, you will be forced to acknowledge the necessity of granting to us more extensive powers, wherewith to clear our way amidst the innumerable difficulties which reiterated changes of Government have heaped around us.

The absolute veto of the executive; a Judiciary placed above the authority of the Legislature; provisions only obscure sometimes contradictory, which furnish individuals, whose private interests is in opposition to the public welfare, with the means of creating doubts upon the most important subjects; powers and functions imperfectly defined; a complicated Jurisprudence; an entangled chicane, in the vortex of which our business and fortunes are precipitated; public officers, who often, have no idea of our municipal laws, and do not understand the language of the great majority of our population; no voice in their election; no check on their conduct; no confidence, no harmony; such is, Legislators, the present state of Government in the Territory of Orleans. It would even be more grievous, if the chief of our executive, to whom we owe this public testimony of our acknowledgment, had not united his efforts to ours, to better our situation.

But the palliative measures to which we recur, offer little resistance to the torrent of disorder which flows from our Constitution it self. The only efficacious means to employ is to drain the source of the evil, by changing entirely the actual system of our government.

That remedy, Legislators, is in your hands. No constitutional obstacle prevents you from using it. The condition which you have put to our admission into the Union, that of waiting until the territory should possess sixty thousands inhabitants, can be repealed by the same authority which has imposed it. It does not emanate from the constitution of the United States: it emanates from your will. If you think the emancipation of this territory to be a necessary measure, because of the Physical and of the political situation of this Country, because of its remoteness from the seat of the federal Government, where we are now obliged to apply even for the details of our Local administration, because of the Confusion into which that administration has been plunged by the successive changes which it has experienced, if you think that emancipation to be a salutary measure, as tending to bind more closely to the interests of the Union a population already known by their loyalty: if you think that emancipation to be a Just measure as the recompense of the irreprochable conduct which that Population has pursued in critical and tempestuous times; nothing can, nay nothing ought to prevent you from pronouncing the decree which we sollicit.

In vain would it be objected that our demand is premature, that our population does not yet amount to sixty thousand free inhabitants, as is required by the ordinance of 1787 Originally made for the Territory north west of the Ohio. The Articles of *Compact* which are included in that ordinance cannot be considered as obligatory on us, since we stipulated, approved, accepted nothing; and the Ordinance with regard to us is a law like the others, emanating solely from your will. If those articles are obligatory on your part, they can be so only as containing an engagement not to retard our incorporation into the union beyond the epoch when our population shall amount to sixty thousand inhabitants; but by contracting the obligation not to deprive us of certain advantages, you did not part with your right of granting to us further favors.

Such was your consideration of the subject, even with respect to those who were considered as contracting parties in the ordinance of 1787, when you erected in 1802, the territory of Ohio into a State, long before it possessed the number of inhabitants required by the Ordinance.

But Although the law which you have established over us can be revoked by the same power that has dictated it, if through respect for ancient institutions, if through attachment for a plan of Government, which was successively applied to your several territories, you should persist in requiring, as a condition of our incorporation, that our population should amount to sixty thousand free inhabitants, then we might abandon the hope ever to see the change which is the object of our wishes. Our territory, though vast cannot admit of any large increase of population. Nearly all the lands conveniently situated are occupied; immense swamps cover a great proportion of the remaining part of the Country; and such aninhabited lands as are cultivable are chiefly to be found towards the limits of our territory. Such a situation threatens therefore at least the present generation, never to see the epoch of their emancipation if your honorable Assembly should not yield to the powerful reasons which now make it convenient, or rather necessary.

Must we add to what has been above represented, that we are capable of appreciating the advantages of the government which we pray you to extend to us? Do you suppose it possible that we should have enjoyed during several years a portion of that precious liberty which you alone have preserved amidst the subjection of all the Civilized nations, and that we should not wish to possess it entirely? Do you doubt that we would receive with transport the favor which we sollicit from your liberality and your Justice? And do you hesitate to believe that, once in possession of our independence, it shall not be wrested from us, but with our lives? No, Legislators, your reason must persuade you that the emancipation of the territory of Orleans is ar-

dently desired by its inhabitants; and your heart must tell you that by extending independence to them, you will for ever secure their friendship and their devotion.

Thos. Urquhart
Speaker of the House of Representatives

J. D Degoutin Bellechasse
President of the Legislative Council

Source: Territorial Papers of the United States (Washington, D.C.: Record Group 59, Microfilm Copy M116 [Florida], T260 [Orleans]), NA, vol. 9: 873–877.

43 Congressional Debate over Louisiana Statehood

The Territory of Orleans requested that it be permitted to write a state constitution in March 1810. Congress debated whether to let the territory write a constitution in the winter of 1810–1811 but did not actually consider statehood itself until the spring of 1812, by which time delegates had received permission to convene a convention and had written a constitution. Nonetheless, the debates were so similar in the central points of dispute that they seem a continuous deliberation. These excerpts present the two major camps of the argument: those representatives and senators who were convinced that the residents of the Territory of Orleans were not yet ready for statehood and those who were convinced that to deny statehood would be to renege on American principles while fostering dangerous resentment west of the Mississippi.

Representative Daniel Sheffey (VA), 2 January 1811 (484): Whilst he was disposed to treat the inhabitants of Orleans Territory, as brothers, and not as vassals, he was not ready to transfer the inheritance purchased by the blood of our fathers to foreigners. While he looked upon these people as equals, and was disposed to do them justice, he thought all they could demand at his hands was to be placed on the equality to which they were entitled.

Representative John Miller (NY), 4 January 1811 (495–496): It has been objected against the bill that the population of the State proposed will not be American. Without intimating how far this consideration may have influence on my mind, under the circumstances in which that country has been lately placed, I cannot, however, but re-

mark that it is natural for a man to carry his feelings and prejudices about him. I was born in Virginia, sir, and I have not yet lost some of my Virginia feelings, notwithstanding an absence of fifteen years, and I cannot see why we should expect the people or Orleans to act and feel differently from other people, more particularly, when the French nation is towering so far above the other nations of the earth; they will have a secret pride in their glory, they will have some attachments, to what extent I cannot say; but, inasmuch as we know that if we send Paddy to Paris, that Paddy he will come back, the idea is certainly not unworthy of our consideration.

Representative Josiah Quincy (MA), 14 January 1811 (524–538): To me, it appears that it [Louisiana Statehood] would justify a revolution in this country; and that, in no great length of time, may produce it. . . . I recur, in the first place, to the evidence of history. . . .

But, says the gentleman from Tennessee (Mr. RHEA) 'these people have been seven years citizens of the United States.' I deny it. Sir—as citizens of New Orleans, or of Louisiana, they never have been, and by the mode proposed never will be, citizens of the United States. . . This Constitution never was, and never can be strained to lap over all the wilderness of the West, without essentially affecting both the rights and convenience of its real properties. It was never constructed to form a covering for the inhabitants of the Missouri, and the Red River country. And whenever it is attempted to be stretched over them, it will rend asunder. . . . You have no authority to throw the rights and liberties, and property of this people, in a 'hotch-pot' with the wild men on the Missouri, nor with the mixed, though more respectable race of Anglo-Hispano-Gallo Americans, who bask on the sands, in the mouth of the Mississippi. I make no objection to these from their want of moral qualities or political light. The inhabitants of New Orleans are, I suppose, like those of all other countries, some good, some bad, some indifferent.

Congressman Nathaniel Macon (NC), 2 January 1811 (485): There ought to be no question as to what stock they sprung from; the true question was, ought they to be a State? The true policy, Mr. M. thought, was, as they were to become a part of the United States, to make them one and indivisible as soon as possible. They had already served a sufficient apprenticeship to the Untied States, but not under a free government, for the Territorial governments were not free. The advantage of exacting of them the condition of using the same language, was a great one. How could they be made one with the United States unless by the use of the same language? Mr. M. wished to treat this Territory as well as the others, and no better; he would not treat one as a daughter and the other as a step-daughter. He was as willing now to make Orleans a State as he

had been to make Ohio a State. The great object is to make us one people; to make this nation one. As to the Mississippi Territory, it had not served a much longer apprenticeship than Orleans, having only been acquired by the treaty with Spain in 1795. The people of Orleans possessed certainly as strong an attachment to the nation as could be expected from the time they had belonged to it. When the Spaniards invaded the Territory, they stepped forward promptly to repel them; and when some citizens of the old States forgot the love every honest heart owes to his country, they showed their attachment to the Union by the readiness with which they lent their aid to repel them. To make them a State would make the attachment still greater, and it was therefore advisable to act on the subject.

Representative Nathaniel Macon (TN), 4 January 1811 (506–507): There are various political considerations which operate in favor of the formation of such a State. The people of the Territory of Orleans are petitioning to become an independent State, and I for one hope the prayer of their petition will in substance be granted. It is said that the French population of the city of New Orleans are unfriendly to the American Government. That they have strong prejudices in favor of France. Although, sir, I do not attach so much importance to that circumstance as some gentlemen do, I am willing to admit that French emigrants in Louisiana feel an attachment to their native country. I do not blush to say that were I in France, or in any other foreign country, I could never forget that I was born an American citizen . . . therefore . . . I cannot doubt that many influential French inhabitants of New Orleans entertain a predilection for the country which gave them birth. But . . . there is an American population at least sufficient to neutralize every exotic prejudice which may exist in New Orleans. . . . A powerful State on the southern seacoast of the United States is an object of great magnitude in perpetuating the Union, which, for the happiness of the great American family, ought never to be dissolved.

Representative John Rhea (TN), 4 January 1811 (498–502): [The Louisiana Purchase and the guarantees of incorporation in Article III are] the act of this nation; it is a solemn compact, made between the United States and the French Republic; it is by the Constitution a supreme law of the land, irrevocable and peremptorily commanding execution in every part to the full extent—it is strange, wonderful strange, indeed, that attempts shall now be made to prevent those people [the residents of the Territories of Orleans and Louisiana] from the enjoyment of all those rights, advantages, and immunities, which the French Republic secured to them and the United States have confirmed by ratification of that treaty. The people of Orleans are anxiously desirous to become a State, and by the best information had, their population appears sufficient . . . It is with states as with individuals; if an individual, the head of a family, purchases a farm adjoining that on which he lives and resides, and probably acquires all the right and title thereto, will any one deny it to be his? Will any one say that the has not power to incorporate it with his former farm, so that both shall be one, or in other words, that purchased with the other shall be but one?

. . . In place of a waste, wild, and uncultivated territory, the United States obtained in honest and righteous manner, without blood and carnage, a fruitful, luxuriant territory, covered by a great number of people, who, since the time of their being ceded to the United States, have manifested, as much as in their power, their attachment and allegiance to the United States . . .

It has been said that Orleans is vulnerable, and therefore you ought, sir, to keep the government in your own hands. I draw a conclusion directly contrary. If Orleans be vulnerable, give the people thereof everything to defend; they have now themselves, their wives and children, and their property to defend; give them all the rights of freemen and citizens, to the full extend of the term, to defend; let them have self-government; let them have all the rights of citizens; let them have a constitution and State government, and a

sovereignty to defend, and then, and not until then, you will make them warriors indeed; they will then fight for themselves and for the United States, if invaded, because they will then have everything worth contending for, and because you have liberally endowed them with all these things, their grateful hearts with irresistible vigor will strengthen their arms to wield the sword against the enemies of the United States.

The object of the bill is not to transfer a part of a State to a foreign territory, nor is it to favor a French population at the expense of the rights of the United States, nor is it the object of the bill to transfer to foreigners what has been obtained by the blood of the old States. The Territory of Orleans is not a foreign territory; it is a territory of the United States made and declared to be so by two solemn laws of the Congress of the united States, bottomed o the irrevocable treaty of Paris. The population of the Orleans Territory is not a French population; whatever the population was, before the treaty alluded to, it is now and for about seven years past has been a population composed of citizens, to a certain extend of the United States . . . let them be a State, and the United States will be more powerful, because the more numerous an agreeing family is, the more powerful it is; let them be a State, and they will be more induced as citizens to acquire wealth by industry, and every increase of their wealth will be an increase to that of the United States.

Representative Thomas Gholson (VA), 4 January 1811 (503–4): It has been with extreme regret, sir, that I have heard so often, and upon so many former occasions, as well as in the present debate, the charges of French influence and disaffection to this Government, made either in express terms, or else intelligibly insinuated, against the people of New Orleans. Suffer me to ask, sir, where are the evidences to support these imputations? Certainly not before this House—if we examine the history of these people since their connexion with us, abundant testimony will be found, not only to exonerate them from the charge of disaffection, but to demonstrate their fidelity to the American

Government. When on the acquisition of that country the most radical innovations upon its laws, customs, usages, and civil proceedings were introduced, these people peaceable submitted without any symptoms of insurgency. When they saw many of their dearest rights endangered or prostrated by new and unprecedented modes of judicial proceeding, and by the chicanery of desperate adventurers, they made no unlawful appeals for redress. When their port of entry was most unwarrantably wrested from them and delivered into the possession of an individual, they awaited the ordinary process of law to be reinstated in that use of it which nature had decreed for them, and of which they could by no earthly power be rightfully deprived. And when, in fine, your very borders were invaded they, as faithful citizens, were ready to defend them.

Source: Annals of Congress: Debates and Proceedings of the Congress of the United States (Washington, D.C.: Gales and Seaton), 11th Cong., 3d sess.

---

44   Forming a Constitution and State Government in the Territory of Orleans, February 20, 1811

Chap. XXI.—*An Act to enable the people of the Territory of Orleans to form a constitution and state government, and for the admission of such state into the Union, on an equal footing with the original states, and for other purposes.*

Be it enacted . . . That the inhabitants of all that part of the territory or country ceded under the name of Louisiana, by the treaty . . . between the United States and France, contained within the following limits, that is to say: beginning at the mouth of the river Sabine, thence by a line drawn along the middle of said river, including all islands to the thirty-second degree of latitude; thence due north to the northernmost part of the thirty-third degree of north latitude; thence along the said parallel of latitude to the river Mississippi; thence down the said river to the river Iberville, and from thence along the middle of said river and lakes Maurepas and Pontchartrain to the gulf of Mexico; thence bounded by the said gulf to the place of beginning, including all islands within three leagues of the coast. . . .

SEC. 2. *And be it further enacted,* That all free male white citizens of the United States, who shall have arrived at the age of twenty-one years, and resided within the said territory, at least one year previous to the day of election . . . and all persons having in other respects the legal qualifications to vote for representatives . . . are hereby authorized to choose representative to form a convention. . . .

SEC. 3. *And be it further enacted,* That the members of the convention . . . are hereby authorized to meet . . . to form a constitution and state government, for the people within the said territory. . . . *Provided,* the constitution to be formed . . . shall be republican, and consistent with the constitution of the United States; that it shall contain the fundamental principles of civil and religious liberty; that it shall secure to the citizen the trial by jury in all criminal cases, and the privilege of the writ of *habeas corpus.* . . .

SEC 4. *And be it further enacted,* . . . the said convention . . . is hereby required to cause to be transmitted to Congress the instrument, by which its assent to the constitution of the Untied States is thus given and declared . . . and if the same shall not be disapproved by Congress, at their next session after the receipt thereof, the said state shall be admitted into the Union. . . .

APPROVED, February 20, 1811.

Source: The Public Statutes at Large of the United States of America (Boston: Charles C. Little and James Brown, 1845), vol. 2: 641–643.

45

The Louisiana Constitution of 1812

We, the Representatives of the People of all that part of the Territory or country ceded under the name of Louisiana, by the treaty made at Paris, on the 30th day of April 1803, between the United States and France, contained in the following limits, to wit: beginning at the mouth of the river Sabine, thence by a line to be drawn along the middle of said river including all its islands, to the thirty second degree of latitude—thence due north to the Northernmost part of the thirty third degree of north lattitude—thence along the said parallel of latitude to the river Mississippi—thence down the said river to the river Iberville, and from thence along the middle of the said river and lakes Maurepas and Pontchartrain to the Gulf of Mexico—thence bounded by the said Gulf to the place of beginning, including all Islands within three leagues of the coast—in Convention Assembled by virtue of an act of Congress, entitled "an act to enable the people of the Territory of Orleans to form a constitution and State government and for the admission of said State into the Union on an equal footing with the original States, and for other purpose;" In order to secure to all the citizens thereof the enjoyment of *the right of life, liberty and property,* do ordain and establish the following constitution or form of government, and do mutually agree with each other to form ourselves into a free and independent State, by the name of the State of Louisiana.

ARTICLE 1ST CONCERNING THE DISTRIBUTION OF THE POWERS OF GOVERNMENT.

SECT. 1st. The powers of the government of the State of Louisiana shall be divided into three distinct departments, and each of them be confided to a separate body of Magistracy viz—those which are legislative to one, those which are executive to another, and those which are judiciary to another.

SECT. 2d. No person or Collection of persons, being one of those departments, shall exercise any power properly belonging to either of the others; except in the instances hereinafter expressly directed or permitted.

ARTICLE II CONCERNING THE LEGISLATIVE DEPARTMENT

SECT. 1st. The Legislative power of this State shall be vested in two distinct branches, the one to be styled the House of Representatives, the other the senate, and both together, the General Assembly of the State of Louisiana.

SECT. 2d. The Members of the House of Representatives shall continue in service, for the term of two years from the day of the commencement of the general election.

SECT. 3d. Representatives shall be chosen on the first Monday in July every two years, and the General Assembly shall convene on the first Monday in January in every year, unless a different day be appointed by law, and their sessions shall be held at the Seat of Government.

SECT. 4th. No person shall be a Representative who, at the time of his election is not a free white male citizen of the United States, and hath not attained to the age of twenty one years, and resided in the state two years next preceding his election, and the last year thereof in the county for which he may be chosen or in the district for which he is elected in case the said counties may be divided into separate districts of election, and has not held for one year in the said county or district landed property to the value of five hundred dollars agreeably to the last list.

SECT. 5th. Elections for Representatives for the several counties entitled to representation, shall be held at the places of holding their respecting courts, or in the several election precincts, into which the Legislature may think proper, from time to time, to divide any or all of those counties.

SECT. 6th. Representation shall be equal and uniform in this state and shall be forever regulated and ascertained by the number of qualified electors therein. In the year one thousand eight hundred and thirteen and every fourth year thereafter, an enumeration of all the electors shall be made in such manner as shall be directed by law. The number of Representatives shall, in the several years of making these enumerations be so fixed as not to be less than twenty five nor more than fifty.

SECT. 7th. The House of Representatives shall choose its speaker and other officers.

SECT. 8th. In all elections for Representatives every free white male citizen of the United States, who at the time being, hath attained to the age of twenty one years and resided in the county in which he offers to vote one year not preceding the election, and who in the last six months prior to the said election, shall have paid a state tax, shall enjoy the right of an elector: provided however that every free white male citizen of the United States who shall have purchased land from the United States, shall have the right of voting whenever he shall have the other qualifications of age and residence above prescribed—Electors shall in all cases, except treason, felony, breach or surety of peace, be privileged from arrest during their attendance at, going to or returning from elections.

SECT. 9th. The members of the Senate shall be chosen for the term of four years, and when assembled shall have the power to choose its officers annually.

SECT. 10th. The State shall be divided in fourteen senatorial districts, which shall forever remain indivisible, as follows; the Parish of St. Bernard and Plaquemine including the country above as far as the land (Des Pécheurs) on the east of the Mississippi and on the west as far as Bernoudy's canal shall form one district. The city of New-Orleans beginning at the Nuns' Plantation above and extending below as far as the above mentioned canal (Des Pécheurs) including

the inhabitants of the Bayou St. John, shall form the second district, the remainder of the county of Orleans shall form the third district. The counties of German Coast, Acadia, Lafourche, Iberville, Point Coupée, Concordia, Attakapas, Opelousas, Rapides, Natchitoches and Ouachitta, shall each form one district, and each district shall elect a Senator.

SECT. 11th. At the Session of the General Assembly after this constitution takes effect, the Senators shall be divided by lot, as equally as may be, into two classes; the seats of the Senators of the first class shall be vacated at the expiration of the second year, of the second class at the expiration of the fourth year; so that one half shall be chosen every two years, and a rotation thereby kept up perpetually.

SECT. 12th. No person shall be a Senator who, at the time of his election, is not a citizen of the United States, and who hath not attained to the age of twenty seven years; resided in this state four years next preceding his election, and one year in the district, in which he may be chosen; and unless he holds within the same a landed property to the value of one thousand dollars agreeably to the tax list.

SECT. 13th. The first election for Senators shall be general throughout the state, and at the same time that the general election for Representatives is held; and thereafter there shall be a biennial election of Senators to fill the places of those whose time of service may have expired.

SECT. 14th. Not less than a majority of the members of each house of the general assembly, shall form a quorum to do business; but a smaller number may adjourn from day to day, and shall be authorized by law to compel the attendance of absent members, in such manner, and under such penalties as may be prescribed thereby.

SECT. 15th. Each house of the general assembly shall judge of the qualifications, elections and returns of its members, but a contested election shall be determined in such manner as shall be directed by law.

SECT. 16th. Each house of the general assembly may determine the rules of its proceedings, punish a member for disorderly behaviour, and with the concurrence of two thirds, expel a member, but not a second time for the same offence.

SECT. 17th. Each house of the general assembly shall keep and publish weekly a Journal of its proceedings, and the yeas and nays of the members of any question, shall, at the desire of any two of them, be entered on their Journal.

SECT. 18th. Neither house, during the session of the general assembly, shall without the consent of the other, adjourn for more than three days, nor to any other place than that in which they may be sitting.

SECT. 19th. The members of the general assembly shall severally receive from the Public Treasury a compensation for their services, which shall be four dollars per day, during their attendance on, going to and returning from the sessions of their respective houses; Provided that the same may be increased or diminished by law; but no alteration shall take effect during the period of service of the members of the house of Representatives, by whom such alteration shall have been made.

SECT. 20. The members of the general assembly shall in all cases except treason, felony, breach or surety of the peace, be privileged from arrest, during their attendance at the sessions of their respective houses, and in going to or returning from the same, and for any speech or debate in either house, they shall not be questioned in any other place.

SECT. 21. No Senator or Representative shall, during the term for which he was elected, nor for one year thereafter, be appointed or elected to any civil office of profit under this State, which shall have been created, or the emoluments of which shall have been encreased during the time such Senator or Representative was in office, except, to such offices or appointments as may be filled by the elections of the people.

SECT. 22. No person while he continues to exercise the functions of a clergyman, priest or teacher of any religious persuasion, society or sect, shall be eligible to the general assembly, or to any office of profit or trust under this State.

SECT. 23. No person who at any time may have been a collector of taxes for the State, or the assistant or deputy of such collector shall be eligible to the general assembly, until he shall have obtained quietus for the amount of such collection, and for all public money for which he may be responsible.

SECT. 24. No bill shall have the force of a law until, on three several days, it be read over in each house of the general assembly, and free discussion allowed thereon; unless in case of urgency, four-fifths of the house where the bill shall be depending, may deem it expedient to dispense with this rule.

SECT. 25. All bills for raising revenue shall originate in the House of Representatives, but the Senate may propose amendments as in other bills; Provided that they shall not introduce any new matter under the colour of an amendment which does not relate to raising a revenue.

SECT. 26. The general assembly shall regulate, by law, by whom and in what manner writs of election shall be issued to fill vacancies which may happen in either branch thereof.

ARTICLE III CONCERNING THE EXECUTIVE DEPARTMENT

SECT. 1. The supreme executive power of the State shall be vested in a chief magistrate, who shall be styled the Governor of the state of Louisiana.

SECT. 2. The Governor shall be elected for the term of four years in the following manner, the citizens entitled to vote for representatives shall vote for a Governor at the time and place of voting for Representatives and Senators. Their votes shall be returned by the persons presiding over the elections to the seat of government addressed to the president of the Senate, and on the second day the general assembly, the members of the two houses shall meet in the House of Representatives, and immediately after the two candidates who shall have obtained the greatest number of votes, shall be balloted for and the one having a majority of votes shall be governor.—Provided however that if more than two candidates hath obtained the highest number of votes, it shall be the duty of the general assembly to ballot for them in the manner above prescribed, and in case several candidates should obtain an equal number of votes next to the candidate who has obtained the highest number, it shall be the duty of the general assembly to select in the same manner the candidate who is to be balloted for with him who has obtained the highest number of votes.

SECT. 3. The governor shall be ineligible for the succeeding four years after the expiration of the time for which he shall have been elected.

SECT. 4. He shall be at least thirty five years of age, and a citizen of the United States, and have been an inhabitant of this state at least six years preceding his election, and shall hold in his own right a landed estate of five thousand dollars value, agreeably to the tax list.

SECT. 5. He shall commence the execution of his office on the fourth Monday succeeding the day of his election, and shall continue in the execution thereof, until the end of four weeks next succeeding the election of his successor, and until his successor shall have taken the oaths or affirmations prescribed by this Constitution.

SECT. 6. No member of Congress, or person holding any office under the United States, or minister of any religious society, shall be eligible to the office of Governor.

SECT. 7. The governor shall at stated times, receive for his services a compensation which shall neither be encreased nor diminished during the term for which he shall have been elected.

SECT. 8. He shall be commander in chief of the army and navy of this State, and of the militia thereof except when they shall be called into the service of the United States, but he shall not command personally in the field, unless he shall be advised so to do by a resolution of the general assembly.

SECT. 9th. He shall nominate and appoint with the advice and consent of the Senate, Judges, Sheriffs and all other Officers whose offices are established by this Constitution, and whose appointments are not herein otherwise provided for—Provided however that the Legislature shall

have a right to prescribe the mode of appointment of all other offices to be established by law.

SECT. 10. The governor shall have power to fill up vacancies that may happen during the recess of the Legislature, by granting commissions which shall expire at the end of the next session.

SECT. 11. He shall have power to remit fines and forfeitures, and, except in cases of impeachment, to grant reprieves & pardons, with the approbation of the Senate. In cases of treason he shall have Power to grant reprieves until the end of the next session of the general assembly in which the power of pardoning shall be vested.

SECT. 12. He may require information in writing from the officers the executive department, upon any subject relating to the duties of their respective offices.

SECT. 13. He shall from time to time give to the general assembly information respecting the situation of the state, and recommend to their consideration such measures as he may deem expedient.

SECT. 14. He may on extraordinary occasions convene the general assembly at the seat of government, or at a different place if that place have become dangerous from an enemy or from contagious disorders; and in case of desagreement between the two houses with respect to the time of adjournment, he may adjourn them to such time as he may think proper, not exceeding four months.

SECT. 15. He shall take care that the laws be faithfully executed.

SECT. 16. It shall be his duty to visit the different counties at least once in every two years, to inform himself of the state of the militia and the general condition of the country.

SECT. 17. In case of the impeachment of the governor, his removal from office, death, refusal to qualify, resignation, or absence from the state, the president of the senate shall exercise all the power and authority appertaining to the office of governor, untill another be duly qualified, or the governor absent or impeached shall return or be acquitted.

SECT. 18. The president of the Senate, during the time he administers the government shall receive the same compensation which the governor would have received had he been employed in the duties of his office.

SECT. 19. A secretary of state shall be appointed and commissioned during that term for which the governor shall have been elected, if he shall so long behave himself well, he shall keep a fair register, and attest all official acts and proceedings of the governor, and shall when required, lay the same and all papers, minutes and vouchers relative thereto, before either house of the general assembly, and shall perform such other duties as may be enjoined him by law.

SECT. 20. Every bill which shall have passed both houses shall be presented to the governor, if he approve, he shall sign it, if not he shall return it with his objection to the house in which it shall have originated, who shall enter the objections at large upon their Journal and proceed to reconsider it—if after such reconsideration, two thirds of all the members elected to that house, shall agree to pass the bill, it shall be sent, with the objections, to the other house, by which it shall likewise be reconsidered and if approved by two thirds of all the members elected to that house, it shall be a law; but in such cases, the votes of both house, shall be determined by yeas and nays, and the names of the members voting for and against the bill, shall be entered on the journal of each house respectively; if any bill shall not be returned by the governor within ten days (Sundays excepted) after it shall have been presented to him, it shall be a law in like manner as if he had signed it, unless the general assembly by their adjournment prevent its return, in which case it shall be a law, unless sent back within three days after their next meeting.

SECT. 21. Every order, resolution or vote, to which the concurrence of both houses may be necessary, except on a question of adjournment, shall be presented to the governor, and before it shall take effect be approved by him; or being disapproved shall be repassed by two thirds of both houses.

SECT. 22. The free white men of this State, shall be armed and disciplined for its defence; but those who belong to religious societies, whose tenets forbid them to carry arms, shall not be compelled so to do, but shall pay an equivalent for personal service.

SECT. 23. The militia of this state shall be organized in such manner as may be hereafter deemed most expedient by the legislature.

ARTICLE IV CONCERNING THE JUDICIARY DEPARTMENT

SECT. 1st. The judiciary power shall be vested in a supreme court and inferior courts.

SECT. 2d. The supreme court shall have appellate jurisdiction only, which jurisdiction shall extend to all civil cases when the matter in dispute shall exceed the sum of three hundred dollars.

SECT. 3d. The supreme court shall consist of not less than three judges, nor more than five; the majority of whom shall form a quorum; each of the said judges shall receive a salary of five thousand dollars annually. The supreme court shall hold its sessions at the places hereinafter mentioned; and for that purpose the state is hereby divided into two districts of appellate jurisdiction, in each of which the supreme court shall administer justice in the manner hereafter Prescribed. The Eastern district to consist of the counties of New Orleans, German Coast, Acadia, Lafourche, Iberville, and Point Coupée; the western district to consist of the counties of Attakapas, Opelousas, Rapides, Concordia, Natchitoches, and Ouachita. The supreme court shall hold its sessions in each year, for the Eastern district in New-Orleans during the months of November, December, January, February, March, April, May, June, and July; and for the western district, at Opelousas during the months of August, September, and October: for five years: Provided however, That every five years the legislature may change the place of holding said court in the western district. The said court shall appoint its own clerks.

SECT. 4th. The legislature is authorised to establish such inferior courts as may be convenient to the administration of justice.

SECT. 5th. The judges both of the supreme and inferior courts shall hold their offices during good behaviour; but for any reasonable purpose which shall not be sufficient ground for impeachment, the Governor shall remove any of them, on the address of three fourths of each house of the general assembly: Provided however, That the cause or causes for which such removal may be required, shall be stated at length in the address, and inserted on the journal of each house.

SECT. 6th. The judges, by virtue of their office, shall be conservators of the peace throughout the state; the style of all process shall be "The State of Louisiana." All prosecutions shall be carried on in the name and by the authority of the state of Louisiana, and conclude "against the peace and dignity of the same."

SECT. 7. There shall be an attorney general for the state, and as many other prosecuting attorneys for the state as may be hereafter found necessary. The said attorneys shall be appointed the Governor with the advice and approbation of the Senate. Their duties shall be determined by law.

SECT. 8. All commissions shall be in the name, and by the authority of the state of Louisiana, and sealed with the state seal, and signed by the Governor.

SECT. 9. The state treasurer, and printer or printers of the state, shall be appointed, annually, by the joint vote of both houses of the general assembly: Provided, That during the recess of the same, the Governor shall have power to fill vacancies which may happen in either of the said offices.

SECT. 10. The clerks of the several courts shall be removable for breach of good behaviour, by the court of appeals only, who shall be judge of the fact, as well as of the law.

SECT. 11. The existing laws in this territory, when this constitution goes into effect, shall continue to be in force until altered or abolished by the Legislature; Provided however, that the Legislature shall never adopt any system or code of laws, by a general reference to the said system or code, but in all cases, shall specify the several provisions of the laws it may enact.

SECT. 12. The judges of all courts within this state, shall, as often as may be possible so to do, in every definitive judgment, refer to the particular law, in virtue of which such judgment may have been rendered, and in all cases adduce the reasons on which their judgment is founded.

ARTICLE V CONCERNING IMPEACHMENT

SECT. 1. The power of impeachment shall be vested in the House of Representatives alone.

SECT. 2. All impeachments shall be tried by the Senate when sitting for that purpose, the senators shall be upon oath or affirmation, and no person shall be convicted without the concurrence of two thirds of the members present.

SECT. 3. The governor and all the civil officers, shall be liable for impeachment for any misdemeanor in office, but judgment, in such cases, shall not extend further than to removal from office and disqualification to hold any office of honor trust or profit under this State; but the parties convicted shall nevertheless, be liable and subject to indictment, trial and punishment according to law.

ARTICLE VI GENERAL PROVISIONS

SECT. 1. Members of the general assembly and all officers executive and judicial, before they enter upon the execution of their respective offices, shall take the following oath or affirmation: "I (A. B.), do solemnly swear (or affirm) that I will faithfully and impartially discharge and perform all the duties incumbent on me as—according to the best of my abilities and understanding, agreeably to the rules and regulations of the Constitution, and the laws of this State; so help me God!"

SECT. 2. Treason against the State, shall consist only in levying war against it or in adhering to its enemies, giving them aid and comfort. No person shall be convicted of treason, unless on testimony of two witnesses to the same overt act, or his own confession in open court.

SECT. 3. Every person shall be disqualified from serving as governor, Senator or Representative for the term for which he shall have been elected, who shall have been convicted of having given or offered any bribe to procure his election.

SECT. 4. Laws shall be made to exclude from office and from suffrage those who shall thereafter be convicted of bribery, perjury, forgery or other high crimes or misdemeanors, the privilege of free suffrage shall be supported by laws regulating elections and prohibiting under adequate penalties, all undue influence thereon, from power, bribery, tumult, or other improper practices.

SECT. 5. No money shall be drawn from the treasury, but in pursuance of appropriations made by law; nor shall any appropriation of money for the support of an army be made for a longer term than one year; and a regular statement and account of the receipts and expenditures of all public moneys, shall be published annually.

SECT. 6. It shall be the duty of the general assembly to pass such laws as may be necessary and proper to decide differences by arbitrators, to be appointed by the parties, who may choose that summary mode of adjustment.

SECT. 7. All civil officers for the state at large shall reside within the State, and all district or county officers within their respective districts or counties, and shall keep their respective offices at such places therein as may be required by law.

SECT. 8. The Legislature shall determine the time of duration of the several public offices when such time shall not have been fixed by this Constitution, and all civil officers except the governor and judges of the superior and inferior courts shall be removable by an address of two thirds of the members of both houses, except those, the removal of whom has been otherwise provided for by this Constitution.

SECT. 9. Absence on the business of this State or of the United States, shall not forfeit a residence once obtained, so as to deprive any one of the rights of suffrage, or of being elected or appointed to any office under this State, under the exceptions contained in this Constitution.

SECT. 10. It shall be the duty of the general assembly to regulate by law in what cases, and what deduction from the salaries of public offi-

cers shall be made for neglect of duty in their official capacity.

SECT. 11. Returns of all elections for the members of the general assembly shall be made to the secretary of state for the time being.

SECT. 12. The Legislature shall point out the manner in which a man coming into the country shall declare his residence.

SECT. 13. In all elections by the people, and also by the Senate and House of Representatives jointly or separately, the vote shall be given by ballot.

SECT. 14. No members of Congress, nor person holding or exercising any office of trust or profit under the United States, or either of them, or under any foreign powers shall be eligible as a member of the general assembly of this State, or hold or exercise any office of trust or profit under the same.

SECT. 15. All laws that may be passed by the Legislature, and the public records of this State, and the judicial and legislative written proceedings of the same, shall be promulgated, preserved and conducted in the language in which the constitution of the United States is written.

SECT. 16. The general assembly shall direct by law how persons who are now or may hereafter become securities for public officers, may be relieved or discharged on account of such securityship.

SECT. 17. No power of suspending the laws of this State shall be exercised, unless by the Legislature, or its authority.

SECT. 18. In all criminal prosecutions, the accused have the right of being heard by himself or counsel, of demanding the nature and cause of the accusation against him, of meeting the witnesses face to face, of having compulsory process for obtaining witnesses in his favour, and prosecutions by indictment, or information, a speedy public trial by an impartial jury of the vicinage, nor shall he be compelled to give evidence against himself.

SECT. 19. All prisoners shall be bailable by sufficient securities, unless for capital offences, where the proof is evident or presumption great, and the privilege of the writ of Habeas Corpus shall not be suspended unless when in cases of rebellion or invasion the public safety may require it.

SECT. 20. No *expost facto* law nor any law impairing the obligation of contracts shall be passed.

SECT. 21. Printing presses shall be free to every Person who undertakes to examine the proceedings of the Legislature, or any branch of the government, and no law shall ever be made to restrain the right thereof. The free communication of thoughts and opinions is one of the invaluable rights of man, and every citizen may freely speak, write and print on any subject, being responsible for the abuse of that liberty.

SECT. 22. Emigration from the State shall not be prohibited.

SECT. 23. The citizens of the town of New-Orleans shall have the right of appointing the several public officers necessary for the administration and the police of the said city, pursuant to the mode of election which shall be prescribed by the Legislature; Provided that the mayor and recorder be ineligible to a seat in the general assembly.

SECT. 24. The seat of government shall continue at New Orleans until removed by law.

SECT. 25. All laws contrary to this Constitution shall be null and void.

ARTICLE VII MODE OF REVISING THE CONSTITUTION

SECT. 1. When experience shall point out the necessity of amending this Constitution, and a majority of all the members elected to each house of the general assembly, shall, within the first twenty days of their stated annual session, concur in passing a law, specifying the alterations intended to be made, for taking the sense of the good people of this state, as to the necessity and expediency of calling a convention, it shall be the duty of the several returning officers, at the next general election which shall be held for Representatives after the passage of such law, to open a poll for, and make return to the secretary for the time being, of the names of all those entitled to vote for Representatives, who have voted for calling a convention; and if thereupon, it shall appear that a majority of all the citizens of this state, entitled to vote for Representatives, have voted for a convention, the general assembly, shall direct that a similar poll shall be opened, and taken for the next year; and if thereupon, it shall appear that a majority of all the citizens of this state entitled to vote for Representatives, have voted for a convention, the general assembly shall, at their next session, call a convention to consist of as many members as there shall be in the general assembly, and no more, to be chosen in the same manner and proportion, at the same places and at the same time, that Representatives are, by citizens entitled to vote for Representatives; and to meet within three months after the said election, for the purpose of re-adopting, amending or changing this constitution. But if it shall appear by the vote of either year, as aforesaid, that the majority of all the citizens entitled to vote for Representatives, did not vote for a convention, a convention shall not be called.

SCHEDULE

SECT. 1. That no inconveniences may arise from the change of a territorial to permanent state government, it is declared by the Convention that all rights, suits, actions, prosecutions, claims and contracts, both as it respects individuals and bodies corporate, shall continue as if no change had taken place in this government in virtue of the laws now in force.

SECT. 2. All fines, penalties and forfeitures, due and owing to the territory of Orleans shall inure to the use of the state. All bonds executed to the governor or any other officer in his official capacity in the territory, shall pass over to the governor or to the officers of the State and their successors in office, for the use of the State, by him or by them to be respectively assigned over to the use of those concerned, as the case may be.

SECT. 3. The governor, secretary and judges, and all other officers under the territorial government, shall continue in the exercise of their duties of their respective departments until the said officers are superceded under the authority of this Constitution.

SECT. 4. All laws now in force in this territory not inconsistent with this constitution, shall continue and remain in full effect, until repealed by the legislature.

SECT. 5. The governor of this state shall make use of his private seal, until a state seal be procured.

SECT. 6. The oaths of office herein directed to be taken, may be administered by any justice of the peace, until the legislature shall otherwise direct.

SECT. 7. At the expiration of the time after which this constitution is to go into operation, or immediately after official information shall have been received that congress have approved of the same, the president of the Convention shall issue writs of election to the proper officers in the different counties, enjoining them to cause an election to be held for governor and members of the general assembly, in each of their respective districts. The election shall commence on the fourth Monday following the day of the date of the President's proclamation, and shall take place on the same day throughout the state. The mode and duration of the said election shall be determined by the laws now in force: Provided however, that in case of absence or disability of the President of the Convention, to cause the said election be carried into effect, the Secretary of the Convention shall discharge the duties hereby imposed on the President, and that in case of the absence of the secretary a committee of Messrs Blanque, Brown, and Urquhart or a majority of them, shall discharge the duties herein imposed on the secretary of the convention—and the members of the general assembly thus elected shall assemble on the fourth Monday thereafter at the seat of government. The governor and members of the general assembly for this time only, shall enter upon the duties of their respective offices, immediately after their election, shall continue in office in the same manner and during the same would have done had they been elected on the first Monday of July 1812.

SECT. 8. untill the first enumeration shall be made as directed in the sixth section of the second article of this Constitution, the, county of Orleans shall be entitled to Six Representatives to be elected as follows: one by the first senatorial district within the said county, four by the second district, and one by the third district—The county of German Coast, to two Representatives, the county of Acadia, to two Representatives; the county of Iberville, to two Representatives; the county of Lafourche, to two Representatives; to be elected as follows: one by the parish of the assumption, and the other by the parish of the interior; the county of Rapides, to two Representatives; the county of Natchitoches, to one Representative; the county of Concordia, to one Representative; the county of Ouachitta, to one Representative; the county of Opelloussas, to two Representatives; the county of Attakapas, to three Representatives to be elected as follows: two by the parish of St. Martin and the third by the parish of St. Mary, and the respective senatorial districts created by this Constitution, to one senator each.

Done in Convention, at New Orleans, the twenty second day of the month of January, in the year of our Lord one thousand eight hundred and twelve, and of the independence of the United States of America, the thirty-sixth.

J. POYDRAS
President of the Convention

ELIGIUS FROMENTIN
Secretary of the Convention

Source: Francis Newton Thorpe, ed., *The Federal and State Constitutions, Colonial Charters, and Other Organic Laws of the States, Territories, and Colonies Now or Heretofore Forming the United States of America* (Washington, D.C.: Government Printing Office), vol. 3: 1380–1392.

46   Admitting the State of Louisiana into the Union, April 8, 1812

Be it enacted . . . That the said state shall be one, and is hereby declared to be one of the United States of America, and admitted into the Union on equal footing with the original states, in all respects whatever, by the name and title of the state of Louisiana. . . .

SEC 2. *And be it further enacted,* That until the next general census and apportionment of representatives, the said state shall be entitled to one representative in the House of Representatives of the United States; and that all the laws of the United States, not locally inapplicable, shall be extended to the said state, and shall have the same force and effect within the state, as elsewhere within the United States. . . .

APPROVED, April 8, 1812.

Source: The Public Statutes at Large of the United States of America (Boston: Charles C. Little and James Brown, 1845), 701–704.

47   Congress Debates Missouri Statehood

The debates over statehood for Louisiana and Missouri could not have been more different. Both cases generated no end of disagreement within Congress, but that disagreement had profoundly different roots. The Louisiana debate of 1812 was primarily an argument about the attachment of individual residents. As Chapter 10 shows, the Missouri debate, only a few years later, was about constitutional arrangements within the union as a whole. When Rep. James Tallmadge, R-N.Y., argued that Missouri should enter the union with provisions for the gradual elimination of slavery, he unleashed a debate that had been a half-century in the making. Most Americans know that argument primarily as one about the expansion of slavery—and rightly so. But there was more to this debate: did Congress have the right to dictate the provisions of a state constitution?

In these two passages, Reps. John Taylor of New York and Philip Barbour of Virginia debate the constitutionality of imposing any requirements on a state constitution from Missouri other than the most basic provision that it be republican in form. Both men were Jeffersonian Republicans, and both eventually served as Speaker of the House (Taylor in the Sixteenth and Nineteenth Congresses, Barbour in the Seventeenth). That the two men could so vehemently disagree on the matter was an indication of the eventual breakdown of the Jeffersonian coalition. Although Republicans had argued about slavery before 1820, the matter had never dominated political debate as much as it would in the years that followed.

Mr. TAYLOR, of New York, spoke as follows:

Mr. Chairman, if the few citizens who now inhabit the Territory of Missouri were alone interested in the decision of this question, I should content myself with voting in favor of the amendment, without occupying for a moment the attention of the Committee. But the fact is far otherwise: those whom we shall authorize to set in motion the machine of free government beyond the Mississippi, will, in many respects, decide the destiny of millions. . . . Our votes this day will determine whether the high destinies of this region, and of these generations, shall be fulfilled, or whether we shall defeat them by permitting slavery, with all its baleful consequences, to inherit the land. . . .

First. Has Congress power to require of Missouri a Constitutional prohibition against the further introduction of slavery, as a condition of her admission into the Union?

Second. If the power exist, is it wise to exercise it?

Congress has no power unless it be expressly granted by the Constitution, or necessary to the execution of some power clearly delegated. What, then, are the grants made to Congress in relation to the Territories? . . . The whole subject is put at the disposal of Congress, as well the right of judging what regulations are proper to be made, as the power of making them, is clearly granted. Until admitted into the Union, this political society is a territory; all the preliminary steps relating to its admission are territorial regulations. Hence, in all such cases, Congress has exercised the power of determining by whom the constitution should be made, how its framers should be elected, when and where they should meet, and what propositions should be submitted to their decisions. After its formation, the Congress examine its provisions, and if approved, admit the State into the Union, in pursuance of a power delegated by the . . . Constitution. . . . This grant of power is evidently alternative; its exercise is committed to the sound discretion of Congress; no injustice is done by declining it. But if Congress has the power of altogether refusing to admit new States, much more has it the power of prescribing such conditions of admission as may be judged reasonable. The exercise of this power, until now, has never been questioned. . . .

. . . [I]t is said that, by the treaty of 1803, with the French Republic, Congress is restrained from imposing this condition. The third article is quoted as containing the prohibition. . . . The inhabitants of the ceded territory, when transferred from the protection of the French Republic, in regard to the United States, would have stood in the relation of aliens. The object of the article doubtless was to provide for their admission to the rights of citizens, and their incorporation into the American family. The treaty made no provision for the erection of new States in the ceded territory. That was a question of national policy, properly reserved for the decision of those to whom the Constitution had committed the power. The framers of the treaty well knew that the President and Senate could not bind Congress to admit new States into the Union. . . .

. . . The sovereignty of Congress in relation to the States, is limited by specific grants—but, in regard to the Territories, it is unlimited. Missouri was purchased with our money, and, until incorporated into the family of States, it may be sold for money. Can it then be maintained that, although we have the power to dispose of the whole Territory, we have no right to provide against the further increase of slavery within its limits? That, although we may change the political regulations of its free citizens by transferring their country to a foreign Power, we cannot provide for the gradual abolition of slavery within its limits, nor establish those civil regulations which, naturally flow from self-evident truth? No, sir, it cannot; the practice of nations and the common sense of mankind have long since decided these questions.

. . . Gentlemen have now an opportunity of putting their principles into practice; if they have tried slavery and found it a curse; if they desire to dissipate the gloom with which it covers their land; I call upon them to exclude it from the Territory in question; plant not its seeds in this uncorrupt soil; let not our children, looking back to the proceedings of this day, say of them, as they have been constrained to speak of their fathers, "we wish their decision had been different; we regret the existence of this unfortunate population among us, but we found them here: we know not what to do with them; it is our misfortune, we must bear it with patience."

History will record the decision of this day as exerting its influence for centuries to come over the population of half our continent. If we reject the amendment and suffer this evil, now easily eradicated, to strike its roots so deep in the soil that it can never be removed, shall we not furnish some apology for doubting our sincerity, when we deplore its existence. . . .

Mr. P. P. BARBOUR, of Virginia, said that, as he was decidedly opposed to the amendment which had been offered, he asked the indulgence of the House whilst he made some remarks in addition to those which had fallen from the Speaker, for the purpose of showing the impropriety of its adoption. . . .

. . . It is said that the like prohibition has been enacted as it respects Ohio and the other States northwest of the river Ohio. In the first place, the House would recollect that an ordinance was passed by the old Congress, at a period anterior to the present Constitution, ordaining that as a fundamental article in relation to all the northwest territory, and therefore the precedent, if it would otherwise have any weight, failed in its application. But, he said, he did not hesitate to express it as his decided opinion, that the ordinance which he had just mentioned was utterly void, and, consequently, that those States might introduce slavery amongst them, if they so willed, because the territory which composes them originally belonged to Virginia. She had conquered it by her arms, she ceded it to the United States upon the express condition that it should be formed into States, as free, sovereign, and independent as the other States. The prohibition of slavery was ordained by the Continental Congress, after the cession had been made, which would unquestionably render those States less sovereign than the original States of the Federal Union. But it has been said that we imposed conditions on the admission of the State of Louisiana into the Union. What were those conditions? That civil and religious liberty should be established, and the trial by jury secured. It cannot be necessary to remind the House, that these several provisions attached also to the original States, by the most explicit declaration to that effect, in the first, fifth, and seventh amendments to the Constitution of the United States. These requisitions, then, were in perfect consistency with his principle. All that he contended for was, that we could impose no condition upon the new States, which the Constitution had not imposed upon the old ones; as those which were imposed upon Louisiana were clearly of that description, they were within our power; but, as the prohibition of slavery was not of that description, he thought it was as clearly beyond our power. The gentleman from Massachusetts had said that it was competent to the State Legislatures to declare that the progeny of all slaves should be free when they attained a given age; and hence he inferred that Congress might do the same, in relation to the proposed State. Sir, said Mr. B., there is no sort of analogy between the cases; the State Legislatures can do it, because to them appertains the whole business of municipal legislation, and this regulation would be embraced within it; and Congress could do the same, in relation to its Territorial governments, because over them we possess the whole power of municipal legislation; not so in the present case; for the question now before us, is not what regulation we shall prescribe for a territory which is to continue as such, but upon what forms and conditions we will admit a State into the Union. Our business is, then, to create a political community if a particular character, as prescribed by the Constitution; to itself it will belong to regulate its interior concerns, and amongst others, to decide whether it will or will not admit involuntary servitude. . . .

Source: Annals of Congress: Debates and Proceedings of the Congress of the United States, 15th Cong., 2d sess. (Washington: Gales and Seaton, 1834–1856), 1170–1174, 1184–1185, 1187–1188.

48 Forming a Constitution and State Government in the Territory of Missouri, March 6, 1820

An Act to authorize the people of the Missouri territory to form a constitution and state government, and for the admission of such state into the Union on an equal footing with the original states, and to prohibit slavery in certain territories.

Be it enacted by the Senate and House of Representatives of the United States of America, In Congress assembled, That the inhabitants of that portion of the Missouri territory included within the boundaries hereinafter designated, be, and they are hereby, authorized to form for themselves a constitution and state government, and to assume such name as they shall deem proper; and the said state, when formed, shall be admitted into the Union, upon an equal footing with the original states, in all respects whatsoever. . . .

SEC. 8. *And be it further enacted,* That in all that territory ceded by France to the United States, under the name of Louisiana, which lies north of thirty-six degrees and thirty minutes north latitude, not included within the limits of the state, contemplated by this act, slavery and involuntary servitude, otherwise than in the punishment of crimes, whereof the parties shall have been duly convicted, shall be, and is hereby, forever prohibited: *Provided always,* That any person escaping into the same, from whom labour or service is lawfully claimed, in any state or territory of the United States, such fugitive may be lawfully reclaimed and conveyed to the person claiming his or her labour or service as aforesaid.

APPROVED, March 6, 1820.

Source: The Public Statutes at Large of the United States of America (Boston: Charles C. Little and James Brown, 1845), vol. 3: 545–548.

49 The Missouri Constitution of 1820

We, the people of Missouri, inhabiting the limits hereinafter designated, by our representatives in convention assembled at St. Louis, on Monday, the 12th day of June, 1820, do mutually agree to form and establish a free and independent republic, by the name of "The State of Missouri," and for the government thereof do ordain and establish this constitution. . . .

ARTICLE II OF THE DISTRIBUTION OF POWERS

The powers of government shall be divided into three distinct departments, each of which shall be confided to a separate magistracy; and no person charged with the exercise of powers properly be-longing to one of those departments shall exercise any power properly belonging to either of the others, except in the instances hereinafter expressly directed or permitted.

ARTICLE III OF THE LEGISLATIVE POWER

Section 1. The legislative power shall be vested in a General Assembly, which shall consist of a Senate and of a House of Representatives. . . .

ARTICLE IV OF THE EXECUTIVE POWER

Section 1. The supreme executive power shall be vested in a chief magistrate, who shall be styled "The Governor of the State of Missouri." . . .

Sec. 14. There shall be a lieutenant-governor, who shall be elected at the same time, in the same manner, for the same term, and shall possess the same qualifications as the governor. The electors shall distinguish for whom they vote as governor and for whom as lieutenant-governor. . . .

ARTICLE V OF THE JUDICIAL POWER

Section 1. The judicial powers, as to matters of law and equity, shall be vested in a supreme court, in a chancellor, in circuit courts, and in such inferior tribunals as the general assembly may from time to time ordain and establish.

Sec. 2. The supreme court, except in cases otherwise directed by this constitution, shall have appellate jurisdiction only, which shall be co-extensive with the State, under the restrictions and limitations in this constitution provided. . . .

ARTICLE XIII DECLARATION OF RIGHTS

That the general, great, and essential principles of liberty and free government may be recognized and established, we declare—

Section 1. That all political power is vested in, and derived from, the people.

Sec. 2. That the people of this State have the inherent, sole, and exclusive right of regulating the internal government and police thereof, and of altering and abolishing their constitution and form of government whenever it may be necessary to their safety and happiness.

Sec. 3. That the people have the right peaceably to assemble for their common good, and to apply to those vested with the powers of government for redress of grievances by petition or remonstrance; and that their right to bear arms in defense of themselves and of the State cannot be questioned.

Sec. 4. That all men have a natural and indefeasible right to worship Almighty God according to the dictates of their own consciences; that no man can be compelled to erect, support, or attend any place of worship or to maintain any minister of the gospel or teacher of religion; that no human authority can control or interfere with the rights of conscience; that no person can ever be hurt, molested, or restrained in his religious profession or sentiments, if he do not disturb others in their religious worship.

Sec. 5. That no person, on account of his religious opinions, can be rendered ineligible to any office of trust or profit under this State; that no preference can ever be given by law to any sect or mode of worship; and that no religious corporation can ever be established in this State.

Sec. 6. That all elections shall be free and equal.

Sec. 7. That courts of justice ought to be open to every person, and certain remedy afforded for every injury to person, property, or character; and that right and justice ought to be administered without sale, denial, or delay; and that no private property ought to be taken or applied to public use without just compensation.

Sec. 8. That the right of trial by jury shall remain inviolate.

Sec. 9. That in all criminal prosecutions, the accused has the right to be heard by himself and his counsel; to demand the nature and cause of accusation; to have compulsory process for witnesses in his favor; to meet the witnesses against him face to face; and, in prosecutions on presentment or indictment, to a speedy trial, by an impartial jury of the vicinage; that the accused cannot be compelled to give evidence against himself, nor be deprived of life, liberty, or property but by the judgment of his peers, or the law of the land.

Sec. 10. That no person, after having been once acquitted by a jury, can, for the same offence, be again put in jeopardy of life or limb; but if in any criminal prosecution the jury be divided in opinion at the end of the term, the court before which the trial shall be had, may, in its discretion, discharge the jury, and commit or bail the accused for trial at the next term of such court.

Sec. 11. That all persons shall be bailable by sufficient sureties, except for capital offences, when the proof is evident or the presumption great; and the privilege of the writ of habeas corpus cannot be suspended; unless when, in case of rebellion or invasion, the public safety may require it.

Sec. 12. That excessive bail shall not be required, nor excessive fines imposed, nor cruel and unusual punishments inflicted.

Sec. 13. That the people ought to be secure in their persons, papers, houses, and effects from unreasonable searches and seizures; and no warrant to search any place, or to seize any person, or thing can issue, without describing the place to be searched, or the person or thing to be seized, as nearly as may be, nor without probable cause, supported by oath or affirmation.

Sec. 14. That no person can, for an indictable offence, be proceeded against criminally, by information, except in cases arising in the land or naval forces, or in the militia when in actual service, in time of war or public danger, or, by leave of the court, for oppression or misdemeanor in office.

Sec. 15. That treason against the State can consist only in levying war against it, or in adhering to its enemies, giving them aid and comfort; that no person can be convicted of treason unless on the testimony of two witnesses to the same overt act, or on his own confession in open court; that no person can be attainted of treason or felony by the general assembly; that no conviction can work corruption of blood or forfeiture of estate; that the estates of such persons as may destroy their own lives shall descend or vest as in cases of natural death; and when any person shall be killed by casualty, there ought to be no forfeiture by reason thereof.

Sec. 16. That the free communication of thoughts and opinions is one of the invaluable rights of man, and that every person may freely speak, write, and print on any subject, being responsible for the abuse of that liberty; that in all prosecutions for libels the truth thereof may be given in evidence, and the jury may determine the law and the facts, under the direction of the court.

Sec. 17. That no *ex post facto* law, nor law impairing the obligation of contracts, or retrospective in its operation, can be passed; nor can the person of a debtor be imprisoned for debt after he shall have surrendered his property for the benefit of his creditors in such manner as may be prescribed by law.

Sec. 18. That no person who is religiously scrupulous of bearing arms can be compelled to do so, but may be compelled to pay an equivalent for military service, in such manner as shall be prescribed by law; and that no priest, preacher of the gospel, or teacher of any religious persuasion or sect, regularly ordained as such, be subject to militia duty, or compelled to bear arms.

Sec. 19. That all property, subject to taxation in this State, shall be taxed in proportion to its value.

Sec. 20. That no title of nobility, hereditary emolument, privilege, or distinction, shall be granted nor any office created the duration of which shall be longer than the good behavior of the officer appointed to fill the same.

Sec. 21. That emigration from this state can not be prohibited.

Sec. 22. That the military is, and in all cases and at all times shall be, in strict subordination to the civil power; that no soldier can, in time of peace, be quartered in any house without the consent of the owner nor in time of war but in such manner as may be prescribed by law; nor can any appropriation for the support of an army be made for a longer period than two years. . . .

Source: Francis Newton Thorpe, ed., *The Federal and State Constitutions, Colonial Charters, and Other Organic Laws of the States, Territories, and Colonies Now or Heretofore Forming the United States of America* (Washington, D.C.: Government Printing Office), vol. 4: 2150–2169.

50

The Qualified Admission of the State of Missouri into the Union, March 2, 1821

RESOLUTION *providing for the admission of the State of Missouri into the Union, on a certain condition.*

Resolved by the Senate and House of Representatives of the United States of America, in Congress assembled, That Missouri shall be admitted into this union on an equal footing with the original states, in all respects whatever, upon the fundamental condition, that the fourth clause of the twenty-sixth section of the third article of the constitution submitted on the part of said state to Congress, shall never be construed to authorize the passage of any law, and that no law shall be passed in conformity thereto, by which any citizen, of either of the states in this Union, shall be excluded from the enjoyment of any of the privileges and immunities to which such citizen is entitled under the constitution of the United States: *Provided,* That the legislature of the said state, by a solemn public act, shall declare the assent of the said state to the said fundamental condition, and shall transmit to the President of the United States, on or before the fourth Monday in November next, an authentic copy of the said act; upon the receipt whereof, the President, by proclamation, shall announce the fact; whereupon, and without any further proceeding on the part of Congress, the admission of the said state into this Union shall be considered as complete.

APPROVED, March 2, 1821.

Source: The Public Statutes at Large of the United States of America (Boston: Charles C. Little and James Brown, 1845), vol. 3: 645.

---

51   Letter from James Madison to William C. C. Claiborne, November 18, 1805

SIR. You will find enclosed a list of your letters which remain unacknowledged.

From the public papers you will have learnt the unfavorable result of the negotiations for the settlement of the controversy with Spain. In truth Mr Monroe left Madrid without being able to accomplish any object of his mission; the councils of Spain obstinately rejecting our demands & declining not only to accept our proposals of compromise, but to offer any of their own. Under such appearances of an obstinate and unfriendly temper on her part, heightened by the reinforcements lately landed at Pensacola, the similar movements reported to have taken place on the western frontier accompanied by the violent and predatory acts committed by the Spanish troops in that quarter, as communicated to the Secretary of War by Dr Sibley, the President has come to the resolution, that the Marquis Casa Calvo and all other persons holding commissions or retained in the service of His Catholic Majesty should be ordered to quit the Territory of Orleans as soon as possible. As the pretext for the Marquis remaining as a Commissioner for delivering possession has ceased, or seems to be exchanged for another arising from his character of Commissioner for settling limits, it may be proper to remark that he has never been accredited in any such character and that no arrangement has ever been proposed to us for setting such a Commission on foot, that the Marquis and nearly all his attendants are military characters, some of them of considerable rank, and that as long as such a difference of opinion continues respecting the lines to be run, there can be no necessity for the commission. You will therefore lose no time in notifying the Presidents order upon this subject to the Marquis and through him to the persons whom it comprehends, in such terms as may leave no room for a further discussion, and as whilst they are attempered to the present state of things may not wear the aspect of hostility. In what manner the relations between the United States & Spain may be affected by the views of Congress on the subject will be known at the approaching Session. With them also it will lie to extend the intermediate provisions for the safety of the Country, in case the new posture of things in Europe should draw Spain into manifestations of a readiness to terminate the difference with us on reasonable & amicable grounds.

Source: Clarence Edward Carter, ed., *The Territorial Papers of the United States* (Washington: Government Printing Office), vol. 9: 533–534.

52   Letter from James Monroe to John Quincy Adams, December 10, 1815

Sir,—Reports continue to circulate that the Spanish Government has ceded to Great-Britain the Floridas and Louisiana. It is also stated that measures are taken for an equipment of an expedition to that quarter, to consist of so large a body of men as would not be contemplated if it was the intention of the British Government to preserve the existing friendly relations between the two countries. Ten thousand men it is said are likely to be sent from Great Britain and Ireland and it has been intimated that some foreign troops will be taken into British pay and employed in the expedition. The Prussian troops near the channel are spoken of.

If the British Government has accepted a cession of this territory from Spain and is taking measures for its occupancy her conduct must be considered as decidedly hostile to the United States. As well might the British Government send an army to Philadelphia or to Charlestown as to New Orleans, or to any portion of Louisiana westward of the Perdido, knowing as it does the just title of the United States to that limit. To send a considerable force to East-Florida even should the British Government state that that it had accepted the cession of that province only, could not be viewed in a friendly light. Why send a large force there if Spain has ceded and is ready to surrender the Province unless the British Government has objects in view, unjust in their nature, the pursuit of which must of necessity produce war with the United States? East-Florida in itself is comparatively nothing but as a post in the hands of Great Britain it is of the highest importance. Commanding the Gulph of Mexico and all its waters including the Mississippi with its branches and the streams emptying into the Mobile, a vast proportion of the most fertile and productive parts of this Union, on which the navigation and commerce so essentially depend, would be subject to its annoyance, not to mention its influence on the Creeks and other neighboring Indians. It is believed if Great Britain has accepted the cession of East Florida and of it only, that she has done it with intention to establish a strong post there and to avail herself of it for all the purposes above suggested. If the cession has greater extent, the design is more apparent.

If none has been made the British Government will it is presumed take an interest in removing the impression which these reports coming from so many quarters could not fail to make. If a cession has been made to Great Britain of East Florida, and her views in regard to it have undergone such a change it will be agreeable to this government to obtain it of her at a fair equivalent.

The revolution which is making rapid progress in South America becomes daily more interesting to the United States. From the best information that we can obtain there is much cause to believe that the Provinces will separate from the Mother Country. Several of them have already abrogated its authority and established independent governments. They insist on the acknowledgment of their governments by the United States and when it is considered that the alternative is between governments which, in the event of their independence, would be free and friendly, and the relation which, reasoning from the past, must be expected from them as Colonies there is no cause to doubt in which scale our interest lies. . .

Source: Stanislaus Murray Hamilton, ed., *The Writings of James Monroe* (New York: Putnam's), vol. 5: 380–382.

53 Letter from James Monroe to Thomas Jefferson, May 1820

By 1820 Thomas Jefferson was long since retired and James Monroe faced no serious opposition in his campaign for a second term as president. With the Senate balking at final approval of the Transcontinental Treaty, both men were eager to reach a resolution with Spain so that the United States could turn to the more troubling question of whether to recognize the new regimes arising in Spanish America. As Monroe discussed these matters, he nonetheless continued to set matters in the context of the Mississippi, the Louisiana Purchase, and the new order that had taken form in North America since 1803.

Dear Sir,—I have receiv'd your letter of the 14. containing a very interesting view of the late treaty with Spain, and of the proceedings respecting it here. If the occurrence involv'd in it nothing more, than a question between the U States & Spain, or between them & the Colonies, I should entirely concur in your view of the subject. I am satisfied, that we might, regulate it, in every circumstance, as we thought just, & without war, that we might take Florida as an indemnity, and Texas for some trifle as an equivalent. Spain must soon be expelled from this Continent, and with any new govt. which may be form'd in Mexico, it would be easy to arrange the boundary in the wilderness, so as to include as much territory on our side as we might desire. No European power could prevent this, if so disposed. But the difficulty does not proceed from these sources. It is altogether internal, and of the most distressing nature and dangerous tendency. You were apprized by me, on your return from Europe, of the true character, of the negotiation, which took place in 1785-6. with the Minister of Spain, for shutting up the mouth of the Mississippi, a knowledge of which might have been deriv'd in part from the secret journal of Congress, which then came into your hands. That, was not a question with Spain, in reality, but one among ourselves, in which her pretensions were brought forward, in aid of the policy, of the party at the head of that project. It was an effort to give such a shape to our Union, as would secure the dominion over it, to its eastern section. It was expected that dismemberment by the Allegheny

Mountains, would follow the occlusion of the river, if it was not desir'd, tho' the latter was then & still is my opinion. The Union then consisted of eight navigating and commercial States, with five productive, holding slaves; and had the river been shut up, and dismemberment insured, the division would always have been the same. At that time Boston ruled the four New England States, and a popular orator in Fanuel hall, ruled Boston. Jays object was to make N. York a New England State, which he avowed on his return from Europe, to the dissatisfaction of many in that State, whose prejudices had been excited in the revolutionary war by the contest between N. York and those States respecting interfering grants in Vermont. It was foreseen by these persons, that if the Mississippi should be open'd, and new States be established on its waters, the population would be drawn thither, the number of productive States be proportionally encreased, & their hope of dominion, on that contracted sectional scale, be destroyed. It was to prevent this that that project was formed. Happily it failed, & since then, our career, in an opposite direction, has been rapid & wonderful. The river has been open'd, & all the territory dependent on it acquir'd, eight states have already been admitted into the Union, in that quarter; a 9th is on the point of entering, & a 10th provided for, exclusive of Florida. This march to greatness has been seen with profound regret, by them, in the policy suggested, but it has been impelled by causes over which they have had no control. Several attempts have been made to impede it, among which, the Harford Convention in the late war, and the proposition for restricting Missouri, are the most distinguished. The latter measure contemplated, an arrangement on the distinction solely, between slave holding and non-slave holding States, presuming that on that basis only, such a division might be formed, as would destroy, by perpetual excit'ment, the usual effects proceeding from difference in climate, the produce of the soil, the pursuits & circumstances of the people, & marshall the States, differing in that circumstance, in unceasing opposition & hostility with each other.

To what account, this project, had it succeeded, to the extent contemplated, might have been turn'd, I cannot say. Certain however it is, that since 1786, I have not seen, so violent & persevering a struggle, and on the part of some of the leaders in the project, for a purpose so unmasked & dangerous. They did not hesitate to avow that it was a contest for power only, disclaiming the pretext of liberty, humanity, &c. It was also manifested, that they were willing to risk the Union, on the measure, if indeed, as in that relating to the Mississippi, dismemberment was not the principal object. You know how this affair terminated, as I presume you likewise do, that complete success, was prevented, by the patriotic devotion of several members in the non slave holding States, who preferr'd the sacrifice of themselves at home, to a violation, of the obvious principles of the Constitution, & the risk of the Union. I am satisfied that the arrangement made, was most auspicious to the Union, since had the conflict been pursued, there is reason to believe that, the worst consequences would have followed. The excitement would have been kept up, during which it seemed probable, that the slave holding States would have lost ground daily. By putting a stop to the proceeding, time has been given for the passions to subside, & for calm discussion & reflection, which have never failed to produce their proper effect in our country. Such too was the nature of the controversy, that it seem'd to be hazardous, for either party to gain a complete triumph. I never doubted the right of Congress, to make such a regulation in [the] territories, tho' I did not expect that it would ever have been exercised.

From this view, it is evident, that the further acquisition, of territory, to the West & South, involves difficulties, of an internal nature, which menace the Union itself. We ought therefore to be cautious in making the attempt. Having secur'd the Mississippi, and all its waters, with a slight exception only, and erected States there, ought we not to be satisfied, so far at least as to take no step in that direction, which is not approved, by all the members, or at least a majority of those who accomplished our revolution. I could go into further details had I time. I have thought that these might afford you some satisfaction. When we meet in Albemarle we will communicate further on the subject.

Source: Stanislaus Murray Hamilton, ed., *The Writings of James Monroe* (New York: Putnam's), vol. 5: 119–123.

54   The Transcontinental Treaty

Often called either the Transcontinental Treaty or the Adams-Onís Treaty, this agreement made an official end to many of the diplomatic conflicts that came with the Louisiana Purchase. First and foremost, it settled the boundary disputes between the United States and Spain. In addition to establishing the terminus between the western United States and Spanish North America, the treaty also ceded the Floridas to the United States. This concession was something of a fait accompli, because the United States had already seized most of the land east of the Mississippi, whether through centralized action, like James Madison's annexation of West Florida in 1810, or by local aggression, like Andrew Jackson's various incursions into the Gulf Coast and the Florida Peninsula during and after the War of 1812. Nonetheless, a formal agreement between the two countries was essential to Monroe, and it came as welcome news to his predecessors, Madison and Thomas Jefferson.

The United States of America and His Catholic Majesty, desiring to consolidate, on a permanent basis, the friendship and good correspondence which happily prevails between the two parties, have determined to settle and terminate all their differences and pretensions, by a treaty, which shall designate, with precision, the limits of their respective bordering territories in North America.

With this intention the President of the United States has furnished with their full powers John Quincy Adams, Secretary of State of the said United States; and His Catholic Majesty has appointed the Most Excellent Lord Don Luis De Onís, Gonzales, Lopez y Vara, Lord of the Town of Rayaces, Perpetual Regidor of the Corporation of the city of Salamanca, Knight Grand Cross of the Royal American Order of Isabella the Catholic, decorated with the Lys of La Vendee, Knight Pensioner of the Royal and Distinguished Spanish Order of Charles the Third, Member of the Supreme Assembly of the said Royal Order; of the Council of His Catholic Majesty; his Secretary, with Exercise of Decrees, and His Envoy Extraordinary and Minister Plenipotentiary near the United States of America.

And the said Plenipotentiaries, after having exchanged their powers, have agreed upon and concluded the following articles:

ARTICLE I

There shall be a firm and inviolable peace and sincere friendship between the United States and their citizens and His Catholic Majesty, his successors and subjects, without exception of persons or places.

ARTICLE II

His Catholic Majesty cedes to the United States, in full property and sovereignty, all the territories which belong to him, situated to the eastward of the Mississippi, known by the name of East and West Florida. The adjacent islands dependent on said provinces, all public lots and squares, vacant lands, public edifices, fortifications, barracks, and other buildings, which are not private property, archives and documents, which relate directly to the property and sovereignty of said provinces, are included in this article. The said archives and documents shall be left in possession of the commissaries or officers of the United States, duly authorized to receive them.

ARTICLE III

The boundary-line between the two countries, west of the Mississippi, shall begin on the Gulph of Mexico, at the mouth of the river Sabine, in the sea, continuing north, along the western bank of that river, to the 32d degree of latitude; thence, by a line due north, to the degree of latitude where it strikes the Rio Roxo of Nachitoches, or Red River; then following the course of the Rio Roxo westward, to the degree of longitude 100 west from London and 23 from Washington; then, crossing the said Red River, and running thence, by a line due north, to the river Arkansas; thence, following the course of the southern bank of the Arkansas, to its source, in latitude 42 north; and thence, by that parallel of latitude, to the South Sea. The whole being as laid down in Melish's map of the United States, published at Philadelphia, improved to the first of January, 1818. But if the source of the Arkansas River shall be found to fall north or south of latitude 42, then the line shall run from the said source due south or north, as the case may be, till it meets the said parallel of latitude 42, and thence, along the said parallel, to the South Sea: All the islands in the Sabine, and the said Red and Arkansas Rivers, throughout the course thus described, to belong to the United States; but the use of the waters, and the navigation of the Sabine to the sea, and of the said rivers Roxo and Arkansas, throughout the extent of the said boundary, on their respective banks, shall be common to the respective inhabitants of both nations.

The two high contracting parties agree to cede and renounce all their rights, claims, and pretensions to the territories described by the said line, that is to say: The United States hereby cede to His Catholic Majesty, and renounce forever, all their rights, claims, and pretensions, to the territories lying west and south of the above-described line; and, in like manner, His Catholic Majesty cedes to the said United States all his rights, claims, and pretensions to any territories east and north of the said line, and for himself, his heirs, and successors, renounces all claim to the said territories forever.

ARTICLE IV

To fix this line with more precision, and to place the landmarks which shall designate exactly the limits of both nations, each of the contracting parties shall appoint a Commissioner and a surveyor, who shall meet before the termination of one year from the date of the ratification of this treaty at Nachitoches, on the Red River, and proceed to run and mark the said line, from the mouth of the Sabine to the Red River, and from the Red River to the river Arkansas, and to ascertain the latitude of the source of the said river Arkansas, in conformity to what is above agreed upon and stipulated and the line of latitude 42, to the South Sea: they shall make out plans, and keep journals of their proceedings, and the result agreed upon by them shall be considered as part of this treaty, and shall have the same force as if it were inserted therein. The two Governments will amicably agree respecting the necessary articles to be furnished to those persons, and also as to their respective escorts, should such be deemed necessary.

ARTICLE V

The inhabitants of the ceded territories shall be secured in the free exercise of their religion, without any restriction; and all those who may desire to remove to the Spanish dominions shall be permitted to sell or export their effects, at any time whatever, without being subject, in either case, to duties.

ARTICLE VI

The inhabitants of the territories which His Catholic Majesty cedes to the United States, by this treaty, shall be incorporated in the Union of the United States as soon as may be consistent with the principles of the Federal Constitution, and admitted to the enjoyment of all the privileges, rights, and immunities of the citizens of the United States.

ARTICLE VII

The officers and troops of His Catholic Majesty, in the territories hereby ceded by him to the

United States, shall be withdrawn, and possession of the places occupied by them shall be given within six months after the exchange of the ratifications of this treaty, or sooner if possible, by the officers of His Catholic Majesty to the commissioners or officers of the United States duly appointed to receive them; and the United States shall furnish the transports and escort necessary to convey the Spanish officers and troops and their baggage to the Havana.

ARTICLE VIII

All the grants of land made before the 24th of January, 1818, by His Catholic Majesty, or by his lawful authorities, in the said territories ceded by His Majesty to the United States, shall be ratified and confirmed to the persons in possession of the lands, to the same extent that the same grants would be valid if the territories had remained under the dominion of His Catholic Majesty. But the owners in possession of such lands, who, by reason of the recent circumstances of the Spanish nation, and the revolutions in Europe, have been prevented from fulfilling all the conditions of their grants, shall complete them within the terms limited in the same, respectively, from the date of this treaty; in default of which the said grants shall be null and void. All grants made since the said 24th of January, 1818, when the first proposal, on the part of His Catholic Majesty, for the cession of the Floridas was made, are hereby declared and agreed to be null and void.

ARTICLE IX

The two high contracting parties, animated with the most earnest desire of conciliation, and with the object of putting an end to all the differences which have existed between them, and of confirming the good understanding which they wish to be forever maintained between them, reciprocally renounce all claims for damages or injuries which they, themselves, as well as their respective citizens and subjects, may have suffered until the time of signing this treaty.

The renunciation of the United States will extend to all the injuries mentioned in the convention of the 11th of August, 1802.

2. To all claims on account of prizes made by French privateers, and condemned by French Consuls, within the territory and jurisdiction of Spain.

3. To all claims of indemnities on account of the suspension of the right of deposit at New Orleans in 1802.

4. To all claims of citizens of the United States upon the Government of Spain, arising from the unlawful seizures at sea, and in the ports and territories of Spain, or the Spanish colonies.

5. To all claims of citizens of the United States upon the Spanish Government, statements of which, soliciting the interposition of the Government of the United States have been presented to the Department of State, or to the Minister of the United States in Spain, the date of the convention of 1802 and until the signature of this treaty.

The renunciation of His Catholic Majesty extends,

1. To all the injuries mentioned in the convention of the 11th of August, 1802.

2. To the sums which His Catholic Majesty advanced for the return of Captain Pike from the Provincias Internas

3. To all injuries caused by the expedition of Miranda, that was fitted out and equipped at New York.

4. To all claims of Spanish subjects upon the Government of the United States arizing from unlawful seizures at sea, or within the ports and territorial Jurisdiction of the United States.

Finally, to all the claims of subjects of His Catholic Majesty upon the Government of the United States in which the interposition of his Catholic Majesty's Government has been solicited, before the date of this treaty and since the date of the convention of 1802, or which may have been made to the department of foreign affairs of His Majesty, or to his Minister of the United States

And the high contracting parties, respectively, renounce all claim to indemnities for any of the recent events or transactions of their respective commanders and officers in the Floridas.

The United States will cause satisfaction to be made for the injuries, if any, which, by process of law, shall be established to have been suffered by the Spanish officers, and individual Spanish inhabitants, by the late operations of the American Army in Florida.

ARTICLE X

The convention entered into between the two Governments, on the 11th of August, 1802, the ratifications of which were exchanged the 21st December, 1818, is annulled.

ARTICLE XI

The United States, exonerating Spain from all demands in future, on account of the claims of their citizens to which the renunciations herein contained extend, and considering them entirely cancelled, undertake to make satisfaction for the same, to an amount not exceeding five millions of dollars. To ascertain the full amount and validity of those claims, a commission, to consist of three Commissioners, citizens of the United States, shall be appointed by the President, by and with the advice and consent of the Senate, which commission shall meet at the city of Washington, and, within the space of three years from the time of their first meeting, shall receive, examine, and decide upon the amount and validity of all the claims included within the descriptions above mentioned. The said Commissioners shall take an oath or affirmation, to be entered on the record of their proceedings, for the faithful and diligent discharge of their duties; and, in case of the death, sickness, or necessary absence of any such Commissioner, his place may be supplied by the appointment, as aforesaid, or by the President of the United States, during the recess of the Senate, of another Commissioner in his stead.

The said Commissioners shall be authorized to hear and examine, on oath, every question rela-

tive to the said claims, and to receive all suitable authentic testimony concerning the same. And the Spanish Government shall furnish all such documents and elucidations as may be in their possession, for the adjustment of the said claims, according to the principles of justice, the laws of nations, and the stipulations of the treaty between the two parties of 27th October, 1795; the said documents to be specified. when demanded, at the instance of the said Commissioners.

The payment of such claims as may be admitted and adjusted by the said Commissioners, or the major part of them, to an amount not exceeding five millions of dollars, shall be made by the United States, either immediately at their Treasury, or by the creation of stock, bearing an interest of six per cent. per annum, payable from the proceeds of sales of public lands within the territories hereby ceded to the United States, or in such other manner as the Congress of the United States may prescribe by law.

The records of the proceedings of the said Commissioners, together with the vouchers and documents produced before them, relative to the claims to be adjusted and decided upon by them, shall, after the close of their transactions, be deposited in the Department of State of the United States; and copies of them, or any part of them, shall be furnished to the Spanish Government, if required, at the demand of the Spanish Minister in the United States.

ARTICLE XII

The treaty of limits and navigation, of 1795, remains confirmed in all and each one of its articles excepting the 2, 3, 4, 21, and the second clause of the 22d article, which, having been altered by this treaty, or having received their entire execution, are no longer valid.

With respect to the 15th article of the same treaty of friendship, limits, and navigation of 1795, in which it is stipulated that the flag shall cover the property, the two high contracting parties agree that this shall be so understood with respect to those powers who recognize this principle; but if either of the two contracting parties shall be at war with a third party, and the other neutral, the flag of the neutral shall cover the property of enemies whose government acknowledge this principle, and not of others.

ARTICLE XIII

Both contracting parties, wishing to favor their mutual commerce, by affording in their ports every necessary assistance to their respective merchant-vessels, have agreed that the sailors who shall desert from their vessels in the ports of the other, shall be arrested and delivered up, at the instance of the consul, who shall prove, nevertheless, that the deserters belonged to the vessels that claimed them, exhibiting the document that is customary in their nation: that is to say, the American Consul in a Spanish port shall exhibit the document known by the name of articles, and the Spanish Consul in American ports the roll of the vessel; and if the name of the deserter or deserters are claimed shall appear in the one or the other, they shall be arrested, held in custody, and delivered to the vessel to which they shall belong.

ARTICLE XIV

The United States hereby certify that they have not received any compensation from France for the injuries they suffered from her privateers, Consuls, and tribunals on the coasts and in the ports of Spain, for the satisfaction of which provision is made by this treaty; and they will present an authentic statement of the prizes made, and of their true value, that Spain may avail herself of the same in such manner as she may deem just and proper.

ARTICLE XV

The United States, to give to His Catholic Majesty a proof of their desire to cement the relations of amity subsisting between the two nations, and to favor the commerce of the subjects of His Catholic Majesty, agree that Spanish vessels, coming laden only with productions of Spanish growth or manufactures, directly from the ports of Spain, or of her colonies, shall be admitted, for the term of twelve years, to the ports of Pensacola and St. Augustine, in the Floridas, without paying other or higher duties on their cargoes, or of tonnage, than will be paid by the vessels of the United States. During the said term no other nation shall enjoy the same privileges within the ceded territories. The twelve years shall commence three months after the exchange of the ratifications of this treaty.

ARTICLE XVI

The present treaty shall be ratified in due form, by the contracting parties, and the ratifications shall be exchanged in six months from this time, or sooner if possible.

In witness whereof we, the underwritten Plenipotentiaries of the United States of America and of His Catholic Majesty, have signed, by virtue of our powers, the present treaty of amity, settlement, and limits, and have thereunto affixed our seals, respectively.

Done at Washington this twenty-second day of February, one thousand eight hundred and nineteen.

JOHN QUINCY ADAMS. [L. S.]
LUIS DE ONIS. [L. S.]

Source: Charles E. Bevans, ed., *Treaties and Other International Agreements of the United States of America, 1776–1949* (Washington: Government Printing Office, 1971), vol. 11: 529–535.

Section V (Documents 55–63): Building a Map

The domestic and diplomatic turmoil after 1803 was always bound by a single theme: the effort to realize the potential of and resolve the problems created by the Louisiana Purchase. Mapmaking was a part of this process. In 1803 members of the Jefferson administration admitted privately that they did not know the first thing about the people or the landscape of Louisiana. This was a matter of no small importance, because the territories carved from the Louisiana Purchase would become the responsibility of the federal government. Meanwhile, Madison concluded that his own efforts to orchestrate diplomacy to settle the disputed boundaries of Louisiana could not proceed without a set of fixed points of geographical reference. In addition, Jefferson had a personal fascination with demography and natural science, and so a map of Louisiana became all the more important.

It took almost two decades for the United States to acquire a map of Louisiana that seemed both accurate and acceptable. The process began with the seemingly simple task of learning about the territory's landscape. This would prove a monumental goal, however, and one that required American explorers to take on a series of challenging ventures. Even with the geographic information provided, there was little the United States could do to press its claims on contested land. Only the dwindling diplomatic fortunes in Madrid made Spain willing to negotiate on terms agreeable to the United States.

This is a story of a metaphorical map—not the physical rendering of the Louisiana Purchase, but the efforts to acquire knowledge of the land, understand its residents, and describe it in words. It is also a story of how the Louisiana Purchase transformed Thomas Jefferson's plans to explore North America. What had been a matter of great personal interest to Jefferson for decades became a vital matter of public policy, as the United States attempted to settle the political, diplomatic, and constitutional ramifications of the Louisiana Purchase.

Documents 56–57:
Mountains of Salt, Lakes of Whiskey

Immediately after the Louisiana Purchase, a variety of publications told fantastic stories of the western landscape. The two newspaper articles shown in documents 56 and 57 provide two particularly extreme examples. The *Alexandria (Virginia) Advertiser* recounted a tale that was quite common. For years, rumors had abounded on both sides of the Atlantic of a tremendous mountain of salt somewhere in the continental interior. Most accounts were like those in the *Advertiser,* attesting to the validity of the claim and pronouncing the benefits that would come about through this natural wonder. At the time, such a mountain would have been a godsend: salt was, of course, a common food additive. It was also the most important preservative at a time when year-round refrigeration was almost impossible.

The article from the *Connecticut Courant* was a tongue-in-cheek response to these stories, but one with a political bite. A Federalist newspaper, the *Courant* persistently ridiculed the Jefferson administration and was among the newspapers that most vehemently criticized the administration's Louisiana policy. In addition, the *Courant* reflected the nativism—especially the anti-Irish variety—that, by 1803, so many in New England embraced. The article refers to discoveries by "Capt. Lewis." By January 1804 the Lewis and Clark expedition was public knowledge, though it had not actually left its winter encampment near the Mississippi.

Documents 58–59: Planning Expeditions

The most famous American effort to explore the Louisiana Purchase is the Lewis and Clark expedition, also known as the Corps of Discovery. Yet Jefferson dispatched that team long before he heard of the Louisiana Purchase. In 1802 Jefferson began discussing an expedition with his personal secretary, Meriwether Lewis, a fellow Virginian and a captain in the U.S. Army. The primary purposes of this expedition would be commercial and scientific. Lewis was supposed to locate the Northwest Passage, a mythical water route connecting the North American interior to the Pacific Ocean. At the time, Jefferson expressed no interest in acquiring the land through which Lewis traveled. His goals were only to create commercial networks with Indians along the Missouri and Columbia Rivers and, ideally, the means for Americans to participate in the trans-Pacific trade. In 1803 Lewis asked William Clark to join him in leading the expedition.

Not only did the Louisiana Purchase transform the meaning of Lewis and Clark's venture, but it also led the United States to launch various attempts to explore the land acquired by the Louisiana Purchase. In the summer of 1806 the United States dispatched two other expeditions. First, Jefferson sent another scientific expedition, this one under the leadership of surveyor Thomas Freeman and physician Peter Custis. Like Lewis and Clark, they traveled mostly by boat, exploring the Red River that flows through what is now Texas, Arkansas, and Louisiana. Later, Lieutenant Zebulon Montgomery Pike led an expedition on foot into the Rocky Mountains, where he was to establish diplomatic and commercial ties with Indians, breaking old linkages that connected Indians to the Spanish outpost at Santa Fe.

The Spanish logically concluded that these expeditions were American efforts to destabilize Spain's North American frontier, and they sent troops to intercept all three expeditions. Lewis and Clark avoided contact with the Spanish or any other European representatives. The other expeditions were not so lucky. Spanish troops forced Freeman and Custis to return to New Orleans after only a few weeks. In the winter of 1807 the Spanish arrested Pike's men, transporting them to Mexico City, where they endured several months of imprisonment before their release and return to the United States.

The two letters from Jefferson shown in documents 58 and 59 exemplify the way the Louisiana Purchase shaped American efforts at continental exploration. They specifically show just how much more important the Lewis and Clark expedition became after April 1803. No longer just an expression of Jefferson's curiosity, the Corps of Discovery became a vital matter of public policy. Establishing the boundaries of Louisiana, building alliances with Indians, and providing information about the landscape suddenly gained new importance when applied to an American Louisiana.

Document 60: Results

The expeditions produced a complicated mixture of scientific knowledge, international controversy, and (eventually) diplomatic settlement and racial dominance. Jefferson's personal interests were satisfied beyond his wildest dreams. Lewis and Clark, Freeman and Custis, and Pike all gathered details on the North American interior that continued to fascinate Jefferson long after his retirement. In the short term, the expeditions angered Spain. In the long term, however, they provided the sort of geographic information that both the United States and Spain needed to settle on fixed boundaries. Likewise, the Indians of North America initially found the Americans to be respectful guests. But eventually that detailed knowledge of North America laid the foundation for the near-extermination of native peoples during the nineteenth century.

The leaders of the expeditions found that the Louisiana Purchase continued to shape their lives. Lewis and Clark both served as territorial governors. Overwhelmed by political, commercial, and personal failures as governor of the Territory of Louisiana, Meriwether Lewis committed suicide in 1809. Clark was more successful. He served with Lewis as Indian agent and commander of the territorial militia. He inherited the mantle of territorial governor in 1813 and oversaw the division of the Louisiana Territory and the eventual creation of the Missouri Territory. When Missouri became a state, Clark returned to work in Indian affairs. Thomas Freeman became a surveyor in the Louisiana Territory. Zebulon Pike continued his army career. He spent an extended period in the Territory of Orleans before the War of 1812, leading to his rapid promotion. Pike died after being wounded in battle on the U.S.-Canadian border. Only Peter Custis left Louisiana for good, returning to his native Virginia.

Documents 61–63: Mapping the People

Even as Americans were creating visual representations of Louisiana that possessed the literal specificity they considered so important in an accurate map, they were equally hard at work compiling the demographic data about the territory that had been in such short supply in 1803. Not only did this information help transform Louisiana from a vague idea into a specific place, but it also charted the transformation of North America in the first half of the nineteenth century. Economic collapse and soil exhaustion in the East, combined with increasing immigration at midcentury, led to a flood of white newcomers to the Mississippi Valley and the Eastern Plains. In addition, the booming plantation system of the antebellum South fueled a massive increase in the enslaved African American population. And finally, Andrew Jackson's removal policy led to the eradication or forced migration of Indians.

55   Population Estimates for Louisiana, 1803

In late 1803 Congress asked Thomas Jefferson to submit whatever information he had on Louisiana. This soon was put in the public record, and publishers quickly released the material under a number of names, most common of which was An Account of Louisiana. Although these figures provide a general estimate of the population, they are inaccurate. Most observers based their own figures on a 1785 Spanish census. In almost two decades since that enumeration, the European and African populations had grown dramatically.

District	White	% White	Slaves	% Slaves	Free People of Color	% Free People of Color	Total
Balize to New Orleans	—	—	—	—	—	—	2,388
San Bernardo or Terre aux boeufs on a creek running from the Englishturn East to the Sea and Lake Borgna	—	—	—	—	—	—	661
City of New-Orleans and suburbs. . .	3,948	49.01%	2,773	34.42%	1,335	16.57%	8,056
Bayou St. Jean and Chantilly between the City and Lake Pontchartrain	—	—	—	—	—	—	489
Coast of Chapitoulas, or along the Banks of the Mississippi 6 leagues upwards	—	—	—	—	—	—	1,444
First German Coast, from 6 to 10 leagues upwards on both banks	688	28.42%	1,620	66.91%	113	4.67%	2,421
Second do. from 10 leagues and ending at 16 do.	883	45.28%	1,046	53.64%	21	1.08%	1,950
Catahanose, or first Acadian Coast, commencing at 16 leagues above the City and ending at 23 on both banks	1,382	62.82%	818	37.18%	0	0.00%	2,200
Fouche or second Acadian Coast from 23 to 30 leagues above town	677	59.33%	464	40.67%	0	0.00%	1,141

continues

(continued)

District	White	% White	Slaves	% Slaves	Free People of Color	% Free People of Color	Total
Valenzuela or settlements on the Bason de la Fouche running from the West side of the Mississippi to the sea, & called in old maps Fourche, or Riviere des Chilimachas	1,797	87.06%	267	12.94%	0	0.00%	2,064
Iberville Parish, commencing at about 30 leagues from Orleans and ending at the river of the Same name	658	62.25%	386	36.52%	13	1.23%	1,057
Galveztown, situated on the river Iberville, between the Mississippi & Lake Maurepas, opposite the mouth of the Amet	213	86.23%	26	10.53%	8	3.24%	247
Pointe Coupee and False River between it, 50 leagues from Orleans, on the West side of the Mississippi	547	25.44%	0	0.00%	1,603	74.56%	2,150
Atacapas, on the River Teche and Vermillion, &c. to the west of the Mississippi, and near the sea	859	59.36%	530	36.63%	58	4.01%	1,447
Opelousas adjoining to, and to the North East of the foregoing	1,646	67.07%	808	32.93%	—	—	2,454
Ouachita on the river of the same name or upper part of the Black river, which empties into the River Rouge	—	—	—	—	—	—	36
Avoyelles on the red river, about 50 leagues from the Mississippi	336	77.78%	94	21.76%	2	0.46%	432
Rapide on do. about 50 leagues higher up	584	77.56%	169	22.44%	0	0.00%	753
Natchitoches on do. about 75 leagues from the Mississippi	785	48.13%	846	51.87%	0	0.00%	1,631
Concord, an infant settlement on the banks of the Mississippi, opposite Natchez (numbers unknown)	—	—	—	—	—	—	0
Total:	15,003	53.58%	9,847	35.16%	3,153	11.26%	28,003

Source: *An Account of Louisiana* (Washington: Duane, 1803).

56   *Alexandria Advertiser,* December 18, 1803

IN Mr. Jefferson's communication of the 14th . . . respecting Louisiana, he states, among other things, the existence of a *Salt Mountain.* The story is thus told:

"One extraordinary fact relative to salt, must not be omitted.—There exists about 1000 miles up the Missouri, and not far from that river *a salt mountain*! The existence of such a mountain might well be questioned, were it not for the testimony of several respectable and enterprising traders. . . . This mountain is said to be 180 miles long, and 45 in width, composed of solid rock salt, without any trees, or even shrubs on it. Salt springs are very numerous beneath the surface of this mountain, and they flow thro' the fissures and cavities of it. . . ."

The President speaks of this as a well authenticated fact, and therefore it is presumed to be true.

On reading this story, it occurred to me that a body which is *solid, rarely* had *"fissures* and cavities,"* in it, yet this *strange* mountain has the two singular properties of being "solid rock salt," and containing various empty apartments or vacancies, probably sufficient for "dry docks" for the present navy. . . .

Will not Louisiana be effectually protected from the operation of all fiery bodies, and from being eventually burnt up with the other parts of the earth, since it is an universally admitted principle, that Salt is more efficacious in extinguishing fire than any and all other substances? At least may we not safely assert that no meteor or comet will ever affrighten or destroy that garden of this western world?

But admitting that the salt of this mountain extends downwards only to the surface of our earth, then there is a body of it about as *wide* as from Connecticut River to the line of the state of New-York, and about as long as from Hartford to Philadelphia.—The height of it Mr. Jefferson does not mention, but the reader will recollect that he calls it a *mountain.*—Say then (for all historical tracts should *avoid* exaggeration) that it is *half a mile high.* Now such a body . . . certainly *measure out* 800 millions of bushels of good rock salt. . . . This, at 150 cents per bushel which Mr. Jefferson says is the price of salt in that country, will nett 12 hundred millions of dollars.—With this we can pay off our national debt—lend Great Britain enough to pay her debt—leave more than six hundred millions of dollars in the treasury, without "taking any bread from the mouth of labor." All this is purchased for 15 millions of dollars, and with it we obtain "an immense prairie" . . . into the bargain. What a *great* mountain! What a *wise* administration! O the ECONOMIES of Livingston and Monroe!!! . . .

In this view of the subject I think the "enlightened" eye of a modern philosopher can now see the Mississippi, the Missouri, and the other great rivers of Louisiana, covered with American ships, laden with the riches of the earth—and the whole extensive region to the Pacific Ocean, peopled with a *virtuous and happy race of democrats,* enjoying all the luxuries of life, and constantly chaunting the praises of Mr. Jefferson, in the song of Jefferson and Liberty, which shall echo through the "fissures and cavities" of the "mountain of solid rock salt" and extend across that "immense prairie."

Source: Alexandria Advertiser.

57 Another Rumor

We have heard it intimated that Capt. Lewis has lately discovered, in the interior of Louisiana, a considerable lake of pure *Whiskey,* which is said very nearly to resemble good old *Irish Usquebaugh.* Should this rumour prove to be well founded, it is believed that most of our newly imported citizens will speedily remove to that country for the sake of securing the free navigation of those *waters.* . . . .

Source: Connecticut Courant, January 4, 1804.

58 Letter from Thomas Jefferson to Meriwether Lewis, June 20, 1803

To Merryweather Lewis, esquire, Captain of the 1st regiment of infantry of the United States of America. [Meriwether Lewis]

Your situation as Secretary of the President of the United States has made you acquainted with the objects of my confidential message of Jan. 18, 1803, to the legislature. You have seen the act they passed, which, tho' expressed in general terms, was meant to sanction those objects, and you are appointed to carry them into execution.

Instruments for ascertaining by celestial observations the geography of the country thro' which you will pass, have been already provided. Light articles for barter, & presents among the Indians, arms for your attendants, say for from 10 to 12 men, boats, tents, & other travelling apparatus, with ammunition, medicine, surgical instruments & provision you will have prepared with such aids as the Secretary at War can yield in his department; & from him also you will receive authority to engage among our troops, by voluntary agreement, the number of attendants above mentioned, over whom you, as their commanding officer are invested with all the powers the laws give in such a case.

As your movements while within the limits of the U.S. will be better directed by occasional communications, adapted to circumstances as they arise, they will not be noticed here. What follows will respect your proceedings after your departure from the U.S.

Your mission has been communicated to the Ministers here from France, Spain, & Great Britain, and through them to their governments: and such assurances given them as to it's objects as we trust will satisfy them. The country of Louisiana having been ceded by Spain to France, the passport you have from the Minister of France, the representative of the present sovereign of the country, will be a protection with all its subjects: and that from the Minister of England will entitle you to the friendly aid of any traders of that allegiance with whom you may happen to meet.

The object of your mission is to explore the Missouri river, & such principal stream of it, as, by it's course & communication with the water of the Pacific ocean may offer the most direct & practicable water communication across this continent, for the purposes of commerce.

Beginning at the mouth of the Missouri, you will take observations of latitude and longitude at all remarkable points on the river, & especially at the mouths of rivers, at rapids, at islands & other places & objects distinguished by such natural marks & characters of a durable kind, as that they may with certainty be recognized hereafter. The courses of the river between these points of observation may be supplied by the compass, the log-line & by time, corrected by the observations themselves. The variations of the compass too, in different places should be noticed.

The interesting points of the portage between the heads of the Missouri & the water offering the best communication with the Pacific ocean should be fixed by observation, & the course of that water to the ocean, in the same manner as that of the Missouri.

Your observations are to be taken with great pains & accuracy to be entered distinctly, & intelligibly for others as well as yourself, to comprehend all the elements necessary, with the aid of the usual tables to fix the latitude & longitude of the places at which they were taken, & are to be rendered to the war office, for the purpose of having the calculations made concurrently by proper persons within the U.S. Several copies of these as well as of your other notes, should be made at leisure times, & put into the care of the most trustworthy of your attendants, to guard by multiplying them against the accidental losses to which they will be exposed. A further guard would be that one of these copies be written on the paper of the birch, as less liable to injury from damp than common paper.

The commerce which may be carried on with the people inhabiting the line you will pursue, renders a knolege of these people important. You will therefore endeavor to make yourself acquainted, as far as a diligent pursuit of your journey shall admit,

with the names of the nations & their numbers;
the extent & limits of their possessions;
their relations with other tribes or nations;
their language, traditions, monuments;
their ordinary occupations in agriculture, fishing,
    hunting, war, arts, & the implements for these;
their food, clothing, & domestic accommodations;
the diseases prevalent among them, & the
    remedies they use;
moral and physical circumstance which distinguish
    them from the tribes they know;

peculiarities in their laws, customs & dispositions;
and articles of commerce they may need or
    furnish, & to what extent.

And considering the interest which every nation has in extending & strengthening the authority of reason & justice among the people around them, it will be useful to acquire what knolege you can of the state of morality, religion & information among them, as it may better enable those who endeavor to civilize & instruct them, to adapt their measures to the existing notions & practises of those on whom they are to operate.

Other objects worthy of notice will be
the soil & face of the country, it's growth &
    vegetable productions, especially those not of
    the U.S.
the animals of the country generally, & especially
    those not known in the U.S.
the remains & accounts of any which may be
    deemed rare or extinct;
the mineral productions of every kind; but more
    particularly metals, limestone,
pit coal & saltpetre; salines & mineral waters,
    noting the temperature of the last & such
circumstances as may indicate their character;
volcanic appearances;
climate as characterized by the thermometer, by
    the proportion of rainy, cloudy & clear
days, by lightening, hail, snow, ice, by the access
    & recess of frost, by the winds, prevailing
at different seasons, the dates at which particular
    plants put forth or lose their flowers, or
leaf, times of appearance of particular birds,
    reptiles or insects.

Altho' your route will be along the channel of the Missouri, yet you will endeavor to inform yourself, by inquiry, of the character and extent of the country watered by its branches, & especially on it's Southern side. The Rorth river or Rio Bravo which runs into the gulph of Mexico, and the North river, or Rio colorado which runs into the gulph of California, are understood to be the principal streams heading opposite to the waters of the Missouri, and running Southwardly.

Whether the dividing grounds between the Missouri & them are mountains or flatlands, what are their distance from the Missouri, the character of the intermediate country, & the people inhabiting it, are worthy of particular enquiry. The Northern waters of the Missouri are less to be enquired after, because they have been ascertained to a considerable degree, and are still in a course of ascertainment by English traders & travellers. But if you can learn anything certain of the most Northern source of the Mississippi, & of it's position relative to the lake of the woods, it will be interesting to us. Some account too of the path of the Canadian traders from the Mississippi, at the mouth of the Ouisconsin river, to where it strikes the Missouri, and of the soil and rivers in it's course, is desirable.

In all your intercourse with the natives treat them in the most friendly & conciliatory manner which their own conduct will admit; allay all jealousies as to the object of your journey, satisfy them of it's innocence, make them acquainted with the position, extent, character, peaceable & commercial dispositions of the U.S., of our wish to be neighborly, friendly & useful to them, & of our dispositions to a commercial intercourse with them; confer with them on the points most convenient as mutual emporiums, & the articles of most desirable interchange for them & us. If a few of their influential chiefs, within practicable distance, wish to visit us, arrange such a visit with them, and furnish them with authority to call on our officers, on their entering the U.S. to have them conveyed to this place at the public expense. If any of them should wish to have some of their young people brought up with us, & taught such arts as may be useful to them, we will receive, instruct & take care of them. Such a mission, whether of influential chiefs, or of young people, would give some security to your own party. Carry with you some matter of the kine pox, inform those of them with whom you may be, of it's efficacy as a preservative from the small pox; and instruct & encourage them in the use of it. This may be especially done wherever you may winter.

As it is impossible for us to foresee in what manner you will be received by those people, whether with hospitality or hostility, so is it impossible to prescribe the exact degree of perseverance with which you are to pursue your journey. We value too much the lives of citizens to offer them to probably destruction. Your numbers will be sufficient to secure you against the unauthorised opposition of individuals, or of small parties: but if a superior force, authorised or not authorised, by a nation, should be arrayed against your further passage, & inflexibly determined to arrest it, you must decline it's further pursuit, and return. In the loss of yourselves, we should lose also the information you will have acquired. By returning safely with that, you may enable us to renew the essay with better calculated means. To your own discretion therefore must be left the degree of danger you may risk, & the point at which you should decline, only saying we wish you to err on the side of your safety, & to bring back your party safe, even if it be with less information.

As far up the Missouri as the white settlements extend, an intercourse will probably be found to exist between them and the Spanish posts at St. Louis, opposite Cahokia, or Ste. Genevieve opposite Kaskaskia. From still farther up the river, the traders may furnish a conveyance for letters. Beyond that you may perhaps be able to engage Indians to bring letters for the government to Cahokia or Kaskaskia, on promising that they shall there receive such special compensation as you shall have stipulated with them. Avail yourself of these means to communicate to us, at seasonable intervals, a copy of your journal, notes & observations of every kind, putting into cypher whatever might do injury if betrayed.

Should you reach the Pacific ocean, inform yourself of the circumstances which may decide whether the furs of those parts may not be collected as advantageously at the head of the Missouri (convenient as is supposed to the waters of the Colorado & Oregon or Columbia) as at Nootka sound or any other point of that coast; & that trade be consequently conducted through the Missouri & U.S. more beneficially than by the circumnavigation now practised.

On your arrival on that coast, endeavor to learn if there be any port within your reach frequented by the sea-vessels of any nation, and to send two of your trusty people back by sea, in such way as shall appear practicable, with a copy of your notes. And should you be of opinion that the return of your party by the way they went will be eminently dangerous, then ship the whole, & return by sea by way of Cape Horn or the Cape of Good Hope, as you shall be able. As you will be without money, clothes or provisions, you must endeavor to use the credit of the U.S. to obtain them; for which purpose open letters of credit shall be furnished you authorizing you to draw on the Executive of the U.S. or any of its officers in any part of the world, in which draughts can be disposed of, and to apply with our recommendations to the consuls, agents, merchants or citizens of any nation with which we have intercourse, assuring them in our name that any aids they may furnish you shall be honorably repaid, and on demand. Our consuls Thomas Howes at Batavia in Java, William Buchanan of the Isles of France and Bourbon, & John Elmslie at the Cape of Good Hope will be able to supply your necessities by draughts on us.

Should you find it safe to return by the way you go, after sending two of your party round by sea, or with your whole party, if no conveyance by sea can be found, do so; making such observations on your return as may serve to supply, correct or confirm those made on your outward journey.

In re-entering the U.S. and reaching a place of safety, discharge any of your attendants who may desire & deserve it: procuring for them immediate paiment of all arrears of pay & cloathing which may have incurred since their departure and assure them that they shall be recommended to the liberality of the legislature for the grant of a souldier's portion of land each, as proposed in my message to Congress: & repair yourself with your papers to the seat of government.

To provide, on the accident of your death, against anarchy, dispersion & the consequent danger to your party, and total failure of the enterprise, you are hereby authorised, by any instrument signed & written in your own hand, to name the person among them who shall succeed to the command on your decease, & by like instruments to change the nomination from time to time, as further experience of the characters accompanying you shall point out superior fitness: and all the powers & authorities given to yourself are, in the event of your death, transferred to & vested in the successor so named, with further power to him, & his successors in like manner to name each his successor, who, on the death of his predecessor shall be invested with all the powers & authorities given to yourself.

Given under my hand at the city of Washington, this 20th. day of June 1803.

Th:Jefferson, Pr. U.S. of America.

Source: Thomas Jefferson Papers (Washington, D.C.: Library of Congress Microfilm Collection).

59

Letter from Thomas Jefferson to Meriwether Lewis, November 16, 1803

Dear Sir

I have not written to you since the 11th & 15th of July, since which yours of July 15. 22. 25. Sep. 8. 13. & Oct. 3. have been recieved. The present has been long delayed by an expectation daily of getting the inclosed 'account of Louisiana' through the press. The materials are received from different persons, of good authority. I inclose you also copies of the Treaties for Louisiana, the act for taking possession, a letter from Dr. Wistar, & some information collected by myself from Truteau's journal in MS. all of which may be useful to you. The act for taking possession passes with only some small verbal variations from that inclosed, of no consequence. Orders went from hence, signed by the King of Spain & the first Consul of France, so as to arrive at Natchez yesterday evening, and we expect the delivery of the province at New Orleans will take place about the close of the ensuing week, say about the 25th inst. Govr. Claiborne is appointed to execute the powers of Commandant & Intendant, until a regular government shall be organized here. At the moment of delivering over the posts in the vicinity of N. Orleans, orders will be dispatched from thence to those in Upper Louisiana to evacuate & deliver them immediately. You can judge better than I can when they may be expected to arrive at these posts, considering how much you have been detained by low waters, how late it will be before you can leave Cahokia, how little progress up the Missouri you can make before the freezing of the river; that your winter might be passed in gaining much information by making Cahokia or Kaskaskia your head quarters, & going to St. Louis & the other Spanish posts that your stores &c. would thereby be spared for the winter, as your men would draw their military rations, all danger of Spanish opposition avoided. We are strongly of opinion here that you had better not enter the Missouri till the spring. But as you have a view of all circumstances on the spot, we do not pretend to enjoin it, but leave it to your own judgment in which we have entire confidence. One thing however we are decided in: that you must not undertake the winter excursion which you propose in yours of Oct. 3. Such an excursion will be more dangerous than the main expedition up the Missouri, & would, by an accident to you, hazard our main object, which, since the acquisition of Louisiana, interests every body in the high-

est degree. The object of your mission is single, the direct water communication from sea to sea formed by the bed of the Missouri & perhaps the Oregon. By having Mr. Clarke with you we consider the expedition double manned, & therefore the less liable to failure, for which reason neither of you should be exposed to risques by going off of your line. I have proposed in conversation, & it seems generally to be assented to, that Congress shall appropriate 10. or 12.000 D. for exploring the principal waters of the Missisipi & Missouri. In that case I should send a party up the Red river to it's head, then to cross over to the head of the Arcansa, & come down that. A 2d party for the Pani & Padouca rivers, & a 3d perhaps for the Moingona & St. Peters. As the boundaries of interior Louisiana are the *high lands inclosing all the waters which run into the Missisipi or Missouri directly or indirectly,* with a greater breadth on the gulph of Mexico, it becomes interesting to fix with precision by celestial observations the longitude & latitude of the sources of these rivers, and furnishing points in the contour of our new limits.

This will be attempted distinctly from your mission, which we consider as of major importance, & therefore not to be delayed or hazarded by any episodes whatever.

The votes of both houses on ratifying & carrying the treaties into execution have been precisely party votes, except that Genl. Dayton has separated from his friends on these questions & voted for the treaties. I will direct the Aurora & National Intelligencer to be forwarded to you for 6. months at Cahokia or Kaskaskia, on the presumption you will be there. Your friends & acquaintances here & in Albemarle are all well as far as I have heard: and I recollect no other small news worth communicating; present my friendly salutations to Mr. Clarke, & accept them affectionately yourself.

Th: Jefferson

Source: Thomas Jefferson Papers (Washington, D.C.: Library of Congress Microfilm Collection).

60   Letter from Meriwether Lewis to Thomas Jefferson, September 23, 1806

The Lewis and Clark expedition returned to St. Louis in September 1806, none the worse for wear despite more than two years of rough travel. Although one man had died of illness early in the venture, the physical health and the military order of the expedition were both holding up well. Lewis and Clark set to work writing lengthy reports to the president. These reports and the journals they kept during the expedition eventually became known primarily for their scientific value. But in this letter, Meriwether Lewis provides a reminder of the diplomatic, commercial, and administrative affairs that were always of paramount importance. He gave Thomas Jefferson the news he least wanted to hear: there was no Northwest Passage. He also indicated something of the complex Indian diplomacy that reigned in western North America. But Lewis was also confident that by fostering commerce and building strong ties with Indians, the United States would be able to convert sovereignty from an abstract notion in the text of the Louisiana Purchase into a functional reality on the frontiers of North America.

St. Louis September 23rd 1806.

Sir,

It is with pleasure that I announce to you the safe arrival of myself and party at 12 OClk. today at this place with our papers and baggage. In obedience to your orders we have penitrated the Continent of North America to the Pacific Ocean, and sufficiently explored the interior of the country to affirm with confidence that we have discovered the most practicable rout which dose exist across the continent by means of the navigable branches of the Missouri and Columbia Rivers. Such is that by way of the Missouri to the foot of the rapids five miles below the great falls of that river a distance of 2575 miles, thence by land passing the Rocky Mountains to a navigable part of the Kooskooske 340; with the Kooskooske 73 mls. a South Easterly branch of the Columbia 154 miles and the latter river 413 mls. to the Pacific Ocean; making the total distance from the confluence of the Missouri and Mississippi to the discharge of the Columbia into the Pacific Ocean 3555 miles. The navigation of the Missouri may be deemed safe and good; it's difficulties arrise from it's falling banks, timber imbeded in the mud of it's channel, it's sand bars and steady rapidity of it's current, all which may

be overcome with a great degree of certainty by taking the necessary precautions. The passage by land of 340 miles from the Missouri to the Kooskooske is the most formidable part of the tract proposed across the Continent; of this distance 200 miles is along a good road, and 140 over tremendious mountains which for 60 mls. are covered with eternal snows; however a passage over these mountains is practicable from the latter part of June to the last of September, and the cheep rate at which horses are to be obtained from the Indians of the Rocky Mountains and West of them, reduces the expences of transportation over this portage to a mere trifle. The navigation of the Kooskooske, the South East branch of the Columbia itself is safe and good from the 1st of April to the middle of August, by making three portages on the latter; the first of which in decending is that of 1200 paces at the great falls of the Columbia, 261 mls. from the Ocean, the second of two miles at the long narrows six miles below the falls, and the 3rd also of 2 miles at the great rapids 65 miles still lower down. The tides flow up the Columbia 183 miles, or within seven miles of the great rapids, thus far large sloops might ascend in safety, and vessels of 300 tons burthen could with equal safety reach the entrance of the river Multnomah, a large Southern branch of the Columbia, which taking it's rise on the confines of Mexico with the Callarado and Apostles river, discharges itself into the Columbia 125 miles from it's mouth. From the head of tide water to the foot of the long narrows the Columbia could be most advantageously navigated with large batteauxs, and from thence upwards by perogues. The Missouri possesses sufficient debth of water as far as is specifyed for boats of 15 tons burthen, but those of smaller capacity are to be prefered.

We view this passage across the Continent as affording immence advantages to the fur trade, but fear that the advantages which it offers as a communication for the productions of the Eeast Indies to the United States and thence to Europe will never be found equal on an extensive scale to that by way of the Cape of Good hope; still we believe that many articles not bulky brittle nor of a very perishable nature may be conveyed to the United States by this rout with more facility and at less expence than by that at present practiced.

The Missouri and all it's branches from the Chyenne upwards abound more in beaver and Common Otter, than any other streams on earth, particularly that proportion of them lying within the Rocky Mountains. The furs of all this immence tract of country including such as may be collected on the upper portion of the River St. Peters, Red river and the Assinniboin with the immence country watered by the Columbia, may be conveyed to the mouth of the Columbia by the 1st of August in each year and from thence be shipped to, and arrive in Canton earlier than the furs at present shipped from Montreal annually arrive in London. The British N. West Company of Canada were they permitted by the United States might also convey their furs collected in the Athabaske, on the Saskashawan, and South and West of Lake Winnipic by that rout within the period before mentioned. Thus the productions [of] nine tenths of the most valuable fur country of America could be conveyed by the rout proposed to the East Indies.

In the infancy of the trade across the continent, or during the period that the trading establishments shall be confined to the Missouri and it's branches, the men employed in this trade will be compelled to convey the furs collected in that quarter as low on the Columbia as tide water, in which case they could not return to the falls of the Missouri untill about the 1st of October, which would be so late in the season that there would be considerable danger of the river being obstructed by ice before they could reach this place and consequently that the comodites brought from the East indies would be detained untill the following spring; but this difficulty will at once vanish when establishments are also made on the Columbia, and a sufficient number of men employed at them to convey annually the productions of the East indies to the upper establishment on the Kooskooske, and there exchange them with the men of the Missouri for their furs, in the begining of July. By this means the furs not only of the Missouri but those also of the Columbia may be shiped to the East indies by the season before mentioned, and the comodites of the East indies arrive at St. Louis or the mouth of the Ohio by the last of September in each year.

Although the Columbia dose not as much as the Missouri abound in beaver and Otter, yet it is by no means despicable in this rispect, and would furnish a valuable fur trade distinct from any other consideration in addition to the otter and beaver which it could furnish. There might be collected considerable quantities of the skins of three speceis of bear affording a great variety of colours and of superior delicacy, those also of the tyger cat, several species of fox, martin and several others of an inferior class of furs, besides the valuable Sea Otter of the coast.

If the government will only aid, even in a very limited manner, the enterprize of her Citizens I am fully convinced that we shal shortly derive the benifits of a most lucrative trade from this source, and that in the course of ten or twelve years a tour across the Continent by the rout mentioned will be undertaken by individuals with as little concern as a voyage across the Atlantic is at present.

The British N. West Company of Canada has for several years, carried on a partial trade with the Minnetares Ahwayhaways and Mandans on the Missouri from their establishments on the Assinniboin at the entrance of Mouse river; at present I have good reason for beleiving that they intend shortly to form an establishment near those nations with a view to engroce the fur trade of the Missouri. The known enterprize and resources of this Company, latterly strengthened by an union with their powerfull rival the X. Y. Company renders them formidable in that distant part of the continent to all other traders; and in my opinion if we are to regard the trade of the Missouri as an object of importance to the United States; the strides of this Company towards the Missouri cannot be too vigilantly watched nor too firmly and speedily opposed by our government. The embarrasments under which the navigation of the Missouri at present labours from the unfriendly dispositions of the Kancez, the several bands of Tetons, Assinniboins and those tribes that report to the British establishments on the Saskashawan is also a subject which requires the earliest attention of our government. As I shall shortly be with you I have deemed it unnecessary here to detail the several ideas which have presented themselves to my mind on those subjects more especially when I consider that a thorough knowledge of the geography of the country is absolutely necessary to their being unde[r]stood, and leasure has not yet permited us to make but one general map of the country which I am unwilling to wrisk by the Mail.

As a sketch of the most prominent features of our perigrination since we left the Mandans may not be uninteresting, I shall indeavour to give it to you by way of letter from this place, where I shall necessarily be detained several days in order to settle with and discharge the men who accompanyed me on the voyage as well as to prepare for my rout to the City of Washington.

We left Fort Clatsop where we wintered near the entrance of the Columbia on the 27th of March last, and arrived at the foot of the Rocky mountains on the l0th of May where we were detained untill the 24th of June in consequence of the snow which rendered a passage over the those

Mountains impracticable untill that moment; had it not been for this detention I should ere this have joined you at Montichello. In my last communication to you from the Mandans I mentioned my intention of sending back a canoe with a small party from the Rocky Mountains; but on our arrival at the great falls of the Missouri on the 14th of June 1805, in view of that formidable snowey barrier, the discourageing difficulties which we had to encounter in making a portage of eighteen miles of our canoes and baggage around those falls were such that my friend Capt. Clark and myself conceived it inexpedient to reduce the party, lest by doing so we should lessen the ardor of those who remained and thus hazard the fate of the expedition, and therefore declined that measure thinking it better that the government as well as our friends should for a moment feel some anxiety for our fate than to wrisk so much; experience has since proved the justice of our dicision, for we have more than once owed our lives and the fate of the expedition to our number which consisted of 31 men.

I have brought with me several skins of the Sea Otter, two skins of the native sheep of America, five skins and skelitons complete of the Bighorn or mountain ram, and a skin of the Mule deer beside the skins of several other quadrupeds and birds natives of the countries through which we have passed. I have also preserved a pretty extensive collection of plants, and collected nine other vocabularies.

I have prevailed on the great Cheif of the Mandan nation to accompany me to Washington; he is now with my frind and colligue Capt. Clark at this place, in good health and sperits, and very anxious to proceede.

With rispect to the exertions and services rendered by that esteemable man Capt. William Clark in the course of late voyage I cannot say too much; if sir any credit be due for the success of that arduous enterprize in which we have been mutually engaged, he is equally with myself entitled to your consideration and that of our common country.

The anxiety which I feel in returning once more to the bosom of my friends is a sufficient guarantee that no time will be unnecessarily expended in this quarter.

I have detained the post several hours for the purpose of making you this haisty communication. I hope that while I am pardoned for this detention of the mail, the situation in which I have been compelled to write will sufficiently apologize for having been this laconic.

The rout by which I purpose traveling from hence to Washington is by way of Cahokia, Vincennes, Louisvill Ky., the Crab orchard, Abington, Fincastle, Stanton and Charlottsville. Any letters directed to me at Louisville ten days after the receipt of this will most probably meet me at that place. I am very anxious to learn the state of my friends in Albemarle particularly whether my mother is yet living. I am with every sentiment of esteem Your Obt. and very Humble servent.

Meriwether Lewis Capt.
1st. U.S. Regt. Infty.

N.B. The whole of the party who accompanyed me from the Mandans have returned in good health, which is not, I assure you, to me one of the least pleasing considerations of the Voyage.

M.L.

Source: Thomas Jefferson Papers (Washington, D.C.: Library of Congress Microfilm Collection).

61   Census Returns

The first two states created from the Louisiana Purchase—Louisiana and Missouri—exemplified demographic as well as political change. The U.S. Census returns from 1810 to 1860 reveal in stark figures the black and white population boom west of the Mississippi. The next slave state— Arkansas—and the first free state from the Louisiana Purchase—Iowa, created in 1846—provide useful counterpoints.

Year	State (or territory)	White Population	Slave Population	Free People of Color	Total
1810	Territory of Orleans	34,311	34,660	7,585	76,556
	Territory of Louisiana	17,227	3,011	607	20,845
1820	Louisiana	73,383	69,064	10,897	153,407
	Territory of Missouri	55,988	10,222	347	66,586
1830	Arkansas	25,671	4,576	141	30,388
	Louisiana	89,231	109,588	16,710	215,529
	Missouri	114,795	25,096	569	140,455
1840	Arkansas	77,174	19,935	465	97,574
	Iowa	42,924	16	172	43,112
	Louisiana	158,457	168,452	25,502	352,411
	Missouri	323,888	58,240	1,574	383,702
1850	Arkansas	162,189	47,100	608	209,897
	Iowa	191,881		333	192,214
	Louisiana	255,491	244,809	17,462	517,762
	Missouri	592,004	87,422	2,618	682,044
1860	Arkansas	324,143	111,115	144	435,450
	Iowa	673,779		1,069	674,904
	Louisiana	357,456	331,726	18,647	708,002
	Missouri	1,063,489	114,931	3,572	1,182,012

Source: U.S. Census Bureau.

62 The Louisiana Purchase and Native Americans

Throughout the first half-century following independence, relations between the United States and Indian groups had followed a predictable course. The United States would sign a formal treaty or reach an informal agreement with a particular Indian group. White settlers would move to the borderlands between U.S. and Indian sovereignty. Violent encounters followed, and the United States would side with its citizens. Despite occasional military victories, most eastern Indians found themselves incapable of withstanding the apparatus created by the federal and state constitutions. The United States then sought subsequent agreements that usually left Indians with control over less land. The Louisiana Purchase offered a solution to these problems.

An Act to provide for an exchange of lands with the Indians residing in any of the states or territories, and for their removal west of the river Mississippi.

Be it enacted by the Senate and House of Representatives of the United States of America, in Congress assembled, That it shall and may be lawful for the President of the United States to cause so much of any territory belonging to the United States, west of the river Mississippi, not included in any state or organized territory, and to which the Indian title has been extinguished, as he may judge necessary, to be divided into a suitable number of districts, for the reception of such tribes or nations of Indians as may choose to exchange the lands where they now reside, and remove there; and to cause each of said districts to be so described by natural or artificial marks, as to be easily distinguished from every other.

SEC. 2. *And be it further enacted,* That it shall and may be lawful for the President to exchange any or all of such districts, so to be laid off and described, with any tribe or nation of Indians now residing within the limits of any of the states or territories, and with which the United States have existing treaties, for the whole or any part or portion of the territory claimed and occupied by such tribe or nation, within the bounds of any one or more of the states or territories, where the land claimed and occupied by the Indians, is owned by the United States, or the United States are bound to the state within which it lies to extinguish the Indian claim thereto.

SEC. 3. *And be it further enacted,* That in the making of any such exchange or exchanges, it shall and may be lawful for the President solemnly to assure the tribe or nation with which the exchange is made, that the United States will forever secure and guaranty to them, and their heirs or successors, the country so exchanged with them; and if they prefer it, that the United States will cause a patent or grant to be made and executed to them for the same: *Provided always,* That such lands shall revert to the United States, if the Indians become extinct, or abandon the same.

SEC. 4. *And be it further enacted,* That if, upon any of the lands now occupied by the Indians, and to be exchanged for, there should be such improvements as add value to the land claimed by any individual or individuals of such tribes or nations, it shall and may be lawful for the President to cause such value to be ascertained by appraisement or otherwise, and to cause such ascertained value to be paid to the person or persons rightfully claiming such improvements. And upon the payment of such valuation, the improvements so valued and paid for, shall pass to the United States, and possession shall not afterwards be permitted to any of the same tribe.

SEC. 5. *And be it further enacted,* That upon the making of any such exchange as is contemplated by this act, it shall and may be lawful for the President to cause such aid and assistance to be furnished to the emigrants as may be necessary and proper to enable them to remove to, and settle in, the country for which they may have exchanged; and also, to give them such aid and assistance as may be necessary for their support and subsistence for the first year after their removal.

SEC. 6. *And be it further enacted,* That it shall and may be lawful for the President to cause such tribe or nation to be protected, at their new residence, against all interruption or disturbance from any other tribe or nation of Indians, or from any other person or persons whatever.

SEC. 7. *And be it further enacted,* That it shall and may be lawful for the President to have the same superintendence and care over any tribe or

nation in the country to which they may remove, as contemplated by this act, that he is now authorized to have over them at their present places of residence: *Provided,* That nothing in this act contained shall be construed as authorizing or directing the violation of any existing treaty between the United States and any of the Indian tribes.

SEC. 8. *And be it further enacted,* That for the purpose of giving effect to the provisions of this act, the sum of five hundred thousand dollars is hereby appropriated, to be paid out of any money in the treasury, not otherwise appropriated.

Source: The Public Statutes at Large of the United States of America (Boston: Charles C. Little and James Brown, 1845), vol. 4: 411–412.

---

63   Andrew Jackson, First Annual Message, December 8, 1830

Thomas Jefferson, James Madison, and James Monroe all showed a certain sentimentality for Indians even as their administrations pursued policies that favored either eradicating or displacing them. Andrew Jackson had no such qualms. A ruthless Indian fighter, the wars he initiated with Indians of the Deep South and the Gulf Coast in the 1810s—usually motivated by his interest in providing new land for white settlers—also served the administration's effort to establish federal sovereignty east of the Mississippi. As president, Jackson did what none of his predecessors would do: he proclaimed once and for all that white settlers and Indians were incompatible. In his first annual message, Jackson expressed his own support for the Removal Act.

It gives me pleasure to announce to Congress that the benevolent policy of the Government, steadily pursued for nearly thirty years, in relation to the removal of the Indians beyond the white settlements is approaching to a happy consummation. Two important tribes have accepted the provision made for their removal at the last session of Congress, and it is believed that their example will induce the remaining tribes also to seek the same obvious advantages.

The consequences of a speedy removal will be important to the United States, to individual States, and to the Indians themselves. The pecuniary advantages which it Promises to the Government are the least of its recommendations. It puts an end to all possible danger of collision be-

tween the authorities of the General and State Governments on account of the Indians. It will place a dense and civilized population in large tracts of country now occupied by a few savage hunters. By opening the whole territory between Tennessee on the north and Louisiana on the south to the settlement of the whites it will incalculably strengthen the southwestern frontier and render the adjacent States strong enough to repel future invasions without remote aid. It will relieve the whole State of Mississippi and the western part of Alabama of Indian occupancy, and enable those States to advance rapidly in population, wealth, and power. It will separate the Indians from immediate contact with settlements of whites; free them from the power of the States;

enable them to pursue happiness in their own way and under their own rude institutions; will retard the progress of decay, which is lessening their numbers, and perhaps cause them gradually, under the protection of the Government and through the influence of good counsels, to cast off their savage habits and become an interesting, civilized, and Christian community. These consequences, some of them so certain and the rest so probable, make the complete execution of the plan sanctioned by Congress at their last session an object of much solicitude.

Toward the aborigines of the country no one can indulge a more friendly feeling than myself, or would go further in attempting to reclaim them from their wandering habits and make them a happy, prosperous people. I have endeavored to impress upon them my own solemn convictions of the duties and powers of the General Government in relation to the State authorities. For the justice of the laws passed by the States within the scope of their reserved powers they are not responsible to this Government. As individuals we may entertain and express our opinions of their acts, but as a Government we have as little right to control them as we have to prescribe laws for other nations.

With a full understanding of the subject, the Choctaw and the Chickasaw tribes have with great unanimity determined to avail themselves of the liberal offers presented by the act of Congress, and have agreed to remove beyond the Mississippi River. Treaties have been made with them, which in due season will be submitted for consideration. In negotiating these treaties they were made to understand their true condition, and they have preferred maintaining their independence in the Western forests to submitting to the laws of the States in which they now reside. These treaties, being probably the last which will ever be made with them, are characterized by great liberality on the part of the Government. They give the Indians a liberal sum in consideration of their removal, and comfortable subsistence on their arrival at their new homes. If it be their real interest to maintain a separate exis-

tence, they will there be at liberty to do so without the inconveniences and vexations to which they would unavoidably have been subject in Alabama and Mississippi.

Humanity has often wept over the fate of the aborigines of this country, and Philanthropy has been long busily employed in devising means to avert it, but its progress has never for a moment been arrested, and one by one have many powerful tribes disappeared from the earth. To follow to the tomb the last of his race and to tread on the graves of extinct nations excite melancholy reflections. But true philanthropy reconciles the mind to these vicissitudes as it does to the extinction of one generation to make room for another. In the monuments and fortresses of an unknown people, spread over the extensive regions of the West, we behold the memorials of a once powerful race, which was exterminated or has disappeared to make room for the existing savage tribes. Nor is there anything in this which, upon a comprehensive view of the general interests of the human race, is to be regretted. Philanthropy could not wish to see this continent restored to the conditions in which it was found by our forefathers. What good man would prefer a country covered with forests and ranged by a few thousand savages to our extensive Republic, studded with cities, towns, and prosperous farms, embellished with all the improvements which art can devise or industry execute, occupied by more than 12,000,000 happy people, and filled with all the blessings of liberty, civilization, and religion?

The present policy of the Government is but a continuation of the same progressive change by a milder process. The tribes which occupied the countries now constituting the Eastern States were annihilated or have melted away to make room for the whites. The waves of population and civilization are rolling to the westward, and we now propose to acquire the countries occupied by the red men of the South and West by a fair exchange, and, at the expense of the United States, to send them to a land where their existence may be prolonged and perhaps made perpetual. Doubtless it will be painful to leave the graves of their fathers; but what do they more than our ancestors did or than our children are now doing? To better their condition in an unknown land our forefathers left all that was dear in earthly objects. Our children by thousands yearly leave the land of their birth to seek new homes in distant regions. Does Humanity weep at these painful separations from everything, animate and inanimate, with which the young heart has become entwined? Far from it. It is rather a source of joy that our country affords scope where our young population may range unconstrained in body or in mind, developing the power and faculties of man in their highest perfection. These remove hundreds and almost thousands of miles at their own expense, purchase the lands they occupy, and support themselves at their new homes from the moment of their arrival. Can it be cruel in this Government when, by events which it can not control, the Indian is made discontented in his ancient home to purchase his lands, to give him a new and extensive territory, to pay the expense of his removal, and support him a year in his new abode? How many thousands of our own people would gladly embrace the opportunity of removing to the West on such conditions! If the offers made to the Indians were extended to them, they would be hailed with gratitude and joy.

And is it supposed that the wandering savage has a stronger attachment to his home than the settled, civilized Christian? Is it more afflicting to him to leave the graves of his fathers than it is to our brothers and children? Rightly considered, the policy of the General Government toward the red man is not only liberal, but generous. He is unwilling to submit to the laws of the States and mingle with their population. To save him from this alternative, or perhaps utter annihilation, the General Government kindly offers him a new home, and proposes to pay the whole expense of his removal and settlement. . . .

May we not hope, therefore, that all good citizens, and none more zealously than those who think the Indians oppressed by subjection to the laws of the States, will unite in attempting to open the eyes of those children of the forest to their true condition, and by a speedy removal to relieve them from all the evils, real or imaginary, present or prospective, with which they may be supposed to be threatened.

Source: James D. Richardson, ed., *A Compilation of the Messages and Papers of the Presidents, 1789–1897* (Washington: Government Printing Office, 1896–1899), vol. 2: 519–522.

Section VI (Documents 64–67): Building a Memory

Within a generation, the initial fears that had abounded with the Louisiana Purchase had faded. The ambivalence that policymakers felt when they considered the practical difficulties of expansion gave way to the spirit of manifest destiny. By midcentury, Americans were so zealous about expansion that they overwhelmingly supported a war of aggression against Mexico in pursuit of new land. The Louisiana Purchase itself underwent its own transformation. Throughout the nineteenth century, Americans referred to it as a way of explaining or rationalizing a broad range of ideas. Documents 64–67 show the shifting meaning of the Louisiana Purchase in the years immediately following its creation, at midcentury, and at the turn of the twentieth century as recorded by Presidents Monroe, Roosevelt, and Wilson.

64   Thomas Jefferson, the Louisiana Purchase, and National Pride

By the late-nineteenth century, the Louisiana Purchase had become a mainstay of American education and civic memory. Not only did writers consider it a moment of tremendous change for the young republic, but they also found in the Louisiana Purchase an ideal opportunity to talk about broader themes. In the process, they usually engaged in a hefty dose of nation building and national pride. Meanwhile, the collective memory of Thomas Jefferson was undergoing a change. Throughout much of the nineteenth century, George Washington was celebrated as the ideal American. Only later would people turn their attention to Jefferson. This article, from New England Magazine, *shows not only how one author attempted to situate the Louisiana Purchase in American history but also how Americans were beginning to revere Jefferson in a new way.*

Among our American statesmen there are few whose lives and thought present more interesting subjects for study than Thomas Jefferson's. As Member of Congress, Minister to France, Secretary of State, and finally as President, his political career is one of the longest and most important in our history. There are so many sides to his character, so many points of view from which his life may be regarded, that anything like an exhaustive discussion of them would far overstep the limits of an Old South lecture. Something of the same difficulty confronts us in the consideration of the Louisiana Purchase. We may look at it merely with reference to the bare history of the great transaction; we may regard it from a purely political standpoint; we may trace in detail the mighty effects of which it was a primary cause. I should like, however, to speak here of Thomas Jefferson and the Louisiana Purchase, mainly with reference to the general subject of "America and France."

From their earliest foundation the history of the English colonies in America was deeply influenced by France. This influence, I think, may be said to have flowed in two channels. First, there is that influence which France exerted by virtue of her explorations and occupation of territory,—an influence which constantly increased for a century and a half, until it reached its climax in that struggle for the continent which was settled at Quebec, and which suddenly revived forty years later, only to cease forever with the cession of Louisiana to the United States. The other influence, subtle but none the less real, we recognize first in the effect of French thought upon the American mind, an influence which, from being purely intellectual, in time became political and, strengthened by the cannon of D'Estaing and the bayonets of Rochambeau, so increased that admiration for France and sympathy with her became a cardinal principle in the creed of one of our earlier parties. How far this influence really extended, in just what measure the thought of our statesmen was actually affected by France, to what extent they employed friendship for her as a mere party cry, is a vexed question, but it is certain that this influence, such as it was, finds its best exponent in Thomas Jefferson.

The rise and decay of the former influence we need here only glance at. Fifteen years before the Pilgrims sought freedom to worship God on the shores of Massachusetts, the Seigneur De Monts established the first French settlement in Canada; and three years later Champlain founded the trading-post of Quebec. While the Puritans of New England were making good their foothold upon the coast, the traders and missionaries of New France were working their way up the St. Lawrence, and along the northern shores of the Great Lakes to the head-waters of the Mississippi. In the wigwams of every Indian tribe as far west as Minnesota, the black robe of the Jesuit became a familiar sight. The wonderful story of these heroic men,—what they dared, what they suffered, what they accomplished,—can be read in the glowing pages of Parkman.

Meanwhile the restless enterprise of one determined man was opening up to France another vast domain. In 1673, Father Marquette had floated part way down the Mississippi; but it was reserved for La Salle to explore the great river, "the father of waters," as the Indians called it, to its mouth, and to dedicate the whole region to France, under the name, "Louisiana." It was the aim of La Salle to erect a state in the valley of the Mississippi such as Champlain had founded on the St. Lawrence. Working back up the river, he would at length connect the two centres of French power in America by a chain of forts which should hem in and completely strangle the growing life of the English colonies. Although La Salle did not live to carry out his scheme, the idea did not wholly perish. In 1699 the first settlement of Louisiana was established, and in 1718 New Orleans began its eventful history.

Had New France and Louisiana been permitted to develop their resources, in time the great aim of La Salle might have been accomplished, and France have become the dominant power on the North American continent; but with an obstinate infatuation, her rulers relinquished this opportunity of a magnificent empire in the new world, as the price of a glorious, but utterly profitless, career in the old. More than once Louis XIV paid for his European aggressions with liberal slices of his American territory, until at last, in 1763, New France itself passed into English hands. During these years Louisiana maintained a sickly existence. In 1716 it was handed over to John Law, who made it the basis of a vast speculation which brought France to the brink of financial ruin. Finally, in 1762, the French possessions west of the Mississippi were ceded to Spain. For the next forty years we may think of Louisiana as continuing her dreamy life, little moved by the rush of outside events. She listened to "the shot heard round the world," little thinking that for her it meant the dawning of a new era. She heard, perhaps with more interest, the distant rumble of volcanic Paris, since a large part

of her population was of French descent; but it is safe to say that by neither of the two great revolutions of the eighteenth century was Louisiana much disturbed. Still, largely as a result of these two revolutions, the trans-Mississippi territory increased in importance, and became a bone of diplomatic contention at more than one court. Especially did it occupy a large place in the policies of two men: one, Napoleon Bonaparte, by virtue of his own intellect and ambition, First Consul of France; the other, Thomas Jefferson, by the will of the people, President of these United States. . . .

To Jefferson also Louisiana had a deep interest. In the years just succeeding the Revolution, the English settlers on the coast for the first time began to break through the mountain barrier which had so long confined them, and to take possession of the Ohio valley. But the road over the mountains was a hard one, and for many years there was surprisingly little intercourse between the people on opposite sides. Those on the west slope looked to the Mississippi as the natural outlet for their products. Spring and fall great fleets of flat-boats, laden with flour, tobacco, and hams, floated down the stream to New Orleans, where the merchandise was sold or exported. They were gallant souls, those early pioneers and state builders, men in whom the sterner qualities predominated. They had won their heritage bit by bit from the bear, the catamount, and the red man, and they were little disposed to suffer the insolence of the Spaniards at New Orleans. When therefore the Spanish governor closed the Mississippi to American commerce, from all the country west of the mountains a great cry went up. Wherever a number of frontiersmen were gathered together, some new tale of Spanish cruelty would come out. Now it was that one Thomas Amis, a settler on the Ohio, had been stopped at Natchez, his goods confiscated, and himself turned adrift in the forest to get home as best he could. The story would be told with a rude eloquence that would fire the hearts of the hearers. And then would follow curses, loud and deep, against the proud, cruel Spaniards, and against the Union which left them defenceless and without a remedy. More than once the whole West was in a blaze, and it seemed inevitable that the country must split asunder on the great line of the Appalachian Mountains. Washington himself declared that the western states stood, as it were, upon a pivot, and it needed but a touch to move them in either direction.

The pioneers had no more sincere friend than Jefferson. As governor of Virginia he had taken a deep interest in the beginnings of Kentucky. Later, as Secretary of State, he had been unremitting in his efforts to gain the right of navigation of the Mississippi by treaty. This had at length been attained in 1795, but when in 1802 the Spanish authorities at New Orleans, acting in the name of France, once more closed the river to American commerce, Jefferson found himself again called upon to interfere. Moreover, he felt that the nation which should hold New Orleans must be our natural enemy, and he realized how much more serious the situation would be if, for that enemy, instead of the decaying power of Spain, we should have France under Napoleon. At the first rumor of the cession he instructed our minister to France, Robert R. Livingstone, to make overtures to Bonaparte, looking towards the acquisition of Louisiana, or part of it, by this country. Affairs in Europe, however, had not yet reached that critical condition which they afterwards assumed, and Napoleon merely answered Mr. Livingstone politely, and went on with his preparations for establishing a colony.

Meanwhile the whole West was stirred to its depths. That a mongrel population of thirty thousand, half of them slaves, should longer stand in the way of the rights of three large states containing twenty times as many inhabitants, was absurd. The frontiersmen proposed to descend the river in force and occupy New Orleans, despite the Federal Government, European diplomacy, or the legions of Napoleon. We have seen that Jefferson had been elected president as the candidate who appealed to the feeling in this country favorable to France. Naturally he dreaded war with that power above all things. At

the same time he was too thoroughly patriotic to place a sentimental liking of any foreign nation above the true welfare of his own country. Accordingly, while on the one hand he held back the western settlers from violent measures, his language in regard to France took a more decided tone. Louisiana included both banks of the river as far north as Natchez. Could Jefferson obtain the east bank, together with the island of New Orleans, he might feel that the right of navigation of the river would be reasonably secure. He therefore dispatched James Monroe as a special envoy to France, to negotiate upon this basis, it being well understood by the latter, however, that the ultimate object was the acquisition of all Louisiana. Congress placed at his disposal two millions of dollars to pay expenses. We have seen how European affairs operated to assist Jefferson's diplomacy. Instead of accepting Monroe's offer, Bonaparte made the counter offer of the whole region for one hundred and twenty-five millions of francs. A little judicious haggling reduced the price to eighty millions, or about sixteen millions of dollars a fourth of which was to be paid to American citizens as satisfaction for claims against France. After a few days for consideration, the American ambassadors accepted these terms, and signed the treaty, April 30, 1803. "Of all our services to our country," said Livingstone, "this is the greatest." "I have given England a maritime rival who will one day humble her pride," said Napoleon, as he ratified the treaty on behalf of France. The treaty was forwarded to America, where it was approved by Jefferson and ratified by Congress. At noon, on the 29th of December, 1803, in the presence of a large part of the population of Louisiana, the French tri-color was lowered from its staff in the public square of New Orleans, and in its place the people saw waving above them the stars and stripes of the Federal Union.

Let us briefly consider the results of this Louisiana Purchase,—what it meant to France, to the United States, and to Jefferson. To France the cession of Louisiana meant the final relinquishment of her interest in the North American continent. From the time when Verazzano sailed along the coast, in 1524, it had been the cherished dream of heroic souls to win an empire in the new world,—perhaps for the Jesuit, perhaps for the Huguenot, but at all events for France. For this cause Coligny and Colbert had labored at Paris, and Champlain and Frontenac at Quebec. For this cause Jean Ribaut had perished in the swamps of Florida, Marquette by the Great Lakes, La Salle on the coast of Texas, and Montcalm on the Plains of Abraham. The struggle forms a grand yet pathetic story. Slowly, mournfully, the tri-color is lowered from its staff in the square of New Orleans. It is the last time that a French flag shall float over American soil in token of sovereignty.

Next, as to Jefferson. We have seen how his fondness for laying down abstract doctrines of political morality, combined with his intense democracy, had taken form in the theories of strict construction and state rights. He had attacked the Federalists for going beyond the letter of the Constitution. Nowhere could he find in that instrument any authority for the purchase of territory by the general government. He had drawn up a series of resolutions for Kentucky, explicitly declaring the individual state superior to the national government. Surely he realized that the acquisition of Louisiana must shatter this theory; for whatever might be the application of the doctrine of state rights to one of the original thirteen colonies, like Virginia, or however it might be twisted to apply to an offshoot from it, like Kentucky, it certainly could have no rightful connection with a state formed out of territory bought and paid for by the whole nation. Moreover, the purchase might furnish a precedent and a power for future administrations to use badly. It certainly would supply a political weapon to the Federalists, and would strongly impeach Jefferson's own reputation for consistency. These scruples and objections doubtless passed through Jefferson's mind; but the great importance of the purchase to the United States was sufficient to overbalance them all. It was a case in which a great acquisition must be paid for by a great concession. On the one hand were the principles which had guided his own political life, and upon which he had founded the Republican party; on the other, true statesmanship and the real welfare of the nation. The statesman and the political theorist in Jefferson met face to face, and the former triumphed. The Louisiana Purchase, contrary alike to the Constitution and to Jefferson's own political faith, was, nevertheless, accomplished; and to-day almost a century of history bears unbroken record to the wisdom and statesmanship which dictated it.

If we ask what the purchase meant to Jefferson's fellow-citizens and contemporaries, we have to answer, Very little. They had come into possession of a territory extending from the Mississippi to the Mexican border and the Rocky Mountains, but as yet they comprehended but vaguely their new acquisition. So little was known about the region that the most marvellous tales were set in circulation, and even transmitted to Congress by Jefferson in his report. There were tribes of Indians, veritable Goliaths in size, curious plants and animals and, most wonderful of all, a mountain of salt, one hundred and eighty miles long by forty-five wide. Of all this, as of the purchase generally, the Federalist papers made unlimited fun. One inquired, with great innocence, if this mountain might not be the remains of Lot's wife. They scouted the price. Why, William Penn had obtained Pennsylvania for five thousand pounds, and Gorges had paid only twelve hundred and fifty for all Maine! Even good Republicans felt that a debt of sixteen millions of dollars was a very dangerous affair. Some cautious people suggested that when emigration to the new regions set in, the entire East would be depopulated, and there would not be enough people left on the sea-board to keep out a foreign army. Others feared that a new state would arise beyond the Mississippi. Josiah Quincy opposed the purchase on the ground that it would strengthen the slave power. These alarms, however, proved for the most part to be imaginary. The growing wealth of the country soon put at rest any fears on the score of the debt. The emigration from the East did not prove as violent as was feared. Before the new country had time to think of secession, it was bound to the older states by bonds of steel. It is true that the Louisiana Purchase added three new states to the slave power; but these were far outbalanced by the great free Northwest.

It was said of Chatham that he found his country an island and left her an empire. Scarcely less is the verdict of history upon Thomas Jefferson. When Jefferson became president he found no less than three European powers "hanging on the flanks and rear of the republic,"—on the north, the British; on the south, the Spaniards; on the west, the French. He found the republic itself tending towards disunion, and the North American continent in a fair way to become but a shuttlecock in the game of European politics. By the Louisiana Purchase he left the country doubled in size, united in domestic interests, and with its political union greatly strengthened. He increased the power and prestige of the United States at home and abroad; he prepared the way for that assertion of her supremacy throughout the western hemisphere to which James Monroe was to give his name; and wrote the acquisition of Florida, of Texas, of California, and of Alaska in the book of national destiny.

But, after all, if we would consider the Louisiana Purchase in its highest phase, we must look at it from the standpoint of its world-wide im-portance. We must reflect how much smaller would be the capability of our country of playing the part assigned it in the great drama of the world, with Chicago to-day a frontier city and the Mississippi for our western limit; how changed the course of the world's history, with a French empire stretching from Oregon to the Isthmus.

This brings us again to the question of America and France. Says Mr. John Richard Green: "In the centuries which lie before us, the primacy of the world will lie with the English people;" and a recent magazine article speaks as a matter of course of the time when Italian, Spanish, and French will be of as little practical importance as the Erse or Welsh, and adds: "Whether we welcome or deplore the prospect, the fact is unmistakable,—the future of the world is English." Perhaps the historian of the twentieth century, as he looks out upon a world dominated by the English language, English laws, and English civilization, together with American liberty, equality, and ideas of self-government, will review the steps by which the great result has been attained. He will see in the long career of France in America one of the most determined attempts made by another race to win for itself this supremacy; and among the men and events that saved the North American continent to the Anglo-Saxon, as second only to James Wolfe and the capture of Quebec, he will mark Thomas Jefferson and the Louisiana Purchase.

Source: Robert Morss Lovett, "Thomas Jefferson and the Louisiana Purchase," *New England Magazine* VII (1889–1890): 569–577.

65

James Monroe on the Louisiana Purchase

No sooner did they conclude negotiations with France than James Monroe and Robert R. Livingston engaged in battle over who should receive credit for the Louisiana Purchase. A particularly egocentric pair of men, each believed that he was responsible for the purchase, and each interpreted the other's assertions as personal slights.

Of course, the activities of two American diplomats were of relatively little importance compared with Napoleon's reaction to events in Saint Domingue, but both Americans continued to claim credit nonetheless. Monroe already believed that his activities overseas in a number of diplomatic posts would be critical to his public reputation and his political prospects. The subject so dominated Monroe's thinking that when, in retirement, he composed the draft of an autobiography, he focused the vast majority of his discussion of events before 1807 not on his service during the Revolution, in the Senate, or as governor of Virginia but instead on his work as a diplomat. Monroe devoted particular attention to the Louisiana Purchase. Referring to himself in the third person, he provided a narrative based on his own recollections and published accounts by other participants. This excerpt from Monroe's story begins by describing his decision to leave Virginia for Paris.

The intimate and cordial friendship and great harmony in political life which he had so long enjoyed with the President and Secretary of State, with his high respect for their talents and merit, rendered it impossible for him to decline a cooperation with them in support of this great cause in which they were engaged. Under these circumstances Mr. Monroe did not hesitate to accept the appointment, although he knew that his relinquishment of the bar and absence from the country would increase the debts then existing and feared that the new mission, however short it might be, would subject him to still further difficulties, especially as he was informed that no outfit would be allowed to him. . . .

He sailed from New York with his family on the 8th of March, 1803, and arrived at Havre de Grace, in France, on the 8th of April following. Colonel John Mercer of Fredericksburg, the son of General Hugh Mercer, who fell at Province-town in our Revolutionary war, accompanied him as a friend, and with intention to afford him all the aid in his power. Mr. Monroe was not allowed a secretary. Colonel Mercer was a young man of talents and great worth. From Baltimore, his family took under their protection Mrs. Ben-thalou, the wife of Colonel Benthalou who had

been an officer in Count Pulaski's Corps, distinguished for his gallantry and wounded in the attack on Savannah. He was then in France in pursuit of claims, and she went to join him.

On landing at Havre de Grace, he was saluted from the battery, and as soon as he reached the hotel to which he was conducted, a guard with an officer and 50 men were sent to his quarters as a further tribute of respect. To have sent back the whole guard might have wounded the feelings of the commanding general. Two sentinels only were retained, and by the officer who commanded and led back the others an acknowledgment was made to the General for his kind attention, with an assurance that by permitting two only to remain the sensibility would be increased. In the morning the General with his *état-major* attended to pay their respects in person to Mr. Monroe, and on the ensuing day the commanding officer of the Navy, with all the officers of the corps at that port, called to pay their respects in like manner. This attention, if it proceeded from the parties themselves, was a strong proof of the favorable impression which Mr. Monroe had made on the nation in his first mission, and if it was shown in obedience to the orders of the government, it was equally a proof of that effect on the nation, as of a corresponding feeling of those at its head. It is believed that no examples of a like attention had been shown to a minister from any other power. On entering the territory, they are usually furnished with passports which specify their grade and the sovereign whom they represent, under which protection they pass from the frontier to the city. Mr. Monroe advised Mr. [Robert R.] Livingston of his arrival on the 8th, the day on which he reached Havre, and the government was advised of it, as he understood, on the same day by the telegraph. . . .

Mr. Monroe left Havre on the 10th of April and reached Paris on the 12th and took the quarters which had been provided for him by his friend Mr. Skipwith, who had accompanied him as Secretary in his first mission [and who] was appointed soon after his arrival as Consul for Paris, which office he still held, having discharged its duties with integrity, ability and diligence. Mr. Monroe received in reply to his letter to Mr. Livingston of the 8th, one of the 10th by Colonel Benthalou, who had advanced by the route to Havre to meet his wife. In this letter Mr. Livingston gave a very discouraging prospect of the success of the mission. He congratulated Mr. Monroe on his safe arrival and expressed an anxious hope that his mission might answer his and the public expectation. War, he said, might do something for us; nothing else would. He had paved the way for him by his memoirs and if he could add an assurance that we were in possession of New Orleans, we should do well. On the evening of his arrival, he waited on Mr. Livingston accompanied by Colonel Mercer and Mr. Skipwith, on which occasion a conversation occurred on the state of affairs in the United States at the period of Mr. Monroe's departure, and in which Mr. Livingston asked what had been the fate of Mr. Ross's resolutions. On being informed that they had been rejected he expressed his regret, with a remark that force only could give us New Orleans and that nothing but the actual possession of the country could give success to the mission in which they were associated. In this interview Mr. Livingston observed to Mr. Monroe

that as he had seen that part of his correspondence with the French government which had reached the Department of State before he sailed, he presumed it would be agreeable to him to peruse that which had followed to the present period. To this Mr. Monroe promptly assented and, in consequence, it was agreed that he should attend there at an early hour the next day, when it should be submitted to him. He attended accordingly, accompanied b Colonel Mercer, and perused the whole. Among the letters of Mr. Talleyrand, that of the 24th of March drew their particular attention because it afforded strong ground on which to presume that the mission would succeed in all its great objects. The sentiment which it expressed was conciliatory, and in regard to Louisiana, it stated that the First Consul considered the possession of it, whereby new means were afforded him to convince the government and people of the United States of his friendly disposition for them, in the number of the advantages which he ought to derive from that acquisition. In regard to any negotiation on that subject, the Minister observed that as Mr. Livingston had announced to him the approaching departure of Mr. Monroe, whom the President had appointed Envoy Extraordinary to treat on it, he had concluded that his government expected that that Minister should be waited for and heard, that every matter susceptible of contradiction should be completely and definitely discussed. He requested him to assure his government that the First Consul, far from thinking that their new position in Louisiana should operate to the injury of the United States, he would receive the new Minister whom the President had appointed with the greatest pleasure, and that he hoped, to the satisfaction of both countries. (See Mr. Talleyrand's letter of March 24, 1803.) As nothing had been done respecting the Mississippi, the great object of the mission, before Mr. Monroe's arrival, and the Minister had pointed to it as an event which he deemed important to that object, Mr. Monroe concluded, notwithstanding the unfavorable impressions of Mr. Livingston arising from what had passed between him and the government, that the First Consul looked to it as one which would form a new relation between the United States and France. Mr. Monroe inferred, therefore, from that letter, that a negotiation would be immediately opened, and in a spirit corresponding with the sentiment expressed in it.

Some incidents of a very interesting nature occurred at the moment of Mr. Monroe's arrival in Paris, which it is proper to notice here. So far as any circumstance in either was connected with the mission, in that degree should the order of time be respected. The first to which we shall advert we should be sorry to postpone, because it relates to an individual in whose welfare and fame the whole nation take a deep interest.

On Mr. Monroe's arrival at his quarters in Paris, a message was delivered to him from his estimable friend, General Lafayette, requesting that he would call on him as soon as convenient at his aunt's, Madame de Tascher, where he lodged, and with whose address he was apprised. He was informed by Mr. Skipwith that he [Lafayette] was confined to his bed in consequence of a fall on the ice in the winter, by which his hip joint had been dislocated, and that he could not rise or change his position. Mr. Monroe called on him the next day and found him in the state described. Their interview was affecting, by a recollection of the incidents which had occurred between them and those relating to Madame Lafayette on Mr. Monroe's first mission, when the General was confined at Olmutz. The President, Mr. Jefferson, had committed to Mr. Monroe the act of Congress which allowed to the General the land and commutation which officers of his rank were entitled to for service in our Revolutionary war, and to which he had set up no claim, preferring to bear his own expenses and to render his service gratuitously. Mr. Jefferson had likewise committed to Mr. Monroe a letter for the General, explanatory of the motive which led to the act, with a renewed assurance of his own undiminished attachment. Mr. Monroe delivered to the General the letter and act, and was most sensibly affected by the impression which they made on him. He was evidently overwhelmed. You are the only people on the earth, said he, from whom I would accept it. Mr. Monroe assured him that this grant allowed him nothing more than what was due to him and what all our officers of the same rank who had served the same time had received. Mr. Monroe heard from other sources that at that time he possessed the estate of La Grange only, a chateau with about 300 acres, the sale of which his condition then pressed, and that Madame Lafayette, who had signed deeds for the conveyance of his other property for the payment of debts, was then hesitating whether she ought to sanction he sale of the last remaining resource and home for her husband, herself, and children. The grant, by the act of Congress, relieved him and the family from the pressure and preserved to them that domicile. It is proper to mention that this relief was promptly obtained by an advance which was generously made to him by the House of Baring on the credit of the land thus granted. The claim of General Lafayette on the citizens of the United States and the friends of liberty everywhere was the stronger from the consideration that the First Consul had offered to him a seat in the Senate, which was entitled to a liberal compensation, and which, as Mr. Monroe understood, he had declined from a fear that the government was taking a direction which he disapproved.

In this interview General Lafayette communicated to Mr. Monroe an incident which excited his surprise. He informed him that General Bernadotte, who had been appointed some short time before Minister to the United States, had left town for Rochfort, the port from which he expected to sail, on the 10th in obedience to the order of his government. General Lafayette and General Bernadotte had served together in the commencement of the Revolution and were intimately acquainted with each other. Knowing that it was the wish of General Bernadotte to see Mr. Monroe before his departure, and that he was on the route from Havre and expected to arrive in Paris on that day, he sent a messenger to apprise him of it that he might remain and have the interview he desired. His orders, however, were so positive as to compel his immediate departure, depriving him of the opportunity. From this communication it appeared that the movement of General Bernadotte was connected by the French government with the arrival of Mr. Monroe, the motive for which he could not comprehend.

In the morning of the day which ensued Mr. Monroe's arrival, he was called on by a confidential friend, who informed him that on the Sunday preceding (the 10th of April), the First Consul had held a cabinet council at St. Cloud in which he apprised his Ministers of his decision to cede to the United States the province of Louisiana, and that he should commit the arrangement of the negotiation to Mr. Marbois. This friend enjoyed likewise the confidence of the two great Houses of Hope and Baring. He stated that the object of Mr. Monroe's mission was known to those Houses, as it was, that he might and probably would require the loan of a considerable sum of money to accomplish it. He assured Mr. Monroe that he was authorized by those Houses to inform him that they would make the loan for any sum he might require. Mr. Monroe asked to what amount and on what conditions would they make it? For ten millions, should you desire that sum, and on the terms your government will approve, at six per cent per annum. Mr. Monroe replied that he did not expect to have occasion for anything like that sum but that it was important and gratifying to him to know that he might obtain it if necessary. As this communication was confidential and differed so entirely from the opinion entertained by Mr. Livingston, as expressed in his letter to Mr. Monroe of the 8th, and in the interview which took place at his own house on the evening of Mr. Monroe's arrival, no notice was taken of it when he called in the morning to peruse his correspondence with the French government, according to appointment.

Mr. Monroe was gratified by a communication which he received at this period from the Consul Cambaceres, through his secretary, Mr. Monvil, a young man of merit, that he should be glad to receive him whenever it might be convenient for him to call on him. He observed that by rule a Foreign Minister might be presented to the First Consul before he was received by the other two, but that that rule would be dispensed with in his case. He assured him, on meeting, that he recollected, with due sensibility, the kind attention and hospitality which had been shown to him by Mr. Monroe in his former mission, and was happy to have it then in his power to evince it. A like was immediately afterwards sent to them that the appointment had been conferred on Mr. Marbois, and from whom an intimation was received that he would commence the negotiation as soon as it might be convenient to them. They were unwilling to lose a day. The negotiation immediately commenced, and terminated in a treaty and two conventions, bearing date on the 30th of April, by which the whole province of Louisiana was ceded to the United States and provision made for the payment of the sum stipulated to be given for it.

Our government contemplated only the acquisition of the Island of New Orleans and the territory eastward of the river, for which our Ministers were authorized to give ten millions of dollars. It was ascertained in the first conference that the First Consul would cede no part of the province if he did not cede the whole, and on a comparison of the value and the condition on which they were able to obtain it with that of the part sought and the sum they were authorized to give for it, our Ministers did not hesitate between the alternatives thus presented to them. The province extended, under any view which could be taken of its limits, far to the south and west on the right of the river, and on the left it was understood to extend to the river Perdido. Should France retain the right bank or should it fall into the hands of another power, of Great Britain for example, disputes might arise which might involve us in war, the charge of which would exceed in a single instance more than the sum for which the whole might be acquired. The mere adjustment of the presiding controversy with France, by the removal of the obstruction to the free navigation of the river, with the content which it would spread over the union and particularly the part dependent on it, would afford an ample indemnity for the price given for the whole.

Eighty millions of livres were stipulated to be given for it, of which sixty were to be paid to France and twenty to our citizens in discharge of the debts due to them by France. The sum to be paid to France, equal to eleven million, two hundred and fifty thousand dollars, was to be paid in stock, with a credit of fifteen years, on the payment of six per cent annually. At the expiration of that term, the principal was to be discharged by installments, by the payment of three millions each year. Cash instead of stock was asked for the sum to be paid to France, and a perpetual exemption of French vessels from foreign duties, instead of one for twelve years, which was agreed on. The negotiation was conducted by the Ministers on each side in a spirit of great candor and liberality. They had been long and intimately acquainted and had great confidence in each other.

This very important transaction being thus concluded, the agent of the two Houses of Hope and Baring, who had communicated with Mr. Monroe on his arrival, requested our Ministers to place them on the same ground with the French government which they had held with them, which they readily undertook and for which an opportunity was immediately afforded. It being the object of the French government to convert the stock into cash, Mr. Marbois asked our Ministers to whom it might be disposed of with most advantage to both nations. They designated to him those two great Houses, with an assurance that they thought them competent in Europe, and that they would act with great candor and liberality. They had had occasion to mention them in the course of the negotiation, to show the estimation in which our stock was held. In the present instance they were more full and explicit. A contract was formed by the French government with these Houses, by this the stock was sold to them at a fair price, and who fulfilled their engagement with great punctuality and credit.

Whether the employment of Mr. Monroe contributed in any degree to the success of the mis-

sion, a correct opinion may be formed by the facts just stated and others which preceded. Mr. Marbois has composed a work entitled, *The History of the Province of Louisiana, and of Its Cession to the United States,* which furnishes useful light on the subject. This history is a well-digested and able work. It commences with the discovery of the province and gives a detailed account of all the incidents attending it from that period to the cession, and of the causes which led to it, and of many of the most interesting circumstances attending the negotiation. We shall confine ourselves to those which bear immediately on the special objects of inquiry. It appears by this work that until the 10th of April, 1803, the First Consul had given no intimation to his Cabinet of his intention to cede the province to any power. Till then, the idea of the cession had not occurred to any of them, nor had they any suspicion that he contemplated it. On that day he opened the subject in a conference with two of his Ministers, one of whom advised, and the other opposed it. The prospect of a war with England, and the loss of it by her preponderance at sea, which he suggested, was the argument used by the one, and the uncertainty of that war and his preponderance on the Continent, which would enable him to take Hanover, by which, by exchange, he might recover Louisiana, was that which was urged by the other. It appears through the whole discussion that he had made up his mind to cede the province, although he did not declare it in that conference. On the next morning, the 11th, at the dawn of day, he sent for the Minister who had advised the cession, declared to him his decision to make it on conditions which he then stated, and committed to him the management of the negotiation. On the 10th it was known to the First Consul, as may fairly be concluded, that Mr. Monroe had arrived at Havre and might be expected in a day or two at Paris. It wa known to Mr. Livingston on that day that he had arrived, as his letter to Mr. Monroe in reply to one from him announcing it from Havre, bears that date. If the report that his arrival had been announced by the telegraph to the French government was correct, and which the manner of his reception at Havre seems to sanction, it must have been known to the First Consul on the 8th. That the movement should have been delayed to that moment and acted on then with such promptitude and decision can admit of no other conclusion.

Other facts are stated by Mr. Marbois which confirm it. In the conference with the Minister to whom the negotiation was committed [Mr. Marbois], the First Consul observed that Mr. Monroe was on the point of arriving, and as his government was distant 2,000 leagues, the President must have given him explicit instructions, more extensive as to the sum to be paid for the territory which might be ceded than could be inferred from the proceedings of Congress. That fact alone proves that he thought that nothing could be done until he did arrive; that he delayed the movement until he knew that he had arrived, and hastened afterwards to make the necessary arrangement for the commencement of the negotiation as soon as he should reach the city.

The war with England was anticipated from the debates in the British Parliament and particularly from the speeches of Lord Grenville and Mr. Canning, as early as the 23d of November, 1802, and it is obvious from the communication of the First Consul to the Corps Legislative of the 20th of February following, in which he proposed that 500,000 men should be raised to defend and revenge the Republic in that war, that he then deemed it inevitable. Had the war with England been the sole or even the ruling motive to the cession, it being known that it would occur at the period referred to, and particularly on the 20th of February, before any account of the mission which had been adopted by the President had reached France, advances would have been made to Mr. Livingston in reference to it or his communications met in a very different spirit; but such was the impression made on him, as is shown by the statement which he expressed in his conference with Mr. Marbois after Mr. Monroe's arrival, notwithstanding the assurance given him that the cession would be made, that it is obvious he had no confidence in it. The impression which

he made on Mr. Marbois was that he thought the overture to cede the province illusory, to avoid the payment of the sum due for the prizes they had taken. So sudden had been the change in the temper of the French government as previously manifested to him, that he could view it in no other light.

The first and only communication of the French government which authorized a presumption that any accommodation would be afforded to us respecting the Mississippi, which was much before Mr. Monroe's arrival, is to be found in Mr. Talleyrand's letter to Mr. Livingston of March 24th, at which time he was at sea on his voyage to France. In that letter Mr. Talleyrand speaks in friendly terms of the United States, acknowledges in like manner the effort made by the President to remove the ferment which had been excited among our citizens by the suppression of the deposit at New Orleans, and intimates the desire of the First Consul to meet us in such an arrangement as would be advantageous and satisfactory to both countries. He refers also, in a marked manner, to the mission of Mr. Monroe, and states that his arrival would be waited for and that the First Consul would receive him with the greatest pleasure.

That the approaching war with England contributed to the cession there can be no doubt, but that it was his sole motive is not believed. We were satisfied, on the contrary, that the excitement produced in the United States by the suppression of our right of deposit at New Orleans and the menace of restoring it by force, which he knew that we could accomplish, and the measure adopted by the President to prevent a rupture and settle the affair by a friendly mission and amicable arrangements, gave the first and a decided impulse to his mind to make the cession. Had the deposit not been suppressed and the affair turned on the relation between France and England only, we do not think that any proposition of cession to our government, or even the idea of it, [would] have occurred. A contempt of danger was a marked feature in the character of the First Consul, and this applied as well to

France, whose power he wielded and whose fame was connected with his own, as to himself personally. He estimated her strength and resources, of which he had seen so many, and the decisive proofs too highly to adopt any measure, and especially the cession of territory, under a different impression. That the statement made by Mr. Marbois of what passed in the conference is correct is readily admitted, but still that statement leaves the subject open to other views as to the policy of the individual in whom the government was vested.

Source: Stuart Gerry Brown, ed., *The Autobiography of James Monroe* (Syracuse: Syracuse University Press, 1959), 154–155, 158–161, 164–167.

66   Theodore Roosevelt on the American West

Theodore Roosevelt was a historian of considerable literary skill. Although he came of age just as American universities were developing modern systems for training historians, Roosevelt did not receive any formal preparation. Instead, the aspiring politician threw himself into his writing with the same zeal that governed many of his endeavors. Between 1894 and 1897 Roosevelt published a multivolume study entitled The Winning of the West. *Telling the triumphal story of the victory of Anglo-American civilization over the barbarism of Indians and European rulers, Roosevelt helped instill in readers' minds what would become the standard narrative of nineteenth-century history. Although he was the advocate of a larger, professionalized government, Roosevelt eschewed an emphasis on political leaders for a celebration of white settlers.*

A great and growing race may acquire vast stretches of scantily peopled territory in any one of several ways. Often the statesman, no less than the soldier, plays an all-important part in winning the new land; nevertheless, it is usually true that the diplomatists who by treaty ratify the acquisition usurp a prominence in history to which they are in no way entitled by the real worth of their labors. . . .

So it was with the acquisition of Louisiana. Jefferson, [Robert R.] Livingston, and their fellow-statesmen and diplomats concluded the treaty which determined the manner in which it came into our possession; but they did not really have much to do with fixing the terms even of this treaty . . . the Americans would have won Louisiana . . . even if the treaty of Livingston and Monroe had not been signed. The real history of the acquisition must tell of the great westward movement begun in 1769, and not merely of the feeble diplomacy of Jefferson's administration. . . . The winning of Louisiana was due to no one man, and least of all to any statesman or set of statesmen. It followed inevitably upon the great westward thrust of the settler-folk; a thrust which was delivered blindly, but which no rival race could parry, until it was stopped by the ocean itself.

Louisiana was added to the United States because the hardy backwoods settlers had swarmed into the valleys of the Tennessee, the Cumberland, and the Ohio by hundreds of thousands; and had hardly begun to build their raw hamlets on the banks of the Mississippi, and to cover its waters with their flat-bottomed craft. Restless, adventurous, hardy, they looked eagerly across the Mississippi to the fertile solitudes where the Spaniard was the nominal, and the Indian the real, master; and with a more immediate longing they fiercely coveted the Creole province at the mouth of the river. . . .

It was these two timid, well-meaning statesmen [President Thomas Jefferson and Secretary of State James Madison] who . . . found themselves pitted against Napoleon, and Napoleon's

Minister, Talleyrand; against the greatest warrior and lawgiver, and against one of the greatest diplomats, of modern times; against two men, moreover, whose sodden lack of conscience was but heightened by the contrast with their brilliant genius and lofty force of character; two men who were unable to so much as appreciate that there was shame in the practice of venality, dishonesty, mendacity, cruelty, and treachery.

Jefferson was the least warlike of presidents, and he loved the French with a servile devotion. But his party was strongest in precisely those parts of the country where the mouth of the Mississippi was held to be of right the property of the United States; and the pressure of public opinion was too strong for Jefferson to think of resisting it. The South and the West were a unit in demanding that France should not be allowed to establish herself on the lower Mississippi. Jefferson was forced to tell his French friends that if their nation persisted in its purpose America would be obliged to marry itself to the navy and army of England. Even he could see that for the French to take Louisiana meant war with the United States sooner or later; and as above all things else he wished peace, he made every effort to secure the coveted territory by purchase. . . .

. . . The steady westward movement of the Americans was the all-important factor in determining the ultimate ownership of New Orleans, Livingston, the American minister, saw plainly the inevitable outcome of the struggle. He expressed his wonder that other Americans should be uneasy in the matter, saying that for his part it seemed as clear as day that no matter what trouble might temporarily be caused, in the end Louisiana was certain to fall into the grasp of the United States.

There were many Americans and many Frenchmen of note who were less clear-sighted. Livingston encountered rebuff after rebuff, and delay after delay. Talleyrand met him with his usual front of impenetrable duplicity. He calmly denied everything connected with the cession of Louisiana until event the details became public property, and even then admitted them with unblushing equanimity. . . . but Livingston, and those he represented, soon realized that it was Napoleon himself who alone deserved serious consideration. . . .

Jefferson took various means, official and unofficial, of impressing upon Napoleon the strength of the feeling in the United States over the matter; and his utterances came as near menace as his pacific nature would permit. To the great French Conqueror however, accustomed to violence and to the strife of giants, Jefferson's somewhat vacillating attitude did not seem impressive; and the one course which would have impressed Napoleon was not followed by the American President. Jefferson refused to countenance any proposal to take prompt possession of Louisiana by force or to assemble an army which could act with immediate vigor in time of need. . . .

. . . Napoleon could not afford to hamper himself with the difficult defence of a distant province, and to incur the hostility of a new foe, at the very moment when he was entering on another struggle with his old European enemies. Moreover, he needed money in order to carry on the struggle. . . .

The treaty was signed in May, 1803. The definition of the exact boundaries of the ceded territory was purposely left very loose by Napoleon. . . .

Source: Theodore Roosevelt, *The Winning of the West* (New York: Current Literature Publishing Company, 1900), VI: 184, 187, 188–189, 198–199, 204–205, 206, 207, 208.

67   Woodrow Wilson on American Political Leadership

When Theodore Roosevelt published The Winning of the West, *Woodrow Wilson was a professor at Princeton University. By 1902, just as* The Winning of the West *was about to begin a new printing, Wilson became the university's president. Eight years later, he began a two-year tenure as governor of New Jersey, an office he left in 1912 to become President of the United States. In that election, Wilson defeated both William Howard Taft, Roosevelt's secretary of war and hand-picked successor, and Roosevelt himself, who had become so disillusioned with Taft and the whole Republican Party that he ran on the insurgent Progressive Party. Unlike Roosevelt, Wilson was a trained academic, and spent much of his career writing studies of American political institutions.* History of the American People *was one of those studies. Like* The Winning of the West, *this study filled several volumes. But the two books exemplified the differences that would eventually create a considerable gap between academic and public history. Where Roosevelt provided stories that celebrated the achievements of individuals or nations, Wilson wrote in the emerging academic style that eschewed literary flourishes for the more direct narration of the social sciences. In addition, where Roosevelt venerated the achievements of individual settlers—almost to a fault—Wilson was more interested in the decisionmaking of public leaders. This difference only made sense given their different audiences. While Roosevelt hoped his books would foster patriotic zeal among a broad readership, Wilson wanted his books to provide an academic analysis of policymaking and useful models for students who might later pursue careers in public service.*

Mr. Monroe was sent to join Mr. Livingston at the French court. He was authorized to purchase Florida and a strip of the coast which should include New Orleans. He found Bonaparte willing to sell the whole of Louisiana or nothing. The American commissioners, therefore, exceeded their authority and agreed to buy the whole of the vast territory for fifteen million dollars. Bonaparte congratulated himself that he had replenished his purse for a war with England and had turned over to the United States lands and resources which should make them able themselves some day to humble England, even on the high seas and in trade.

Mr. Jefferson admitted that he could find nowhere in the constitution authority to buy foreign territory, and professed himself very anxious about the awkward situation that had arisen. He believed that such a purchase would be beyond the precedent even of Mr. Hamilton's "implied powers," and wished a constitutional amendment passed to make good what his representatives had done and he could not decline to accept. "I had rather ask an enlargement of power from the *nation,* when it is found necessary," he said, "than to assume it by a construction which would make our powers boundless. Our peculiar security is in the possession of a written constitution. Let us not make it a blank paper by construction." But in the same breath with which he urged his scruple he declared his readiness to abandon it. "If our friends think differently," he said, "certainly I shall acquiesce with satisfaction, confiding that the good sense of our country will correct the evil of construction when it shall produce ill effects"; and the houses agreed to the treaty and voted the money for the purchase without so much as proposing an amendment (1803). The President acquiesced with startling facility in the apparent "necessity of shutting up the constitution" in such exigent cases of imperative policy. No one but the more extreme and partisan Federalists would patiently hear of any scruples in the matter. Nowhere except in New England was there sharp and acrid dissent.

Mr. Jefferson had given the country its first taste of his real quality in action. He was a Democrat a people's man, upon conviction, genuinely and with a certain touch of passion; but he was no lawyer. He stickled for a strict construction of the constitution only when he thought that a strict construction would safeguard the rights of common men and keep the old Federalist theories of government at arm's-length: not because he disliked to see the country have power as a nation, but because he dreaded to see it put in bondage to an autocratic government. He wanted as little governing from the federal capital as might be; but as much progress as might be, too, and as much access of power and of opportunity to the people as a body of free men, unshackled-by any too meddling government. It was his weakness to think it safe for the friends of the people to make "a blank paper" of the constitution, but the very gate of revolution for those who were not Democrats. If only Democrats led, "the good sense of the country would correct the evil of construction when it should produce ill effects"!

Source: Woodrow Wilson, *History of the American People* (New York: Harper & Brothers, 1906).

Index